Simplicius Simplicissimus

The "Phoenix Copper"

Frontispiece from the 1669 edition

Gerhardo Dünnhaupt

L. M. Q. D.

G. Sch-B.

1998 reprint of second revised edition
First published 1993 by Camden House
Transferred to digital printing 2007

Camden House is an imprint of Boydell & Brewer Inc.
668 Mt. Hope Avenue, Rochester, NY 14620, USA
www.camden-house.com
and of Boydell & Brewer Limited
PO Box 9, Woodbridge, Suffolk IP12 3DF, UK
www.boydellandbrewer.com

ISBN: 1–879751–37–2 (Cloth)
ISBN: 1–879751–38–0 (Paper)

Library of Congress Cataloging-in-Publication Data

Grimmelshausen, Hans Jakob Christoph von, 1625–1676.
    [Simplicissimus. English]
    The adventures of Simplicius Simplicissimus / Hans Jakob Christoffel
von Grimmelshausen; a modern translation with an introduction by
George Schulz-Behrend. — 2nd rev. ed.
        p. cm. — (Studies in German literature, linguistics, and culture)
    Includes bibliographical references.
    ISBN: 1–879751–37–2 (cloth: acid-free paper)
    ISBN: 1–879751–38–0 (paper: acid-free paper)
        I. Schulz-Behrend, George, 1913–   II. Title.   III. Series: Studies in
German literature, linguistics, and culture (Unnumbered)

OT1731.A7E5 1993
833'.5—dc20
                                                        92-33514
                                                        CIP

This publication is printed on acid-free paper.
Printed in the United States of America.

The Adventures of Simplicius Simplicissimus

by

Hans Jacob Christoffel von Grimmelshausen

A modern translation, with an Introduction,
by
George Schulz-Behrend

second, revised edition

CAMDEN HOUSE

taught in Egypt by men like Claude Ptolemy, who lived in the second
century A.D. During the Renaissance it experienced a revival which
lasted well into the seventeenth century, after which time a separation
was made between astrology and astronomy. Astrology, though hardly
taken seriously, survives even today if space given to it in certain maga-
zines and newspapers means anything. However, astrology has left an
important impact on the visual arts and literature. Grimmelshausen was
acquainted with its lore and used it when he wrote his almanac *The
Adventurous Simplicissimus' Ever-Lasting Calendar* (1671), an interesting
combination of farmer's almanach and collection of stories that plugs
his major novel and offers much conventional astrological advice and
entertainment.

According to astrological beliefs, macrocosm and microcosm are
closely interrelated, and the seven planets — Saturn, Jupiter, Mars, the
Sun (Sol), Venus, Mercury, and the Moon (Luna) — exert their influence over practically everything on Earth, the center of the universe.
The planets in combination with the signs of the zodiac have a variety
of functions: Saturn's chief domain is the soil along with the hard-
working peasants who cultivate it; Saturn is also the planet of the
beginning and end; its color is black. Mars, as is well known, has its
influence on everything connected with warfare; its color is red. Sol is
identified with gold and good sense. Jupiter is the master of the hunt;
it deals also with riches, liberality, and the association with prominent,
powerful persons. Venus' domain is luxury, leisure, love, and music; its
color is green. Mercury exerts its influence on commerce, the arts and
sciences, especially medicine; it counts thieves and cheats among its
children. The Moon, silvery, wet and cold, rules over water in all its
forms; its domain also includes the phenomena of change and inconstancy.

Instead of letting his hero live his entire life under the tutelage of
the one planet dominant at the hour of his birth, Grimmelshausen chose
to place entire segments of his novel with plot, major and minor characters, locations, etc. under the influence of consecutive planets. Let us
briefly look at two representative segments of *Simplicius Simplicissimus*
and ascertain how Rehder/Weydt assign them to planetary influences
or dependencies.

Book I starts with a sentence calling attention to Saturn, the planet
of beginning and end. Then, in a satirical mode, with ironic references
to the noble origin of the boy, the knan is introduced. He is a typical
saturnine character, an old, hard-working tiller of the soil who lives in
a lonely place and is clumsy with his instruction to the boy. Ironically
this ineptness leads to a sudden change in which the next planetary

of the work. Simplicius serves to unify the following themes and components of the novel: (1) a critical, moralizing attitude toward the world; (2) preoccupation with sin and repentance; (3) preoccupation with the inconstancy of the world; and (4) an episodic structure. While functioning to hold these elements together, Simplicius as an individual is not affected by them. Like an actor he slips into a role, soon to lay it aside for another. He has certain traits by which we recognize him, but they do not go beyond type characteristics. When viewed in this light, the story need not close with Book V; it can be expanded without violating any preconceived plan or symmetry.

One might think that the developmental theory must exclude the figure theory, but at least one interpreter, Johannes Alt,[3] has combined the two into the "type-sequence" theory. According to Alt, Grimmelshausen started his story with a hero who was a folk character, a simple fool. However, realizing that such a story would have relatively limited appeal, he created diversity by introducing a different type as the central character of successive units of the story and surrounding him with other type characters. Because of the author's ingenious technique for concealing the seams of the various units, an unsuspecting reader gains the impression that development takes place, whereas, in reality, only type sequences are found.

In 1968 two scholars, Helmut Rehder,[4] an American, and Günther Weydt,[5] a German, published their discovery that Grimmelshausen had deliberately based his *Simplicius Simplicissimus* on an astrological foundation. This discovery, identical in substance, except for one aspect of sequence, had in either case been suggested by a series of seven woodcuts called *Planetenkinder* by Georg Pencz, a student of Albrecht Dürer (1471-1528).

Astrology, a body of pseudo-scientific knowledge, goes back in its Chaldaic form to ancient Babylonian priests, to those Old Testament times when Chaldean was synonymous with wise man. Astrology was accepted by the Greeks and Romans, and an improved version was

---

[3] Johannes Alt, *Grimmelshausen und der Simplicissimus* (Munich: C. H. Beck, 1936).

[4] Helmut Rehder, "Planetenkinder: Some Problems of Character Portrayal in Literature," *The Graduate Journal, The University of Texas* 3 (1968): 69-97.

[5] Günther Weydt, *Nachahmung und Schöpfung im Barock: Studien zu Grimmelshausen* (Berne: Francke, 1968); see especially Part IV: "Planetensymbolik im barocken Roman, 1. Die astrologische Struktur des Romans."

phase, that of the planet Mars, is anticipated. Mars was already mentioned when the simple agricultural activities of the knan were described in military terms. Now a troop of cavalrymen ransack the farmstead, inflict torture and rape; what they can't carry off they ruin; they torch the buildings. The boy finds refuge with another saturnine figure, the old hermit. A martian interlude ensues: peasants take diabolic revenge on a number of soldiers who have lost their way in the woods; but the troopers, having received reinforcements, raise the level of violence by brutalizing the peasants. Meanwhile the boy is once again leading a saturnine existence, a mode of life that comes to an end with the death of Simplicius' hermit father. When Simplex goes for help and advice to the parson of the nearest village he sees the minister beaten up; village and parsonage are in flames. Simplex's dream shows him the tree of Mars that covers all of Europe. With the discovery that his provisions for the winter have been stolen by soldiers, life as a hermit becomes impossible and Simplex realizes that he has to escape into the unknown world. After Saturn and Mars a new planet takes over at Hanau.

One more example must suffice: Venus, the planet of music, joy and leisure, assumes its short domain in Paris, where handsome Simplicius (Beau Alman) in a court performance at the Louvre plays the major role in an opera on the theme of Orpheus and Eurydice. Orpheus, the divine singer, having lost his beloved Eurydice, persuades Pluto, the god of the lower world, to allow her to return to Earth. But there is one condition: Orpheus must not look back at her until they are in broad daylight. When he disobeys the agreement he loses Eurydice forever. In despair Orpheus curses all womankind and is punished for his antifeminism by maenads, frantic followers of the wine god Bacchus. They throw him in a lake where (according to *this* version) a dragon devours him. Simplicius plays his part so well that a number of courtly ladies become enamored of him and he is half drawn, half coerced into a series of sexual encounters. At the point where Simplex realizes the despicable nature of his life under these circumstances, the tutelage of the planet Venus ends and Mercury takes over. The segment after that comes under the influence of the Moon. *Simplicius Simplicissimus* ends in Book VI as it began, under Saturn, planet of beginning and end.

In evaluating these interpretations, one must observe that the developmentalists applied to *Simplicius* a nineteenth-century concept of unique personality development which was alien to seventeenth-century prose fiction. The German *Bildungsroman*, at its best exemplified by Goethe's *Wilhelm Meister*, portrays its hero in depth and lets him progress by way of manifold experiences from naiveté to his own *Weltan-*

schauung (personal philosophy of the purpose of life). It has been suggested that instead of calling *Simplicius* a *Bildungsroman* (novel of inner development) it might be called an *Entwicklungsroman* (novel of outer development). But this term is so general that it could be applied with equal justification to every biographical novel, inasmuch as every human being goes through the phases of childhood, youth, manhood, and old age. However, this sort of progress is far different from genuine *Bildung*, which implies growth of personality rather than merely chronological progress.

Alt's type-sequence theory is limited by its many compromises; conceivably it might apply to any picaresque novel. The figure theory also oversimplifies; it fails to consider the many indications of character in Simplicius, for he does remember earlier events, he is careful to explain the reasons for his actions (not always, to be sure, but often enough), he emphasizes repeatedly that he wants his story to be complete; in these and other ways he exhibits at least the beginnings of being a character.[6]

While the astrological interpreters of *Simplicius Simplicissimus* found abundant evidence for their view in the novel (and in other writings of Grimmelshausen), one of their most convincing critics expressed the general objection: "The basic defect in the astrological interpretation ... is that of putting a theoretical cart before a creative horse."[7] Grimmelshausen, these critics assert, nowhere professes a clear belief in astrology. His attitude is ambivalent at best (even in the *Everlasting Calendar*), but more often he voices doubt and disbelief, frequently hiding his views behind irony or, worse yet, satire. Why should Grimmelshausen have based his major work on a preconceived pattern he did not wholeheartedly believe in? Moreover, Weydt and his disciples are accused of emphasizing only those items that validate *their* theory while ignoring those that do not. For example, the 360-odd gold pieces in III, 16 are pressed into service to affirm the influence of the Sun on Simplicius: — they stand for the 365 or 366 days of the solar year. But the 893 gold pieces and the 80 thalers Simplex finds in III, 12 are passed over in utter silence. A third objection is that Grimmelshausen blurs the distinction among planetary deities and gods of Graeco-Roman mythology. The

---

[6] Werner Hoffmann, "Grimmelshausens Simplicius Simplicissimus nicht doch ein Bildungsroman?" *Germanisch-Romanische Monatsschrift*, N. S. 17 (1967): 166-80.

[7] Blake Lee Spahr, "Grimmelshausen's Simplicissimus: Astrological Structure?" *Argenis* 1 (1977): 7-29; quotations on p. 12.

In Grimmelshausen's day learned journals and writers of the courtly novel completely disregarded *Simplicius Simplicissimus*, for its author was not, on the face of it, a really learned man and he belonged to no literary group that might have, in effect, "promoted" the book. The best indication of the novel's enormous appeal to contemporary readers is the six editions that appeared during the author's lifetime, plus three additional posthumous ones, the last in 1713. After that the novel was forgotten for a number of decades.

Since its rediscovery by German Romantic authors (*ca.* 1800 ff.), numerous interpreters have regarded *Simplicius* as a novel of character development. Friedrich Gundolf[1] was the first to draw a parallel between *Simplicius* and *Wilhelm Meister*, Goethe's novel of character development. The heroes of both novels, Gundolf asserts, share the urge for personal fulfillment and in both works the world is pictured as a realm of development through trial and error. In light of this interpretation, the adventures of Simplicius assume importance to the degree that they contribute to the maturing of the hero's personality. Accordingly Grimmelshausen makes use of outer events to unfold inner growth: Simplicius develops from a naive child into a sophomoric fool; then he deteriorates into a show-off, a rake, and a male prostitute. His illness serves as a turning point, after which his character improves until he retreats from the world and becomes, once more, as in childhood, a saintly hermit. The events of his life are shown to form a well-defined arc whose zenith of worldly success corresponds to a nadir of spiritual depravity. Book VI, with its numerous extraneous episodes and Simplicius' second retreat from the world, does not readily fit into this scheme, and developmentalists point out that the *Continuation* was not a part of the novel's first edition, that it constitutes an afterthought inspired by commercial rather than artistic considerations, and that it may almost be disregarded.

More recently, Günter Rohrbach[2] has maintained that Simplicius is not at all a character or individual in the modern sense. He is, rather, a "figure" whose purpose is strictly functional. An *individual* arouses our interest through the growth of his personality; a *figure* does so because of the function he assumes in relation to the various elements

---

[1] Friedrich Gundolf, "Grimmelshausen und der Simplicissimus," *Deutsche Vierteljahrsschrift für Literaturwissenschaft und Geistesgeschichte* 1 (1923): 339-58.

[2] Günter Rohrbach, *Figur und Charakter: Strukturuntersuchungen an Grimmelshausens Simplicissimus*, Bonner Arbeiten zur deutschen Literatur, 3 (Bonn: H. Bouvier & Co., 1959).

tales growing out of his main novel. Of the ten components of what Grimmelshausen called the Simplician cycle only one has achieved a certain modern fame, and that because Bertold Brecht was inspired by *The Life of the Arch-Cheat and Runagate Courage* (1670) to write his brilliant play *Mother Courage* (1939), to which he gave the subtitle "A Chronicle Play of the Thirty Years' War."

Nor was the latter part of Grimmelshausen's life peaceful. King Louis XIV of France had in 1672 started a war with the Dutch, a war that put some French-German border territories under considerable stress. In July of 1675, for example, Marshal Turenne invaded and occupied Renchen and the surrounding country. The inhabitants, remembering dire events experienced by them or their elders during the Thirty Years' War, once more fled to the woods. Presumably Mayor Grimmelshausen stayed behind and organized a citizen volunteer force with which to preserve what modicum of order was possible in the chaos of war. Grimmelshausen died on August 17, 1676, at the age of 55. His sons, though dispersed at the time, were able to be at his side in the hour of his death. In a brief entry in the parish register the priest referred to him as an honest man of great genius and learning.

II

When *Simplicius Simplicissimus* appeared, creditable prose fiction in Germany was not concerned with the sordid realities of the recent war, with the struggle for survival on the level of the lower and middle classes. Members of sophisticated circles, if they read fiction at all, read translations or adaptations of highly stylized courtly romances or novels of state. Works like d'Urfé's *Astrée*, Sannazaro's *Arcadia*, and Sidney's novel of the same title, Montemayor's *Diana*, Madeleine Scudéry's exotic *Ibrahim Bassa,*, and John Barclay's *Argenis* come to mind. Understandably, middle-class readers — the lower classes were, as today, by and large non-readers — found them meaningless and dull. Instead they enjoyed, in translation of course, the picaresque (or rogue's) novel, which had originated in Spain with the anonymous *Lazarillo de Tormes* (1554, translation 1617); other picaresque novels available were Mateo Alemán's *Guzmán de Alfarache* (1599/1605, trl. 1615), López de Ubeda's *Picara Justina* (1605, trl. 1620/27), and Quevedo's *Historia de la vida del Buscon* (1626, trl. via the French, 1671). An example of the French *roman comique*, another form of the "middle-brow" novel, is Charles Sorel's *Histoire comique de Francion* (1623/26/33, trl. 1662).

In 1639 we find Grimmelshausen as a musketeer in the imperial regiment of Colonel Hans Reinhard von Schauenburg at Offenburg. The colonel must have noticed the intelligent young soldier, for he assigned him as a clerk to the administrative office of his regiment. In 1648 he became the secretary of Colonel Johann von Elter, the brother-in-law of H. R. von Schauenburg. Elter had orders to prevent French and Swedish troops from marching on Vienna, but the Peace of Westphalia put an end to all hostilities and Hans Christoph could return to Offenburg. Having converted to the Catholic faith, Grimmelshausen now married Catharina Henninger, the daughter of an ex-sergeant major in Schauenburg's regiment. Not only did the marriage bring with it an improvement in Grimmelshausen's social status, it also marked the end of a soldier's restless life and the beginning of a solid bourgeois existence. About this time Johann Jacob Christoph added *von* to his name, the predicate of nobility cherished by family tradition.

His first peacetime job was that of administering the country estates of his former commander H. R. von Schauenburg and those of a cousin, C. B. von Schauenburg. The Grimmelshausens lived from 1649 to 1660 in the village of Gaisberg near Oberkirchen in a house that came with the job. Here they prospered in a modest way, running a wine tavern on the side and acquiring some real estate. Then, from 1662 until 1665 Grimmelshausen became the steward of a wealthy Strasbourg physician, Dr. Johannes Küffer. The doctor, having acquired and renovated an old castle, employed Grimmelshausen as the caretaker of it. But soon Grimmelshausen changed jobs once more: he again opened an inn which he called "Zum silbernen Stern" (The Silver Star, i.e. the Moon) and devoted himself to writing. During 1667 he managed to publish two books, neither very successful, the didactic tract *The Satyrical Pilgrim* and the Old Testament tale *Joseph the Chaste*.

Not that Grimmelshausen could now devote the major part of his time to writing: in 1667 he was appointed mayor of Renchen, a town that belonged to the Bishop of Strasbourg. He was kept busy with administrative duties, police work, meting out justice, and collecting taxes. Still, in 1668 his publisher in Nuremberg was able to put on the market Grimmelshausen's major work, *Der abentheuerliche Simplicissimus* (*The Adventurous Simplicissimus*), a novel in five books; it was followed by a sixth book, the *Continuation*, in 1669. Although he kept writing until 1676, he never repeated the resounding success of *Simplicius Simplicissimus*, a novel that was several times reprinted, "improved," and imitated. It is hard to imagine how a busy civil servant, the mayor of a bustling village, managed to find the leisure to write a wheelbarrowful of entertaining stories, novels of courtly love, almanacs, and

Introduction

I

Relatively little is known about the life of Hans Jacob Christoph[el], who later called himself von Grimmelshausen, for he lived at a time when records were either not kept at all or, like other valuables, were often lost in the course of the Thirty Years' War or one of the many that followed. And so it is not surprising that the date of his birth is in doubt. To arrive at likely biographical facts in Grimmelshausen's life generations of scholars have used documented historical events in combination with "facts" derived from his autobiographical writings, chiefly the novel *Simplicius Simplicissimus*. Reference books state that Grimmelshausen was born in March of 1621 (or 1622) in the ancient Hessian town of Gelnhausen, some twenty-five miles northeast of Frankfurt am Main. When his father died while the boy was still young and his mother remarried, his grandparents took on the responsibility of his upbringing. Grandfather Melchior, a baker by trade and the keeper of a wine tavern, had dropped the *von* from his name because his bourgeois way of making a living contradicted the implication of nobility conveyed by the *von*. Hans Jacob was probably attending the (Lutheran) Latin school when Gelnhausen was looted and ravaged by Swedish troops in September of 1634 and many of its inhabitants fled into the woods or to the relative safety of the fortress of nearby Hanau, especially after the battle of Nördlingen (October 6, 1634) had swamped the countryside with Bavarian and imperial troops.

Among the refugees at Hanau was probably Hans Jacob Christoph, but his stay appears to have been short: while playing on the ice of the fortress moat, he was kidnapped by Croatian soldiers and taken to their Colonel Corpus at Hersfeld. In February 1635 he was picked up by Hessian soldiers and taken to Cassel. At the siege of Magdeburg in 1636 he probably worked as a stable boy and he was present at the battle of Wittstock in October 1636 when Swedish forces defeated the imperials. In 1637 he seems to have been with the regiment of Field Marshal von Götz in Soest, Westphalia; and from March 1638 on he took part in Götz's unsuccessful campaign to lift the siege of the important fortress of Breisach.

planetary Jupiter presumably does not know about the events that took place at Peirithous' wedding (III, 7). Nor can the planetary Jupiter justifiably ask non-planetary deities like Pallas Athena and Vulcan to assist the German hero in III, 4. And though there are many more faults that can be found with the astrological theory of interpretation, we conclude with the observation that it does not exactly help the theory when the two discoverers of it disagree on the sequence of the planets, to wit:

Rehder and Weydt		
in agreement	Saturn, Mars,	Venus, Mercury, Moon
Rehder	Jupiter, Sun	
Weydt	Sun, Jupiter	

III

Neither these nor a number of other interpretations that have been advanced by earnest and well-meaning critics are altogether satisfactory. The reason being that most of them stress one aspect of the novel, only to lose sight of the whole of it. In order to gain something approaching an adequate understanding of *Simplicius Simplicissimus* let us turn to the author himself and find out from him what he intended.

The place where the modern author addresses his (prospective) reader is the preface. Here he states his theme, expresses his reasons for writing the book, gives a concise outline of its content, anticipates and refutes criticism, and tells the reader how he can benefit from his book. But, alone among seventeenth-century novels, *Simplicius Simplicissimus* has no preface. This omission must be intentional, for Grimmelshausen furnished his first publication, *The Satyrical Pilgrim* (1666) with *three* prefaces! In his major novel the function of a verbal foreword is taken over by an emblem-like frontispiece, the so-called phoenix copperplate. This illustration, like most others found in the writings of Grimmelshausen, reflects the author's own ideas and is therefore of more than passing interest. The eight-line poem explaining the picture will also furnish hints and indications.

The frontispiece shows, standing amid seven human masks, a most unusual figure. A human head with horns and the ears of a horse is set on a human trunk with arms; the human part is supported by an animal body with feathered wings and a scaly fish tail. The left leg is a goat's, while the right ends in a webbed foot. The creature wears a rapier on a baldric and in his right hand holds a picture book on whose open pages are shown various objects: a crown, a cannon with a pile of balls, a tree, ointment jars, insects, a chalice, a baby in swaddling clothes, a drawn goose, dice and dice box, and so on. In the verses beneath the picture, the creature says that like the phoenix he was born from fire; that he flew through the air without being lost; that he traveled through water and over land; that in his wanderings he acquainted himself with much that was sad, and with but little that gladdened him; that he put all of it into his book, so that the reader, like the creature himself, may withdraw from folly and live in peace.

Although the grotesque creature possesses a horned head, a human trunk, and a goat's leg, he is clearly intended to represent the satirical author/hero of the novel. The legend on the banner above him seems to confirm this. While the weirdly composed figure resembles no single creature on earth, its determining features — smiling face, horns, tail, and goat's leg — are those of a satyr. We usually consider the satyr as the personification of unrestrained, particularly sexual, activity; but during the Renaissance and well into the seventeenth century the satyr was regarded equally as a wise being who, "under the abuse of that name [of satyr]," might guide human beings through the world without participating in its folly.[8] That is obviously the meaning here, but the satyr is also the symbol for satirical writing, and Grimmelshausen was acutely aware of it.

Simplicius, then, is a strangely constituted being whose experience as a wanderer in various realms qualifies him as a guide for others. The verses beneath the figure allude more specifically to the fact that Simplicius was born a Christian through the fire with which the troopers burned his knan's house. He flew through the air to the assembly of witches and to Magdeburg without being lost. He traversed the waters of the Mummelsee to the center of the earth, and over land through many countries. Simplicius' adventures have been told not so much for entertainment as for guidance, particularly in achieving salvation of the soul. The pictures to which the satyr is pointing refer to various events in Books I through V, and the masks on the ground

[8] Ellen Leyburn, *Satiric Allegory: Mirror of Men*, Yale Studies in English, 130 (New Haven: Yale University Press, 1956), 7.

signify the masks Simplicius has pulled from the faces of persons and things, during his journey through the world.[9]

The poem preceding Book VI, the *Continuation*, is also important to any consideration of the author's purpose. In it Grimmelshausen justifies taking Simplicius out of the solitude of his Black Forest retreat. Simplicius ponders the concatenation of events that made him suppose, wrongly, that he had found enduring quietude. A fall, swift and unaccountable as death, has overtaken him, and, we may infer, the search for tranquility begins once more, for nothing except inconstancy is constant. The prefatory section of Book VI, 1 repeats Grimmelshausen's previously announced purpose in writing his novel: he wants to instruct, but not in the moralizing, theological style of the day. Rather, he wants to sugarcoat the bitter pill of his teaching so that the reader will continue to read and profit. He claims (rather conventionally) that his "satyrical" style scores general vices and not specifically personal ones. If a reader is satisfied with the husks of his story (the entertainment) when he might profit from the kernels of instruction, he has only himself to blame.

Finally, the title page of the first edition also gives us certain indications of the author's intentions. In the exuberant style of baroque titles, it summarizes the contents of the novel, explaining that "The Adventurous Simplicissimus [in] German" is "the biography of a curious rogue named Melchior Sternfels von Fuchshaim; where and how he came into this world; what he saw, learned, experienced, and suffered therein; and why he voluntarily quit it again. Exceedingly jolly to read and useful for everyone. Edited by German Schleifheim von Sulsfort."[10]

---

[9] A very comprehensive discussion of the frontispiece "monster" or "chimera" is given by Karl-Heinz Habersetzer in his article "'Ars Poetica Simpliciana.' Zum Titelkupfer des *Simplicissimus Teutsch*," *Daphnis* 3 (1974): 60-82 and 4 (1975): 57-78. Habersetzer points to the opening lines of Horace's *Ars poetica* as a place that probably suggested the figure in the phoenix copperplate.

[10] Grimmelshausen had a penchant for onomastic mystification. He juggled the letters of his name until he came up with anagrams like the two just mentioned, but he also used Samuel Greifnson von Hirschfeld, Erich Stainfels von Grufensholm, and half a dozen others. Since no copyright was available to authors and publishers with pseudonyms, the situation practically invited unscrupulous printers to produce pirated editions. Another disadvantage resulted from this practice: for centuries the works of Grimmelshausen were listed in library catalogs and reference books under these pseudonyms. It was not until the nineteenth century that the author was identified and the

Once again the author, who hides behind two pseudonyms, insists that his book is not only entertaining but useful.

In an effort to find out how Grimmelshausen intended to fulfill the double function of entertainment and instruction, one may investigate the way in which Simplicius, our fictional autobiographical hero, communicates with the reader. At times he writes as if he were keeping a diary[11] — for example, in the scene in which he explains his identity to the hermit (Bk. I, 8). At other times, but still using the first person and past tense, Simplicius tells the story of his life from the standpoint of the worldly-wise hermit of the island — for example, in the ironic description of the knan's farm, with remarks and references which a ten-year-old could not possibly make (Bk. I, 1-2). The two different views of reality are intermingled so that the reader often does not know which of the two chronologically distinct but personally identical reporters is writing. In addition, the author himself makes an occasional remark — for example, he asks how he could have transported Simplicius from near Hersfeld to Magdeburg so quickly without using the witches' ride (Bk. II, 18).

Young Simplicius usually tells his entertaining stories in diary form while old Simplicius looks over his shoulder, making observations and offering evaluations. The retrospective attitude may be kept up throughout whole chapters, but often a retrospective comment is no longer than a single sentence or even a subordinate clause — for example, "If I had [by that time] read the heathen poets, I would have thought of the Eumenides" (Bk. II, 6). The retrospective "I" is used to point out the lapse of time between the event and the writing, and it justifies moral reflections and admonitions (which usually come at the opening or the close of chapters). The "later ego" also gives the author: (1) the writer's omniscience; (2) the chance to impart miscellaneous information; and (3) the chance to make value judgments and to use satire. Naive Simplex sees only the outer appearances, the masks of the world; the "satyr" Simplicius knows what is behind them, tears them off, and points out the discrepancy.

If the two egos are represented by two lines, their purely chronological progression may be indicated by straight, converging lines. But under the aspect of progression toward God, the mature ego is a straight line in relation to which the line of the younger ego fluctuates

confusion gradually cleared up.

[11] I am here following Lothar Schmidt, "Das Ich im 'Simplicissimus,'" *Wirkendes Wort* 10 (1960): 215-20.

widely. Young Simplex in the woods with his father is certainly closer to the island hermit than are the Hunter of Soest or Simplicius in Paris. Resolutions of repentance, even if quickly forgotten, decrease the distance between the lines; and when, in Book V, 23 Simplicius takes stock of his life and decides to become a hermit once more, the lines meet. But backsliding causes another divergence, which lasts until Simplex, having renounced the gimmickry of Europe, decides to remain on the island, where he praises God and seeks spiritual perfection.[12]

Viewed thus, the novel presents a unified picture of one Christian's life. It tells of Simplicius' pre-Christian ignorance; his instruction in the essentials of Christianity; his fall at Hanau, where he accepts the parson's specious advice to go along with the world; his enthusiastic but essentially sinful involvement with worldly concerns during youth; the numerous ineffectual attempts at repentance — in France, in Einsiedeln, on the tree in the river, and so on; the self-appraisal induced by the realization that his life so far has been futile; his interlude as a restless hermit who soon returns into the world; and his final contentment in a truly ideal life. Certainly the novel is meant to be an example for all Christians — and since Grimmelshausen was anything but narrowly sectarian, one might say for all religious people to follow. Nevertheless, *Simplicius* is entertaining, even if we fail to see or neglect to follow its message. (This is all the easier to do since for long stretches the author himself — writing in the picaresque mode — seems to have done so.) The novel constitutes good entertainment chiefly because Simplicius is the kind of man to whom all sorts of interesting adventures happen. He is, of course, a direct descendant of the Spanish *picaro*, and before stressing his peculiarly German traits, one should consider what he has in common with Lazarillo de Tormes, ancestor of all the picaros. Lazarillo, narrator and hero of his own story, is a talented fellow of humble origin who learns many of his tricks from a blind beggar. He soon develops into a social parasite, but he engages in his nefarious activities with tremendous gusto and *joie de vivre*. He has no high regard for the society on which he preys; he blames his misfortunes on bad luck and credits his successes to God and his own cleverness. Although Lazarillo is an antihero like Don Quixote, his outlook on life

---

[12] As far as this novel is concerned, that is the end of the plot. However, Grimmelshausen brings Simplicius back and makes him participate in a number of shorter pieces, for example, calendar stories and in the *Life of Jump-up*. Aside from the fact that the word *Simplician* had the power of endorsement, Grimmelshausen may well have sensed that a hermit's life, be it ever so exemplary, fell short of the biblical "Love thy neighbor as thyself."

is more closely related to that of Sancho Panza, the realist. At the end
of his story Lazarillo obtains a government appointment — "For nowadays nobody prospers except those who work for the government"; he
becomes a town crier and shares his wife with the archpriest of San
Salvador.

Translations and adaptations of Spanish picaresque novels had
appeared in Germany, but Grimmelshausen mentions by name only the
adaptation of Cervantes' exemplary work, *Rinconete y Cortadillo*. He
specifically acknowledges indebtedness to a French adaptation, Charles
Sorel's *Histoire comique de Francion*,[13] praising its jolly style and borrow-
ing from it the figure of Mad Jupiter in Book III.

Grimmelshausen modernized and Germanized his picaro by making
him the child of noble parents (though he is not allowed to benefit from
his nobility), by letting him participate in historical events, and, above
all, by making him a searcher for salvation. Like the author of *Lazarillo
de Tormes*, Grimmelshausen borrowed and adopted all sorts of literary
and subliterary material, like folk tales and anecdotes, using his special
knack of narration to give them relevance and new life. In his enthusiasm for telling a good story Grimmelshausen was often carried away,
and, forgetting his high purpose of furnishing instruction, created
scenes that are unforgettably amusing. Many such incidents could be
mentioned — for example, the scene in which Simplex steals the parson's bacon (Bk. II, 31) and the meeting of Heartbrother and Simplicius
in Villingen (Bk. IV, 25).

Grimmelshausen is, furthermore, one of the first German authors to
capture the sweep and beauty of landscape; the description of the view
from his hermitage on the Black Forest is justly famous (Bk. VI, 1). His
powers of observation and association are such that he can highlight the
salient feature of a person or an object by a striking comparison: his
aged knan is as chipper as a beetle; a pilgrim's staff is like a Bohemian
earpick; a lady is more *mobilis* than *nobilis*; and a beard is shaped like
a Swiss cheese. Nor is his observation only visual; he has a fine ear for
levels of speech, for dialects and sounds: the peasants in the Black
Forest speak broad Swabian (Bk. V, 17), while the blackamoor in the
chest pleads for his life in Westphalian Low German (Bk. III, 8). This
flair for freshness and accuracy has deservedly earned Grimmelshausen
the label of "realist."

Humor has undoubtedly contributed much to the enduring popular-
ity of *Simplicius*. Grimmelshausen's humor spans a broad range from

---

[13] See Manfred Koschlig, "Das Lob des 'Francion' bei Grimmelshausen,"
Jahrbuch der Deutschen Schillergesellschaft 1 (1957): 30-73.

subtle irony (for instance, in the description of the knan's farm in terms of knighthood, Bk. I, 1), through comic situations (the scene of Oliver and the cat, Bk. IV, 22), to homespun and even crude folksiness (Simplex' dilemma after his escape from the goose pen, Bk. II, 2).

Surprising as it may seem, Grimmelshausen was the only German writer with personal experience of the Thirty Years' War who made that war the setting of a novel. No one else appears to have had the ability or the courage for such an undertaking. Although his perspective is that of a simple trooper, his descriptions of the war are vivid, typical, and realistic. In addition to personal experience Grimmelshausen used published accounts of the war, but unless the reader consults a detailed source study he is unable to tell which passages are based on experience and which come from reading. Because Grimmelshausen stays remarkably close to historical facts, Germans have long used *Simplicius* as "readings in historical background." A comparison of the plot events with the facts of recorded history points up the close connection.

Two days after the battle of Höchst, Simplicius' father appears at a country parson's home and is at first mistaken for General Mansfeld himself. Grimmelshausen is careful to explain that remnants of the defeated army were dispersed as far as the Spessart hills. Simplicius' mother also finds herself in the Spessart, where a few days after the battle of Höchst, she gives birth to a boy. Thus the date of the hero's birth can be fixed as shortly after June 20, 1622. The child stays in the forest until after the hermit's death; on his way into the world he passes by Gelnhausen, where he eats grain and sleeps in sheaves that the peasants could not harvest because the battle of Nördlingen had frightened them away. That was in the fall of 1634, and according to the chronicles winter came early that year and was unusually severe. James Ramsay, a Scotsman by birth, had been appointed commander of Hanau by Prince Bernhard of Weimar in 1634, and in January of 1635 Simplicius was presumably present at the revels with which his uncle celebrated the fall of Braunfels, while refugees inside Hanau were starving. The imperial colonel Corpus, whose men took Simplex with them, is mentioned in the annals of the war, as is the Hessian (Protestant) general Melander Holzappel.

The second siege of Magdeburg, where Simplicius was carried through the air, took place in 1635/6; the city fell to the imperials on July 13, 1636, and Simplicius stayed in the service of the cavalry captain's wife until after Weberschanze, Havelberg, and Perleberg were taken, in the fall of 1636. The two armies, the Saxon and the imperial, then allied, broke camp because the Swedish forces under Banér were approaching. The ensuing battle of Wittstock, on October 4, 1636, brings Simplicius welcome release from his arrest as a sorcerer and spy. After the winter of 1636/7, during which he is a servant of the imperial dragoons in Paradise convent, Simplicius as the Hunter of Soest harasses the garrisons of Dorsten, Lippstadt, and Coesfeld, which Count von Götz had been unable to take from the Swedish. Count von der Wahl, mentioned as concentrating troops for an expedition to Meppen, Lingen, and other places, was in Westphalia in 1637. The commander of Lippstadt, where Simplicius is interned for six months during the winter of 1636/7, *was* a Colonel St. André. (Simplicius, only fifteen at the time, was at first addressed as "my child.") Several events mentioned only incidentally are authentic — for instance, a siege of Lippstadt was expected but did not materialize because Johann von Werth was defeated in the Breisgau and von Götz had to go to the upper Rhine to fight Bernhard of Weimar.

After his trip to Paris and his reluctant service in imperial Philippsburg, Simplicius joins the Merode Brothers until the day before the battle of Wittenweier, in which von Götz was defeated by Bernhard (August 9, 1638). On July 29, then, Simplicius is caught by the Weimarers and made a musketeer in Colonel Hattstein's regiment. He has to work with pick and shovel in the siege of Beisach, but receives permission to return to Lippstadt before Breisach capitulates on December 17, 1638. In Villingen he meets Heartbrother, who calls himself Count von Götz's intimate friend and factotum. With Heartbrother Simplicius goes to Vienna in the spring of 1640, and the two again become involved in the war. Historically, von Götz was cleared in August 1640 of charges of collaborating with the enemy. He was killed in the battle of Jankau (March 1645), and although neither date nor place of his death is mentioned in the novel, Grimmelshausen must have been aware of the date, for in Book V, 5 Mad Jupiter asks Simplex about news from Münster. The peace conference had convened there in December of 1644, but six months were wasted in deciding who was to precede whom into the meeting hall, and Simplex has nothing to report.

The next definite date alluded to is the Duc d'Enghien's expedition, from which the knan fled into the woods near the Mummelsee (Bk. V, 12). That expedition took place in August 1644, and the Mummelsee episode must therefore be dated after that time. The promises that Torstensson made to the Swedish officer quartered in Simplicius' house must have come before the autumn of 1646, when Torstensson retired. Finally, Simplicius' return from his trip to Russia, after an absence of three years and some months, is placed after the German peace had been concluded, that is, after 1648.

Thus it is evident that the framework of historical facts and dates is substantial and that Grimmelshausen has carefully arranged the war experiences of his hero within the realm of the probable. Simplicius' adventures in Russia are entirely unhistorical, as is his life on the un-named island in the Indian Ocean. But those chapters will find a ready response in readers familiar with the adventures of Robinson Crusoe. Exactly fifty years before Defoe's classic was published, Grimmels-hausen created his island paradise by using a British pamphlet, *The Isle of Pines* (London, 1668), a satire by Henry Neville, and supplementing it with a description of the Dutch island of Mauritius.

Fashionable baroque novels usually contained vast quantities of encyclopedic information. Hoping to satisfy this demand, Grimmels-hausen provided his readers with similar material — copied from handbooks. Such "learned" matter generally consists of references to the Bible, to Greek and Roman mythology, and to major and minor classical authors. But it also includes treatises such as the one on the influence of drugs on memory (Bk. II, 8), or an essay on the life and customs of the Merode Brothers (Bk. IV, 13), about whom Grimmels-hausen was the first to write. In the present translation, much of this "scholarly" material is summarized or omitted.

Such embellishments, which were of considerable factual interest to contemporary readers, could be made to serve more than one purpose — for instance, in the episode of the Mummelsee (Bk. V, 12-17). Superfi-cially, the adventure is a retelling of local folk tales, to which are added reminiscences from an essay by Paracelsus on nature spirits. But in addition the readers, many of whom still believed the earth was a flat disk, were given the length of the earth's radius, are informed why some wells have medicinal qualities and why these waters are more effective when first discovered, and so on. Moreover, one becomes acquainted with the utopia of an intelligent race of little people who live happily in their appointed tasks except that they, being without souls, cannot participate in the benefits granted to mortals through the redemption of Christ. The sprites want to learn about life on earth, for when the earth is destroyed by fire because of human sinfulness, they too must perish. Simplicius assures their king that the sprites need not fear, for mortals are paragons of virtue and live according to God's commands. The king then awards Simplicius a magic stone; when placed on the ground it will produce a mineral well "which will en-hance and advance you, [Simplicius], to the extent that you have merit-ed by revealing the truth to us." But Simplex has been lying, and there-fore he loses the stone accidentally and barely escapes being beaten for causing a well to spring up where it is not wanted.

This episode, containing beautiful description, "scientific" information, satire on conditions on earth, and bitter irony, is an allegory with
deep religious implications. Despite its seeming irrelevance, its fairy-
tale quality, and its scientific inaccuracies, for seventeenth-century
readers it carried the message that the soulless sprites envy us mortals
the chance of looking upon the face of God and that we should exert
ourselves harder to deserve that chance.

The satire of Mad Jupiter also has serious overtones, and even Simplicius' sober discourse with the parson in Lippstadt has a double
purpose: Simplex discusses the various brands of Christianity with the
minister, but his real purpose is to divert the man's attention so that
Simplex can keep up his erotic activities. In this, as in other instances,
one must distinguish between the "tongue-in-cheek" meaning and the
true meaning of the passage.

For didactic purposes Grimmelshausen also makes extensive use of
proverbs and maxims, and for admonition there is hardly a more impressive device than the litany, a series of prayerlike repetitions and
invocations such as the one quoted from Guevara in Book V: "Farewell,
World!"

IV

Having considered a number of different interpretations, one may
conclude that Grimmelshausen himself provides the best clues to an
understanding of his major work. A perceptive seventeenth-century
reader would have needed no lengthy introduction in order to understand Grimmelshausen's intentions, for he had an immediate relationship to the work, and he could hardly help being in sympathy with the
author's goal. We, however, being children of a different age, are apt to
view the novel in a different light. The modern reader, like his seventeenth-century counterpart, is perfectly capable of finding humor, satire,
and entertainment in the novel; on the age-old problem of how to be a
Christian in a world that makes the Christian life all but impossible, we
must avail ourselves of what we can in *Simplicius*, even if we enjoy only
the husks and do not penetrate to the kernel of the tale. Furthermore,
if our religious concerns are somewhat different from those of an earlier
age, the condition of the world is not. Even now we sense the historical
relevance of *Simplicius* for our own time when the vicious world,
steeped in perverseness, deceit, hatred, and war, is still crying out for
improvement.

G. Sch.-B.

Book One

CHAPTER 1: *Simplicius' peasant origin and rustic education*

*I*n this our day and age when many think the world is coming to an end, a disease is rampant among common people, an affliction that makes those suffering from it want to be knights and nobles of ancient lineage. As soon as they have by hook or crook scraped together a handful of pennies, they sashay in clothes of the latest foolish fashion, or if by lucky chance they have gained a bit of a reputation for bravery, these people then claim to be of noble family, when the fact is that their forebears were day laborers, hod carriers, or peddlers with pushcarts. Their cousins were mule skinners, their brothers cops and bailiffs, their sisters bawds, their mothers go-betweens or even witches; and — to tell the truth — their whole clan with its thirty-two ancestors is as sullied and soiled as a street gang in Prague that called itself the Sugarmaker's Clique.[1] Indeed, the present-day members of this squirarchy are often as black as if they had been born and bred in African Guinea.[2]

I don't like to put myself on par with these foolish people, though — to come right out with it — I have often thought I must have some grand seigneur or at least an ordinary, run-of-the-mill nobleman for an ancestor, for by nature I am inclined toward the business of nobility, if only I had the necessary tools and investment capital for it. But joking aside, my origin and education might be compared to that of a prince (if only you don't stress the differences too much). My "knan" — that's

---

[1] Reference to a translation (1617) of one of Cervantes' novelas ejemplares, *Rinconete y Cortadillo*, by Niclas Ulenhart, who had transposed the events of Cervantes' story from Spain to Bohemia. The gang is called "Zuckerbastels Zunft" (= Sugarmaker's Guild).

[2] The color gradation, here used symbolically runs from implied white (= virtuous) by way of soiled (sullied, off-white) to black (= evil); cf. Shakespeare's [Black-a-] Moor of Venice.

what they call a father in the Spessart[3] — owned a palace as good as the next man's. It was so attractive that not one single king could have built one like it with his own two hands; he would rather have put off the construction for all eternity. It was well chinked with adobe, and instead of being covered with barren slate, cold lead, or red copper, it was thatched with straw, on which grows noble grain. In order not to show off his ancient nobility (which went back as far as Adam) and his wealth, he had the wall about his castle made not of fieldstone picked by the wayside, or of indifferently manufactured brick — no, he used oak planking, from a noble and useful tree on which grow pork sausages and juicy hams,[4] and which requires more than a hundred years to reach its full height. Where is the monarch to imitate that? Where is the sovereign wanting to do likewise? The rooms, halls, and chambers had been tinted black by smoke — only because black is the most durable color in the world, and paintings in that color need more time to acquire perfection than even the most skillful painters give their best work. The tapestries were of the most delicate texture in the world, for they were made by a creature who in antiquity vied in spinning with Minerva herself.[5] His windows were dedicated to St. Noglass for no other reason than that he knew windows woven of hemp and flax took more time and trouble than the most precious Venetian glass. His station in life made him think that everything produced with a lot of trouble was for that very reason more precious; and whatever is precious is most becoming to nobility.

Instead of page boys, lackeys, and stable boys, he had sheep, rams, and pigs, each neatly dressed in its own uniform. They often waited on me in the fields until, tired of their service, I drove them off and home. His armory was sufficiently and neatly furnished with plows, mattocks, axes, picks, shovels, manure forks, and hay rakes. He drilled and exercised with these weapons daily; hoeing and weeding was his military discipline, as in peacetime among the Romans. Hitching up the oxen was his captaincy; taking manure to the fields, his science of fortification; plowing, his campaigning; splitting fire wood, his troop

---

[3] The Spessart is a hilly district northeast of Frankfurt am Main. Around 1620 it was sparsely settled and densely forested.

[4] Formerly acorns that dropped off the trees in the fall were used to feed and fatten the pigs roaming the oak forests.

[5] Arachne, a Lydian woman, was weaving in competition with Minerva (Athene); she lost and was changed into a spider.

movements and maneuvers; and cleaning out the stables, his war games and most noble diversion. With these activities he made war on the whole earth — as far as his resources went — and thereby obtained rich harvest every fall. I mention all this only incidentally and without boasting, for I don't think I was any better than my knan, whose residence was situated in a pleasant location, the Spessart Hills (a place hardly anybody has ever heard of). Only brevity keeps me from telling you about my knan's family, and mentioning his name and ancestry here and now. Suffice it to say that I was born in the Spessart.

Just as my knan's household was aristocratic, so my upbringing was similarly superior; in my tenth year I had already absorbed all the rudiments of the above-mentioned exercises, drills, and maneuvers. In book learning, on the other hand, I was equal to the famous Amplistides,[6] of whom Suidas[7] reports that he could not count beyond five. My father was much too bright for organized studies and observed herein the usage of modern times, that is, people don't think much of useless knowledge, because you can hire flunkies for that kind of drudgery. Otherwise I was an excellent musician on the bagpipes, on which I could produce splendid dirges.

Concerning theology, there was no one like me in all Christendumb; I had heard of neither God nor man, heaven nor hell, angel nor devil, and I did not even know the difference between good and evil. You can easily imagine that with such theology I lived like our first parents in paradise; in their innocence they also knew nothing of sickness, death, or dying, not to mention resurrection. Oh, aristocratic (or asinine) life in which one does not worry about medicine either! My studies in the law (and all the other arts and sciences in the world) were similar. I was so perfect and excellent in ignorance that I could not possibly have known that I knew nothing at all. Once more I say, Oh, happy life that I was leading then!

But my knan did not want me to enjoy such bliss any longer. He thought I should live and act in accordance with my aristocratic birth. So he started to draw me toward higher things and to assign me more difficult lessons.

[6] Amplistides is the typical nitwit in Greek comedy.

[7] Suidas compiled a biographical dictionary, *ca.* 10th or 11th century.

CHAPTER 2: *The first rung on the ladder of success which Simplicius climbed, together with praise of shepherds and appended excellent advice*

HE ENDOWED ME WITH the office most dignified not only in his household but in the whole world, namely, the ancient appointment of herdsman. He entrusted me first with the hogs, then with the goats, and finally with the whole flock of sheep, and had me mind, pasture, and protect them from the wolf, particularly with my pipes, the sound of which, according to Strabo, helped to fatten the lambs and sheep of Arcadia. At that time I resembled David, but instead of bagpipes he had only a harp; that was not a bad start for me, for I took the omen to mean that in time I too might be world famous. Since the beginning of time prominent men have started as herdsmen; in Holy Writ we read of Abel, Abraham, Isaac, Jacob and his sons, and Moses (who had to mind his brother-in-law's sheep before he became the leader and legislator of six hundred thousand Israelites).

Someone may object here that the aforementioned were devout and holy men, not peasant lads from the Spessart who did not know God. I grant you it is so; but my innocence had to make up for my other shortcomings. Examples can be found among the ancient heathens as well; among the Romans there were noble families who without doubt were called Bubulcus (ox herd), Statilius Taurus (bull), Pomponius Vitulus (calf), Vitellius (baby beef), Annius Capra (goat), and others who were so named because they handled such critters, and probably herded them too.

But to get back to my own flock, you must know that I was as unacquainted with the wolf as I was with my own ignorance. For that reason my father was all the more diligent with his instruction. He said, "Boy, pay attention! Don't let no sheep stray too far, and play on yer bagpipes so the wolf don't come and cause a lot of damage. He's a kind of four-legged rascal and thief who gobbles up men and animules. And if you don't watch good I'll tan yer hide." With equal graciousness I replied, "I ain't never seen a wolf." "Go on, ya muttonhead," he answered, "you'll stay stupid all your life. I wonder what'll become of ya. You're a big lunk already, not knowing that a wolf is a big four-legged rascal." He gave me some more instructions, and finally he got mad and walked off grumbling. He suspected that my crude understanding, which had not yet been sufficiently refined by his instruction, could not grasp his subtle teachings.

CHAPTER 3: *The sympathetic suffering of a loyal bagpipe*

I STARTED TO MAKE such a hullabaloo with my bagpipe that you could have killed toads with it. That way I thought I was safe from the wolf. And as I remembered that my mother had often told me she was afraid her chickens would die from my singing, I started to sing, too, so that the remedy against the wolf would be all the more effective. I sang a song she had taught me, about us peasants and the valuable work we were doing.

I got as far as the tenth verse in my mellifluous melody when suddenly my flock and I were surrounded by a troop of heavy cavalry. They had lost their way in the woods and had been attracted by my music and herdsman's song.

'Aha!' I thought, 'what have we here? These are the four-legged rascals and thieves of whom your knan spoke.' For at first I thought (as did the American Indians when they first saw Spanish cavalry) that horse and man were but one creature, and must be wolves. I wanted to chase them off like dogs and get rid of them, but I had hardly inflated my bagpipe when one of them picked me up by the wing and set me down so hard on one of the peasant horses they had liberated that I tumbled off and fell on my beloved bagpipe. It gave off a pitiful scream, as if it wanted to call upon the mercy of all the world. But although it used up all its breath to lament my fall, it did not do any good. I had to get back on. What troubled me most was that the soldiers pretended I had hurt the bagpipe by falling on it and that's why it had screamed so savagely. Well, like the *primum mobile*, my mare carried me in a steady trot to my knan's farm. Very strange notions and outlandish ideas were percolating in my head; I imagined myself transformed into one of the iron men (for the ones taking me with them were dressed in iron armor). But because the change did not take place, other notions entered my silly head. I thought these foreign creatures had come only to help me drive home the sheep, especially as none of them was devouring my sheep, but all were hurrying straight to my knan's farm. I was on the lookout to see if my knan and my mother were coming out to meet us and bid us welcome. But in vain. He and mother, together with Ursula, my knan's only and dearest daughter, had taken French leave by the back door. They did not want to welcome these guests.

CHAPTER 4: *Simplicius' residence is taken by storm, plundered, and destroyed; warriors make a mess of it*

THOUGH I HADN'T INTENDED to take the peace-loving reader into my father's home and farm along with these merry cavalrymen, the orderly progress of my tale requires me to make known to posterity the sort of abysmal and unheard-of cruelties occasionally perpetrated in our German war, and to testify by my own example that all these evils were necessarily required for our own good by the kindness of our Lord. For, my dear reader, who would have told me that there is a God in heaven if the warriors hadn't destroyed my knan's house, if they hadn't forced me to be among the people who taught me well enough? Shortly before this event I could neither know nor imagine but that my knan, mother and Ursula, myself and the hired hands were the only humans on earth, for no people or dwellings were known to me except my knan's house, where I went in and out daily. But I soon discovered where people come from, and that they have no permanent abode, but often have to move on again before they can look around. I had been human in shape alone, and a Christian in name only; in reality I was an animal! But the Almighty looked upon my ignorance with forgiving eyes, and wanted me to come to the recognition of both Him and myself. And though he had a thousand different ways for this purpose, undoubtedly he wanted to use as an example to others the manner in which my knan and mother were punished for my negligent upbringing.

The first thing these horsemen did in the nice black rooms of the house was to put in their horses. Then everyone took up a special job, a job having to do with death and destruction. Although some began butchering, heating water, and rendering lard, as if to prepare for a banquet, others raced through the house, ransacking upstairs and down; not even the privy chamber was safe, as if the golden fleece of Colchis might be hidden there. Still others bundled up big bags of cloth, household goods, and clothes, as if they wanted to hold a rummage sale somewhere. What they did not intend to take along they broke and spoiled. Some ran their swords into the hay and straw, as if there hadn't been hogs enough to stick. Some shook the feathers out of beds and put bacon slabs, hams, and other stuff in the ticking, as if they might sleep better on these. Others knocked down the hearth and broke the windows, as if announcing an everlasting summer. They flattened out copper and pewter dishes and baled the ruined goods. They burned up bedsteads, tables, chairs, and benches, though there were yards and yards of dry firewood outside the kitchen. Jars and crocks, pots and casseroles all were broken, either because they preferred their meat broiled or because they thought they'd eat only one meal with us. In the barn, the hired girl was handled so roughly that she was unable to walk away, I am ashamed to report. They stretched the hired man out flat on the ground, stuck a wooden wedge in his mouth to keep it open, and emptied a milk bucket full of stinking manure drippings down his throat; they called it a Swedish cocktail. He didn't relish it and made a very wry face. By this means they forced him to take a raiding party to some other place where they carried off men and cattle and brought them to our farm. Among these were my knan, mother, and Ursula.

Then they used thumbscrews, which they cleverly made out of their pistols, to torture the peasants, as if they wanted to burn witches. Though he had confessed to nothing as yet, they put one of the captured hayseeds in the bake-oven and lighted a fire in it. They put a rope around someone else's head and tightened it like a tourniquet until blood came out of his mouth, nose, and ears. In short, every soldier had his favorite method of making life miserable for peasants, and every peasant had his own misery. My knan was, as I thought, particularly lucky because he confessed with a laugh what others were forced to say in pain and martyrdom. No doubt because he was the head of the household, he was shown special consideration; they put him close to a fire, tied him by his hands and feet, and rubbed damp salt on the bottom of his soles. Our old nanny goat had to lick it off and this so tickled my knan that he could have burst laughing. This seemed so clever and entertaining to me — I had never seen or heard my knan laugh so long — that I joined him in laughter, to keep him company or perhaps to cover up my ignorance. In the midst of such glee he told them the whereabouts of hidden treasure much richer in gold, pearls, and jewelry than might have been expected on a farm.

I can't say much about the captured wives, hired girls, and daughters because the soldiers didn't let me watch their doings. But I do remember hearing pitiful screams from various dark corners and I guess that my mother and our Ursula had it no better than the rest. Amid all this horror I was busy turning a roasting spit and didn't worry about anything, for I didn't know the meaning of it. In the afternoon I helped water the horses and that way got to see our hired girl in the barn. She looked wondrously messed up and at first I didn't recognize her. In a sickly voice she said, "Boy, get out of this place, or the soldiers will take you with them. Try to get away; you can see they are up to no good!" That is all she could say.

CHAPTER 5: *How Simplicius uses his legs and is frightened by rotten trees*

SUDDENLY I BEGAN NOTICING the misery about me and started thinking about how to get out of it as soon as I could. But where should I go? My mind was much too shallow to give me a suggestion, but toward evening I succeeded in escaping to the woods and I didn't even leave my beloved bagpipe behind. But what now? I didn't know the roads any better than I knew the lanes through the frozen sea to Nova Zembla. There was some safety in the pitch-dark night that covered me, but to my dim wit it wasn't half dark enough. So I hid in thick bushes where I could hear the screams of the tortured peasants and the song of the nightingales; I shut my eyes and fell fast asleep. But when the morning star rose brightly in the east I saw my knan's house go up in flames, and no one was there to put out the fire.

In hopes of finding someone I knew, I crept out of hiding, but at once five cavalrymen saw me, and one shouted, "Boy, come here, or by God I'll drill you so the smoke will come out of your ears!" Since I didn't know what the soldier wanted, I stopped in my tracks, forgetting to shut my mouth, and stared at them as a cat looks at a new barn door. They wouldn't have become angry with me if a bog hadn't kept them from getting at me. One of them fired his carbine at me, and I was so scared by the flash and the noise (made more frightening by a multiple echo) that I fell to the ground and lay there for dead. As a matter of fact, I never moved a muscle. And when the horsemen rode off, thinking I was dead, I did not feel like sitting up or looking about me all day.

When night came around once more, I got up and walked a long way into the woods, until in the distance I saw a rotten tree sending out an eerie light. That frightened me again. I turned on my heels and kept walking till I saw another such tree, and I ran from this one too. I spent the whole night like this, running from one rotten tree to another. Finally daylight came to my aid by bidding the trees to stop being luminous, but this was no great help, for my heart was full of fear, my legs full of tiredness, my empty stomach full of hunger, my mouth full of thirst, my brain full of silly notions, and my eyes full of sleep. I kept on walking without knowing where I was headed. The farther I walked, the farther I went away from people and into the forest. At that time (though I didn't know it) I felt the effects of ignorance and unreason; if a dumb beast had been in my shoes, it would have known better what to do than I. But when night came a third time, I had enough sense to crawl into a hollow tree (taking good care of my beloved bagpipe, too), and I firmly resolved to sleep all night.

CHAPTER 6: *This chapter is short and so devout that Simplicius faints over it*

I HAD HARDLY MADE myself comfortable for sleeping when I heard a voice saying, "O great love shown to us ungrateful men! O my only solace, my hope, my treasure, my God!" and more in this vein that I could not altogether understand.

These words might well encourage, console, and gladden the heart of a Christian in the shape I was in at that time. But — oh, ignorance and simplicity! — it was all Greek to me and I couldn't make head or tail of it. But when I heard that the speaker's hunger and thirst would be appeased, my own unendurable hunger and my stomach, which from lack of food had become the size of a walnut, advised me to invite myself too. So I told myself to be courageous, crawled out of the tree, and approached the voice.

I saw a man with long grayish-black hair that lay disheveled about his shoulders; his tousled beard had the shape of a Swiss cheese. His face, though haggard and sallow, was kind, and his long cloak was patched and mended with more than a thousand snippets of different materials. Around his throat and body he wore a heavy iron chain. To my eyes he looked so frightening and ghastly that I started trembling like a wet dog. But my fear was increased by the fact that he was hugging a crucifix about six feet high. Since I didn't know him, I could not but imagine that this old man must be the wolf of whom my knan had recently warned me.

In my fear I whipped out my bagpipe (which I had rescued from the cavalrymen as my only treasure), blew it up and started to make a horrendous sound to drive off this wolf. The anchorite was caught up in astonishment. No doubt he thought a devilish ghost had come to trouble him, like the great St. Anthony, and to disturb his meditation. As soon as he had recovered a little he reviled me, his tempter in the hollow tree (for I had retreated to it once more); he was even bold enough to come right up to me and rail at the fiend of men. "Hah!" he said, "you are just the one to trouble the godfearing.... " I did not understand another word, for his approach frightened me so hard that I fainted dead away.

CHAPTER 7: *Simplicius is given a friendly welcome in a poor inn*

I DON'T KNOW HOW I came to, but I was out of the tree, my head was in the old man's lap, and he had opened my jacket. When I had recovered a little, seeing the hermit so close to me, I screamed as if he were about to rip the heart from my chest. But he said, "Son, be still; I won't hurt you; calm yourself," and so on. But the more he comforted and soothed, the more I shouted, "You'll eat me!" "Now, now, my son," he said, "be quiet; I won't eat you." This sort of wrangling went on for some time until I calmed down and went with him into his hut. Here Poverty herself was the major domo, Hunger was cook, and Want was the purveyor. My stomach was given some vegetables and a drink of water, my mind, which was altogether confused, was straightened out and put at ease by the old man's comforting friendliness. Soon Sleep tempted me to pay nature her tribute. When the hermit saw this he left the hut, because there was enough room for only one person to sleep in it. About midnight I awoke again and heard him sing the following song, which I later learned by heart:

> Come, nightingale, O balm of night,
> Come, let your voice cheerful and bright
> Sing out in lovely rapture.
> The other birds have gone to sleep,
> But you a tuneful vigil keep,
> Your Maker's praise to capture.
>> Loudly raise your brilliant voice
>> And rejoice.
>> Show you love
> God who is in heaven above.

> Although the sunshine now has left
> And we of daylight are bereft,
> Yet we may now compete
> To praise his mercy, praise his might,
> Nor darkness hinder us nor night
> To offer praise replete.

Therefore raise your brilliant voice
    And rejoice.
        Show you love
God who is in heaven above.

True Echo with her wild reply
Wants also to be heard close by
When your praise is ringing.
She bids us to avoid all sloth,
That we be active, never loth
She joins in happy singing.
    Therefore raise your brilliant voice, etc.

The stars which in the sky are found
In praise of God do still abound
And show their veneration.
The songless owl with ugly screech
Does yet a noble lesson teach:
Praise God in every nation!
    Therefore raise your brilliant voice, etc.

O come then, sweetest bird of night,
Inspire us with your song's delight.
In bed let us not linger.
Instead let's sing to God in praise
Till Dawn the somber pall doth raise
From woods with rosy finger.
    Loudly raise your brilliant voice
    And rejoice.
    Show you love
God who is in heaven above.

While this song went on, it seemed almost as if the nightingale, the owl, and Echo had joined in, and if I had ever heard the morning star sing, or could have imitated its melody on my bagpipe, I would have slipped out of the hut to join in, because this harmony seemed so lovely.

But I fell asleep again and did not wake up until well into the day. When the hermit stood in front of me and said, "Get up, little one, I'll give you something to eat and show you the way out of the woods, so you get back to your people in the village before night falls," I asked him, "What's that, 'people,' 'village'?" He said, "Have you never been in a village? Don't you know what 'humans' or 'people' are?" "No," I said, "I've been nowhere but here; but tell me, what *are* 'people,' 'humans' and 'village'?" "God preserve us!" answered the hermit. "Are you foolish or bright?" "I am ma and pa's boy. My name is neither Foolish nor Bright." The hermit heaved a sigh, crossed himself, and said, "My dear child, for God's sake I'd like to keep you here and teach you." The next chapter will tell of our dialogue.

CHAPTER 8: *How Simplicius uses elevated speech and thereby gives evidence of his excellent qualities*

Hermit. What is your name?
Simplex. My name is Boy.
Herm. I can see you're not a girl. But how did your father and mother call you?
Sim. I never had a father and mother.
Herm. Then who gave you that shirt?
Sim. My mither, of course.
Herm. How did your "mither" call you, then?
Sim. She called me "boy," also "rascal," "clumsy lout," and "jailbird."
Herm. Who was your mother's husband?
Sim. Nobody.
Herm. But with whom did your mother sleep at night?
Sim. With my knan.
Herm. How did your knan call you?
Sim. He called me "boy."
Herm. What was your knan's name?
Sim. Why, "knan"!
Herm. But how did your mother call him?
Sim. "Knan," and sometimes "boss."
Herm. Did she ever call him anything else?
Sim. Yes, she did.
Herm. What?
Sim. "Belch," "roughneck," "boozehound," and several other names when she was riled.
Herm. You are an ignoramus not to know your own name or that of your family.
Sim. Well, smarty, you don't know it either!
Herm. Do you know how to pray?
Sim. Naw, Annie and mither did all the praying at the house.
Herm. I'm asking you if you know the Lord's Prayer.
Sim. Sure.
Herm. Let me hear it.
Sim. Our dear father, who art heaven hallowed be name, kingdom come your will done heaven on earth, give us debts as we give our debtors. Lead us never in no evil attempts, but save us from the kingdom and the power and the glory in eternity. Emma.
Herm. Didn't you ever go to church?
Sim. Sure. I'm a good climber and stole a whole shirtful of churries.

Herm. I didn't say *cherries*; I mean *church*.

Sim. Ha, ha, you mean the little blue ones? Don't you?

Herm. Heaven help me! Don't you know anything of our Lord God?

Sim. You bet! He hung in the corner behind the kitchen door. Mither brought him home from the fair and fastened him up there.

Herm. Oh dear Lord! Only now I see the great benefice of grace in Thy presence and how man is nothing if he does not know Thee. Listen, Simpleton — for I cannot call you anything else — when you say the Lord's prayer you must speak thus: "Our Father, who art in heaven, hallowed be thy name. Thy kingdom come, thy will be done, on earth as it is in heaven. Give us this day our daily bread."

Sim. Cheese, too?

Herm. Alas, dear child, be silent and learn. You need that more than cheese. Your mother was right when she called you clumsy. Boys like you should not interrupt an old man, but be silent, listen, and learn. If only I knew where your parents live, I'd be glad to take you to them and teach them how to bring up children.

Sim. I don't know where to go. Our house burned down; my mither ran off and came back with Ursula; my knan ran off too; the hired girl was sick and lay in the barn. She told me to run away and not to hang around.

Herm. Who burned down the house?

Sim. Well, iron men came riding on animals as big as oxen, but without horns; these men stuck the sheep and cows and hogs, broke the windows and the oven; then I ran off, and later the house burned down.

Herm. Where was your knan?

Sim. Well, the iron men tied him up; then our old nanny goat licked his feet; this made him laugh and he gave the iron men lots of silver coins, yellow ones too, and nice shiny things and strings of white beads.

Herm. When did this happen?

Sim. When I was supposed to herd the sheep. They wanted to steal my bagpipe too.

Herm. When were you supposed to herd the sheep?

Sim. Don't you get it? When the iron men came. Later our tousleheaded Annie told me to run away; otherwise the warriors would take me along. She meant the iron men, and I ran away and came here.

Herm. Where do you want to go now?

Sim. I sure don't know. I want to stay here.

Herm. It isn't good to keep you here, neither for you nor for me. Eat, and then I'll take you to some people.

Sim. Well, tell me what this "people" is.

Herm. People are humans like you and me. Your knan and mither and your Annie are humans. And when some of them get together, they are called "people."
Sim. Hoho!
Herm. Now go and eat!

This was the conversation we had together. The hermit often looked at me and sighed from the bottom of his heart; I don't know whether he pitied me in my excessive simplemindedness, or for a reason I discovered only some years later.

CHAPTER 9: *Simplicius turns from a mere beast into a Christian*

I STOPPED CHATTING AND started eating. This lasted only until I had had enough and the old man asked me to go away. Then I chose the tenderest words in my peasant vocabulary and used them all to persuade the hermit to let me stay with him. Surely he thought it would be hard to keep me around, but still he decided to put up with me, more to instruct me in Christianity than to let me help him in his old age. His greatest worry was that my tender youth might not be able to endure his severe and frugal way of living.

My trial period lasted about three weeks. It was spring and I worked so well in the garden that the anchorite took a special liking to me, not so much because of the work I did (I was used to it), but rather because he saw I was eager to hear his instruction and my heart was apt to benefit from it.

For these reasons he was the more ambitious to introduce me to all sorts of good principles. He started his teaching with the fall of Lucifer. From there he proceeded to the Garden of Eden, and when we with our parents were run out of it, he passed through the law of Moses and taught me, through God's ten commandments (and their interpretation) to tell virtues from vices, to do good and avoid evil. Finally he got around to the gospels and told me of Christ's birth, suffering, death, and resurrection. He concluded with doomsday and depicted heaven and hell as I could best grasp and understand it, clearly but not with too much detail. When he had finished one topic he started another; my questions guided our progress, and he could not possibly have been a better teacher. His life and his words were one continuous sermon from which, through God's grace, my mind — not exactly inert or stupid — derived much benefit. In three weeks I not only learned what a

Christian must know, but I experienced so much the love of being taught that I couldn't sleep for it at night.

The hermit was so successful in teaching me mainly because the smooth tablet of my mind was altogether blank; when he started writing on it, he did not have to crowd out or erase anything. Nevertheless, compared to other folks there still was plenty of simplicity in me, and for this reason the hermit called me "Simplicius," since neither of us knew my real name.

I learned from him how to pray, and when he had decided to let me stay, the two of us built a hut for me. It was just like his, made of logs, brush, and dirt, and shaped almost like a soldier's tent or (to use a different comparison) like a turnip cellar on a farm, hardly big enough for me to sit upright in it. My bed was made of dry leaves and grass; it was the same size as the hut, and I can't decide whether to call this sort of shelter a covered bed or a hovel.

CHAPTER 10: *How he learned to read and write in a wild forest*

THE FIRST TIME I saw the hermit reading the Bible, I could not imagine with whom he was carrying on his secretive and, as I thought, very serious conversation. I saw his lips move and heard him mumbling, but I saw and heard no one with whom he was talking. And though I knew nothing of reading and writing, I noticed by his eyes that he was carrying on with something inside the book. I paid close attention to the book, and after he had put it aside I took hold of it, opened it, and happening on the first chapter of the Book of Job, with a beautifully colored illustration, I asked the picture some strange questions. But when no answer was forthcoming I became impatient and — just as the hermit came up behind me — I said, "You little rascals, can't you open your mouths anymore? Only a moment ago you were gossiping with my father." (That is what I had to call the hermit.) "I can see very well that you too are driving the sheep home for your poor knan and that you have set the house on fire. Wait, wait, I can still put it out so it won't do any more damage." With those words I got up to get a bucket of water, because I felt something had to be done. "Where are you going, Simplex?" said the hermit, whom I hadn't noticed behind me. "Oh, father," I said, "these soldiers have sheep and want to drive them off. They took them from the poor man you were just talking with. His house is on fire too, and if I don't help put it out it'll burn to the ground." And I pointed with my finger to what I saw.

"Don't rush off," said the hermit, "there is no danger." I answered politely, "But are you blind? *You* see about the sheep and *I'll* get the water." "Boy," said the hermit, "these pictures are not reality. They've been made to give us an idea of events long past." I answered, "But you were talking with them a while ago. Why shouldn't they be real?"

Contrary to his habit, the hermit laughed at my childish simplicity or simple-minded childishness and said, "Dear child, these pictures cannot talk. But I can tell from these black lines what they mean. It's called 'reading,' and when I read, you think I am talking with the pictures, but it's not so." I answered, "Since I am a human being like you, I should also be able to read the black lines. How am I to take your words? Dear father, tell me what to make of this." Then he said, "All right then, son, I shall teach you and you'll be able to talk with the pictures just as I can, but it will take time; I shall have to show patience, while you need diligence."

On birch bark he wrote the letters as they appear in print, and when I had learned them, I learned how to spell, then how to read and write; and since I imitated the printed letters I could write better than my teacher.

CHAPTER 11: *Of vittles, household utensils, and other things necessary for this life on earth*

I STAYED IN THE forest for about two years before the hermit died, and a little longer than six months after his death. Therefore, I think I should tell the curious reader (who often wants to know even the most minute details) of our activities and how we spent our life there.

For food we had all sorts of vegetables like carrots, cabbage, beans, peas, lentils, and such. We did not turn up our noses at beechnuts, wild apples, pears, and cherries; even acorns often tasted good. Our bread (or perhaps I had better call it cake) of ground Indian corn was baked in hot ashes. In the winter we snared birds; in the spring and summer God kept us supplied with nests full of their young. We sometimes ate snails and frogs, and we didn't mind fishing with pots and line, since not far from our camp ran a creek with plenty of fish and crawfish. We used its water for cooking and drinking. For a while we kept a wild pig in a pen and raised it on acorns and beechnuts; later we butchered and ate it. My hermit knew that it is no sin to use what God grants to man. We needed but little salt and no spices at all, for we did not want to stimulate thirst because we had no wine cellar. We received the necessary salt from a parson who lived about fifteen miles from us. I'll have to tell more about him later.

We had a complete supply of utensils to maintain our household — a shovel, a mattock, an ax, a hatchet, and a Dutch oven for cooking; the iron kettle wasn't ours, having been borrowed from the parson. Each of us had a worn-down blunt knife. These things and nothing else were our property. As for the rest, we did not need dishes, plates, spoons, forks, skillet, frying and roasting pan, salt shaker or other table or kitchen utensils, for our Dutch oven also served as our dish, and our hands as forks and spoons. When we wanted to drink we inserted a reed in the water of our well or we lowered our heads into the creek, like Gideon's warriors. Of all sorts of proven material, like wool, silk, cotton, and linen (for beds, table cloths, and drapes), we possessed nothing except what we wore. We thought we had enough as long as we were protected from the rain and cold. Our household had no special schedule except on Sundays and holidays. On these days we started walking at midnight in order to be on time for services in the parson's church before anybody else arrived. We always sat upstairs by the broken organ, from where we could see the altar and the pulpit. The first time I saw the parson getting into his pulpit, I asked my hermit what he intended to do in the big tub! After services we went home just as secretly as we had come; and after we had returned, with feet and bodies tired, we ate poor food with good teeth. The rest of the time the hermit spent in prayers or in teaching me pious lore.

On weekdays we did what was most necessary according to the season. One day we'd work in the garden; another we spent collecting fertile soil in shady places or in hollow trees, in order to improve our garden even without manure. Other times we wove baskets or fish pots, split fire wood, went fishing, or did anything else but loaf. And amidst all this activity the hermit did not cease instructing me faithfully in all good knowledge; and in such a severe life I learned to endure hunger, thirst, heat, cold, hard work, but fist of all to know God and how to serve him honestly. And that was the most important. Beyond this, my hermit did not want to instruct me, for he considered it enough for a Christian to reach his goal through prayer and hard work. And that is why I stayed a simpleton, for when I left the woods I had been quite well instructed in spiritual matters, pronounced my German exactly as it is spelled, knew Christianity very well, and yet was such a plain idiot in worldly matters that I didn't amount to a hill of beans.

CHAPTER 12: *A pretty way of experiencing a blessed death and getting buried at next to no cost*

I HAD SPENT ABOUT two years here and had barely become used to the hard life of a hermit when my best friend on earth took his mattock, gave me a shovel, and led me by the hand into the garden where we usually said our prayers. "Well, Simplex, dear child," he said, "since the time has come when I must depart the earth, pay my debt to nature and leave you behind in this world, and as I see the future events of your life approaching, knowing well that you will not stay long in this lonely place, I have done my best to encourage you on the path of virtue by giving you instruction. By means of this you are to guide your life as by a compass so that you, along with all the other chosen souls, will be deemed worthy of looking forever upon the Lord's face in the coming life."

These words made my eyes water and I said, "Dear father, do you want to leave me alone in this forest? Shall I ... " That is all I could utter; my heart was so troubled for love of the hermit that I fainted at his feet. He picked me up, consoled me as best he could, and pointed out my mistakes by asking if I wanted to rebel against the order instituted by the Almighty. "Don't you know," he continued, "that neither heaven nor hell is able to do that? Don't *you* try it, son! Do you ask me to tarry longer in this vale of tears? Ah no, my son, let me depart, for I will be kept here in this misery neither by your tears nor by my own desire. I am called away by God's express will, and I prepare joyfully to obey his command. Instead of crying foolishly, pay attention to my last words. They are: Know yourself, the longer you live the more so. And if you grow as old as Methuselah, do not give up trying. Most men were lost because they did not know who or what they were, what they could have become or had to become." Then he advised me to stay away from bad company, because the damage done by evil companions was inexpressible. He gave me an example of it by saying: "If you put a drop of sweet wine into a crockful of vinegar, the wine turns to vinegar, but if you put a drop of vinegar into sweet wine, the vinegar will go unnoticed." "Dearest son," he said, "most of all, remain steadfast, for whoever perseveres to the end shall be saved. But if against my expectation you should fall because of weakness of the flesh, quickly arise through honest repentance!"

These three admonitions — to know oneself, to avoid evil companions, and to remain steadfast — this pious man considered good and necessary because he had practiced them and he had not gone wrong.

After he had come to know himself, he fled not only bad companions but the whole world; in this resolution he persisted till the end, and in his end he was doubtless saved — how, I shall soon tell.

After he had finished speaking, he started digging his own grave with the mattock. I helped him as best I could and as he had requested, but I couldn't imagine his purpose. Then he said, "My dear and only true son — for I have begotten no creature but you to honor our Creator — when my soul has gone to its resting place, pay your due respect to my body. Cover me with the same dirt we have just now dug out of this pit." Then he embraced me, kissed me, and pressed me much harder to his chest than I thought a man like him could. "Dear child," he said, "I commend you to God's protection and die joyfully, for I hope He will protect you." But I could not help crying and bawling; I clung to the chains he wore around his neck, thinking I might thus keep him from getting away. But he said, "My son, let go of me so I can see if the grave we have dug is long enough." He unfastened the chains, took off his cloak, and, lying down in the grave like someone going to sleep, he said, "Great God, take back the soul that Thou hast given me. Into Thy hands, O Lord, I commend my spirit," and so on. Then he gently closed his lips and eyes while I stood there like a stick, not believing that his dear soul had left the body, because I had seen him in such seizures before.

As was my custom in these situations, I stayed a few hours by him and prayed. But when my very dear hermit did not make any effort to get out of the grave, I climbed down to shake, kiss, and stroke him. But life had left him; grim relentless death had robbed poor Simplex of his company. I sprinkled the lifeless body (maybe I should say I embalmed it) with my tears and after I had run to and fro, had cried pitifully for some time and torn my hair, I started to bury him, with sighs more than with shovels of dirt. And when I had hardly covered his face, I climbed down and uncovered it, to see it and kiss it once more. I carried on like this all day, until I had finished the funeral altogether alone. Anyway, bier, coffin, shroud, candles, pallbearers, mourners, and clergy were not available to sing a dirge and take care of the burial rites.

CHAPTER 13: *Simplicius lets himself drift, like a piece of reed on a pond*

A FEW DAYS AFTER the hermit's demise, I made my way to the parson mentioned above, reported my master's death to him, and asked his advice on how to act in this situation. Although he tried very hard to dissuade me from staying longer in the woods, I followed in my predecessor's footsteps bravely, and all summer long carried on as a pious anchorite should. But as time changes everything, the grief I felt for my hermit gradually lessened, and the severe cold of winter outside extinguished the ardor of my intentions inside. The more I began to waver, the lazier I became about my prayers, and instead of contemplating divine and heavenly things, I was overcome by a desire to look at the world. And since I wasn't much good anymore in the forest, I resolved to see the parson again and to find out if he would still advise me to leave the woods. To this end, I walked toward the village, and when I got there I saw it in flames; a troop of cavalry had just plundered it, set it on fire, killed some of the peasants, run off many and captured a few, among them the parson. Oh my God! How full of trials and tribulations is a man's life?! One misfortune hardly stops before another overtakes us.

The cavalrymen were about to leave, and the parson was led by a rope like a poor sinner and slave. Some were screaming, "Shoot the bastard!" Others wanted money from him. He raised his hands and begged them, for the sake of their souls, to spare him and treat him with Christian mercy — in vain, for one of them rode roughshod over him and hit him such a wallop over the head that blood trickled down; he collapsed, commended his soul to God, and lay there like a dead dog. The captured peasants didn't fare much better.

When it looked as if these horsemen had lost their minds in their tyrannical cruelty, an armed gang of peasants like an angry swarm of yellow jackets came charging out of the woods. They raised such a ghastly war whoop, attacked so furiously, and fired so savagely that my hair stood on end, for I had never attended this kind of free-for-all. Nobody's likely to make monkeys of our peasants from the Spessart or the Vogelsberg region — nor the ones from Hesse, Sauerland or the Black Forest! The horsemen made tracks, not only leaving the stolen cattle behind, but also throwing away the loot as they ran, giving up their prey lest they fall prey to the peasants. Still, a few were captured.

This introductory entertainment almost spoiled my desire to see the world; I thought if this is the way things are, the wilderness is far more attractive. Still, I wanted to hear the parson's explanations, but he was rather faint from his injuries and the beating he had received. He admonished me that he couldn't help or advise me because at present he had been reduced to such a condition, he would soon have to eke out a living as a beggar, and even if I wanted to stay in the woods, he wouldn't be able to give me any help, because, as I could see, his church and parsonage were at that very moment going up in smoke.

With these words I trotted sadly back toward the woods and my home. Since I had experienced little comfort on my journey (rather, I had become much more devout again), I decided never to leave the wilderness. I was already figuring out how to get along without salt (which the parson had previously given me) and thus do without anybody's help.

CHAPTER 14: *A strange story of five peasants*

SO THAT I MIGHT follow my decision at once and be a genuine hermit, I dressed in the late hermit's hair shirt and put on his chain — not because I needed to mortify my rebellious flesh, but to resemble my predecessor in appearance as well as in manner of living and also to protect myself better against the cold of winter.

Two days after the village had been plundered and burned, I was just sitting in my hut roasting yellow turnips and praying at the same time, when some forty or fifty musketeers surrounded me. Although they hardly believed their eyes when they saw me, these boys turned my place upside down looking for something that absolutely wasn't there, for I had only a couple of books, and they threw them helter-skelter because they were no good to them. After a while, when they had taken a second look at me and seen by the feathers what kind of a useless bird they had caught, they decided there was no hope of booty. Then they wondered about my hard way of living and took pity on my tender youth, particularly the officer in charge. He did me the honor of requesting me to show them the way out of the woods, in which they had been lost for some time. I did not refuse for a moment. To get rid of these unfriendly guests as soon as possible, I led them by the nearest road to the village where the parson had been manhandled. Truth to tell, that was the only road I knew.

But before we got out of the woods we saw about ten peasants, some armed with guns, the others busy burying something. The soldiers approached them and shouted, "Halt!" The peasants answered with their guns. And when they saw how many soldiers there were, they rushed off this way and that so that the musketeers (who were tired) couldn't catch any of them. Then the soldiers wanted to uncover what the peasants had covered up — an easy job because the spades and picks were still there. They had hardly started when a voice came up from below and said, "You bloody rascals! You dirty crooks! You damn bastards! Do you think heaven will let you go unpunished for your un-Christian cruelty? There are plenty of stout fellows who will retaliate for your bestiality, so that nobody will come to kiss your ass!" The soldiers looked at each other and didn't know what to do next. Some thought they were hearing a ghost, but I thought I was dreaming. Their officer told them to go on digging. Soon they struck a barrel, opened it, and found inside a man whose nose and ears had been cut off. But he was still alive. As soon as this fellow had recovered enough to recognize some of the group, he told how the peasants had captured six soldiers who had been reconnoitering for feed. Only an hour ago, they had shot five of these, standing them one behind the other; since the bullet, having had to go through five bodies before him, had not killed him, the sixth in the line, they had cut off his nose and ears. But first they had forced him (I beg the reader's pardon) to lick their asses. When he saw himself so degraded by these dishonorable and dastardly knaves, he called them the vilest names he could think of, hoping to trick them into killing him, though they had vouchsafed his life, but in vain. After he had embittered them, they stuck him in his barrel and buried him alive, saying that since he tried so hard for death, for reasons of spite they did not want to humor him.

While this man was telling of his misery, another group of soldiers, infantry, came up out of the woods. They had captured five of the fugitive peasants and shot the others. Among the captives were four peasants to whom the mistreated cavalryman had been forced to do as he was told. Now, when both groups of soldiers discovered they were from the same army, the horseman had to tell once more what had happened to him and his comrades in arms.

You should have seen what happened to the peasants there! Some of the soldiers in their first fury wanted to fill them full of lead, but others said that these vile s.o.b.s ought to be tortured a little; they ought to get a taste of what they did to our buddy. In the meantime, their ribs were being tickled with musket stocks. Finally a soldier stepped forward and said, "Gentlemen, since it is a crying shame for all soldiers that five peasants abused this rascal (he pointed to the cavalryman), it is no more than fair for us to erase this blot and let these bastards kiss our friend a hundred times." Another said, "This rat is not worthy of the honor. If he hadn't been such a numbskull he would have died a thousand times rather than act in a manner unbecoming to a soldier."

Finally they resolved that each of the cleansed peasants was to reciprocate on ten soldiers. Then they wanted to decide what else to do to the peasants. But the peasants were so obstinate that they in no way could be coerced. One soldier took the fifth peasant aside and promised to let him go where he pleased, if he denied God and all his saints. The peasant answered that he had never given a damn for the saints and his personal acquaintance with God had been slight. He swore he did not know God and wanted no part of his kingdom. The soldier fired a bullet at his head, but it ricocheted as if it had hit a steel wall. Then he pulled out his broadsword and shouted, "Is that the kind you are? I promised to let you go to heaven, I am now sending you to hell!" And he split his head apart down to the teeth. "This is the way to get revenge," said the soldier. "Send these villains to hell now and keep 'em there forever!"

Meanwhile the soldiers tied the other four peasants (the same whom the soldier had had to lick) over a fallen tree in such a way that their rumps stuck up. After removing their trousers, they took yards and yards of fuse cord, made knots in it, and neatly ran the knotted cord through the cleft of their behinds until they drew blood. "This is the way to dress their clean backsides," they said. The peasants screamed like pigs, but a lot of good it did them! The soldiers didn't stop until they struck the bone. I was sent back to my hut because the second troop knew the way, so I didn't find out what else they did to the peasants.

CHAPTER 15: *Simplicius is raided, and has a wondrous dream about peasants and how it goes in time of war*

WHEN I GOT HOME I found that all my firewood, my utensils, and all the paltry food I had saved and harvested in the garden all summer for the coming winter — all was completely gone. 'What now?' I thought. At that moment, need taught me to pray, I called on all my modest wit to decide what would be best for me. But since my worldly experience was limited and slight, I could not come to a good decision. The best I could do was commend myself to God and to put my trust in Him; otherwise I would surely have despaired and perished. Moreover, the things I had heard and seen that day were constantly on my mind, and I thought not so much about food and survival as about the hatred that existed between soldiers and peasants. But in my simplicity I could not help thinking that since Adam's creation there must surely be not one but two kinds of people on earth — wild ones and tame ones — who cruelly persecute each other like unreasoning animals. I was cold and troubled, and with such thoughts I fell asleep, on an empty stomach.

Then, as in a dream, I saw how all the trees standing around the place where I lived were suddenly changing and taking on an utterly different appearance. On top of each tree sat a cavalier; and instead of bearing leaves, the branches were decorated with all sorts of men. Some of these fellows had long pikes, others muskets, pistols, halberds, small flags, and drums and fifes. The sight was a pleasure to look at, for everything was neatly divided by rank. The root was made up of lowly people like craftsmen, day-laborers, peasants, and such, who nevertheless gave the tree its strength and imparted vigor anew when it had been lost. In fact, to their own great disadvantage and even peril they made up for the deficiency caused by absent leaves. They were complaining about those sitting in the tree; and they had good cause, for the whole load rested on them so hard that all their money was being squeezed out of their pockets and even out of the strongboxes which they had secured with seven locks. But if money was not forthcoming, certain commissioners curried them with combs (a process called military execution), and because of this, there came sighs from their hearts, tears from their eyes, blood from their nails, and marrow from their bones. Yet among them there were some jokers called funny birds who were little troubled by it all. They took everything easy, and in their misery they came up with all sorts of raillery so that they needed no consolation.

CHAPTER 16: *Omissions and commissions of modern soldiers, and how hard it is for a common soldier to get a commission*

THE ROOTS OF THESE trees had sheer wretchedness to contend with, but the men on the lowest branches had to endure even greater trouble, hardship, and discomfort. And though the branch-dwellers were jollier, they were also more defiant, tyrannical, and for the most part ungodly; and they constituted at all times an unsupportable burden for the roots. About them there appeared these lines:

Hunger, thirst, and poverty,
Heat and cold and tyranny,
Whence, whatever, where the ache,
Mercenaries give and take.

Those words were all the more truthful because they described the men's work perfectly; for their entire activity consisted of hard drinking, suffering hunger and thirst, whoring and pederasty, rattling dice and gambling, overeating and overdrinking, killing and being killed, harassing and being harassed, hunting down and being hunted down, being afraid and causing fear, robbing and being robbed, mugging and being mugged, inflicting misery and suffering it, beating and being beaten — in a few words, spoiling and harming, and being despoiled and harmed in turn. And neither winter nor summer, rain nor wind, mountain nor valley, fields nor swamps, ditches, passes, seas, walls, water, fire, nor ramparts, danger to their own bodies, souls, consciences, nay, not even loss of life, heaven, or any other things of whatsoever name kept them from it. On the contrary, they continued eagerly in their works until after a while they finally gave up the ghost, died and croaked in battles, sieges, storms, campaigns, and even in their quarters (where soldiers enjoy paradise on earth, especially when they run into well-to-do peasants) — except only a few oldsters who (unless they had stashed away stolen or extorted goods) made the very best panhandlers and beggars. Right above these troubled people sat some old chicken thieves who had squatted and suffered a few years on the lowest branches and who had been lucky enough to escape death till now. These looked a little more serious and respectable than the lowest bunch, for they had climbed up one level. But above them there were some still a little higher, and they also aspired to grandeur. Being the lowest in the chain of command, they were called jacket-dusters: they beat the pikemen and musketeers and with their abuse and cursing dusted their backs and heads. Above these the tree had a kind of break or separation, a smooth section without branches which was greased with the soap of envy so that no one (unless he was of the nobility) could climb up, no matter how brave or smart or skillful he was. This section was polished more smoothly than a marble column or a steel mirror. Above this place sat those with flags or ensigns, some young, some much older. The young ones had been given a boost by their cousins. The old ones had climbed up under their own power, either by means of a silver ladder called bribery, or else by means of a rope which luck had let them catch because there were no better men present just then. A little further up sat still higher ones, and they also had their afflictions, cares, and troubles. They did, however, enjoy the advantage of being able to line their purses most conveniently with a liner they were cutting out of the roots; and for this they were using a knife known as forced contributions. The situation became most pleasant when a commissioner happened along and emptied a tubful of money above the tree to refresh it. Then those on top caught almost all of what dropped, while practically nothing arrived below. For this reason more of the lower squatters died of hunger than were killed by the enemy. The upper echelon seemed to be entirely exempt from either danger.

For that reason there was constant wrangling and climbing in this tree, for every one wanted to sit in the highest, most blessed place. And yet, there were some lazy, devil-may-care louts who hardly tried for a better position and who sleepily did what they had to do. The lowest men with any ambition were hoping for the fall of the uppermost so that they might sit in their places. The struggle was fiercest and least rewarding in the slippery section, for whoever had a good sergeant did not want to lose him through promotion. So they found scribblers, valets, ex-pages, impoverished noblemen, poor cousins, and other parasites and starvelings, and made ensigns out of them, and these were taking the bread out of the mouths of meritorious old soldiers.

CHAPTER 17: *Though in wartime noblemen are preferred over commoners (as is just and proper), many men of low origin attain great heights*

[In a discussion between an old sergeant and a nobleman about the advantage of having only noblemen for officers, the nobleman quotes the Bible, ancient writers, and a proverb to prove his point. The sergeant asserts that hope of promotion makes the soldier do his best; and the nobleman admits that some men of lowly station have risen to be great soldiers, for example, the imperial general Johann von Werth, the Swedish Stalhans, the Hessian St. André, and a few others. But as a rule, concludes the sergeant, noblemen keep the door locked when commoners seek preferment.]

CHAPTER 18: *Simplicius takes his first leap into the world, and has bad luck*

I DID NOT FEEL like listening any longer to this argument; and, turning to the trees again, I saw that they were moving and colliding. These men came tumbling down lickety-split, and the noise of falling and cracking up was all around me. One man lost an arm, another a leg, a third even a head. While I was still staring, it seemed as if all the trees were only one tree and on its top sat Mars, the god of war. He was covering all of Europe with the branches of this tree. As I figured it, this tree could have cast its shadow over the whole world, but because strong northern gales of envy and hate, distrust and jealousy, pride, haughtiness and greed and other such pretty virtues were howling through it, the tree appeared rather tenuous and transparent. For this reason somebody had attached these rhyming lines to its trunk:

> The giant oak when battered by storm and badly hurt
> Casts off a branch or two, worse damage to avert:
> Through internecine wars and through fraternal strife
> All things are overturned and suffering grows rife

I was awakened from my sleep by the tremendous clatter of the destructive winds and the mutilation of the tree and found myself alone in my hut. Therefore I began thinking what in the world I was to do now. To stay in the woods was impossible, for I had been robbed so completely of everything that I could no longer subsist there. Nothing was left except a few books that lay scattered pell-mell here and there. While I was picking them up with tears in my eyes, and calling on God to guide my steps where I was meant to go, by chance I found a letter the hermit had written while he was still alive. It read: "Dear Simplici, when you find this letter, leave the woods at once and save the parson and yourself from present hardship, for he has done me many a kindness. God, whom you should ever have before you and to whom you should pray, will take you to the place most suitable for you. However, always keep Him in mind and always try to serve Him as if you were still with me in the woods. You will be able to endure, provided you always remember my last words and act accordingly. Farewell!"

I kissed this letter and the hermit's grave many thousand times, and without tarrying longer I started out to look for people until I should find them. I continued walking straight ahead for two days, and when night overtook me I looked for a hollow tree to sleep in. My only food was the beechnuts I picked up along the way. On the third day, not far from Gelnhausen,[8] as luck would have it, I came upon a level field. There I enjoyed a meal like a wedding banquet, for everywhere lay sheaves of wheat which the peasants, having been scattered after the momentous battle of Nördlingen,[9] had not been able to harvest. Their loss was my gain. I made a shelter of some of the sheaves, for it was cruelly cold, separated out some grain and ate it. I hadn't tasted anything like it in a long time.

CHAPTER 19: *How Hanau is conquered by Simplicius, and Simplicius by Hanau*

AT DAYBREAK, I ATE some more wheat and then walked toward Gelnhausen, where I found the city gates wide open. One or two gates had been burned; some still were barricaded with manure. I walked in, but though I saw no living people, the streets were littered with corpses, some stripped of all their clothes. This miserable sight frightened me, as you can well imagine. In my simple-mindedness I could not imagine what kind of disaster might have left the place in such a shambles. But after a while I found out that imperial troops had surprised some of Prince Bernhard of Weimar's[10] men, and this is how they had been treated. I had hardly gone a stone's throw or two into town when I had seen enough of it. So I turned around, made my way through the fields, and came to a busy highway that took me to the lordly fortress of Hanau.[11] As soon as I saw the first guard I wanted to

[8] Grimmelshausen's birthplace, a town on the Kinzig River.

[9] On September 6, 1631, the Swedish under Duke Bernhard of Saxe-Weimar and Count Horn were defeated by the imperial forces at Nördlingen.

[10] Duke Bernhard of Saxe-Weimar (1604-1639) was one of the most famous generals of the Thirty Years' War. When Gustavus Adolphus of Sweden was killed in the battle of Lützen, Bernhard took charge and saved the day for the Protestants.

[11] Located east of Gelnhausen on the Main River and not far from Frankfurt. The commander of the fortress, James Ramsay, a Scotsman in Swedish service, was a historical personage; he died in 1639.

run like a rabbit, but two musketeers stopped me and took me to their guardhouse.

Before I go on, however, I must tell the reader about my droll appearance at that time, for my clothing was very strange and wondrously odd; the governor later had me painted that way. To begin with, my hair had not been cut in two and a half years, either in the Greek, German, or French fashion, nor had it been curled, teased, or combed. Rather it reposed on my head in its natural dishevelment, covered with more than a year's outdoor dust instead of powder (meal dust, puff stuff or whatever the name of this foolish material is that's made for male and female fops), and my waxen, pallid face peered out from under it like a hoot owl about to light out at a mouse. And as I went bare-headed all the time and my hair was naturally curly, I looked as if I wore a Turkish turban. The rest of my outfit matched my coiffure perfectly, for I wore the hermit's coat, if coat it could still be called, since the original cloth from which it was cut had altogether disappeared and there was nothing left but the shape of it, barely held together by more than a thousand snippets of multicolored cloth meticulously joined and patched. Over this threadbare and multifariously mended coat I wore the hair shirt instead of a cape, for I had cut off the sleeves and was using them for stockings. My body was girded with iron chains crossing neatly in front and back, the way St. William is usually painted. I looked almost like one of those persons captured and released by the Turks who wanders about begging for ransom to free his friends. My shoes were carved from a piece of wood and tied on with ribbons of basswood bark; my feet looked as red as if I was wearing a pair of Spanish red stockings or had colored my skin with brazilwood dye. I imagine, if at that time some charlatan, quack, or mountebank had owned me, and exhibited me for a flat-faced Samoyede or a Greenlander, he would have found plenty of fools willing to pay a pretty penny to stare at me. Though anybody with brains could easily see from my lean and hungry looks and my neglected exterior that I was not a run-away from a restaurant kitchen or a lady's parlor, much less from some great gentleman's household, still I was closely questioned in the guard room; and as the soldiers stared at me, so I stared at the crazy attire of the officer whose questions I had to answer.[12] I did not know whether he was a "he" or a "she," for he wore his hair and a beard long *à la française*; on either side of his face long braids hung down like pony tails, and his beard was so miserably dressed and botched that between his mouth and his nose only a few

[12] Specific, identifying military uniforms were not yet in vogue.

scraggly hairs showed. Concerning his gender I was no less puzzled by his wide trousers; to me, they looked more like a woman's skirt than a pair of men's pants. I thought to myself, 'If he's a man he ought to have a regular beard, for this dandy isn't as young anymore as he pretends. But if he is a woman, why does the old harlot have so many hairs straggling about her face?' 'Surely it must be a woman', I thought, 'for an honest man won't have his beard ruined in such a deplorable way. Even billy goats won't set foot in a strange herd when their beards have been clipped — they are that bashful.' And though I was in doubt, not knowing the current fashion, I finally decided he was a man and a woman at the same time.

This male woman (or female man) had me searched thoroughly, but found nothing on me save a little book mad of birch bark in which I had written my daily prayers; in it lay the slip of paper that the pious hermit (as reported above) had left me as a memento and a good-by present. He took it away. But since I did not want to lose it, I knelt before him, took hold of his knees and said, "Alas, dear Mr. Hermaphrodite, leave the prayer book with me!" "You fool," he answered, "who in hell told you my name was Herman Phrodite?" I had noticed right away that this joker couldn't read or write; he gave the book to two soldiers and ordered them to take me to the governor.

Well, they led me through town and everybody came out to stare at me like a sea monster and made a big fuss over me. Some thought I was a spy; others, an idiot; still others, a bogey, a ghost, a spook, or an apparition of some kind of evil omen. A few thought I was a fool, and they might have been nearest the mark — if I hadn't had knowledge of God.

CHAPTER 20: *How he was saved from prison and torture*

WHEN I WAS LED before the governor, he asked me where I came from. I replied that I did not know. He continued, "Where do you want to go? And what do you do for a living?" I kept answering I didn't know. He asked, "Where's your home?" And when I answered again that I didn't know, his expression changed, whether from anger or astonishment I can't say. But since everybody likes to suspect the worst, especially when the enemy is close by (Gelnhausen had been taken only recently, and a regiment of dragoons had been wasted there), the governor agreed with those who thought me a traitor and a spy. He ordered me searched. But when he heard from the soldiers who had brought me in that it had already been done, and that they had found only the small book they had handed over, he read a few lines in it and asked me who had given me the book. I answered that it had always been mine, for I had made it up myself and written in it. He asked, "But why on birch bark?" I answered, "Because the bark of other trees isn't suitable for the purpose." "You rascal," he said, "I am asking you why you did not write on paper." "Well," I said, "we didn't have any in the woods." The governor asked, "Where? In what woods?" I answered again, in the same vein, that I didn't know.

Then the governor turned to several of the officers in attendance and said, "This fellow is either a bad egg or a simpleton. Well, he can't be a simpleton because he can write so well." And as he thumbed through the book to show them my beautiful handwriting, the hermit's letter fell out. He had it picked up, but I turned pale because I considered this my dearest possession and treasure, and almost like a holy relic to me. The governor noticed and again suspected me of treason, especially after he opened the letter and read it, for he said, "I know this hand and know it was written by a distinguished soldier, but I can't recall who it is." The contents puzzled him, too, for he said, "This is undoubtedly some kind of code no one understands except the one with whom it was arranged." Then he asked me my name and when I answered, "Simplicius," he said, "Well, well, I know the likes of you! Get him out of here and put chains on his hands and feet. Maybe then he'll change his tune." The two soldiers went with me to my newly appointed lodging, that is, the stockade, and there turned me over to the warden, who according to his orders decorated me with handcuffs and leg irons, as if it weren't enough to carry the hermit's chain I had around me.

This first welcoming reception nevertheless did not satisfy the world. Next came hangmen and executioners with their instruments of torture who (although I was satisfied with my innocence) made my miserable life altogether hell. "Oh, my God!" I said to myself, "this serves me right. Simplicius left God's service and joined the world so that this caricature of a Christian could get his just reward. I had it coming with my irresponsible actions. Oh, unhappy Simplici, where does your ingratitude take you? Behold, God had hardly got you into His service and cognizance when you quit Him and turned your back on Him. Couldn't you have kept on eating acorns and beans in order to serve your Creator without let or hindrance? Didn't you know that your faithful hermit and teacher fled the world and chose the wilderness? Oh, you blind blunderhead. You left the woods hoping to satisfy your shameful desires and see the world. But now look; while you think you are feasting your eyes, you needs must perish in this dangerous labyrinth. Could you not have imagined, you numbskull, that your late predecessor would not have exchanged the joys of the world for the hard life in the loneliness of the woods if he had been confident of obtaining true peace, real rest, and the salvation of his eternal soul in the world? You benighted Simplici, now you get the reward for your vain thoughts and insolent foolishness! You can't complain of injustice and protest your innocence, because you rushed into this martyrdom and the death that's sure to follow."

Thus I accused myself, begged forgiveness of God, and commended my soul to Him. Meanwhile we were approaching the jail for common thieves, and when my need was greatest, God's help was nearest. For when I was surrounded by police and stood waiting (together with a multitude of people) for the jail to be opened to let me in, the parson whose village had lately been robbed and burned wanted to see what was going on, for he too was under arrest. Looking out of the window he saw me and shouted wildly, "Oh, Simplici, is it you?" When I heard and saw him, I couldn't help raising both hands toward him and crying, "Oh, father! Oh, father! Oh, father!" He asked what I had done. I answered that I didn't know; I had surely been brought here because I had escaped from the forest. But when he found out from the bystanders that I was considered a traitor, he begged them to stop until he had reported my circumstances to the governor. That would be good for his and my release, especially since he knew me better than anyone else.

CHAPTER 21: *Fickle Fortune throws a friendly glance in Simplicius' direction*

HE WAS PERMITTED TO see the governor; and half an hour later I, too, was summoned and told to go to the servants room, where there were two tailors, a shoemaker with a pair of shoes, a haberdasher with hats and hose, and someone else with all sorts of cloth to dress me up at once. They got me out of my coat, and took off the chain and the hair shirt so the tailors could take my measurements. Then a soldier barber came in with strong cleansers and scented soap, and just as he was about to start on me, another order arrived which scared me out of a year's growth. Though I worried, it didn't mean anything; it said I was to put my old weeds right back on, for a portrait artist was on his way with the tools of his profession — to wit, minium and cinnabar for my eyelids; lacquer, indigo, and azure for my coral-colored lips; orpiment and yellow lead for my white teeth (which I bared from hunger); and carbon black and umber for my yellow hair, white lead for my ghastly eyes, and lots of other colors for my weather-beaten coat. He also had a whole handful of brushes. This fellow started squinting, drawing outlines, and putting the first coat of paint on; he tilted his head in order to compare his work exactly with my shape. Now he changed my eyes, now my hair, now hurriedly my nostrils and everything he had not done right the first time, until in the end he had produced the spitting image of Simplicius, and I was quite shocked at my own horrid appearance. Only then was the barber allowed to give me the once-over. He washed my hair and worked on it for at least an hour and a half. Finally he cut it according to the latest fashion, for I had hair enough and to spare. After that he put me in a bathtub and scrubbed from my emaciated body the dirt accumulated over the last three or four years. He had hardly finished when I was given a white shirt, shoes and stockings, also a turndown collar and a hat with a feather in it. The trousers were beautifully decorated and trimmed with lace all over. Now the only thing missing was the jacket, and the tailors were hurrying to finish it. The cook came in with a nourishing soup and the kitchen maid brought me a drink. There sat Master Simplicius like a young count, all dressed up and ready to be waited on. I enjoyed the food regardless of my uncertain future, for I had never heard of the hangman's meal! For this reason my magnificent beginning pleased me so much that I can hardly mention it, let alone express it adequately and glory in it. As a matter of fact, I don't think I've ever felt a deeper joy at any time before or since.

When the new coat was ready I put it on, but I made a pitiful appearance and looked like a scarecrow, for the tailors had been ordered to make the coat too big, in the hope I would soon grow in all directions, a hope I amply justified, for with the governor's good vittles I put on weight so fast you could almost see me expand. My rustic dress with its chain and other accessories was put in the museum among other rarities and antiques; my life-size portrait was hung right next to them.

After supper my lord (that was me) was put in a bed the like of which I had never seen, neither at the hermit's nor at home. But there was a roar and a rumble within me all night long so that I could not sleep, perhaps either because my insides did not know yet what was good for them or because they were upset about these newfangled vittles they had had to take on. One way or the other, I stayed in bed (for it was cold) until the sun was shining again. I thought over the strange experiences of the last few days and how the good Lord had faithfully helped me through it all and led me to such a good place.

CHAPTER 22: *The identity of the hermit whose generosity Simplicius enjoyed*

THAT SAME MORNING THE governor's marshal ordered me to go to the preacher and find out what his master had decided about me. A soldier escorted me to the parson, who sat me down in his study. "Dear Simplex," he said, "the hermit with whom you stayed in the woods is not only the governor's brother-in-law, but he was also his dearest friend and protector in the wars.[13] As the governor deigned to tell me, this man never lacked the heroic courage of a soldier nor the godliness and reverence of a monk, two virtues rarely found together. His religious sense and the late troubles so marred the course of his worldly happiness that he scorned and gave up his nobility and his extensive land and holdings in Scotland (which was his home), because all worldly business appeared to him stale, worthless, and reprehensible. To say it in a few words, he hoped to exchange his present high estate for an even brighter future glory, because his high mind was disgusted with all secular splendor, and his thoughts and intentions were set on such a plain and pitiful life as you saw him lead in the woods where you kept him company till he died. In my opinion, he was brought to this pass by reading too many popish books about the lives of ancient hermits.

"But I do not want to conceal from you how he happened to come to the Spessart Hills to fulfill his wish for a poor hermit's life, so you can tell others about it later. The second night after the bloody battle of Höchst[14] had been lost he came all alone to my parsonage, toward morning, when my wife and children had just dropped off to sleep. (We had been kept awake all the previous night and half of this one by

---

[13] It is doubtful that Simplicius' parents, Captain Sternfels von Fuchshaim and Susanna, née Ramsay, have historical prototypes.

[14] The battle near Höchst (now an industrial suburb of Frankfurt) took place on June 10, 1622. The imperial general Tilly defeated "Crazy Christian," Duke of Braunschweig, who fought for Protestantism in the service of Frederick V, the erstwhile king of Bohemia. According to Bk. I, chap. 22 and Bk. V, chap. 8, some Mansfelders must have been involved in this battle.

the commotion caused by refugees and their pursuers.) First there was a timid knock at the door which got louder until he awakened me and my exhausted servants, and when I opened the door after a short, polite exchange of words, I saw him dismount from his spirited steed. His valuable clothes were as much covered with the blood of his enemies as decorated with gold and silver. And since he was still brandishing his sword I became alarmed. But when he put it in the scabbard, and uttered nothing but polite words, I wondered why such a courageous gentleman was asking for lodging at such a poor parson's. Because of his splendid personal appearance, I addressed him as General von Mansfeld, but he answered that only as far as misfortune was concerned could he be compared to him, indeed take precedence over him. He regretted three things, to wit: the loss of his highly pregnant wife; the lost battle; and the fact that, unlike other good soldiers, he had not been privileged to give his life for his faith. I wanted to comfort him, but I soon saw that his magnanimity needed no consolation. I shared with him what my house afforded and had a soldier's bed made up of fresh straw, because — though he needed rest badly — he wanted to sleep in no other. The first thing he did the next morning was to give me his spirited horse and his money (of which he had quite a bit with him, in gold) and to hand out precious rings among my wife, children, and the servants. I did not know what to make of him, because soldiers usually take sooner than give. For that reason I was worried about accepting his precious gifts and insisted I had not deserved such of him, nor knew how to deserve them. Besides, I said, if such riches, and particularly the expensive horse (which could not well be hidden), were found at my place, some people would conclude I had robbed or even helped to kill him. He said not to worry about that; he would give me a letter of donation in his own handwriting; he did not intend to wear his shirt, much less the clothes on his back, when leaving the parsonage. And then he acquainted me with his intention of becoming a hermit. With might and main I tried to dissuade him, for it seemed to me such action smacked of popishness, and reminded him that he could better serve the Gospel with his sword. But in vain, for he talked so much and so long with me that he wore me down, and I furnished him with the books, pictures, and utensils you saw at his place, though in return for everything he had given me, he wanted only the wool blanket with which he had covered himself during the night. From this he had a coat made. I also had to exchange my wagon chain, which he wore from then on, for a golden one on which he had been wearing his beloved wife's picture; thus, he kept neither money nor valuables. My hired man took him to the loneliest spot in the woods and helped him build his hut there. How he spent his life there and how you helped him, you know yourself, and better than I.

"After the Battle of Nördlingen was lost a while ago, and I was stripped clean and, as you know, injured to boot, I fled to this place for safety because my most valuable things were here already. And when my money was about to give out, I took three rings and the gold chain with the picture on it that I had received from the hermit (the ring with his initials was part of the lot) and went to a Jew to make them into money. On account of their high value and good workmanship, he offered them to the governor, who straightway recognized the coat of arms and the picture, sent for me, and asked how I got the jewelry. I told him the truth, showed him the hermit's letter of donation (in his own hand) and told him the whole story — how he had lived and died in the woods. But he refused to believe me and threatened to keep me under arrest until he found out the truth. While the governor was preparing to send out soldiers to look at the hermit's place and to have you brought here, I saw you being led to prison. As the governor no longer has cause to doubt my words, because I referred to the place where the hermit used to live, to you, and to other witnesses, but especially to my sexton, who often let you and him into church before daybreak; and since the note he found in your prayer book gives excellent proof not only of the truth but also of the late hermit's holiness — the governor wants to do you and me as much good as he can, for the sake of his departed brother-in-law, and take good care of us. You have only to make up your mind what you want him to do for you. Do you want to study at a university? He will pay all expenses. Do you want to learn a trade? He'll have you apprenticed. Do you want to stay with him? He'll treat you like his own son, for he said that if even a dog came straying in from his late brother-in-law's, he'd take care of him too."

I answered, whatever the governor wanted to do with me, it would be all the same to me.

CHAPTER 23: *Simplicius becomes a page. How the hermit's wife was lost*

THE MINISTER HAD ME wait in his lodgings until ten o'clock before going with me to see the governor to tell him of my resolve. The reason was that then he might eat with him, since the governor was very hospitable. For at that time Hanau was surrounded, and the common man had a hard time of it, especially the refugees in the fortress; thus, a few of the better ones did not mind picking up from the streets some frozen turnip peels thrown out by the rich. The parson was lucky enough to get a seat opposite the governor. But I waited on table, plate in hand, as the major-domo told me to; I did it with the gracefulness of a jackass playing chess or a hog performing on the harp. But the preacher made up through his conversation what my own clumsiness jeopardized. He said I had been reared in the wilderness, had never been among people, and must therefore be considered excused because I was still ignorant of how to behave. My loyalty to the hermit and the hard life I had endured along with him were admirable, so much so that not only should my clumsiness be excused, but I should be given preference over the finest nobleman's son. He further told how the hermit had thoroughly enjoyed my company, because — as he had often said — I was the very image of his dearly beloved's appearance and because he had often marveled at my perseverance and unswerving intention of staying with him, and many other virtues he had praised in me. In short, he could hardly stress enough how, shortly before his death, the hermit had warmly commended me to him, the minister, and how he had confessed he loved me like his own child.

This speech tickled my ears so well that it seemed to me I had received from it reward and pleasure enough for all I had ever endured at the hermit's. The governor asked whether his late brother-in-law hadn't known that he was in command at Hanau. "Certainly," answered the preacher, "I told him so myself. But he took it (with a joyous face and a little smile) as coldly as if he had never known a Ramsay. As I think of it now, I still have to marvel at the man's constancy and firm resolve, how he could endure not only renouncing the world, but even forgetting his best friend, who was so close by!" The eyes of the governor (who wasn't a bit effeminate, but a tough heroic soldier) filled with tears. He said, "Had I known he was still alive and where to look for him, I would have had him brought here even against his will, that I might have repaid him for his acts of kindness. But since luck failed me in this, I will take care of his son Simplicius and thus show my gratitude after his death." "Alas!" he continued, "that noble cavalier had good cause to mourn his pregnant wife, for she was captured by a troop of imperial horse who were in pursuit. That was in the Spessart Hills too. When I found out about it, not knowing but that my brother-in-law had been killed at Höchst, I immediately sent a trumpeter[15] to the enemy to inquire about my sister

---

[15] Trumpeters or drummers were often used as ad hoc emissaries or agents.

and to ransom her. But I found out only that the troop of cavalry had been broken up by peasants in the Spessart, and that my sister had been separated from them and become lost. To this hour I don't know what happened to her."

This and similar matters, concerning my hermit and his beloved, a pair that was pitied all the more as they had been married only a single year, were the table talk of the governor and the preacher. But I became the governor's page boy, and such a fellow as the people (especially the peasants, when they wanted me to announce them) called Master Young, though one seldom sees a young one who is a master (but many masters that used to be young ones).

CHAPTER 24: *Simplicius reproaches people; he sees many idols in this world*

AT THAT TIME, YOU could find in me nothing but a clear conscience and a pious, upright mind, and this was accompanied and enhanced by noble innocence and simplicity. I knew no more of vices than what I had heard or read about them; and if I actually ran into one it seemed an awful and strange thing to me, because I had been brought up to have God's presence always in my mind and to live seriously according to His holy will; and because I knew His will, I was accustomed to weigh men's actions and character against it. In doing this, I thought I saw about me nothing but wickedness. My God! At first, how surprised I was when I considered the law and the gospel together with Christ's faithful warnings and — on the other hand — the works of those who claimed to be His disciples and followers. Instead of an upright mind which every righteous Christian ought to have, I found nothing but hypocrisy and such egregious folly among the children of this world that I was in doubt whether I was seeing Christians or not. For I could easily notice that many knew the serious will of God, but I noticed no seriousness in trying to achieve it.

Therefore my mind was full of a thousand different whimsies and strange thoughts, and I fell into serious doubt concerning Christ's bidding when he says, "Judge not, lest ye be judged!" Nevertheless, the words of St. Paul, which he wrote to the Galatians, chapter five, entered my mind: "Now the works of the flesh are manifest, which are *these*: adultery, fornication, uncleanness, lasciviousness, idolatry, sorcery, enmities, strife, jealousies, wraths, factions, divisions, hatred, murder, drunkenness, revelings, and such like, of which I forewarn you, even as I did forewarn you, that they who practice such things shall not inherit the kingdom of God." Then I thought, 'Almost everyone is doing these things openly; why can't I honestly conclude from the apostle's words that neither will everyone be saved?'

Besides pride and avarice (and related vices), the wealthy indulged daily in gluttony and drunkenness, fornication and buggery. But what appeared worst to me was this abomination, that some, especially soldier boys (whose vices are usually not too severely punished), made a joke of their godlessness and God's holy will. For example, I once heard an adulterer who wanted to be praised for his deed say these ungodly words, "It serves that patient cuckold right to be wearing a pair of horns because of me, and, to tell the truth, I did it more to hurt him than to please her, that I might have my revenge on him." "Oh, barren satisfaction!" answered an honest fellow who heard it, "whereby one pollutes one's own conscience and acquires the shameful name of an adulterer!" "How so 'adulterer'?" was the sneering answer. "I did not break his marriage, I only bent it a little. The real adulterers are those of whom the sixth commandment speaks, where it says that nobody should climb into another's garden to reap the cherries before the rightful owner gets to them!" And to make his meaning clearer he explained the seventh commandment according to his diabolic catechism. He was so full of such explanations that I sighed and thought, 'Oh, cursed sinner, you call yourself a bender of marriages, and God a breaker of marriages because he separates man and wife through death!' "Don't you think," I said from excessive zeal and chagrin, though he was an officer, "that you commit a greater sin by such godless talk than by adultery itself?" But he answered me, "Shut up, smarty, do you want to get hit?" And I have no doubt, I would have gotten a thrashing if the fellow hadn't been afraid of my master. But I kept silent, and later saw it wasn't at all unusual for single folks to hanker for married ones, and married folks to lust after single ones.

When I was still studying the way to salvation at the hermit's, I wondered why God had so strictly forbidden idolatry to his people. For I imagined that whoever had come to know the true, eternal God would never honor and adore another. In my simple mind I concluded that this commandment was unnecessary and superfluous. But alas, fool that I was, I knew not what I was thinking, for as soon as I entered the world I noticed that, regardless of this commandment, almost every worldling had a god besides God. Some even had more than all the ancient or modern heathens. Some had their god in a strongbox and found all their assurance and consolation in him; others had theirs at court, having put all their trust in a court favorite who often was a more despicable dullard than his worshiper, for his airy godhead consisted only in the prince's flibbertigibbet favor. Others had their idol in reputation and worldly glory, and imagined themselves demigods if only they had fame. Still others had theirs in their head — namely, those to whom the true God had given a sound brain, making them clever in a handful of arts and sciences. These put the kind Creator aside, and relied on His gift in their hope for worldly prosperity. Also, there were many whose god was their own belly, to which they daily delivered those sacrifices the heathens long ago offered to Bacchus and Ceres; and when the belly rebelled or other human frailties appeared, these deplorable creatures made a god of their physician and took lodging, as it were, in a pharmacy, from which they were dispatched straight to the grave. Some fools made she-gods of slick wenches; they called them by different names, worshiped them day and night with a thousand sighs, and made songs praising them and humbly requesting that they take merciful pity on their foolishness, and become she-fools even as they were he-fools.

On the other hand, there were wenches who had set up their own beauty as a god. This one, they thought, will get me a husband; let God in heaven say what he will. In lieu of other sacrifices, this idol was daily entertained and adored with grease paint, jellies, lotions, powders, and other cosmetics. I saw people who considered houses in good locations their gods, for they said that, as long as they had lived there, they had had good luck, and money had, as it were, grown on trees in their back yard. I marveled at this, for I saw the reason for their lucre. I knew a fellow who never got a good night's rest worrying over his tobacco trade, for he had given it his heart, mind, and thoughts, which should be dedicated to God alone; by day and night he sighed a thousand times, for he was doing well by it. But what happened? This splenetic fellow died and was blown away just like tobacco smoke. Then I thought, 'Oh, you miserable man! If the salvation of your soul and our true God's honor had been of the same importance to you as your idol (who is exhibited in your shop as a Brazilian with a roll of tobacco under his arm and a pipe in his filthy mouth), I would be very confident you'd be wearing a golden halo in the other world.' Another fellow, named Jack Ass, I was told, had even more sleazy gods; for when at a party everybody told him he had eked out a living in the days of dreadful famine and high prices, Jack said in so many plain words that snails and frogs had been his lord god. Without them he would have starved. I asked him what he had thought of God himself, who at that time had provided him with these creatures for his survival? The simpleton didn't know what to answer, and I had to marvel all the more for nowhere had I read that either the old heathen Egyptians or the most recent American aborigines had ever proclaimed such vermin their god, as this fop did.

In the company of a distinguished gentleman I once visited a museum full of oddities. Among the paintings, I liked none better than an "Ecce Homo," because of the sad expression that evoked tremendous compassion in the beholder. Next to it hung a large sheet of paper painted in China, with the Chinese idols sitting there in all their majesty. Some looked like veritable devils. The master of the house asked me which piece in his museum I liked best. I pointed to the "Ecce Homo," the image of Christ. But he said I was wrong; the Chinese picture was much rarer and hence more precious; he wouldn't give it up for ten such "Ecce Homos." I replied, "Sir, is your heart like your mouth?" He said, "I try to have them agree." Then I said, "So the god of your heart is the one whose portrait you just now let your mouth declare to be the most precious thing." "Silly," he said, "I am talking about supply and demand!" I answered, "What is rarer and more admirable than that God's son suffered for us, as this picture portrays it?"

CHAPTER 25: *Everything on earth appears strange to Simplicius, and he seems strange to the world, too*

AS MUCH AS THESE and other idols were honored, the majesty of our true God was held in contempt; though I saw no one who cared to keep His commandments, I saw on the other hand many who rebelled against Him and outdid the publicans (who were open sinners in the days when Christ walked on earth) in meanness. Christ says, "Love your enemies; bless those that curse you; do good unto those that hate you; pray for those who insult and persecute you." But I found none who obeyed these orders of Christ; on the contrary, they did exactly the opposite. One time I saw a soldier give another a good blow on the cheek, and imagined that now he would turn the other cheek. (I had never seen a fight before.) But I was mistaken. The victim whisked out his blade and cut the attacker on the head. I shouted at him, "Friend, what are you doing?" "I'd be an s.o.b.," he answered. "I'll get even, goddammit, or I'll croak. Only a bastard would take that lying down!" The noise between the two fighting cocks increased because each one's friends were fighting too. I heard them swear by God and their souls with such nonchalance that I couldn't believe they valued either above a penny. But that was only child's play. Pretty soon someone shouted, "May lightning strike me dead! Let hail and thunder strike me and a hundred thousand others!" The holy sacraments were poured out not by tens and scores but by thousands, by buckets, and barrelfuls and in whole rivers, and again my hair stood on end. I wondered what had become of Christ's commandment in which he says, "Do not swear, rather let your speech be, 'Yea, yea, nay, nay,' and whatsoever is more than these is of the evil one." What I had heard and seen prompted me to decide that these fighting cocks were not Christians, and I sought other company.

I wished everyone had been brought up and taught by my hermit. In my opinion, others would then have seen the ways of the world with the eyes through which I saw it. I was not so smart as to say that if there were only Simpliciuses in the world, there would be fewer vices; but one thing is sure, a Mr. Worldly who is used and inured to every vice and folly is least in a position to know that he and his ilk are taking the primrose path to perdition.

CHAPTER 26: *An amazing new custom of welcoming people and wishing them good luck*

BEING IN SERIOUS DOUBT whether or not I was living among Christians, I went to my parson and told him all I had heard and seen, and also my thoughts — namely, that I suspected people were only mocking Christ and His word, and that they were really non-Christians. I asked him to help me come out of this dream, that I might really know what to think of my fellow men. The parson answered, "Certainly they are Christians, and I wouldn't advise you to call them anything else." "My God," I said, "how can this be? If I remind someone of the sin he is committing against God, I am laughed at and made fun of." "Do not be surprised at that," answered the parson. "I think if the early Christians, even the apostles themselves, were to rise and come back into this world, they would ask the same question as you, and everybody would consider them fools too. What you have seen and heard so far is common knowledge and only child's play in comparison with what else is being committed against God in this world, either secretly or publicly. But do not let it trouble you. You will find few such Christians as the late Mr. Samuel."

While we were talking, some captured enemy soldiers were led across the square, and we interrupted our conversation to go and see the prisoners of war. Then I saw a crazy custom the like of which I never could have dreamed up. This was the new fashion of greeting and welcoming. One of our men, who had previously served on the emperor's side and knew one of the prisoners, went to him, shook hands with him, and shouted full of joy and confidence, "Well, well, let lightning strike me! You still alive, old soak? Holy mackerel! How in hell did you get here!? I thought you had been rotting on the gallows since last year!" The other fellow answered, "By God's bones, old soak, is it you or not? How in hell did *you* get here? I never thought I'd see *you* again. Hasn't the devil whisked you off yet?" And when they parted, instead of "God be with you," they said, "Hell's bells, maybe we'll meet tomorrow, get good and drunk, and have a great time."

"Is that a Christian welcome?" I said to the parson. "If this is the way they speak to each other when they are friends, what will they say when they become enemies? Sir Parson, if these are Christ's lambs and you are their appointed shepherd, it is your job to lead them to better pasture." "Yes, dear child," replied the minister, "that's the way these soldier-boys are. May God have mercy on them. If I preached to them, it would do as much good as preaching to the birds — and what's more, these rascals would come after me with a hatred that's downright dangerous."

I was astonished by this, kept on chatting a while longer, and finally left to call on the governor. At this time I had permission to look at the town and to visit the minister, for my master knew of my simple-mindedness and thought I'd overcome it if I got around a little and was instructed by others or, as they say, was cut down to size and got rid of my rough edges.

CHAPTER 27: *A powerful stench stinks up the secretary's office*

MY MASTER'S FAVOR TOWARD me kept increasing daily, for I resembled not only his sister (who had been the hermit's wife) but also the hermit himself; indeed, the resemblance improved the more our good food and lazy days made me sleek and pleasant to look at. This favor was extended by others as well, for whoever had something to do with the governor showed favor toward me. This was especially true of the governor's secretary, who was supposed to teach me arithmetic and who had a lot of fun with my ignorance and simplicity.

He had only recently graduated, and was still full of students' jokes and pranks, for which he had been famous at school. (Some thought he had bats in the belfry.) He often persuaded me that black was white, and white, black; that's why at first I believed everything he said, and in the end, nothing. Once when I reproached him for his untidy inkwell he answered that was the best thing in the whole office, for he could get out of it whatever he wanted — clothes or money; in fact, he had fished a good many other things out of it. I did not want to believe that such bulky and valuable goods could come out of such a tiny glass. But he asserted the *spiritus papyri* (that's what he called the ink) could do just that, and the inkwell was called a "well" because it was deep enough to hold everything. I asked how one could get them out, since the well wasn't wide enough to stick in two fingers at the same time. He replied he had an arm in his head that could do it, and he had hopes of fishing out some rich and beautiful girl; he was confident that if his luck held he could get real-estate and servants out of it too. And this was nothing new; it had all been done before.

I was dumbfounded at this trick and wondered if other people knew how to do it, or might learn. "Sure," he answered, "all chancellors, doctors, secretaries, managers, lawyers, commissioners, notaries, and innumerable others who commonly become rich if they fish diligently and look out for Number One." I said, "So the peasants and other hardworking people are stupid not to learn this trick instead of eating their bread in the sweat of their brow." He answered, "Some don't know how much good this trick can do, and therefore they don't want to learn it. Others want to learn it, but don't have the arm in the head or something else they need. Some learn the trick, have the arm, but don't know certain little catches or gimmicks the trick requires if you want to get rich. Others know everything and can do everything they need, but they live on Failure Street and haven't the same chances I have to practice the trick."

While we were discussing the inkwell (which reminded me of Fortunatus' purse),[16] a book on epistolary titles and salutations happened to attract my attention and I said to the secretary, "All these people addressed are sons of Adam, creatures like you and me; all are dust and ashes! Why the big difference in salutation? Your Lordship, your Holiness, your Worship, your Grace, your Invincible Highness, your Majesty. Are these divine characters? And why 'Esquire'?" The secretary had to laugh as he explained these things to me, and while I

---

[16] Fortunatus is the hero of a popular tale (*Volksbuch*, chapbook) which appeared at Augsburg in 1509 and was reprinted many times. The goddess Fortuna gave the hero a purse that was always full.

was laughing about so much foolishness I couldn't help letting out such a fiendish fart that it startled both of us.

The smell spread through the office in no time. "Get out, you swine!" the secretary said to me. "Go to the other hogs in the pigsty, where you belong, instead of carrying on a conversation with educated people!" But he was forced to clear out, just as I was; the horrible stink was unbearable. That's how I messed up the good beginning of a promising business training in the secretary's office.

CHAPTER 28: *Someone full of envy teaches Simplicius soothsaying and other gentle tricks*

I HAD GOTTEN INTO this trouble through no fault of my own, for the unusual food and medicines I was made to swallow every day, to straighten out my shrunk stomach and diminished innards, raised many powerful storms inside me, and they bothered me when they urgently sought an exit. And since I did not think it at all bad to let nature take her course (it was impossible to resist her at length, my hermit had never instructed me in this matter, nor had my knan forbidden it), I let the wind pass — until the day I lost face with the secretary. Now, perhaps I might have done without his sympathy, if I had not gone from bad to worse, for I fared like a pious, good man who comes to court, a place where Goliath tried to undo David; Minotaur, Theseus; Circe, Ulysses; *et al., et al.*

My master had another page, a smart aleck and sharp cookie, who had been there several years longer than I. Well, I was chummy with him because we were of the same age. I thought, 'He is Jonathan and you are David.' But he was jealous of my master's great favor toward me, which increased daily. He worried that I might even want to take his place; and therefore he thought secretly of ways to discredit me and through my fall prevent his own. But I, with the gentleness of a dove, confided all my secrets to him, and because these consisted only of childish simplicity and piousness, he could never get at me.

Once, in bed, we talked a long time before falling asleep and while we were talking about soothsaying he promised to teach it to me for nothing. He asked me to stick my head under the covers, this being part of the game. I did so eagerly, and watched closely for the arrival of the spirit of prophecy. Holy cow! It went in at my nose and with such concentration that I couldn't possibly stay under for the stench.

"What is it?" asked my teacher. I answered, "You farted!" "And you," he replied, "are saying sooth and have caught on beautifully."

I did not think this was too bad, for at the time I was still too naive to take offense. I only wanted to know how to let out quiet ones. My fellow page answered, "There's nothing to it. Just raise your left leg like a dog at the corner, whisper *je pète, je pète, je pète,* and push as hard as you can. Then when these travelers come out, they do so as quietly as thieves." "That's good," I said, "and even if there should be a slight smell, everyone will think it was one of the dogs." If I had only known about this in the office earlier today!

CHAPTER 29: *Simplicius picks up two eyes from a calf's head*

ON THE FOLLOWING DAY my master gave a sumptuous party for his officers and other good friends. The occasion was the news that his men had taken Fort Braunfels without losing a single soldier. It was part of my duty to help with carrying in the dishes, pouring the wine, and waiting at table, platter in hand. First, I had to carry in a large, juicy calf's head. As it was well boiled, one eye hung out rather loosely; it looked pleasant and tempting to me. And because the smell of the broth and the ginger dressing made my mouth water, I suddenly felt an irresistible appetite. The calf's eye, smiling at my nose, my mouth, and my eyes, almost begged me to incorporate it into my ravenous stomach. I didn't break a leg fighting back, but, yielding to my desire, in the passageway I lifted out the eye with a spoon and swallowed it quickly. Nobody noticed until the calf's head reached the table and betrayed itself and me. When it was about to be carved up and one of its most delicious parts was missing, my master saw at once why the man with the carving knife hesitated. The cook was called in, and the runners were questioned closely. Finally it came out that I, poor fellow, had been given the whole head and that's as far as anyone could report.

With a frightful expression, as it seemed, my master asked me what I had done with the one eye. I didn't let him scare me, but whipped out the spoon and in a flash demonstrated with the other eye what they wanted to know.[17] "*Par Dieu!*" said my master, "this trick tastes better than ten calves." The gentlemen present praised this bon mot and called

[17] In some countries the eyes of a sheep (or calf) are considered as delicacies reserved for honored guests; see H. Norman Schwarzkopf, *The Autobiography: It Doesen't Take a Hero* (New York: Bantam, 1992), p. 31 f.

my silly action a bright invention, a harbinger of future bravery and unflagging zeal. But the governor warned me not to try anything like that again.

CHAPTER 30: *How a person gets tipsy little by little, and how in the end he becomes plastered without being aware of it*

AT THIS BANQUET, AS at many others, people came to the table like Christians; grace was said very quietly and reverently. During the soup and the first few courses, such reverence continued almost as in a Capuchin convent. But hardly had they said, "God bless us," three or four times when the noise began. I can't describe how everyone's voice became louder as time passed. Perhaps the company could be compared to an orator who starts softly and ends like rolling thunder. There were foods, called *hors d'oeuvres* to be eaten before the drink; they were well seasoned and salty, to make the wine go down more easily. Who knows but that Circe used these foods when she changed Ulysses' companions into swine? I observed once how the guests ate the courses like pigs, then drank like cows, acted like jackasses, and finally puked like dogs. They poured good wine like hock, Bacharach and Liebfraumilch down by the bucketful, and soon the effect in their brains became apparent.

I did not know where their unsteadiness came from, for I had never heard of drunkenness. I saw their strange movements, but did not know the cause of this condition. At first the glasses were easily emptied, but the task became harder as time passed and stomachs filled. I didn't know yet that they regurgitated in order to make room for more of the same. My parson was also present; since he was human, he had to step out, and I followed him. "Sir Parson," I asked, "why do these people act so strangely? Why do they walk unsteadily, as if they have lost their wits? They all have eaten and drunk their fill, and yet they are swearing by hell and damnation they want to drink more. Do they have to do this? Don't their bellies burst? Can they be in God's image and act like swilling swine?" "Shut up!" said the parson. "This is neither the time nor the place to preach. If it were, I'd do it better than you." Hearing this, I looked on silently as food and drink were wilfully wasted, while hundreds of refugees, their eyes dark with hunger, were starving at our doorsteps because their cupboards were bare.

CHAPTER 31: *How Simplicius fails in art and is beaten black and blue*

WHILE I WAS WAITING at table, platter in hand and my mind full of thoughts and notions, my stomach informed me that there were winds demanding passage. Following instructions of the night before, I raised my left leg, put on the pressure, and would have mumbled the magic words *je pète*. But a tremendous, rumbling tornado passed out, and I was so embarrassed I felt like a condemned man, rope around his neck, on the way up the ladder to the gallows. I lost control of my muscles, and my mouth (unwilling to be outdone by the behind) started competing with it in noise. The worse the wind broke below, the louder came out the *je pète* above — as if the entrance and the exit were conducting a contest in decibels. This brought me a lot of internal relief, but it also provoked my master's disfavor.

Almost all of the governor's guests sobered up from the startling sounds of my mortars, trumpets, and bombs, and their reverberating echo. For my failure to control the winds, I received such a good licking that I can feel it to this day.

CHAPTER 32: *More on swilling, and how ministers are to be kept away from it*

WHEN THE STORM WAS over I had to resume serving at table. My parson was still there and, like the others, was asked to drink some more. But his mind wasn't on it, and he said he didn't want to drink like a hog anymore. Then one of the worst topers proved to him that the parson was drinking like an animal, but he (the toper) and his pals, like men. Animals, he said, drink only as much as they like, enough to quench their thirst; they don't know what's good, and don't like wine. But we humans know how to make use of liquor, and we let the good wine infuse us, as our forefathers did. "All right," said the parson, "but it is also human to show moderation." "Right you are," answered the toper, "an honest fellow practices what he preaches." He had a big jug filled moderately full, and with unsteady hand presented it to the man of the cloth. "Now drink up!" he intoned. But the parson bolted from the room, leaving the toper holding the jug.

After the parson had been induced to leave, things went from bad to worse. When one was so full he could not sit or walk or stand, the others shouted, "We're even! You've done me this way before, now it's your turn!" and so on. Those who could last the longest and drink the most boasted and considered themselves to be great men. In the end, they were all reeling as though under a spell. True, something strange had happened to them, and yet no one was surprised at it except me. One man sang, another cried; one laughed, another was sad; one swore and prayed; one hollered, "Courage!"; another could no longer talk; one was peaceful and quiet, another wanted to fight the devil; one slept, another chatted and would let no one else get a word in. One told of his amorous exploits, another spoke of warlike deeds. Some talked of church and theology; others, of politics and world affairs. Some of them were restless as quicksilver; others lay like lead and could not lift a finger, let alone stand upright. Their actions were so droll, foolish, strange, and sinful, and ungodly, too, that the bad smell I produced, and for which I had been beaten, was a joke in comparison. Toward the end serious fighting broke out; they were throwing glasses, tumblers, plates, and dishes, using their fists, chairs and chair legs, swords, and other handy objects to strike at each other, and quite a few were wounded. But my master soon quelled the riot.

CHAPTER 33: *How his honor the governor shot a horrible fox*

WHEN PEACE HAD BEEN restored, the master topers, together with musicians and ladies, promenaded into another building whose hall had been selected for and dedicated to another foolishness. My master reclined on a lounge, for he wasn't feeling well, because he was too full or too angry. I was about to leave the room to let him rest and sleep, but when I reached the door, he tried to whistle for me and couldn't do it. He called, and it came out "Simpls!" I ran to him and found him with eyes rolling like a stuck hog. I stood there like a bonehead, not knowing what to do. He pointed to a washstand and stammered, "Br, bra, bring me the ... you louse, pass the basin. I have to ... sha ... shoot a fa ... fa ... fox." When I got back, he had cheeks like a trumpeter. He grabbed me by the arm and maneuvered me in such a way that the basin was right in front of him. His mouth burst open and let such a mess escape into the basin that I almost fainted from the smell, especially as my face got splattered. I would have joined him, but when I saw how pale he turned, I gave up that idea for fear he might die; for he broke out in a cold sweat, which made his face look like a dying man's. When he recovered, he ordered me to bring him some water with which to rinse the wine conduit he was using his body for.

CHAPTER 34: *How Simplicius spoiled the dance*

I FOLLOWED THE GOVERNOR into a large house where I saw men and women, married and unmarried, moving so quickly and confusedly that my head swam. They were so lively and shouted so loudly that I thought they had all gone stark mad; I simply couldn't imagine what they meant by this raving and raging. When I came closer I saw that they were our guests who had been quite rational in the forenoon. 'My God,' I thought, 'some madness must have come over them.' Now I thought it might be spirits of hell mocking the human race in this pretentious manner, with monkey movements and frivolous steps. If they had human souls and the image of God in them they probably wouldn't act so inhuman.

When my master entered the house, the frenzy had just stopped, but there was still some ducking, swashbuckling, and scraping of feet as if they wanted to erase the tracks made in their rage. By the sweat running down their faces and the huffing and puffing, I could see they had been working hard; but the joy in their faces showed they hadn't minded that in the least.

I wanted to know what it was all about, and asked my comrade and fellow page, who had taught me how to soothsay a few days ago. He told me (for honest truth) that those present had agreed among each other to break down the floor of the hall. "Why else would they carry on so? Didn't you see how they broke the windows awhile ago? It will be the same with the floor," he said. "My God!" I replied, "we'll fall down in the cellar and break our necks." "Yes," said my friend, "that's what they intend to do and they don't give a damn. You will see that each man who exposes himself to this danger will grab a lady or a pretty girl. They say that couples who cling to each other don't get hurt when they fall." Since I believed all I heard, I was greatly frightened, and when the music started again and the boys ran toward the girls, as soldiers do to their guns at the sound of the alarm, I already felt the floor giving way, and every bone in my body breaking. But when the music played the latest hit and everyone started rocking and rolling I thought, 'This is the end. Now Simplex, you have been a man for the last time.' I thought the whole structure would collapse momentarily, and in my fright I grabbed a lady of the highest nobility and most excellent reputation, who was just conversing with a gentleman. I held her by one arm like a bear, and hung on like a burr. When she drew back, not knowing what sort of fool notions filled my head, I went berserk and started screaming as if they were about to kill me. But that's not all. By chance I also soiled my underwear, and the smell was terrific. The musicians suddenly broke off, dancers and their partners stopped, and the good lady to whose arm I clung felt insulted; she thought my master had ordered me to do all this to offend her. Then the governor gave orders to give me a good licking and lock me up, because I had already played other tricks on him that day. The soldiers who were to carry out the orders not only felt sorry for me, but couldn't stay with me because of the stink. For that reason they dispensed with the beating and locked me in a goose-pen under a stairway.

End of the First Book

Book Two

CHAPTER 1: *How a goose and a gander copulated*

I n my goose-pen, I formulated those thoughts about dancing and swilling which I had already laid down in the first part of my book called *Black and White*,[1] therefore to report further on them here is not necessary. Still, I can't deny that at that time I was in doubt whether the dancers were really raging so furiously in order to break down the floor, or whether I had only been fooled into thinking so.

Now I want to tell how I got out of the goose jail. I had to sit and stew in my own juice for a full three hours — that is, until the prelude to venery (I should have said, the respectable dance) was over — before someone sneaked up and rattled the latch. I listened as hard as a hog that's peeing in a puddle, but not only did the fellow open the door, he even slipped in as gladly as I would have slipped out. In addition, he dragged a girl in by the hand, just as I had done at the dance. I did not know what he was up to, but since I had run into various adventures on this foolish day and was getting used to them, so to speak, I decided to await with patience and in silence what fate would send my way. Expecting the worst, I slunk toward the door.

Now between the two intruders there arose a whispered conversation, of which I could make out only that one party was complaining about the rank odor of the place (but it was mainly my trousers). The other party was trying, in turn, to comfort the first. "Fair lady," he said, "I regret with all my heart that an unhappy fate will not grant us the use of a suitable locality wherein to enjoy the fruits of our love. However, I can assure you that your gracious presence makes this despicable corner more lovely than a nook in paradise itself." At this juncture I heard kisses and noticed strange postures, the meaning of which I did not know. So I kept on being quiet as a mouse. When a

---

[1] This was Grimmelshausen's (not Simplicius'!) first publication: *Satyrischer Pilgram, das ist ... Weiß und Schwartz ...* (The Satyrical Pilgrim, i.e. ... White and Black ...), part I, 1666 [but dated 1667]; see also Book III, chapter 13, footnote 18.

quaint noise arose, and the goose-pen (which was only knocked together from some boards, under a stairway) gave off a rhythmical racket, and the wench moaned as if she was in pain, I thought, these are two more of those raving lunatics who wanted to destroy the dance floor. They have come now to do the same here and to kill you. As soon as these thoughts burst into my head, I rushed over to the gate, to escape death. I lit out of the place with a shriek as ghastly as the one that had landed me there in the first place, but I had enough sense to bolt the door behind me and to dash out of the wide-open front door.

Well, this was the first time in my life that I attended a wedding, though I had not been invited. But then, I didn't have to give a present either, though the bridegroom later added up quite a bill for me, and I had to pay every penny of it.

Gentle reader, I'm not telling this story for laughs only, but to make the story complete and to show you what dancing can lead to. This much is sure: at dances some bad, featherbrained bargains are struck, of which, later on, the whole family must be ashamed.

CHAPTER 2: *When it's a good time to take a bath*

THOUGH I HAD LUCKILY escaped from the goose-pen, I still was very much aware of my misfortune, for I didn't know what to do about my trousers. In my master's quarters everyone was asleep and I didn't dare approach the guard on duty before the house; in the guardhouse they wanted none of me because of my aroma; it was too cold to stay in the street — and so I had come to the end of my rope. Long after midnight it occurred to me to take refuge once more with my friend the parson. I was rash enough to knock at the door until the maid let me in, but she didn't like it. When she smelled me (her long nose picked up my scent at once), she became still angrier. She started making a scene and her master, who had almost finished sleeping, heard it. He called the two of us to his bed, but as soon as he smelled a rat and had turned up his nose at me ever so little, he stated, this was an excellent time for taking a bath, never mind what the calendar said. He ordered the maid — or rather, gently begged her — to wash my trousers and hang them up in front of the stove, before daybreak. I was to go to bed, for he saw I was practically frozen stiff with cold.

I had hardly warmed up a little when dawn broke, and the parson came to my bed to hear how I had been doing and how my affairs were coming along. (On account of my wet trousers and underwear I couldn't go to him.) I told him everything, starting with the trick my friend had taught me and how *that* had turned out. Then I reported that the guests had gone stark mad after he, the minister, had left, and how they had tried to break down the floor of the house, and how I had become frightened; how I had wanted to escape annihilation and had been locked in the goose-pen for it; what words and works I had observed in the two who had let me out; and how I had locked them in instead of me. "Simplici," said the parson, "your situation is rotten. You had a good thing going; but I'm afraid it's all off! Hurry, get up and out of the house, or I too will incur your master's anger when they find you here." So, in my damp clothes, I had to move on, and for the first time I found out how fortunate is a person who has his master's favor, and how people look the other way when your favor starts limping and you are about to lose it.

I went to my master's quarters. Everyone was dead asleep except the cook and a couple of maids. They were cleaning the rooms used yesterday for drinking, and the cook was fixing a breakfast — more a snack — from the leftovers. I went to the maids who were working among broken glass and big puddles of spilled and vomited wine and beer. The floor looked like one of those maps picturing various oceans, islands, and continents. The room smelled much worse than the goose-pen, and I didn't stay long. In the kitchen, while I dried my clothes before the fire, I awaited with fear and trembling what fate might have in store for me when my master finished sleeping. I also pondered the foolishness and senselessness of the world and thought about everything that had happened to me during the last day and night, and what else I had seen, heard, and experienced. Such thoughts caused me to consider as happy the poor and miserable life my hermit had led, and to wish that he and I might be back in our old place.

CHAPTER 3: *The other page gets his comeuppance, and Simplicius is chosen to become a fool*

WHEN MY MASTER AROSE, he sent his orderly to fetch me out of the goose-pen. The fellow reported that he had found the door open and a hole behind the latch cut with a knife, and that the prisoner had sprung himself. But before the news reached him, my master heard from others that I had recently been seen in the kitchen.

Meanwhile, the servants had to run to and fro fetching yesterday's guests for breakfast. Among these, of course, was the minister, who had to come earlier than the others because my master wanted to discuss my situation with him before they all sat down to eat. First he asked the minister if he thought I was rational or foolish, simple-minded or mischievous. He told him how scandalously I had behaved the previous day, before table as well as at the dance; how many of the guests (who thought it had all been arranged to mock them) had resented this; how he had me locked in the goose-pen to prevent further mischief; how I had escaped and was now parading in the kitchen like a young squire no longer required to wait on him. In all his born days he had never seen the like of such disrespect — and that in front of so many good and honorable people. All he could think of was having me flogged and sending me clear to hell, because I was just too stupid.

While he was still busy complaining, the guests arrived one after another; and when the governor had finished, the parson answered that, given the chance, he might tell many a lively story about me, not only to prove my innocence, but also to calm the angry mood of those disgusted by my behavior. This was accepted, provided he told his stories at table, so that all the company might hear and enjoy them.

While they were talking about me upstairs, the mad ensign whom I had penned up in place of myself drove a bargain with me downstairs in the kitchen. By threats and a thaler which he secretly slipped in my pocket, he got me to promise to keep my mouth shut about his doings.

The table was set and the guests sat down as they had the day before. Various concoctions of wine with vermouth, sage, elecampane, quince, and lemons, as well as a cordial called "hippocras," were on hand to clear up the heads and smooth out the stomachs of the topers, for all of them were martyrs of the devil. Their first topic of conversation was themselves — how they had managed to get each other drunk yesterday. And yet, not one wanted to admit that he had been really pickled, though the night before they had sworn by all hell they couldn't drink another drop. A few admitted they had been a bit elevated; others asserted that nobody got *drunk* any more since getting *high* had been invented. When they tired of being told or telling their own folly, poor Simplicius had to take the gaff. The governor himself reminded the parson to begin the stories he had promised.

First the preacher begged their pardon for having to use a few words that might not be exactly becoming to him as a man of the cloth. Then he told about the natural causes of the winds bothering me; about the mishap I had had in the secretary's office; and about the trick I had learned for controlling the wind — along with soothsaying — and how badly I had fared trying it out. Next he told how utterly strange the dance had appeared to me, since I had never before seen one; what my friend had told me about it; why I had grabbed the aristocratic lady and had been goose-penned for it.

He told all this in such a pleasant and humorous way that the company couldn't help laughing heartily. Thus he managed to make excuses for my ignorance and simplicity in such a detailed way that I regained my master's grace and was again permitted to wait at table. But the parson did not want to mention my experience inside the goose-pen and how I escaped from it, because he was afraid some saturnian old sourpusses would take offense, thinking a minister must always wear a long face. Instead, to amuse his guests, my master asked me what I had given my friend for teaching me such useful tricks. When I answered, "Nothing," he said, "*I'll* pay him for his instruction." He was given the same licking I got the day before.

My master had now heard enough of my foolishness. He asked me why I had cut the door open and escaped from the pen. I replied that perhaps someone else had done the cutting. "Who?" he asked. "Maybe the one who came inside." "Who came in?" "I dasn't tell anybody." But the governor, being quick-witted, saw at once how to get the better of me, and asked who had forbidden me to tell. Without hesitation I answered, "The mad ensign." The laugh that went up told me that I must have pulled a boner. The ensign, who was there at the table, blushed like a red-hot coal, and I said I wouldn't speak another word unless I first got permission from him. My master motioned the ensign to grant permission, and I was free to tell what I knew. Then the governor asked me what the crazy ensign had been up to in the goose-pen. I answered, "He brought a girl with him." "What then?" said my master. I answered, "I thought he wanted to make water." My master asked, "What about the girl? Wasn't she ashamed?" "Heavens no, sir," I replied. "She raised her skirts as if to keep him company by (may the gentle, honorable, virtuous reader pardon my impolite pen for writing down so coarsely what I said then) shitting." At this point such laughter arose among all the people present that my master could no longer hear me, let alone ask me any more questions. It wasn't necessary either, unless they had wanted to drag the "good" girl through the mud too.

Then the major-domo said that recently I had come in from the ramparts and told him I knew where thunder and lightning came from. I had seen big hollow tree trunks on half a wagon each. They were filled with onion seed and an iron turnip with the tail cut off. When the trunks were tickled a little with a pronged stick, smoke, thunder, and hellfire came out in front. There were more stories of this kind, and it seemed that the conversation and laughter throughout the whole breakfast was about me. They finally decided to keep me well befuddled and in time I'd make a capital jester, one who could be given to the world's mightiest sovereign and who would make even the moribund smile.

CHAPTER 4: *About the man who provides the money, the military service that Simplicius rendered to the Crown of Sweden, and how he received the name "Simplicissimus"*

WHILE THEY WERE HAVING a good time and were about to continue yesterday's celebration, a guardsman handed a letter to the governor and announced that a commissioner, sent by the Swedish war council to inspect the garrison and look over the fortress, was at the gate. This put a hair in the soup, and the diners' enjoyment collapsed like a bagpipe when the air escapes. Musicians and guests dispersed like clouds of tobacco smoke that leave only a faint smell behind. My master, with his adjutant (who carried the keys) and a committee of officers (carrying lights), trundled toward the gate to let in the so-and-so of an inspector. My master wished Old Nick would break the visitor's neck in a thousand pieces before he ever entered the fortress! But when he did let the commissioner in, welcoming him at the inner drawbridge, he almost held his stirrup to prove his sincere devotion to him. In fact, the respect mutually displayed soon grew so monstrous that the inspector dismounted and *walked* to his lodgings. Each of them wanted to show his politeness by getting on the left side of the other, etc. 'Alas,' I wondered, 'what is this strangely false spirit that rules men by making a fool of either one through the folly of the other?'

As we approached the main guard, the sentry shouted, "Who goes there?" — though he saw it was the governor. He didn't answer because he wished to allow the commissioner the honor of replying. So the sentry shouted a second time, twice as loud. Then the inspector answered, "The man who pays you!" As we passed, I, being one of the last ones, heard the sentry (who was a green recruit, a well-to-do young farmer from the Vogelsberg) mutter these words, "I'll bet you are a liar. 'Man who pays!' A filcher and a robber who grabs my money, that's what you are. You've stolen so much money from me, I wish lightning would strike you dead before you leave this town."

At this point, I got the notion that our gentleman in the velvet jacket must be a holy man, not only because curses did not stick to him, but also because even the people who hated him showed him honor, love, and respect. That same night he was entertained like a prince, plied with drink till he was as blind as a bat, and put into a magnificent bed.

At the inspection on the following day, everything went helter-skelter. Even simple-minded I was bright enough to hoodwink and outwit our smart inspector (and for this sort of job they don't usually employ innocent milksops). I was too diminutive to pass for a musketeer; so I took about an hour to become a drummer-boy. They gave me some borrowed clothes (my page-boy knickers would not do for this) and a borrowed drum — probably because I was borrowed myself! — and that is how I passed the inspection. But since they didn't think I could remember an assumed name to which I would have to answer at roll call, I kept "Simplicius." To this the governor himself added a family name and had me recorded in the muster roll as "Simplicius Simplicissimus." Like a harlot's child he made me the first of my family, though in his own opinion I greatly resembled his sister. I later kept this name — until I found out the correct one — and under it I played my role quite well, doing a considerable favor to the governor and only slight harm to the Crown of Sweden. That's all the military service I ever rendered the Crown, and its enemies have no cause to hate me for it.

CHAPTER 5: *Simplicius is taken to hell by four devils and treated to Spanish wine*

WHEN THE COMMISSIONER HAD left, the minister confidentially invited me to his rooms. He said, "O Simplici, I take pity on your youth, and your future misfortune moves me to sympathy. Listen, my child, and let me tell you for sure that your master has decided to rob you of your reason and to make you into a fool. He has already ordered a costume for you. Tomorrow you will be sent to a school where you are taught to forget your reasoning power. No doubt, they'll grill you so hard that you become a weirdo, unless God and natural means prevent it. But since being deprived of one's reason is an uncertain and troublesome matter, I have decided to help you with advice and other good and necessary remedies and medicine — all for faithful Christian charity and the sake of the hermit's piety and your own innocence. Therefore follow my advice and swallow this powder. It will strengthen your mind and memory, so that you may easily overcome every onslaught without hurting your reason. Here I also give you an ointment. Put it on your temples, spine, neck, and nostrils. And use these preventives before you go to bed, for you may be picked up at any hour. But look out and be sure that no one finds out anything about my warning or these medicines; otherwise both of us might be the worse for it. And when they give you their damnable treatment, don't believe everything they want you to believe but act as if you do. Don't talk much or your teachers will find out they are sawing dead wood and they'll make your troubles worse, though I don't know what they will do to you. When you have put on the fool's cap and bells, come back and we'll discuss your situation again. Meanwhile I will pray to God that He save your health and your mind." Then he gave me the powder and the ointment, and I walked home.

The matter proceeded as the parson had said. I was in my first sleep when four big fellows, dressed up like frightful devils, came into my room and stopped before my bed. They jumped around like mountebanks and Shrovetide jesters. One had a red-hot poker, the other carried a torch; the other two whisked me out of bed, danced with me awhile, and forced my clothes on me. I acted as if I thought they were real, natural devils, let out some piteous wails, and made gestures of fear, but they announced I would have to leave with them. They tied a towel around my head, that I might not see or hear or scream. By various roundabout ways, upstairs and down, they led me, trembling like an aspen, into a cellar where a big fire was burning. After they had taken off the towel they began toasting me in Spanish wine and malmsey. It wasn't hard for them to persuade me I had died and gone to the pit of hell, because I purposely pretended to believe everything they were making up. "Go right on drinking," they said, "for you'll be with us forever anyway. But if you don't want to be a regular fellow who joins in, you'll go into that fire!" Those poor devils tried to disguise their voices so I couldn't recognize them, but I noticed right away that they were the governor's quartermaster sergeants. Of course I didn't let on I knew; rather I laughed up my sleeve that these bruisers, who wanted to make a fool out of me, instead must be my fools.

I drank my share of the Spanish wine, but they outdid me because such heavenly nectar is seldom given to such fellows, and I swear they got full before I did. When the time seemed right, I staggered about as I had recently seen my master's guests do. Finally I no longer wanted to drink, only to sleep, but with the poker that was always kept in the fire they chased and pursued me into all the corners of the cellar. They seemed to have become foolish themselves, for they wanted me to drink, not sleep. And when I fell down in the chase (as I did often, on purpose), they picked me up and made as if to throw me into the fire. They kept me awake like a falcon in training, and it was a great trouble and hardship to me.

I might have outlasted them in drinking and waking, but they took turns, and in the end I would have come out the worse for wear. I spent three days and two nights in this smoky cellar, which had no light but that shed by the fire. My head started to buzz and throb as if it was about to burst, and I had to think of something to rid myself of these tortures and torturers. I did as does the fox who urinates in the dogs' eyes when he sees no hope of escaping them. When nature urged me to defecate, I stuck three fingers down my throat, and filled my pants and beslobbered my clothes all at the same time. The stench was so unbearable that even the devils could stay with me no longer. They wrapped me in a bedsheet and beat me so miserably that my innards and my soul almost left me. From this treatment I fainted and lost the use of my senses. I lay there like a corpse and didn't know what else was done to me, I was so far gone.

CHAPTER 6: *Simplicius goes to heaven and is changed into a calf*

WHEN I CAME TO again, I was no longer with the devils in the cellar vault but in a beautiful room, in the hands of three of the ugliest old women the earth has ever seen. At first, when I opened my eyes a little, I thought they were natural spirits of hell. (If I had read the heathen poets, I would have thought of the Eumenides.) One of them had eyes like two will-o'-the-wisps and between them a long bony hawk nose whose tip reached her lower lip. I saw only two teeth in her mouth. They were so long, round, and thick that either could compare with a ring finger in shape, and with gold in color; there was bone enough for a whole mouthful of teeth, but it was badly distributed. Her face looked like Spanish leather and her hoary hair hung strangely disheveled about her head, for she had just been hauled out of bed. I don't know how to compare her two long breasts, except maybe with two cow bladders about half blown up. At the end of each dangled a dun-colored plug half a finger long. Truly, this was a frightening sight that might have been, at best, a good remedy for the mad love of lustful bucks. The other two were just about as ugly, except they had flat monkey noses and their dresses weren't quite so sloppy. When I regained my senses a little better, I saw that one was our dishwasher, the other two, the wives of the two quartermaster sergeants.

I acted as if I couldn't move. As a matter of fact, I didn't feel like dancing. These three old crones stripped me stark naked and cleansed me of all filth like a little child. This did me no end of good, and during their work they showed much patience and sympathy. I almost revealed to them how well I had caught on to everything.

But I thought: 'No, Simplici, do not confide in an old woman. Rather remember you will have glory enough if you, a child, can pull the wool over the eyes of three experienced old hags with whose help one might catch the very devil in an open field. Let this be a harbinger of your future success.'

When they had finished with me they laid me in a marvelous bed where I fell asleep without being rocked. They left, taking the dirty clothes and the washtub with them. As I figure, I slept more than twenty-four hours without interruption, and when I woke up two beautiful winged boys stood by the bed. They were magnificently dressed in white nightshirts, taffeta sashes, pearls, jewels, golden chains, and other precious things. One carried a gold-plated washbasin full of cookies, candy, marzipan, and other goodies; the other held a gold-plated cup. They claimed to be angels and wished to convince me that I was now in heaven, since I had happily gotten out of purgatory and escaped the devil and his dam. For that reason I was to ask for whatever I craved; everything I wished either was on hand or could be sent for. I was bothered by thirst and when I saw the cup before me I asked only for a drink, which was gladly handed to me. However, what I drank was not wine but a gentle sleeping potion, and I fell asleep again as soon as the potion got warm inside me.

The next day I awoke — otherwise I'd be sleeping yet! — and found myself no longer in bed, or in the previous room, or with my angels, or in heaven — but in my old goose-pen. It was as dark and scary as the previous cellar; moreover, I was wearing a suit made of calfskin with the rough side out. My trousers were in the Polish (or Swabian) style and the jacket was even crazier. On my head was a cap like a monk's cowl; it was pulled way down and had a large pair of donkey's ears. I had to laugh at my misfortune, for I saw by the nest and the feathers what sort of bird I was to represent. Only then did I begin to take stock and to think of my welfare. And as I had reason to thank God for not letting me lose my mind, I also ardently begged Him to keep, rule, lead, and guide me. I determined to play the fool as well as I could, and at the same time to bide my time and see what else fate had in store for me.

CHAPTER 7: *How Simplicius behaved in this bestial state*

I COULD HAVE ESCAPED from the pen by means of the hole the mad ensign had cut in the door. But because I was supposed to be a fool, I didn't, but acted like a hungry calf calling for its mother. My mooing was soon heard by those who were assigned to watch me, for two soldiers came and asked who was in the goose-pen. I answered,

"You fools, don't you hear it's a calf?!" They opened the pen, took me out, and acted surprised to hear a calf talking. (But they did this like an actor newly hired and clumsy, who has trouble impersonating the character he is supposed to act. I felt like helping them get into the spirit.) They wondered what to do with me and agreed to give me to the governor as a present. He would give them a larger reward for me, since I could talk, than would a butcher if they sold me.

They asked me how I was doing. I said, "Badly enough." They wanted to know why, and I said, "Because it seems to be customary here to put honest calves in goose-pens. You boys ought to know that if I am to become a regular ox I must be raised like a respectable critter." After this brief discussion they took me across the street toward the governor's quarters. A mob of boys followed me; they all took to mooing just like me, and a blind man would have thought, judging by the noise, that a herd of cattle was being driven by. But on sight it looked like a bunch of fools, some younger than others.

Well, the two soldiers presented me to the governor as if they had just captured me in a military raid. He gave them a tip and promised me the best treatment ever. I had my own thoughts about it — namely, 'All that glitters isn't gold' — but I said, "Sir, do not have us calves confined in goose-pens if you want us to grow up into regular critters." The governor comforted me, thinking he was terribly bright to have made such a cunning fool of me. But my thoughts were 'Just wait! I've passed the baptism of fire and have been strengthened by it. Now we'll see who can best act the other fellow's part.'

Just then a peasant who had fled the countryside drove his cattle to the watering trough. When I saw that, I left the governor and rushed, bleating and bawling, to the cows, as if I wanted to suck their milk. But when I got close, the cows were frightened by me worse than by a wolf. In fact, they stampeded as if a nestful of hornets had been let loose among them, and their owner couldn't keep them together anymore. It was lots of fun. In no time at all, a mob of people gathered who were all looking at my foolishness, and when my master managed to stop laughing a little, he said, "One fool makes a hundred more!" I thought, 'Pinch yourself, sir, for it is yourself you are talking about.'

Since from then on everyone called me the Calf, I in turn gave everybody a special nickname or mock name. Most people (but especially my master) thought them very suitable, for I named everyone as his character seemed to require. To put it in a nutshell, many people thought I was a witless fool, and I thought of people as foolish nitwits. As I see it, this is still the way of the world; everyone is content with his brains, and imagines he is the most intelligent of all.

My pastime with the peasant's cows helped to make the short forenoon even shorter, for it was the time around winter solstice. At the noon meal I waited at table as usual, but I also had a little fun on the side. When I was supposed to eat, I would take no human food or drink. I demanded grass — which was not available at that season. My master sent to the butcher's for two calfskins and ordered them slipped on two little boys. He seated the boys with me at the table and asked us not to be bashful when the food came. Our first course was a tossed green salad. The governor even had a real calf brought in and it was given lettuce sprinkled with salt. First I put on a cold stare as if to express surprise, but under the circumstances I thought I had better join in the game. When some onlookers saw me so disconcerted, they said, "It is nothing new to see calves eat meat, fish, cheese, butter, and other foods. Why, calves even get drunk now and then! These critters know a good thing when they taste it. It's even reached the point where there is hardly any difference between calves and humans. So why should you be the only one to hold out and not join in the fun?"

I was persuaded the more quickly to start eating because I was hungry, and not because I had seen men more piggish than swine, fiercer than lions, more lecherous than billy-goats, more vicious than dogs, more intractable than horses, more stubborn than jackasses, more given to drink than cattle, slyer than foxes, more voracious than wolves, sillier than monkeys, and more venomous than snakes and toads. All of these animals enjoy human food. Yet men differ from them in shape and do not often retain the innocence of a calf.

So I fed myself, along with my fellow calves, as my appetite required, and if a stranger had chanced to see us together at the table he would surely have thought old Circe had returned to change men into animals, an art my master knew and practiced.

My dinner was exactly like my lunch, and as my fellow calves had to eat with me, so they had to sleep with me — unless my master allowed me to sleep in the cow barn. I insisted on this because I wanted to fool those who thought they were making a fool of me. And I concluded that God, who is full of loving kindness, provides each human being with enough intelligence for self-preservation, whatever job he has been given; and the notion many folks (with or without the doctorate) cherish, that they alone are smart, is foolish, for there are people living on the other side of the mountain too.

CHAPTER 8: *Of some people's retentive memories and of others' forgetfulness*

WHEN I AWOKE IN the morning my two vealified companions were gone. So I got up, and when the adjutant went for the keys, to open up the town gates, I sneaked out of the house and went to the minister. I told him everything, how I had survived hell as well as heaven. When he saw that I felt guilty about deceiving so many people, particularly my master, by playing the fool, he said, "That is something you must not worry about. The foolish world wants to be fooled. Use what intelligence they have left you; use it for your own advantage and thank God you came out on top — that's not granted to everyone. Imagine you have been reborn like the phoenix, through fire, from unreason to reason and thus to a new life. But keep in mind that you aren't out of the woods yet. At the risk of losing your mind, you slipped into this jester's outfit, but the times are so strange that no one knows if you can slip out of it without losing your life. Anybody can dash into hell, but to get out again takes sweat and toil. You aren't half the man you think you are, when it comes to escaping imminent danger. For that you'll need more brains and caution than you had when you couldn't tell reason from folly. Remain humble and expect future changes."

His way of speaking was intentionally different from what it had been before, and I imagined he had seen by my facial expression that I considered myself quite a big shot because I was so good at tricks and tomfoolery. In turn I read in his face that he was put out with me — and what good *was* I to him? Accordingly, I changed my tune and thanked him heartily for giving me such wonderful remedies for preserving my mind, and made an impossible promise to repay him everything. This tickled him and changed his mood. He praised his remedies and told me that Simonides Melicus had invented a technique (perfected by Metrodorus Sceptius) by which people could repeat word for word everything they had ever heard or read. This could not have been done, he said, without mind-building drugs of the kind he had given me.

Well, dear parson, I thought, in the books you lent the hermit I read it quite differently — but I was smart enough not to say so. For to tell the truth, it wasn't till I was supposed to have turned foolish that I became prudent and more guarded in my speech. The parson droned on about how Cyrus had been able to call any of his 30,000 soldiers by name and gave many other examples of mnemonics. Finally he said, "I am telling you all this so that you will really believe a man's memory can be improved and strengthened by drugs, just as it can be weakened or even erased by them." And he launched into at least a dozen more examples.

Then he gave me some more medicine and instructions. When I left the house, about a hundred boys again followed me, all bellowing like calves. My master, who had just gotten up, came to the window, saw all these fools in a drove, and had a good laugh.

CHAPTER 9: *Cockeyed praise of a beautiful lady*

AS SOON AS I got home I had to go up to my master's, for some aristocratic ladies were there, and they wanted to see and hear his new jester. I came in and stood there like a mute. After a while, the lady I had grabbed at the dance spoke up, remarking that she had been told this calf could talk, but now she saw it wasn't true. I piped up with, "Well, I heard monkeys couldn't talk, but now I see it isn't true." "How so?" said my master. "Do you think these ladies are monkeys?" I answered, "If they aren't now, they soon will be. Who knows how it all comes out? I never thought I'd be a calf, and yet I am one." My master asked how I could tell that the ladies might be monkeys soon. My answer was, "A monkey is bare behind. The ladies are already bare in front. The girls I've seen cover up better." "You jackanapes, you are a foolish calf, and you talk like one. These ladies show what's worth seeing, but monkeys are bare by necessity. You had better make up in a hurry for putting your foot in your mouth, or I'll have you whipped or get the dogs to run you into the goose-pen, as happens to calves that don't behave. Let us hear how you can praise and compliment a lady." Well, I looked at this lady from tip to toe and up again, and finally I said, "Sir, I see what's wrong. It's the tailor's fault. He used the material that was to cover the neck and breast in the skirt; that's why it drags so behind. If the fellow can't tailor better than that he ought to have his hands cut off." "Lady," I said to her, "get rid of that tailor and use my knan's. His name was Master Littlepaul and he made such pretty pleated skirts for my mither and our Annie and Ursula. They were the same width up and down, and they never dragged in the dirt like yours. You have no idea how he dressed up those cute wenches." My master asked if Annie and Ursula were prettier than this lady. "Heck, no, sir!" I said. "This lady has hair the color of baby dirt and her hair is as straight and white as if hog bristles had been slapped on her head. And her curls are so well rolled they look like hollow pipes, or a dozen candles or sausages hanging on either side of her head. Just look at her nice smooth forehead, isn't it curved more attractively than a backside? And it's whiter than a skull that's been out in the open for years. But what is this in comparison with her delicate body, which I am not privileged to see at all? Isn't it as tender, slim, and graceful as if she had had the skitters for eight weeks running?" At this they all started laughing and I could no longer be heard, nor could I speak anymore. So I took to my heels laughing, letting others make fun of me only so long as I was pleased to put up with it.

CHAPTERS 10-13: *Telling exclusively of notable heroes and artists. On the troubled and perilous lives of rulers. Concerning the judgment and understanding of some brute animals. Containing all sorts of information; if you want to find out, read it yourself or have someone else read it to you*

THEN CAME LUNCH AND I did a lot of talking again, for I had decided to discuss all foolishness and punish all vanity, and my job at that time gave me an excellent excuse for it. No one at table was too great to escape my tongue. And if there was one who wouldn't stand for it he was either laughed at by the others or he was told by my master that no wise man should ever get angry at a fool.

Once my master said, "I don't know what I have in you. For a calf you are much too reasonable. I almost think under your calfskin you are covered with a rogue's hide." I pretended to be angry and answered him, "Do you humans suppose we animals are all fools? You ought not to, for I imagine if the older animals could talk like me they would really tell you off. I might almost say you humans have learned your arts and crafts from us. You eat and drink yourself into the grave; not so with us animals. In the springtime who tells the summer birds to come here and hatch their young? And in the fall, to fly to warmer lands? Who leads them or shows them the way? Or do you humans lend them your compasses, so they don't lose the way? No, dear people, without you they know the way, how long they must travel, and when to leave one place and the next. They don't need your compass or your calendar. If you lived among us animals and saw what we do and don't do, you would find that all of us have our own abilities and virtues. Hence, many ancient philosophers were not ashamed to ask if dumb animals have reason. Go to the bees and observe how they make wax and honey. Then tell me your opinion."

After this speech, my master's table companions delivered diverse opinions about me. The secretary suggested I should be considered mad because I regarded myself as a reasonable animal. Still, he said, lads who have bats in the belfry, and yet considered themselves wise, make the very best and most amusing jesters. My master said he thought me to be a fool because I told everyone the unvarnished truth, and yet my discussions were altogether unlike a fool's. (They said all this in Latin, so I shouldn't understand them.) He asked me if I had been a student while I was still human. I said I didn't know what "student" was and asked if one needed a stud to stude with. The mad ensign thought the devil spoke through me. Then my master asked me whether I was still accustomed to praying like people, and whether I was looking forward to going to heaven. "Sure," I said. "I still have my immortal human soul, and it doesn't long for hell, especially since I didn't get on very well in that place awhile ago. I have only been a little transmogrified, and hope in time to become human again." "I join you in that hope," said my master, and sighed. From this I concluded that he was sorry he had dared make a fool of me. "But let me hear," he continued, "how you pray."

I kneeled down, raised my eyes and hands toward heaven as the hermit had done, and because my master's repentance comforted me, I couldn't hold back my tears. After the Lord's Prayer, I prayed for all Christendom and for my friends and enemies, and I asked that the good Lord might enable me to live according to his will, and that I might become worthy of praising him through all eternity. This prayer was full of reverently composed words the hermit had taught me. Some of the more softhearted listeners almost started crying, for they were full of sympathy for me. There were tears even in my master's eyes.

After the meal, my master sent for the parson, told him everything I had put forward and hinted that he was afraid things might not be as they ought to be and that perhaps I was in league with the devil. Not long before, I had been altogether simple-minded and ignorant, but now I was discussing things that made one's hair stand on end. The parson replied that he should have thought of this before making a fool of me. Human beings, he said, were made in God's image and no one ought to fool with them as with beasts, especially not with one so young. But he did not think the evil one had gained an entrance, for I had always commended myself to God in fervent prayer. But if, contrary to his expectations, I had been lost to the fiend, those who were responsible for it might see how they answered God for it. Surely it was one of the greatest sins to rob a man of his wit, for it made him incapable of God's service and praise, and it was chiefly for these ends that man had been created.

"I assured you," said the parson, "that he had intelligence enough. But he could not adapt himself to the world because he was educated in simple-mindedness by his father, a crude peasant, and by your brother-in-law in the wilderness. A little patience in the beginning would have let him prove his worth. He just happened to be a pious, simple child who didn't know the wicked world. But I have not the least doubt he can be set straight if only one could get him to give up the illusion that he has become a calf."

"I am worried," answered my master, "because though at first he was so ignorant, now he gives out all sorts of information without the least hesitation — things someone older, more experienced, and better read could hardly know. Why, he told me many characteristics of animals, and has described my own characteristics as charmingly as if he had always been a man of the world. His talk astonishes me, and I should perhaps consider it as an oracle or a hint from the Lord."

"Sir," replied the parson, "this might be explained naturally. I know he has read a lot; he and the hermit read through all my books, and there were quite a few. And since the boy has a good memory and his mind is idle now, he can dredge up what he previously stored away. Oh, I am sure he can be restored."

With these words, the parson left the governor dangling between fear and hope. The upshot was that a wait-and-see period followed. The parson had given his advice more for his own sake than for mine, because by pretending to be worried about me and taking a lot of trouble he gained the governor's favor and had himself appointed chaplain of the garrison. In those evil days, that was nothing to be sneezed at, and I was glad for him.

CHAPTER 14: *How Simplicius continued to lead the good life; how the Croatians robbed him of that, too*

FROM THIS TIME ON, I was in my master's favor, grace, and love, and I was completely happy except that I had too much calfskin and too few years — but I didn't know that yet. The parson did not want me to be normal again, as the time for that seemed not to have come yet. When my master saw that I liked music, he arranged to have me instructed in it and apprenticed me to an excellent lutenist, whom I soon surpassed in his art, because I had a better voice than he. Thus I provided entertainment for my master. All the officers showed me their good will, the richest burghers gave me presents, the servants and soldiers wished me well because they saw how much my master liked me. I got presents here, there, and everywhere, for people knew that jesters and fools often have more influence with their masters than straightforward people, and their gifts were meant that way; some gave them that I mightn't tell on them, others to have me do just that, and thus I picked up a pretty penny. I gave the parson much of it because

I didn't know what it was good for. As no one dared to look at me askance, so I had no tribulations, troubles, or cares. I put all my mind to my music and to how I might skillfully reproach someone for his shortcomings. So I grew up like a fool in fairyland; my face got sleek and my muscles grew strong, and anybody could see I was no longer mortifying myself, as in the woods, on water, acorns, beechnuts, roots, and herbs. Instead, Rhine wine and the stout of Hanau washed down my rich food, all of which in those poor times was truly a gift of God; for in those days all of Germany was wholly seared by the flames of war, hunger, and pestilence, and Hanau itself was surrounded by enemies. But none of this bothered me in the least.

My master decided that, after the siege was lifted, he would give me either to Cardinal Richelieu or to Duke Bernhard of Weimar. Besides wanting to earn much gratitude through me, he let on that he couldn't stand the sight of me in jester's garb because in face and figure I reminded him so much of his lost sister, whom I resembled more every day. The parson advised him against getting rid of me. He thought the time had just about come to perform a miracle and change me back into a reasonable human being. He suggested that the governor have some calfskins put on other boys, and then have on hand a third person, in the guise of a doctor, prophet, or traveling showman, who should undress these boys with a lot of hocus-pocus, pretending he could turn animals into men and vice versa. That way I might be straightened out without too much trouble and made to think I (like others) had turned human again.

When the governor had accepted this suggestion, the parson told me of the agreement and easily persuaded me to go along with him. But jealous Fortune was ready neither to let me slip out my fool's dress nor to let me enjoy my luxurious, full-fed life any longer.

While the furrier and the tailor were preparing the clothes that were to be used in the projected comedy, I was moving with some boys on the ice just outside the fortress. Someone — I don't know who — led a raiding party of Croatian soldiers who rounded us up, sat us on farm horses they had just stolen, and trotted us off. To be sure, they were in doubt for a moment whether or not to take me along. Then one of them said in Bohemian, "Mih weme daho Blasna sebao, bo we deme ho gbabo Oberstowi." Another replied, "Prschis am bambo ano, mi ho nagonie possadeime, wan rosumi niemezki, wan bude mit Kratock wille sebao."[2] So I was forced to get on a horse and found out that a

---

[2] Less than perfect Bohemian: "We'll take this fool along and give him to the colonel." "Gad, yes. We'll put him on a horse. The colonel knows German. He'll have fun with him."

single unlucky hour can deprive one of all well-being, happiness, and salvation, and one's whole life is changed.

CHAPTER 15: *Simplicius' life in the cavalry; what he saw and learned among the Croats*

ALTHOUGH THE ALARM WAS sounded at once in Fort Hanau, and cavalry sent out, that bothered the Croats but little and hardly retarded their getaway. Our men retrieved nothing, for the Croats were very mobile and cleverly made for the forest near Büdingen, where they could forage, trade off the Hanau children who were to be ransomed by their parents, and sell their stolen horses and other "liberated" goods to the burghers. Before it had become really dark, they started up again, and quickly crossed the forest toward the monastery of Fulda, everywhere taking along whatever they could carry. Robbing and plundering did not delay their rapid movement the least little bit, for they were just like the devil who, they say, can run and crap at the same time. In the evening we arrived at the monastery of Hersfeld, where their quarters were. Their large loot was shared evenly, and I was given to Colonel Corpes.[3]

Everything here seemed strange and disgusting to me; I had to trade my Hanau delicacies for coarse black bread and lean beef, or for a flitch of stolen bacon — but this was only when times were good. Wine and beer had turned to water, and instead of sleeping in a bed I had to be content with straw in the horse barn. Instead of playing the lute for everyone's delight, I often had to crawl under the table like our other boys, howl like a dog, and take my chances on getting wounded by spurs while looking for food, and that was no fun. Instead of taking walks in Hanau, I could go along on foraging raids, curry the horses, and haul the manure out of the stable.

Foraging is defined as riding out to the villages and, with danger of life and limb, threshing, grinding, and baking, grabbing and stealing whatever is handy, maltreating and abusing peasants and even ruining their women, daughters, and hired girls. And when the poor peasants object to this treatment or get bold enough to rap some forager's knuckles while he is at his work (and there were plenty of such thieves

---

[3] Colonel Corpes served in General Johann Isolani's regiment of Croatians. In January 1635 their headquarters were in Hersfeld. Corpes was stabbed to death on 9 July 1638.

in Hessia at that time), then you strike them down — provided you can — or at least make their houses go up in smoke.

My new master had no wife (this type of soldier doesn't usually take his wife along because any female can take her place), no page, no manservant, no cook, but he did have a swarm of hostlers and boys who waited on him and his horses, and he was not at all ashamed to saddle and feed his own horse. He regularly slept on a straw pallet or on the bare ground, covered only with a fur coat, and that's why lice were sometimes seen wandering all over his clothes. He was not embarrassed about it and laughed when somebody picked one off him. He wore his hair short and had a wide beard like a Swiss; this served him well when he disguised himself in peasant clothing and went reconnoitering. Though he never kept a luxurious table, he was honored, loved, and feared by his men and all who knew him. At that time we were never quiet or in the same place for long, but now here, now there. Now we were raiding, now being raided. But we hadn't enough strength to defeat the Hessians, whose lieutenant general, Melander[4] by name, gave us no rest. He captured many of our men and sent them home to Cassel.

I didn't like this unstable life one bit and often wished I were back at Hanau. My greatest trouble was that since I couldn't really talk with these fellows, I got pushed from pillar to post and had to take beatings and abuse. The colonel's greatest fun was having me sing in German and play the trumpet, but that seldom happened. Mostly I got boxed on the ears so hard that blood came out of my nose and I didn't come back for second helpings. Since, on account of my youth, I wasn't very useful on raiding parties, I took an interest in cooking and keeping my master's guns clean. He liked this so much that I gained his favor and he had a new jester's suit made for me. It was of calfskin again and had ears much larger than the old one. Since my master was not a gourmet, I did not need much skill in cooking. But I really got tired of my job when I was short of salt, fat, and spices (as often happened); so I lay awake nights and thought how I might escape with good grace, especially when spring came around. About this time I made it my job to remove the entrails of butchered sheep and cows, which had been smelling up the camp. The colonel approved. Each time I dragged them farther away, and one fine day, after dark, I escaped into the nearest woods.

---

[4] Peter Holzapfel Melander (1585-1648) was since 1633 Lieutenant General of Landgrave William of Hesse-Cassel. Though a Calvinist, in 1642 he became a field marshal in the imperial army.

CHAPTER 16: *Simplicius picks up a rich loot and becomes a forest-dweller*

MY SITUATION, TO JUDGE by appearances, gradually became worse — so bad, as a matter of fact, that I imagined I had been born only to suffer misfortune. Only a few hours after I escaped from the Croats, some highwaymen picked me up. No doubt they thought they had made a good catch; it was night and they couldn't see my jester's suit. Two of them were ordered to take me to a certain spot far inside the woods. While it was still pitch dark, one of these demanded money from me. He laid down his gun and gloves and started frisking me and asking me who I was and if I had any money.

As soon as he felt my furry suit and the long donkey ears on my cap (he thought they were horns), and saw the brilliant sparks that came from my fur when he stroked it, he was frightened and became edgy. I noticed this, and before he could recover, I rubbed my suit with both hands so that it glowed as if I were full of burning sulphur. In a frightening voice, I answered, "I am the devil, and I'll wring your necks!" This scared the two of them so thoroughly that they made off through shrubs and bushes as if hellfire was after them. The darkness of night did not slow them down; when they fell over sticks, stones, stumps, logs, or even each other, they jumped up again and continued running. They ran until I couldn't hear them anymore. But I laughed so loud that the woods echoed, and that too was awful to hear in such a lonely place.

As I was about to leave I stumbled over a musket, which I picked up and kept, for I had learned from the Croatians how to handle guns. Continuing on, I ran into a knapsack made, like my suit, of calfskin; I looked it over and found dangling from it a pouch containing powder, lead, and everything else I needed. I strapped it on, shouldered the gun like a soldier, and hid nearby in a dense thicket, hoping to get a little sleep. But at daybreak the whole raiding party came back to the place to look for the lost gun and knapsack. I pricked up my ears like a fox and kept quieter than a mouse. When they found nothing they laughed at the two who had run away from me. "Oh, you cowards!" they said. "You ought to be ashamed — scared by a single man, running away and leaving your gun!" But one of them swore the devil should fetch him if I hadn't been Satan himself; had he not touched the horns and the rough skin? The other fellow got cross and said, "Hell, I don't care if it was the devil or his dam. I want my knapsack back." One of them — one of the better ones, I thought — answered, "Why do you think the devil wanted your knapsack and gun? I'd bet my neck, the chap you ran from took both with him." Another replied that it might well have been some peasants who had passed by, found the gun, and picked up the things. They all agreed this might have been the case, and everyone allowed the devil in person had been in their midst, especially because the one who had searched me swore frightful oaths it had been so and made the most of my horns and sparkling skin. I think if I had suddenly appeared, they would all have run off again.

Finally, after they had been looking in vain for a long time, they moved on. I opened the knapsack, looking for something for breakfast. The first thing I found was a purse with 360-odd ducats in it. No one need ask if I was pleased, but let me assure the reader that I liked the knapsack even better when I saw it was well stocked with food. And since among common soldiers ducats and their like are much too scarce to be lugged around on raids, it occurred to me that this fellow must have just gotten them and secretly slipped them into the knapsack, so as not to share them with his companions.

I ate my breakfast joyfully, soon found a pleasant spring to quench my thirst, and then counted my ducats. But to save my life I couldn't say where this happened. I stayed in the woods as long as my food lasted (and I used it very sparingly). But when the knapsack was empty, hunger drove me to the homesteads of the peasants. By night I crawled into their cellars and kitchens, and took what food I found and could carry off. I dragged it with me into the wildest parts of the woods. Here again I led an altogether hermitlike life — except that I stole much and prayed little, and had no settled home but kept moving about widely. Fortunately, summer was on its way.

CHAPTER 17: *How Simplicius rode to dance with the witches*

OCCASIONALLY AS I ROAMED through the woods I happened to meet peasants, but they always ran away from me. I don't know if the war had made them fearful, had perhaps robbed them of their homes, or whether the raiders had broadcast their encounter with me, so that the peasants who saw me thought the fiend himself was walking in their part of the woods.

Once when I had been lost in the forest for several days and was afraid my rations would run out, I was glad to hear two woodcutters. I followed the sound of their axes, and when I saw them I took a handful of ducats out of the purse, sneaked up close to them, showed them this attractive gold, and said, "Gentlemen, if you will take care of me I'll give you this handful of gold." But the minute they saw me and my gold they took to their heels, leaving behind their axes, wedges, and hammers, as well as their lunch of cheese and bread. This I picked up, put it in my knapsack, and got lost in the woods again, almost despairing of ever getting back among people.

After much thinking I reached this conclusion: Who knows what will become of you? But you have money, and if you put it into a safe place with reliable people, you can live on it for a long time. Thus it occurred to me that I should hide it. From the donkey's ears that made people run from me I made two armlets, combined all my ducats, sewed them inside and tied them on above my elbow. When I had thus secured my treasure I again entered peasants' houses and took from their supplies what I needed and could carry off; and though I was still quite simple-minded I had enough sense never to return to a place where I had once stolen the least bit. For this reason I was very lucky and never got caught filching.

Once, toward the end of May, I again wanted to get some food in my usual (though forbidden) manner. I had made my way to a farmstead and gotten into the inner sanctum of the kitchen. When I heard people were still up, I opened wide a door leading out to the yard, to provide a way out in case of necessity. (N.B. I never went where they kept dogs.) I was waiting quietly for everyone to go to bed when I noticed a slit in a small serving window giving on the next room. I sidled up to it, to see if the people were going to bed. But my hope came to nothing, for instead of undressing they had just gotten dressed, and instead of a candle they had a sulfurous blue flame burning on a bench. They were greasing sticks, brooms, forks, chairs, and benches, and, one after the other, were riding out the window on them. I was greatly surprised and rather horrified. But since I was used to greater horrors and had neither heard nor read of ghosts, I did not worry too much.

When everyone was gone and it was quiet, I went into the room to look for whatever I could take along. I sat down astride a bench and had hardly touched the wood when I rode — no, whizzed — on this bench straight out the window. My gun and knapsack stayed behind as carfare! Sitting down, taking off, and landing took place in one instant, it seemed, and all at once I was in a big crowd of people who were all doing a strange dance, the like of which I had never seen. Holding each other by the hand, they had formed many circles, one within another, their backs toward the center, as the three graces are sometimes pictured. The innermost ring consisted of seven or eight persons; the second had twice as many; the third more than the first two, and so on, so that there were over two hundred people in the outer ring. Since one circle danced clockwise and the next counterclockwise, I could not distinguish exactly how many circles there were, or what occupied the center around which they all revolved. The way the heads all reeled past one another looked awfully funny.

And the music was as weird as the dance. I think everyone was singing the tune while dancing, making an extraordinary harmony. The bench that took me there set me down by the musicians who were standing outside the circles. Instead of clarinets, flutes, and whistles, they were busily playing on vipers, asps, and chicken snakes. Some were holding cats and blowing in their bungholes; when they fingered the tails, the sound was like a bagpipe. Others ran a bow across a horse's head as if it were a fiddle, and still others played on a cow's skeleton (as can sometimes be found in a pasture) as on a harp. One old boy was holding a bitch, cranking her tail, and fingering her tits! Then there were devils using their noses for trumpets, and the echo resounded through the woods. When this dance came to an end, the whole hellish mob started racing, shouting, reeling, roaring, howling, raging, and raving as if everyone had gone stark mad. It is easy to imagine how frightened I was.

While this noise was going on, a chap came toward me, carrying on his hip a giant toad, big as a side drum. Its entrails hung out the rear and were stuffed back in again in front. It looked so repulsive that it turned my stomach. "Lookee, Simplex," he said, "I know you are a good lute-player. Let's hear something!" I practically keeled over when I heard him address me by my name. I could not answer and felt as if I were in a deep dream. In my heart I prayed to God Almighty that he help me out of my dream and let me wake up. The chap with the toad looked me straight in the eye and flicked his nose in and out like a turkey; then he struck me such a blow on the chest that I couldn't breathe. I started shouting to God. In no time at all it became pitch dark; I slumped to the ground and crossed myself at least a hundred times.

CHAPTER 18: *Why it is unlikely that Simplicius is telling tall tales*

SINCE THERE ARE PEOPLE — some of them learned and distinguished — who don't believe that witches and wizards exist, let alone fly through the air, there are bound to be those who will say at this point that Simplicius is pulling the wool over their eyes. Well, I don't want to argue with these people. Nowadays four-flushing is a very common practice, and I don't deny that I know how, for otherwise I would be something of a stick-in-the-mud.

But people who doubt that witches ride through the air should remember that Simon Magus[5] was raised on high by an evil spirit and did not fall down until St. Peter had prayed. In Book III of his *History of Northern Nations* (chapter 1, p. 19), Olavus Magnus[6] tells us that Hadingus, king of Denmark, who had been expelled from his kingdom by rebels, returned home on the spirit of Othonus, who had disguised himself as a horse. It is well known from the *History of Doctor Faustus*[7] that he and others (though they were not sorcerers) traveled through the air from one place to another. I myself knew a woman and her maid (both are dead now); this maid was polishing her mistress' shoes, and when she had finished one and set it down by the fire to do the other, the polished one slipped up the chimney in no time. But this story was kept quiet.

I have reported all this only because I want to let you know how witches and wizards have at times actually traveled to their conventions, and not because I want you to believe that *I* traveled that way. It's all the same to me whether you believe it or not; but whoever prefers to be skeptical, let him figure out a better way to get me from Hersfeld or Fulda — I don't know myself exactly where in the woods I was hanging out — to Magdeburg in such a short time.

CHAPTER 19: *Simplicius becomes a fool, just as he had been before*

BUT TO RESUME MY story: I assure the reader that I lay still on my stomach till daylight, for I hadn't the heart to sit up. I was in doubt whether I had dreamed what I have been telling. Though I was rather frightened, I was bold enough to fall asleep, for I thought at worst I might find myself in a wild forest; but even that wouldn't have been

[5] Simon the Sorcerer is mentioned in the New Testament; see Acts of the Apostles 8, 9-13. During the Middle Ages he had become the very incarnation of a wizard.

[6] Olavus Magnus (1490–1558) was a Swedish ecclesiastic and scholar. His *Historia de gentibus septentrionalibus*, Rome 1555, once was the authoritative handbook on everything Scandinavian; German translation Strasbourg 1567.

[7] The theme of Doctor Faust(us), a character truly representative of Renaissance man, has been dealt with in various ways: as a tragedy by Marlowe and Goethe; as an opera by Gounod; as an anonymous puppet play; as a collection of stories by Widmann, for example, and as a novel by Thomas Mann.

too bad, for since leaving home I had spent most of my time there and was quite used to it. About nine o'clock in the morning some foragers came and woke me up. Only then did I notice that I was in the middle of an open field.

The soldiers took me to a windmill and, when their feed had been ground there, to the camp outside Magdeburg.[8] I was assigned to a colonel of the infantry, who asked me where I came from and to whom I belonged. I told everything, down to the smallest detail; since I didn't know the Croatians' names, I described their clothing, gave examples of their speech, and told how I had escaped from them. I carefully neglected mentioning my ducats. The tale of my trip through the air and the witches' dance was considered foolishness and tall talk, especially since the rest of my story was also a little mixed up.

Meanwhile a mob of people collected about me, for one fool makes a thousand more, and among them was one who had been a prisoner of war in Hanau last year; he had joined the forces there, but afterward had gone back to the imperial troops. He recognized me and said immediately, "Ho-ho, this is the commander's calf at Hanau!" The colonel asked for particulars, but the chap knew only that I was good at lute-playing, that Croatians from Colonel Corpes' regiment had taken me away, and that the governor had hated to lose me because I was a good fool and jester. Now the colonel's wife sent to another colonel's wife, who could play the lute quite well, and therefore always carried one with her. She asked for this instrument, and when it was brought I was ordered to show what I could do. But it was my opinion I should be given something to eat first, because my empty stomach was no match for the bulging belly of the lute. This was done, and after I had eaten my fill and had swallowed a good stein of brown beer, I sounded both my own and the lute's voice, talked thirteen to the dozen, and without any trouble got everyone to believe I was what my calf's clothing seemed to indicate.

The colonel asked me where I wanted to go now, and when I answered that it was all the same to me, we soon agreed that I should stay with him and become his page. He wanted to know what had become of my donkey's ears. "Well," I said, "if you found out where they are I should still be wearing them." I kept mum because all my riches were contained in them.

In a short time I became acquainted with most of the high officers in the Saxon as well as in the imperial camp, and with the ladies, too,

---

[8] In the Peace of Prague (1635) Magdeburg had been given to the son of the Elector of Saxony. The Swedes who held the city refused to give it up until Saxon and imperial forces threatened a siege.

who dressed up my cap, sleeves, and cut-off ears with silk ribbons in gay colors. I almost suspect some of today's fancy dressers first got the idea from me. The money I received from the officers I charitably shared with others, for I drank up every last penny of it in the good beer of Zerbst and Hamburg — two varieties that agreed well with me, though I had enough to eat and drink, without it, wherever I went.

When my colonel got a lute for my own use (he thought I'd stay on forever), I was no longer allowed to buzz back and forth between the two camps. He hired a tutor for me, who was to look after me and whom I was to obey. The tutor was a man after my own heart, for he was quiet, understanding, learned, of good conversation but not too talkative and — to mention the most important thing last — pious, well-read, and full of all sorts of arts and sciences. At night I had to sleep in his tent, and by day I was not to get out of his sight. He had been very wealthy, the counselor and official of some prince, but since the Swedes had robbed and utterly ruined him, and his wife died and his only son been forced to give up his studies because of poverty (he had become a regimental clerk in the Saxon army), he stayed with this colonel as a stable master, in order to have something to do while waiting for the dangerous course of the war to change on the banks of the river Elbe, so that the sun of his former good fortune might again shine on him.

CHAPTER 20: *This chapter is rather long and deals with throwing dice and what goes with it*

BECAUSE MY TUTOR WAS along in years he couldn't sleep through the whole night. This was the reason for his finding out during the first week that I wasn't such a fool as I pretended to be. In fact, since he was an expert in physiognomy, he had noticed it right away, in my face. One time I awoke at midnight and made all sorts of remarks about my life and strange experiences; then I got up and rendered to God Almighty thanks for all the benefices he had shown me and all the dangers from which he had saved me. After this, I lay down again with a heavy sigh and went to sleep.

My tutor, who had heard everything, pretended to be fast asleep. But when the prayer was repeated several nights in a row, he felt quite sure I had more sense than many an oldster who thinks he is the cat's whiskers. But he did not discuss it with me in the tent because, he said, the walls were too thin; and for reasons of his own, he did not want

anyone else to know my secret just then — before he himself was sure
of my innocence.

One time I went for a walk behind the camp; he did not mind
because it gave him a chance to look for me and talk to me alone. He
found me in a lonely place and said, "My dear young friend, because
I want only what's best for you, I am glad to be able to talk with you
here alone. I know that you are not a fool, as you pretend, and that you
do not wish to live in this lowly and despicable condition. If your
welfare is dear to you, and you wish with all your heart what you ask
of God every night, and if you will put your trust in me as an honest
man, then tell me about yourself and I shall try in every way to help
you get out of your fool's suit."

At this I embraced him and in my joy acted as if he were a prophet
come to save me from the fool's motley. And then we sat down in the
grass and I told him my whole life's story. He looked at my palm and
was quite taken with my unusual past and future. He advised me not
to take off my fool's clothing in the next few days, for he could tell by
palmistry that I would be a prisoner and in mortal danger. I thanked
him for his good will and advice, prayed that God might reward his
help, and begged him to be my true friend and father because I was
forsaken by all the world.

Then we got up and went to a gambling place, where a contest with
dice was going on and every throw was accompanied by a thousand
curses. The place was about as big as the Old Market in Cologne; coats
lay on the ground, tables stood everywhere, and gamblers were milling
around. Each group had three cubed bones of chance to which they
entrusted their luck in splitting and reapportioning their money. Each
table had a supervisor (or croupier, who reaps the crops!) whose job it
was to be umpire and see to it that no injustice was done. He also lent
coats, tables, and dice, and from the winner collected a fee for it in such
a way that he usually came out best. Yet these operators don't prosper,
for they also gamble and lose; or if they invest their money well, the
canteen keeper gets it, or the surgeon, for after a fight they often have
to have their heads dressed and bandaged.

While I was standing there, looking at the place and all the gamblers
and their foolishness, my tutor asked what I thought of it. I answered,
"I don't like their taking God's name in vain; but as for the rest, I let it
stand on its own merit or lack of it, as something strange to me, which
I do not yet understand." My tutor replied, "You must know that this
is the most wicked and abhorrent place in the whole camp. The people
here covet their neighbor's money and lose their own over it." I asked,
"Dear sir, if gambling is such a horrid and dangerous matter, why do
the people in charge allow it?" My tutor answered, "I shouldn't like to

say it's because the officers themselves join in, but rather because the soldiers don't want to do without it, or can't do without it. For whoever has yielded to gambling once (or who has once been possessed by the gambling devil) gradually becomes so ensnared that he can give it up no more than he can give up sleeping." I crossed myself and wondered why such inventions of the devil should be permitted in a Christian army.

CHAPTER 21: *A bit shorter and livelier than the preceding one*

AS TIME PASSED, MY tutor and I became more and more devoted to each other, and yet we kept our closeness a secret. I was still acting the part of the fool, but my jokes had become more thoughtful than foolish. When our siege of Magdeburg made no progress, I suggested having a big rope made and wrapping it all the way around the town.[9] Then all the men and draft animals in camp should pull on it and thus raze the town in a one-day operation. I thought up plenty of such foolish jokes and gags and always had a good supply on hand. My master's clerk (who was quite a joker and prankster) gave me a lot of material that kept me going along the road of foolishness.

Once I asked him what kind of fellow our regimental chaplain was, and why he dressed differently from other people. The clerk said, "He is Mr. Dicis-et-non-facis. That means a guy who ties the knot for other men but doesn't take a wife of his own. He dislikes thieves because they don't tell what they do, but *he* never does what *he* says. Thieves don't like him, either, because the only time they associate closely with him is at their hanging." Later when I called our good chaplain by that Latin name, he was laughed at, and I was called an evil-minded fool and got whipped for it.

The tutor, on the other hand, whenever he was alone with me, entertained me with conversation of a different kind. He told me a lot about his son, the above-mentioned regimental clerk in the Saxon army. His abilities were much greater than those of our colonel's clerk. Thus our colonel not only liked him but tried to get him released and to make him *his* secretary.

This muster clerk (who, like his father, was called Ulrich Heartbrother) and I became such good friends that we swore each other eternal brotherhood, by virtue of which we would never forsake each

[9] Simplicius' suggestion goes back to the Bible; see 2 Samuel 17, 13.

other, in good luck or bad, fortune or misfortune. And since this was done with the approval of his father, we kept our covenant all the more faithfully. Beyond that we cared only for getting me honorably out of my fool's coat, so that we might serve one another better. But the elder Heartbrother, whom I honored and respected as a father, did not approve; he said in so many words that changing my status now would bring severe imprisonment and grave danger upon me. And because he also predicted great disgrace for himself and his son, he thought we had good reason to live all the more carefully and warily. He did not want to be involved in the affairs of a person whose future danger he clearly foresaw, and he was afraid that if I revealed my true self, my bad luck might strike him as well, for he had known my secret right along, had known me inside and out, as it were, but had not told the colonel.

Shortly afterward I noticed that our colonel's clerk was obviously green with envy of young Heartbrother, in fear that my friend would be promoted ahead of him, and he would lose his job. I saw how worried he was: envy made him sigh whenever he looked at either the older or the younger Heartbrother. From all this I guessed that he was planning to trip them and make them fall. From a sense of affection and duty, I communicated my suspicion to my heart's brother, that he might look out for this Judas. But he made light of the matter, for he was far superior with pen and sword, and in addition had the colonel's love and favor.

CHAPTER 22: *A roguish thieves' trick to wear each other's shoes*

IT IS CUSTOMARY TO choose military constables from among the older, more experienced soldiers, and we also had someone like that in our regiment. He was a crafty gallows' bird and archrogue with far more experience than was required for the job, for he was a necroman-cer, sorcerer, coscinomancer,[10] and exorcist. He was as bulletproof as steel, made others bulletproof, and could put whole squadrons of cavalry into the field. His face looked, quite naturally, very much as painters and poets represent Saturn.[11] Now, although some poor,

---

[10] A person able to discover hidden objects by looking through and turning a sieve; also, the sieve will turn when the name of a thief is mentioned.

[11] Saturn is represented as an old, grey-haired man with a large beard; he carries a scythe or a staff in his right hand and walks bent over forward.

unfortunate soldiers who got nabbed felt very much downhearted because of him, there were others who were glad to have this creepy character for a friend. One of these was Oliver, our clerk, and the more his jealousy of easygoing young Heartbrother grew, the more intimate he became with the constable. I soon concluded that the conjunction of Saturn and Mercury would bode no good for my fairminded, honest young Heartbrother.

About this time the colonel's wife gave birth to a son, and the christening was celebrated in high style. Young Heartbrother was asked to serve on table, and because my friend was glad to do a favor, Oliver took this opportunity to perpetrate a piece of villainy that he had long contemplated. For when all the guests had left, the colonel's large gold-plated cup was missing. It had definitely been used after certain strangers had left, and the colonel wasn't too keen about losing it. The page said he had seen it last in Oliver's hands, but Oliver said he must have been mistaken. They summoned the constable to enlist his aid, asking him to use his magic to regain the cup, and, if possible, to arrange that the thief become known only to the colonel. (He did not want to ruin any of the officers of his regiment if by chance one of them had stolen it.)

Since everyone knew himself to be innocent, we all gathered in the colonel's big tent, where the necromancer was about to perform. Everybody looked at everyone else, wanting to know where the cup had gone and what would come of it. When the constable had mumbled a few words, several young dogs crawled out of one person's pants pocket, another's sleeves, and still another's boots, fly, and any other openings in his clothes. These pups ran all over the tent; they were very pretty, of different colors and each differently marked. It was lots of fun. My own tight Croatian calfskin trousers were filled with puppies, too, and I had to pull them down. During my stay in the woods, my drawers had rotted on me, and I stood there stark naked, all I had before and behind appearing in plain sight! Finally a doggie jumped out of Heartbrother's fly; it was the jolliest of the lot and wore a golden collar. This one swallowed up all the other puppies (there were so many you couldn't put a foot down without stepping on one). When it had gobbled them all up it gradually shrank, but the collar grew until it changed into the colonel's loving cup.

The colonel and everyone else concluded that young Heartbrother, and no one else, had stolen the cup. Therefore the colonel said to him, "Look, you ungrateful guest, is this theft your thanks for all the good turns I've done you? Tomorrow I wanted to make you my secretary, but instead you ought to be hanged, as of today. And it would be done, too, if it weren't for your honest old father. Hurry up, get out of my camp, and don't let me see you as long as you live!"

Heartbrother wanted to explain, but since his theft was so obvious to everybody, he was not heeded, and when he went out his father fainted and we had quite a time bringing him to and comforting him, saying that a good father is not responsible for what a bad child has done. This is how Oliver, with the devil's help, got what he wanted, which he had been unable to get by honest means.

CHAPTER 23: *Ulrich Heartbrother sells himself for a hundred ducats*

AS SOON AS YOUNG Heartbrother's captain found out about the theft, he fired him as a clerk and reduced him to the rank of a pikeman. From this time on everybody began despising him, and even the dogs practically peed on him. For this reason he often wished he were dead. His father was so worried about him that he fell seriously ill and prepared for death. Since he had predicted that he would have to go through mortal danger on the twenty-sixth of July (which day was drawing near), he got permission from the colonel to see his son once more in order to talk about his will. I was the third person at this sad meeting. Well, I saw that the son needed to make no excuses to his father, who knew his character and upbringing well enough and was sure of his innocence. As a wise, understanding, and thoughtful man, he gathered from the circumstances that Oliver had been out to get his son and had schemed with the constable to cause his downfall. But what could he do against a sorcerer? He might be in worse trouble if he avenged himself. Furthermore, he was aware that he might die; yet he could not die in peace so long as his son lived under a cloud of shame. As for the son, the less he relished living under these conditions, the more he wished to die before his father. Surely the suffering of these two men was so pitiful to witness that I had to cry from the bottom of my heart. Finally they decided to be patient and to put their affairs into the hands of God. The son was to think of getting released from his company so that he might try his luck elsewhere. But when they thought it over, he lacked the funds to buy himself free of the captain. And while they pondered and commiserated about the straits in which poverty kept them, cutting off all hope of improving their lot, I remembered the ducats which were still sewn up in the donkey ears. I asked them how much money they needed in this emergency. Young Heartbrother answered, "If someone came along and gave us a hundred thalers, I would be fairly sure to get out of all my trouble." I answered, "Brother, if this will do it, lift up your heart, for I will give you a hundred ducats."[12] "Alas, brother," he answered in turn, "are you really a fool, or are you heartless enough to make fun of my grief?" "No, no," I said, "I'll lend you the money." Taking off my jacket, I peeled one donkey ear from my arm, snipped it open, and let him count out a hundred ducats. I kept the rest and said, "With this I will take care of your sick father if he needs it." At this they embraced me, kissed me, and were beside themselves with joy, calling me an angel whom God had sent for their comfort. They wanted to give me a promissory note and to assure me that I would share in old Heart-brother's inheritance equally with the son, or (if God helped them to their estate again) that they would gladly repay me this amount with interest. I would have none of this but their friendship. Then young Heartbrother wanted to swear that he would have his revenge on Oliver or die trying, but his father forbade it, assuring him that whoever killed Oliver would be done in by Simplex. "Yet," he said, "I am sure neither will kill the other, because you are not fated to die by weapons." After that he made us swear to love and assist each other in trouble.

Having commended his father to my care, young Heartbrother bought himself free with thirty thalers and the captain gave him an honorable discharge. Then he went to Hamburg and with the rest of the money bought two horses and equipment and joined the Swedes as a volunteer cavalryman.

CHAPTER 24: *Two prophecies in a row come true*

NONE OF THE COLONEL'S men was better suited than I to care for old Heartbrother in his sickness, and because the sick man was more than satisfied with me, I was put in charge by the colonel's wife, who also did much good for him. And since he was in such good hands and reassured about his son, he improved from day to day so that he recovered almost completely before the twenty-sixth of July. Yet, he wanted to bide his time and play sick until this fateful day, of which he was truly afraid, should pass.

Meanwhile he was visited by many officers, from either army, who wanted to know their fortunes, and since he was a good astrologer,

---

[12] The (gold) ducat is worth much more than the (silver) thaler. N.B. The word *dollar* is derived from *t(h)aler*: they were first minted in Joachimst(h)al, Bohemia, where silver was mined.

physiognomist, and chiromancer he was seldom wrong. He even named the day on which the battle of Wittstock later took place, for many came to him who felt threatened with violent death. He assured the colonel's wife that she would complete her lying-in period in camp, because Magdeburg would not be surrendered before the end of those six weeks. He expressly told Oliver (that snake-in-the-grass who tried to curry favor with him) that he would have to die a violent death, and that I would avenge his death and kill his murderers. For this reason Oliver was my friend for a while.

He told me my own future life in so much detail that it seemed it had already been completed and he had always been by my side. But I did not pay much attention, and only afterward, after many things had happened, I remembered he had mentioned their coming. He especially warned me of water, for he feared I would perish by it.

Now when the twenty-sixth of July came, he told me and a soldier whom the colonel had assigned to him for his protection, repeatedly and with emphasis, to let no one enter his tent. He was its only occupant, and he prayed constantly. Toward afternoon a cavalry officer came riding up and asked for the colonel's stable master. He was sent to us and immediately denied admission. But he insisted; he pressured the soldier and promised him a reward if he could see the stable master; he *had* to see him this evening. Because this got him nowhere, he started swearing, calling down the Lord's wrath and asserting he had come many times at the stable master's bidding and yet had missed him every time. Now that he'd arrived, he'd be damned if he would be refused. He dismounted and could not be prevented from opening the tent flap. I bit his hand, but he hauled off and hit me in the face.

As soon as he was inside and saw the old man, he said, "Sir, I beg you to excuse the liberty I am taking, but I must talk to you." "All right," said the stable master, "what is it?" The lieutenant said, "I only wanted to ask you to cast my horoscope." The stable master answered, "I hope, most honored sir, you will forgive me and excuse my refusal because of sickness, for my aching head cannot at present do the work, which requires many calculations. If you will be patient until tomorrow I hope to be able to satisfy you." The lieutenant shouted, "Sir! Just read my palm then." "Lieutenant," replied old Heartbrother, "this art is unreliable and deceptive. For that reason, may I insist that you put off your request until tomorrow, when I shall be glad to be of service."

The lieutenant was reluctant to be turned away. He stepped up to Heartbrother's cot, stretched out his hand, and said, "Sir, I only ask you to tell me a few words concerning the end of my life; I assure you if it should be violent, I shall interpret your words as a warning from God to take better care of myself. Therefore I beg you for God's sake to come right out and not conceal the truth from me." The good old man answered him in a few words. "All right then. Look out or you'll be hanged within the hour." The lieutenant (who was drunk as a lord) shouted, "You rascal! You talk this way with a gentleman!?" He drew his blade and killed my dear old Heartbrother on his cot. The soldier and I immediately raised the alarm, and everyone ran for his gun. The lieutenant was on his mount in no time and would have escaped if the Elector of Saxony and his entourage had not come by just then. He had the lieutenant arrested and when he heard what had happened, he turned to our general, von Hatzfeld,[13] and said only, "If a sick man in his bed is not safe from murderers, we certainly have rotten discipline in an imperial camp!" That was a severe sentence and enough to cut short the lieutenant's life. Our general immediately had him hanged by his precious neck, and that procedure choked off his breath.

CHAPTER 25: *Simplicius is metamorphosed from a youth into a virgin and acquires several wooers*

THIS TRUE STORY PROVES that one cannot reject all predictions, as do some smart alecks who think they know everything and believe in nothing. It also shows that a man can hardly avoid the end that was set for him, even though his downfall is foretold by prophecy. As to whether it is necessary, useful, and good to have one's horoscope cast, I only say this: Old Heartbrother told me so many things, but I have often wished, and still wish, that he hadn't. I have never been able to avoid the misfortunes he predicted, and the ones still ahead are turning my hair grey — and all in vain; presumably, like all the rest, they will happen whether or not I prepare myself for them. Concerning the good forecasts, I hold that they are more deceptive and will not help a person as much as the bad predictions.

What good did it do me that old Heartbrother swore to high heaven I was the son of noble parents, while I knew of no other parents than my knan and mither, who were crude peasants in the Spessart? Or, to cite another example, what good did it do Wallenstein, Duke of Friedland, to be told he would be crowned king to the accompaniment of sweet string-music? Everybody knows how *he* was rocked to sleep

---

[13] Melchior von Hatzfeld (1593-1658) was an imperial general. In 1636 he was beaten by Banér (Sweden) at Wittstock; see chap. 27.

at Eger.[14] Let other people ponder these matters. I'll get back to my
story now.

When I had lost both my Heartbrothers, as I have told, I became
disgusted with the camp at Magdeburg; I grew sick and tired of my
jester's garb and my foolery, and I no longer cared to be the butt of
everyone's jokes. I wanted to be free of all this, even if it cost me life
and limb. And because there was no better opportunity, I went about
it in a thoroughly irresponsible way.

Oliver, who had become my tutor when old Heartbrother died,
often allowed me to go foraging with the soldiers. Now, when we came
to a large village and everyone went into the houses to see what he
might take along, I sneaked off to see if I could find some peasant's old
clothes I might slip into. But what I was looking for did not turn up
and I had to be satisfied with a woman's dress. Finding myself alone,
I changed into it, threw my suit into a privy, and imagined that now I
was delivered from all my trouble. In my new outfit I started walking
across the street toward some officers' wives; I was very careful to take
mincing steps. But I had hardly left the house when some of the
foraging party saw me and I speeded up my gait. When they shouted,
"Stop, stop!" I ran all the faster and reached the officers' wives before
they did. I implored the ladies, for the sake of all women's honor and
virtue, to save my virginity from these lusting rascals. Not only was my
wish granted, but a captain's wife hired me as her maid and I stayed
with her until our men had captured Magdeburg, Werberschanze,
Havelberg, and Perleberg.

The captain's wife, who was no longer a spring chicken, though she
wasn't too old either, took such a liking to my pretty face and straight
body that finally, after much hemming and hawing and beating vainly
about the bush, she told me in plain language where the shoe was
pinching her. But at that time I was still very conscientious; I acted as
if I had not understood and gave no indications but those from which
one might conclude that I was a shamefaced maiden.

The captain and his man were infected with the same disease —
lovesickness; and so he asked his wife to get some prettier clothes for
me, so that they need not be ashamed of my ugly peasant dress. Doing
more than she had been told, she dressed me up like a French doll, and
this fed the fire in all three of them. In fact, the ardor of the captain and

[14] Albrecht Eusebius Wenzel von Wallenstein (1583-1634), the greatest general
on the Catholic side, was murdered in the town hall of Eger, Bohemia, on
February 25, 1634. In his drama *Wallenstein's Death*, Schiller presents the last
few days of his life.

his man grew so great that they passionately begged of me what I could not grant them and what I was elegantly refusing the lady.

Finally, the captain determined to create a situation that would enable him to get by force what he couldn't possibly have. His wife got wind of it, and because she hoped ultimately to wear down my scruples, she blocked his every move so that he thought he'd go crazy. The one I really felt sorry for was our man, the poor fellow, for master and mistress could cool their ardor with each other, but this poor chap had nobody. Therefore, one night when man and wife were asleep, the hired man stood by the wagon where I slept. Amid fiery tears he poured out his love for me and asked for my sympathy and pity. But I proved harder than any stone and let him know that I intended to keep my virginity until I got married. When he offered marriage a thousand times and yet heard only that it was impossible for me to marry him, he despaired (or at least acted that way), drew his sword, put the point to his chest and the handle against the wagon, and let on he wanted to kill himself. I thought, 'The devil pushes a man to suicide.' I comforted him and said I would give him my decision in the morning. This satisfied him and he went away to sleep. But I stayed awake all the longer and contemplated my dilemma. I sensed that my situation would come to no good end; the captain's wife was becoming more and more impatient, the captain more daring in his approach, and the man more desperate in his love. I did not know how to escape from this labyrinth.

Often I had to help my mistress catch a flea, but of course this was to get me to see and touch her lily-white breasts and the rest of her body. And because I too was made of flesh and blood, this sort of thing was getting more difficult for me. If the woman left me in peace, the captain pestered me, and if I had a night of respite from these two, the manservant was after me. Thus my women's clothing was much harder to wear than the fool's motley. At that point (but much too late) I thought of the late Heartbrother's prophetic warning, and I imagined I was right in the middle of that danger to life and limb he had predicted for me. The dress held me captive; I could not escape in it, and the captain would have crushed every bone in my body if he had surprised me catching fleas on his pretty wife. What was I to do? I decided to make a clean breast of it to the manservant next morning. I assumed his ardor would cool, and if I gave him some of my ducats he might help me back into men's clothing and thus out of trouble. This would have worked well if luck had been with me, but it wasn't.

John, my foolish lover, got up right after midnight in order to hear my assent. He started rattling and rocking the wagon just after I had fallen into a deep sleep (for I had lain awake worrying for some time).

In a loud voice he called out, "Sabina, Sabina, my sweetheart, get up and keep your promise!" But he woke up the captain before me because his tent was close to the wagon. Undoubtedly the captain was livid and green with envy, but he did not emerge to interfere; he only got up in order to see how the deal would turn out. The manservant woke me up and urged me either to come out of the wagon or to let him in. I gave him a scolding and asked if he thought I was a whore; my promise was based on marriage and without that he could never have me. He asked why I didn't get up; it was beginning to get light and I could make an early start with the breakfast. He would fetch water and firewood and make a fire for me. I answered, "If you want to do that, I can sleep that much longer. You go ahead. I'll be there soon." But since the fool would not leave me in peace, I got up, more to do my work than to be kind to him, especially since yesterday's mood of despair seemed to have left him. I could easily pass for a soldier's hired girl, for I had learned from the Croats how to cook, bake, and launder, and no finer work was required. Whatever I could not do, like arranging the captain's wife's hair, she gladly overlooked, for she knew very well I had never learned it.

When I climbed out of the wagon my John became so enflamed by the sight of my white arms that he could not refrain from kissing me, and I didn't put up much resistance. The captain, who was looking on, could not stand it and came running with drawn sword to dispatch my lover. But he took to his heels and forgot to come back. The captain said to me, "You bloody whore! I'll teach you...." He couldn't say *what* because of his anger. He started beating me as if he were insane. I began screaming and he had to stop to avoid causing an alarm, for the Saxon and the imperial armies were encamped close to each other since the Swedes, under General Banér,[15] were approaching.

CHAPTER 26: *How Simplicius is considered a traitor and a warlock*

WHEN DAYLIGHT CAME AND both armies began to break camp, my master abandoned me to the stable boys. They were a bunch of brutes and the trouble I had with them was bad enough. They chased me toward a clump of bushes where they hoped to satisfy their animal lust, as is the custom of these children spawned by the devil when a

---

[15] Johan Banér (1596-1664), distinguished Swedish general. In the battle of Wittstock (Sept. 24-Oct. 4, 1636) he restored much of the prestige Sweden had lost through the Peace of Prague in 1635.

woman is turned over to them. Many other lads ran out just to watch this pitiful sport, and among these was John, the manservant. He had kept an eye on me, and seeing that things were getting rough, he wanted to save me by main force even if it cost him his head. He got some help by saying I was his fiancée. His friends felt sorry for both of us and wanted to do what they could. But the stable boys, who claimed prior rights and did not want to give up their quarry, took a different view and set force against force. So a fight started and help came running to either side; the situation almost resembled a tournament where everyone does his best for the sake of a beautiful lady.

The riotous noise brought in the assistant constable, who arrived just as they had torn the clothes off me and noticed I was no woman. The appearance of the constable stopped everybody, for he was feared worse than the devil himself, and those who had been fighting evaporated instantly. He quickly got the essential information, and while I was hoping he would rescue me, he put me under arrest because it was most unusual and highly suspicious for a man in women's clothing to be found inside an army camp. On the way to the general provost marshal, the constable and several of his men led me past the different regiments (who were all ready to march). But when we passed my colonel's regiment he recognized me, talked to me, and gave me some clothes, and I was handed over to our old constable who put me in handcuffs and chains.

I found it mighty hard to walk that way, and I would have starved if Oliver, the secretary, had not given me something to eat. I did not dare show my ducats, which I had managed to conceal until now, for surely I would have lost them and drawn even greater suspicion on myself. In the evening Oliver told me why I was given such severe treatment. Our regimental magistrate had received orders to question me at once and to communicate the results to the provost marshal. They thought not only that I was a scout or a spy, but also that I knew witchcraft, for shortly after I disappeared from the colonel, some witches had been burned, who had confessed (and died for it) to seeing me at one of their meetings, at which they had deliberated about drying up the river Elbe so that Magdeburg could be captured sooner.

The regimental magistrate was given a list of seven questions to ask me, but I wanted to tell him my whole story so that the strange circumstances of my life might explain everything neatly and put my answers to the questions in proper context. But the magistrate was not that curious; he was tired and grouchy from marching and wanted only brief answers. When he had finished writing them down he said, "Hm, yes, you are the kind whose tongue needs loosening on the rack." My thought was, "May God help me if things go his addlepated way."

Early next morning the provost marshal sent our constable an order to keep me under arrest because he intended to examine me personally, as soon as the armies stopped moving. Doubtless I would have been tortured if God had not destined it differently. While under arrest I thought constantly of the parson at Hanau and of the late Heartbrother, for both had predicted my fortune after my escape from the fool's cap.

CHAPTER 27: *How the provost weathered the battle of Wittstock*

WE HAD HARDLY PITCHED camp that night when I was taken to the provost marshal. He had my previous answers in front of him and started examining me. I told him how things had come about, but he did not believe me. It *was* hard for the provost marshal to tell whether he was dealing with a fool or a clever scoundrel, for although questions and answers came tripping off my tongue, the whole business was most strange. The provost marshal asked the constable whether anything unusual, like written documents, had been found on me. The constable answered, "No, why bother to frisk him? The camp police brought him in almost naked." But, alas, that wasn't good enough. The provost had to frisk me in everyone's presence, and since he did this most thoroughly, he found the two donkey's ears that were wrapped around my arms and contained my ducats. Then they said, "Do we need any other proof? This traitor undertook to do some big job. Why else would a man put on fool's clothing or a woman's dress? It's best to torture him on the rack tomorrow or, as he is probably guilty, burn him at the stake; since he admits keeping company with sorcerers, he doesn't deserve anything else."

You can easily imagine how I felt. I knew I was innocent and trusted in God, but I also saw the danger, and deplored the loss of my ducats, which had disappeared into the provost marshal's pockets. But before they could give me the third degree, Banér's army and ours started fighting. First they fought for position and then for the heavy artillery, which we promptly lost. Our constable, that clever puppy-maker, stayed pretty far behind the battle lines, with his helpers and the prisoners, and yet we were so close behind our own brigade that we could recognize the individual soldiers by their clothing. When a Swedish squadron clashed with ours, we were in danger of death no less than the fighters, for the air was so full of whizzing bullets that you might think they were fighting exclusively for our personal benefit.

Those who were afraid ducked and cringed, but those with experience and courage let the bullets pass without turning pale. In the battle itself each man tried to prevent his own death by killing the man approaching him. An awful music was performed by the cruel shots, the clashing of armor plate, the splintering of pikestaffs, the screams of the attackers as well as the wounded, by the blare of trumpets, the roll of drums, and the shrill sound of fifes. Heavy dust and dense smoke covered the scene, as if to hide the ghastly sight of the wounded and dead. From the darkness one heard the pitiful moaning of the dying and the joyful shouting of those still full of courage. As time went on, even the horses seemed to become more energetic in the defense of their masters. A few of them fell down dead beneath their riders. They had received wounds through no fault of their own and in recompense for faithful service. For similar reasons, others fell on their masters, and thus, while dying, enjoyed the honor of being supported by those whom they had carried while alive. Still others, in rage and anger, ran away, leaving mankind behind, and for the first time sought their freedom in the open fields. The earth that is accustomed to covering the dead was, herself now covered with corpses. In one place lay heads that had lost their masters, and elsewhere lay bodies without heads. Out of some bodies entrails hung in a cruel and ghastly manner. The heads of others had been crushed and the brains spattered all over. Here one saw lifeless bodies robbed of their blood; there, some still alive and gory with the blood of others. Here lay severed arms with the fingers still twitching as if they itched to get back into the melee. There some fellows who had shed or spilled not one drop of blood were taking to their heels. In one place lay thighs separated from the burden of their bodies; yet they had become heavier than ever they had been in life. In another place mortally wounded men were praying for speedy death, while others were begging for mercy and asking quarter. To sum it all up: it was one pitiful, miserable sight.

The Swedes soon drove our people before them and scattered them in quick pursuit. On this occasion our Mr. Constable and his prisoners also decided to flee, though we — never having fought — did not deserve any hostility; but the constable threatened to kill us if we didn't join him. At that moment young Heartbrother came galloping up with five other horsemen and greeted the constable with a shot from his pistol. "Look at you, you old son of a bitch," he shouted. "Do you still feel like producing puppies? I'll repay you for your trouble!" But the shot didn't hurt the constable any more than it would a steel anvil. "Ho-ho!? Is this the kind you are?" shouted Heartbrother. "I don't want to have made this trip for nothing. You puppy-maker, you'll die even if your soul is sewed to your guts." Then Heartbrother ordered one of the constable's own soldiers to kill him with an ax, if *he* didn't want to get killed.

This is how the constable got his comeuppance. When Heartbrother recognized me, he took off my chains and handcuffs, put me on a horse, and had his man take me to safety.

CHAPTER 28: *Concerning a great battle in which the triumphant conqueror is taken prisoner in the very act of being victorious*

THOUGH MY SAVIOR'S MAN removed me from further danger, his master rode into it, for reasons of honor and a desire for spoils. He was surrounded and taken prisoner. When the victorious Swedes had divided their loot and buried their dead, and Heartbrother was missing, his captain inherited me, the horses, and the man. I had to become the captain's stable boy for no other pay than the promise that he would "set me up," i.e., buy me a mount and an outfit, if I did well and when I had grown a little older. For the time being, I had to be content and patient.

Soon after that my captain was promoted to lieutenant colonel. It was my job to do what David did long ago for King Saul; I had to sing and play the lute. On the march I had to carry his cuirass for him — a job I hated. Though this piece of equipment had been invented to protect against the enemy's thrusts, I found the very opposite to be true, for under the protection of the cuirass the little crawlers that fed on me could persecute me all the better; beneath it they had free passage, fun, and frolic. It seemed I was wearing this piece of armor for *their* protection, not mine, because I couldn't possibly get at them with my hands. I thought of all sorts of strategic devices for eradicating this armada, but I had neither the time nor the opportunity to stamp them out by fire (as is done by baking them in an oven), water, or poison (mercury would do it!). Nor did I have the money to get rid of them by buying all new shirts or a set of new clothes. I had to live with them at the expense of my life's blood. When they were nibbling and irritating me too much, I'd whip out my pistol as if to exchange shots with them, but I only took the ramrod and pushed them away from their food. After a while I put a piece of fur on the end of the rod, tied it with sticky tape, and, reaching under the cuirass with this louse-catcher, I nabbed them by the dozen and hurled them to the ground from high on horseback. But still, it didn't really help.

One time my lieutenant colonel was ordered to ride to Westphalia on a special mission. If he had then had as many men as I had lice, he would have frightened the whole world. But since he hadn't, he had to proceed carefully and hide in a forest between Hamm and Soest.[16] At that time my pedicular enemies had reached the height of their glory. They were plaguing me so much with their undermining tactics that I thought they would soon take up quarters between my skin and my flesh. No wonder the Brazilians eat lice — anger and the spirit of revenge drives them to it! One time, when part of the cavalrymen were feeding their horses, while others slept or kept a lookout, I could no longer stand the annoyance. I stepped aside under a tree to do battle with my enemy. Though others put on their armor when they fight, for this battle I took mine off and started such a murder and massacre that my swords (both thumbs) were dripping blood, and corpses (or dead skins) fell everywhere. The ones I didn't kill I chased out into the cold world and let them take a walk under the tree. I thought of a ditty I had heard:

> And when the slaughter started, my nails they all got red.
> One louse said to her neighbor, "O lousy, we'll be dead!"

When I think of the slaughter my skin still itches. I continued so furiously that I did not notice some imperials charging my lieutenant colonel until they were close upon me, relieved the poor lice, and captured me. My manly courage, with which I had lately slain many thousands, did not impress the imperials. I was given to a dragoon and the best thing about me that he got was my lieutenant colonel's cuirass; he sold it to his commander at Soest (where they were quartered) for a stiff price. I had to be the dragoon's stable boy, and he became my sixth master in this war.

CHAPTER 29: *How, before his death, a pious soldier lived well in Paradise; and how the Hunter took his place after his death*

BECAUSE OUR LANDLADY DID not want me to populate her and her whole house with my pedicular multitudes, I had to get rid of them. She didn't fool around, either, but stuck my ragged clothes in her oven and roasted the lice alive until dead. I began living as if in a rose

---

[16] Westphalia, a district in northwestern Germany, is partly hilly, partly good, level farmland; as a class its farmers are well to do. Various industries flourished there even in the seventeenth century. The towns mentioned were centers of military activities. Soest has one of the finest examples of church architecture in the Catholic cathedral of St. Mary-on-the-Height.

garden; in fact, no one can believe what a relief it was to be rid of this torment. The last few months had been like sitting on an ant hill!

But right after this alleviation I received another cross to bear. My master was one of those soldiers who are sure they'll go to heaven. He was satisfied with his pay and wouldn't hurt a fly. All he owned he had saved out of his weekly wages and extra money from sentry duty. Though this was little enough, he treasured it more than others value Oriental pearls; every two bits he sewed up in his clothing, and his poor horse and I had to help him save. That is why I had to subsist on dry pumpernickel and water or, if prosperity was rampant, on small beer. But I had no taste for this because my throat became rough from coarse unbuttered bread, and my whole body got frightfully emaciated. If I wanted better food I had to steal it — but he instructed me to do it in such a way that he could not be billed for it.

As far as he was concerned, there was no need for gallows, the wooden horse,[17] hangman, bastinadoes, or for surgeons, or tavern-keepers, or the musicians who play taps; his whole life was far removed from gluttony, swilling, gambling, and dueling. When he was ordered on convoy duty, raiding, or some such special job, he straggled along like an old lady on a cane. I am convinced that if it hadn't been for this good dragoon's heroic and martial *virtues* he would never have caught me. He wouldn't have paid any attention to a lousy boy but would have pursued my lieutenant colonel instead. There was no use looking forward to a piece of hand-me-down clothing, for the chap wore clothes that were almost as well patched as my hermit's. His saddle and other gear were hardly worth three bits; his horse was so weak from hunger that neither Swede nor Hessian need fear being pursued by him.

All this persuaded his captain to place him as a guard in a convent at Paradise, near Soest — not because he was good for the purpose, but rather to give him a chance to get ahead and to buy a new mount, and particularly because the nuns had asked for a pious, conscientious, and quiet man. Well, he rode there and I walked along, because unfortunately he had only one horse. Along the way he said, "Tarnation, Shrimpy" — he could never remember "Simplicius" — "we're going to Paradise and how we'll gorge there!" I answered, "The name is a good omen. May God grant that the place lives up to it." "Sure," he said (and he hadn't understood me), "even if we could drink an 'Ohm' of beer — that's forty gallons — every day or two, I'm sure they wouldn't mind. You just be a good boy. I'm going to have a brand new coat made for

---

[17] This is a contraption on which those condemned to a flogging are strapped.

myself and let you have the old one. It'll make you a nice piece of clothing yet."

We found Paradise as we desired it or even better; instead of angels it was full of pretty young women who treated us so well with food and drink that after a while I put on weight. There they had the richest beer, the best Westphalian ham and knockwurst, and very tender and well prepared beef. I learned to put half an inch of salted butter on pumpernickel, and cheese on top of that, to make it slide down better. And when I sat over a leg of mutton (well seasoned and garnished with garlic!) and had a stein of beer by my side, soul and body were refreshed and I forgot all my hardships. This Paradise did me as much good as if it had been the real thing. My only concern was that it wouldn't last forever and that I had to walk around in rags.

But just as bad luck had come to me by the jugful, so good luck came now by the tubful: when my master went to Soest to get the rest of his baggage, I found on the way a package, and in it were several yards of red cloth for an overcoat, and red velvet for lining. I took it along and exchanged it at a cloth merchant's for enough common green cloth to make a suit, together with the buttons. The man also agreed to have the suit made up for me and to give me a hat into the bargain. Since now I needed only a pair of new shoes and a shift, I gave the haberdasher the silver buttons and the braid that went with the red cloth, and for these he gave me the shoes and shirt; and so I had a complete new outfit.

When I returned to Paradise my master was hopping mad because I hadn't brought the package to him first. He even talked of whipping me and taking the suit right off my back (and he would have done it if it had fit him and if he hadn't been ashamed). I thought I had done the right thing all the time!

Now this parsimonious tightwad had to be ashamed that his boy was dressed better than he. For that reason he rode to Soest, borrowed money from his captain, and bought himself a whole new outfit. He promised to repay from his special weekly wages, which he did. Of course he had the money himself, but he was too smart to use it; for if he had done so, he might have lost the lazy man's job of safeguarding Paradise that winter. This way, if the captain wanted his money back he would have to leave him in this sinecure.

From now on we had the laziest life on earth, and bowling was our most strenuous work. When I had curried, fed, and watered my dragoon's nag, I carried on like a rich man's son and went for a walk. The convent was safeguarded also by the Hessians, who had sent a musketeer from Lippstadt. He was a furrier by trade, a good singer and fencer. In order not to get rusty, he practiced fencing with me in all kinds of weapons, and I soon became so good at it that I held my own against him. My dragoon bowled with him, but only for who would have to drink the most beer with the next meal; and so the convent was the loser, whatever the outcome.

The convent had its own game forest and employed a keeper for it. Since I too was dressed in green, I associated with him, and that winter I learned all the tricks of his trade, particularly those concerning small game. For this reason, and because the name "Simplicius" is a little unusual and not easy to pronounce, everyone called me "Hunterboy." I got to know all the roads and trails, and this came in handy later. When I couldn't go out because of the weather, I read all sorts of books that the steward of the convent lent me. But when the noble nuns noticed that I could play the lute, dabbled on the clavichord, and had a good voice, they started paying more and more attention to me. Since I was well proportioned and my face wasn't hard to look at, they all thought my demeanor and bearing were that of a nobleman and altogether becoming to a well-liked young man. Before I knew it, I became popular, and everyone wondered why I was working for such a slovenly dragoon.

In spring, having spent the winter in this pleasant manner, my master was relieved of his job. He took it so hard that he fell ill. A severe fever and some old troubles then set in, and three weeks later I had to bury him. I wrote this inscription for his grave:

> John Starveling lies here, a soldier good and brave.
> He ne'er spilt human blood & now he's in his grave.

By custom and legal usage his captain should have inherited his horse and gun, while the sergeant the rest of his possessions. But since I was an up-and-coming young man who would in time be a good soldier, everything was offered to me if I wanted to join the army in place of my late master. I accepted with enthusiasm, because I knew that my master had left behind quite a number of ducats he had scraped together and sewn into his old breeches. When I gave my name — Simplicius Simplicissimus — to the muster clerk (and his name was Cyriacus) he couldn't spell it and said, "There isn't a devil in hell by that name!" When I asked *him* if there was one by the name of Cyriacus, he didn't know what to say, though he thought he was smart. My captain, who heard this conversation, was so pleased by this that he thought well of me from then on.

CHAPTER 30: *How the Hunter prospered when he began soldiering. Any young soldier can learn a lot from this chapter.*

BECAUSE THE COMMANDER AT Soest needed a stable boy and I seemed to be the kind he liked, he was reluctant to see me become a soldier. He said he'd get me yet, for I wasn't old enough to pass for a man. Then he argued with my captain about it, sent for me, and said, "Listen, Hunterboy, you ought to be my servant!" I asked what I was to do in this position. He answered, "Help wait on the horses." "Sir," I replied, "we are far apart in this matter. I'd rather have a master in whose service the horses wait on me; but since I can't have that kind of job, I'll stay a soldier." He said, "Your beard is too soft yet." "Oh no," I said, "I feel strong enough to outdo a man of eighty. It's not the beard that kills another man; otherwise billy goats would sell at a higher price." He said, "If your courage is as good as your tongue, I'll let it pass." I answered, "This you can find out in the next battle"; and so I let him know I wished to be a stable boy no longer.

Next I performed an autopsy on the dragoon's old pants. With their contents I bought a good horse and the best pistols I could find. Everything had to be spick-and-span, and because I liked the name "Hunterboy" I also had a new green suit made. I gave the old one to my stable boy, for I had outgrown it. So my boy and I rode side by side, and no longer could anyone consider me poor stuff. I was bold enough to decorate my hat with an outrageous plume, like an officer's, and soon I had plenty of enemies who were jealous of me. We exchanged angry words and finally came to blows. But as soon as I had shown a few of them what I had learned from the furrier in Paradise, and that I could repay every thrust in kind, they not only left me in peace but even sought my friendship.

I frequently volunteered to go raiding, either on foot or on horseback, for I was well mounted and faster on foot than many others. When we got involved with the enemy, it was neck or nothing with me, and I always wanted to be one of the first.

This activity soon made me well known and so famous among friend and foe that both sides reckoned with me, especially since the most dangerous tasks were given to me and I was put in charge of whole groups of raiders. About that time I started helping myself to everything, and whenever I got hold of something special I gave my officers such a big share of it that they helped me out and looked the other way when I raided off limits. General Götz[18] had had to leave intact three enemy garrisons in Westphalia, one each at Dorsten, Lippstadt, and Coesfeld. I annoyed them no end, for I was at them with small groups of raiders almost every day, now here, now there; and I took valuable loot. Because I came out on top everywhere, the people grew to think I could make myself invisible and was bulletproof, like iron or steel. Therefore, I was feared like the plague, and thirty of the enemy's men were not ashamed to run like rabbits when they knew me to be nearby with only fifteen men. It got to the point that I was sent to exact "contributions" from towns or to see that they paid what they owed. This benefited my purse and my name; officers and fellow soldiers loved their Hunterboy; the most prominent enemy raiders shook in their boots, and the peasants were kept on my side by love or fear. I punished my enemies and richly rewarded those who had done me even the least favor; I spent almost half of my loot on rewards and information.

For this reason no enemy raiders proceeded, no convoy or expedition by the enemy took place that I didn't know of. I then guessed their intentions and made my plans accordingly. And since, with a little luck, I had for the most part anticipated well, everyone was surprised at my youthful success, and many officers and experienced soldiers, even on the enemy side, wanted to see me. Furthermore, I treated my prisoners with great consideration so that they often cost me more than I gained through them; and whenever I was able to show some courtesy to an enemy, especially to officers, I always did so, if it could be done without violating my duty and loyalty.

With this sort of behavior I would soon have been commissioned as an officer if my youth hadn't prevented it. For if one wanted to command a squadron at my age one had to be of ancient nobility; moreover, my captain could not promote me because at the moment there were no positions vacant in his company. He did not want to lose me, for in me he would have lost more than a milch cow. But he did make me a sergeant.

The honor of being preferred over older soldiers — though it was a slight thing — and the praise I received daily encouraged me to even greater achievements. I lay awake at night thinking of what I could do to make myself even greater, more renowned, and more admirable. I worried over lack of opportunity to show my skill with weapons, and

[18] Count von Götz (1595-1645) was ordered to the upper Rhine to retake the important fortress of Breisach. When he failed he was arrested for dereliction of duty, but ultimately acquitted. (See Book IV, 26.) He died in the battle of Jankow.

often wished for the Trojan War or the Siege of Ostend,[19] but, fool that I was, I did not consider that every grey goose gets caught at last. But when a rash young soldier has luck and pluck and money, that's how it goes. Pride and arrogance are sure to arise in him. Because of my arrogance I kept two hostlers instead of a stable boy. By giving them expensive clothes and horses, I incurred the envy of all the officers.

CHAPTER 31: *How the devil stole the parson's bacon, and how the Hunter got caught in his own trap*

I WANT TO TELL a story or two about the time before I left the dragoons. These events are not of world-shaking importance, but they are entertaining; for I didn't undertake only big things — I didn't scorn the little ones either, if I could just make a name for myself and arouse admiration among the people.

My captain was ordered to proceed with some fifty men to the fortress of Recklinghausen, there to carry out an assignment. Because we thought we might have to hide in the woods for a few days, each of us took along a week's rations. But when the convoy we were waiting for did not come on time, we ran out of food, and we couldn't steal any without giving away our presence and ruining the plan. We were starving and it hurt. Unfortunately in this place I had no helpers (as I had in most others) who would secretly supply me and my men with food and information. So, unless we wanted to return empty-handed, we had to think of something. My comrade, a student who had recently dropped out and joined the army, was longing for the good oatmeal his parents used to provide for him and which he had scornfully left behind. And while he was thinking about breakfast he remembered his studies. "Oh, brother," he said, "isn't it a shame I didn't study the art of feeding my own stomach? ... Hah! If I went to the parson over in the village, for sure *he'd* give me something to eat." I thought about this awhile and then spoke with the captain about making use of the student. Our situation was so bad and his trust in me so great that after some hesitation he consented.

I traded clothes with another soldier and then my student and I, taking the long way around, trotted toward the village, which was only half an hour away as the crow flies. We recognized the minister's house

[19] Ostend (now in Belgium) was under siege from 1601 to 1604 during the struggle for independence on the part of the Low Countries. After heroic resistance the city had to surrender to General Spinola.

because it was close to the church, and because it looked somewhat citified and was built against a wall that enclosed the entire parsonage. I had already instructed my comrade what to say. He was still wearing his threadbare school clothes; I pretended to be a painter's journeyman. (I did not think I'd be called on to paint, because few peasants have painted houses.) The parson was polite, and when my pal addressed him in well-turned Latin phrases and told him (like a seasoned liar) that soldiers had robbed him and taken all his food and money, he was given a sandwich and a mug of beer. I pretended we did not belong together and said I would have a bite to eat at the inn and then come back and holler for him, so that we could travel some distance before nightfall. So I went toward the inn, more to see what could be picked up at night than to satisfy my hunger. On the way I had the good luck to run into a peasant sealing up his oven; it was full of large loaves of pumpernickel and they are baked for twenty-four hours! I thought, 'Go right ahead sealing! One way or another we'll get at this good stuff.'

I didn't stay long at the inn, because now I knew where to get bread, but I bought a few sweet rolls to take to my captain; and when I got back to the parsonage the "student" had already finished eating and had told his host I was a painter on my way to Holland, where I wanted to continue studying art. The minister welcomed me cordially and asked me to accompany him into the church where he had some works of art he wanted repaired. To avoid spoiling the plans, I had to play along. He took us through the kitchen and when he opened the lock on the heavy oak door that led to the yard — oh, marvelous sight! — I saw the black heavens full of black stars — I mean hams, sausages, and sides of bacon hanging in a chimney. I looked at these hopefully, thinking that they were smiling back at me. But *wishing* them off the hooks and into the hands of my comrades in the woods did nothing to move them. Well, I thought of ways and means of aligning them with the aforementioned bread, but nothing good occurred to me right then; the parsonage was enclosed by a wall, all windows were secured with iron bars, and two monstrous dogs were cavorting about the yard — and they probably would not be sleeping at night if somebody tried to steal what they would ultimately chew on if they had guarded it well.

Inside the church, while the parson and I discussed the repair and restoration of some paintings, I made all sorts of excuses, including my present journey, for not wanting to work on them just now, the sexton or sacristan said, "Hey you, you look more like a ragged soldier to me than a painter." I wasn't used to such talk any more, and yet I had to take it; I only shook my head and answered, "Oh you rascal, if you'll give me a brush and some colors I'll paint a jackanapes that looks just like you." The parson took it in fun and warned us that it wouldn't do to tell each other off in this holy edifice. He meant that he trusted neither of us, but he offered the student and me one more drink and let us go. But I had lost my heart to the sausages!

Before nightfall we were back in camp. I changed clothes and weapons again, told the captain of our experience, and selected six stout men to help us carry the bread. We got to the village about midnight and quietly liberated the bread (we had a man along who could sweet-talk the dogs into silence). When we passed the parsonage I just could not go on without a flitch of bacon. I wondered how to get into the parson's kitchen, but I saw no other entrance than the chimney and thought it might, on this one occasion, substitute for a door. We hid the bread inside the charnel house in the cemetery and got a ladder and a rope from a barn. Since I could climb in and out of fireplaces like a chimney sweep (I had learned it in hollow trees as a child), I climbed on the roof with another fellow, and having tied my long hair in a knot, lowered myself down to the supplies, and then tied one ham after another onto the rope. They were hauled to the roof and taken to the cemetery. But dammit! Just when I was ready to quit, the rail on which I was standing broke, and I fell down head over heels and was caught as in a mousetrap. My friends on the roof lowered the rope to pull me up, but it also broke before they could lift me off the ground. I thought, 'Well, Hunterboy, now they'll chase you, and you may get your skin torn.' My fall had awakened the minister, who asked the cook to make a light. She came into the kitchen in a nightshirt, with a housecoat draped over her shoulders, and stood so close that she was touching me with it. She reached for a live coal, held a candle to it, and blew on it. I blew much harder than she, and that frightened the poor biddy so badly that she dropped coal and candle, and retreated to her master. This gave me a chance to think how I might get out of my predicament, but nothing occurred to me. My comrades wanted to break down the door and get me out by main force, but I wouldn't let them. I asked them instead to look to their firearms, to have only one man, Johnny Jump-up, on the roof, and to wait and see whether I could get away without a big commotion, so that our assignment — the surprise attack — should not be betrayed. If this couldn't be done they were on their own and had to act as best they could.

While the parson was striking a light, the cook told him that there was a ghastly two-headed spook in the kitchen. When I heard this, I quickly rubbed soot and ashes all over my face and hands so that I certainly did not look like an angel (as some of the ladies at Paradise had occasionally said). If the sexton had seen me, he would have had to concede that I was a very fast portrait painter! Then I began making a fearful racket by banging pots and pans together; I hung a stove ring around my neck and picked up a poker with which to defend myself in case of necessity. But none of this impressed the pious parson. He and the cook approached in procession. He was dressed in his black gown and stole, book in one hand, aspergillum in the other. The cook held a wax candle in either hand and a bucketful of holy water slung over one arm. He started exorcising me, asking who I was and what I was doing there. Since he thought I was the devil himself, I thought I might appropriately act like him. So I lied and said, like the devil, "I am the devil and I want to wring your neck — and your cook's." He continued his exorcism and reproached me for bothering him and his cook, who had done nothing to deserve this. He adjured me to go back where I came from. In an atrocious voice I answered that I couldn't, even if I wanted to. Meanwhile on the roof, Jump-up,[20] who could imitate animal sounds and was not stupid, caught on to what was needed below and hooted like an owl, barked like a dog, whinnied like a horse, bleated like a billy goat, and heehawed like a jackass; he projected sounds down the chimney now like a bunch of cats mating in February, now like a cackling hen, and finally like a pack of hungry wolves. This frightened the parson and the cook, but I worried that I was being exorcised because the parson had heard or read that the devil likes to wear green.

In the midst of these troubles, which encompassed all of us, I luckily noticed that the door to the yard was not locked, only bolted. I quickly snapped the bolt back and rushed out the door into the church yard (where I found my friends with pistols cocked) and let the parson exorcise all the devils he wanted to. After Jump-up had handed down my hat from the roof and we had put all the food in sacks, we returned to our camp, for we had nothing more to do in the village, except perhaps to return the rope and ladder.

We tarried two more days in the woods, waiting for our convoy. When it finally came we lost not a single man, took thirty prisoners, and found richer spoils than I had ever shared. On account of my courage and meritorious conduct I received two shares — namely, three beautiful Friesland stallions loaded with all the merchandise they could carry off in a hurry. If we had had the time to examine the booty carefully and take it to a secure location everybody would have gotten rich on his share. As it was, we had to leave more behind than we could carry off. We retreated to Rehnen, where we fed the horses and divided our spoils.

---

[20] Grimmelshausen wrote several sequels to his main novel. Two of the more important ones are *Der seltzame Springinsfeld* (Strange Johnny Jump-up) and *Trutz Simplex*; see Book V, 6, esp. footnote 7.

There I got to thinking again about the parson and how I had carried off his bacon. The reader can imagine what an ambitious and arrogant chap I was. Not only had I robbed the pious minister and frightened him nearly out of his wits, now I wanted to feel proud of it, too! Therefore, I took a gold ring with a sapphire, which I had liberated on the same raid, and sent it together with a letter by messenger to the good parson.

Your Reverence,

if lately in the forest I had not run out of food, I should have had no reason to steal your Reverence's bacon. I hereby assure you by everything that's holy that I frightened you against my will and hope for your pardon. Concerning the bacon itself, it is only fair to pay for it, and in lieu of cash I am sending you this ring, furnished by the parties for whose sake the smoked pork had to be carried off. I hope your Reverence will accept it. Moreover, I assure you that I shall be your faithful and humble servant in all emergencies, even though your sexton doesn't think I am a painter.

Your devoted,
Hunterboy

The farmer whose oven had been emptied of pumpernickel was sent sixteen thalers out of the raiders' common kitty, for I had taught my comrades that they ought thus to get the farmers on their side, because in a pinch they can either help you out or give you away and sell your neck. A few days later I received this answer from the parson:

Honored Hunter,

if the victim of your bacon raid had known you would appear in devil's guise, he would never have wished to see the famous Hunterboy. But inasmuch as the "borrowed" bacon and bread have been so generously paid for, the fright you gave us will be more easily forgotten, especially as it was inflicted reluctantly and by such a famous person. All is forgiven, and when you pass through here again, do not hesitate to look in at the house of one who is not reluctant to exorcise the devil. Farewell!

This is how I carried on everywhere. I became very famous, and the more I spent and wasted, the more booty came to me. Though it was worth around a hundred thalers, I thought I had invested the ring well. And that's the end of this book.

End of the Second Book

The hermit with young Simplex

Book Three

CHAPTER 1: *How the Hunter begins to stray from the path of righteousness*

*I*n the previous book the gentle reader learned how ambitious I had become in Soest, and how I sought and found honor, glory, and favor through behavior which in other men would be considered punishable. Now I want to tell how I allowed my foolishness to mislead me further into extreme danger. As I have mentioned, I was so eager for honor and glory that I could hardly sleep, and when I lay awake many a night thinking up new tricks, some curious notions came to me. For instance, I invented shoes one could wear hind end front, with the heels under one's toes. I ordered some thirty pairs of these, of different sizes; I gave them out to my companions, and when we went raiding, it was impossible to track us, for we wore now these, now our regular shoes, carrying the other pair in our knapsacks. When an observer came to a place where my men had changed shoes, the tracks would lead him to think that two parties had met and disappeared again. But if I kept wearing my backward pair, one would think I was going where I had already been or had come from a place to which I was just then going. Thus my tracks were more confusing than a maze, and those who wanted to capture me by tracking me could never find me or catch me in their net.

Often I was very close to the enemy, who was supposed to look for me far away, and even more often I was miles from the woods they were surrounding and combing through to catch me. And as I managed the raiding parties on foot, so did I those on horseback; I thought nothing of getting off at a fork or crossroads and having the mounts reshod with the irons pointing the other way. The common tricks that are used on raids, if one is weak and yet wants to be judged strong from the tracks left behind, or if one is strong and wants to be considered weak, were such an everyday matter that I don't want to tell about them here.

Besides, I invented an instrument by which, on calm nights, I could hear a horn signal three hours away, a horse neighing or dogs barking two hours away, and human beings talking at an hour's distance. I kept this invention very secret and I derived much glory from it, because everyone considered such reception to be downright impossible. The instrument (which I usually carried in my breeches along with the telescope) wasn't very practical by day, unless it was used in a lonely and quiet place, for otherwise everything, from horses and cows down to birds and frogs, became as audible as if one stood in a market square surrounded by crowds of people and many animals.

When I could not go raiding with a group, I went out stealing by myself, and then neither horses, cows, pigs, nor sheep were safe. I collected them from their stables for miles around. I put shoes or boots on cattle and horses until I got them to a busy road where no one could trace them. Then, too, I reversed the shoes on the horses or, in the case of cows or oxen, put boots on them, and so spirited them to safety. When I brought my loot home I shared it honestly with my comrades and officers. And that is why they let me go out time and again, and if my theft was betrayed or found out, they covered up for me. As for stealing from poor people, taking chickens or other trifles, I considered myself above that.

Eventually I began to lead an Epicurean life, eating and swilling, for I had forgotten the precepts of my hermit, and there was no one who would tell me off or whom I'd have to mind. The officers joined me in malfeasance by enjoying my payoffs, and those who should have punished and corrected me encouraged me in further vices. Finally I became so godless, bold, and despicable that there wasn't a piece of roguery I wouldn't have tackled. As time went on, I was secretly envied by my comrades for having a luckier hand at stealing than anyone else, and by the officers for carrying on in grand style, raiding and getting more famous than any of them. I am sure if I hadn't been so generous someone would have turned me in before this.

CHAPTER 2: *How the Hunter of Soest gets rid of the Hunter of Werle*

WHILE I WAS CARRYING on this way, being about to have some devil's masks made, plus frightful clothes with horse and oxen feet to go with them, so that I could scare the enemy and also, in this disguise, take loot from my friends, I heard of a fellow in Werle, a renowned raider, who was wearing a green suit and, under my name, committing all sorts of monstrosities like robberies and attacks on women, especially among people contributing to our maintenance. Extremely insistent complaints came in about my conduct, and I should have lost face if I hadn't clearly shown and proven that when *he* was pulling a job under my name *I* was somewhere else. Having informed the commander in Soest, I invited the stranger to swords or pistols in an open field. But when he hadn't the heart to appear, I sent word that I wanted to avenge myself, even if I had to do it in the castle of the commander at Werle, who did not punish him. I also let him know that if I caught him on a raid, I would treat him as an enemy. For this reason, not only did I not use the devil's masks, for which I planned something important, but I even chopped up all my green suits and had them publicly burned in Soest, disregarding the fact that the clothes alone, without the feathers and harness, were worth more than a hundred ducats. In my rage, furthermore, I swore that the next man calling me a hunter would have either to kill me or to be murdered by me, even if I'd hang for it. And I would not lead any more raiding parties (not being an officer, I didn't have to), until I avenged myself on the phony hunter in Werle. So I stayed home and did nothing more military than stand my watch, and if I received orders I carried them out very indifferently, like any other sleepyhead. This soon became known in the neighborhood, and the enemy raiders became so cocksure and daring that they practically camped on our turnpikes, and I couldn't stand this either. I found hardest to bear the fact that the Hunter of Werle continued to operate under my name and to take rich booty.

Meanwhile, when everyone thought I had gone to sleep on my laurels and wasn't about to get up, I scouted my opponent's activities and found out that he was not only imitating me in dress and name but also, at night, stealing anything he could get. So I awoke to the challenge and made my plans accordingly. In the course of time I had gradually trained my two hired men like bird dogs, and both were so devoted to me that in case of need they would have walked across red-hot coals for me because I gave them plenty to eat and drink, and plenty of loot.

I sent one of those men to Werle to my enemy. My man pretended that since I had promised never to go raiding again and was beginning to live like a lazybones, he didn't want to stay with me but had come to offer his services to him who had assumed his former master's hunting dress. He hoped he might be employed as a regular trooper. He knew all the highways and byways, could tell him many tricks for getting plenty of booty, and so on. This good simpleton believed my man and was talked into hiring him. Then my man persuaded him and his fellows to go to a sheep farm to pick up some fat rams. But I and Johnny Jump-up, with several others, were already lying in ambush.

We had bribed the sheepman to tie up his dogs and let the arrivals go into the barn for their nefarious work without interference. I promised to bless their mutton. When they had broken a hole in the wall, the Hunter of Werle wanted my man to climb in first. But he said, "No, someone might be watching inside and brain me as I came in. I see you are still inexperienced at filching. Let me look around a little first." He drew his sword, put his hat over the point, advanced the hat a few times into the hole, and said, "This is the way to find out if the boss is home!" After this the Hunter of Werle himself crawled in, but right away Jump-up caught him by the arm that held the sword and asked if he wanted quarter. His pal heard it and started to rush off. But since I didn't know one of them was the Hunter and since I was faster than the fugitive, I caught up with him and grabbed him after a few steps. I asked, "What army?" He answered, "Imperial." "What regiment? I am imperial too; only a rascal denies his colors." He answered, "We are dragoon from Soest who have come to get some mutton. If you are imperial, I hope you'll let us pass." I asked again, "Who are you from Soest?" He answered, "My friend inside the barn is the Hunter of Soest." "You are rascals!" I shouted. "Why do you rob your own people? The Hunter of Soest isn't a fool who gets caught in a sheep-fold." "Oh, I mean from Werle," he answered in turn. And while we were arguing, my man and Jump-up arrived with my enemy. "Look at him, the jailbird," I said. "Is this where we meet? If I did not respect the imperial arms you took up against our enemies, I'd fire a bullet through your head! Until now *I* have been the Hunter of Soest, and I call you a dirty dog until you take up one of these swords and fight with me." My man (who, like Jump-up, wore a ghastly devil's mask with ram's horns) laid two identical swords before us and let the Hunter of Werle choose one. But the poor Hunter did exactly as I had done in Hanau when I spoiled the dance, for he spoiled a good pair of pants and no one could stand him for the smell. He and his comrade trembled like two wet dogs; they got down on their knees and begged for mercy. But Johnny Jump-up hollered, in a voice that sounded like it came out of a rain barrel, "You'll have to fight or I'll twist your neck!"

"Oh, my dear devil," answered the Hunter, "I didn't come here to fight. If you'll excuse me, sir, I'll do whatever you want." Amid such confused babble my man put one of the swords in his hand and the other in mine. But the Hunter was shaking so hard that he couldn't hold his. The moon shone brightly, and the sheepman and his help could see and hear everything. I called him closer so that I'd have a witness to this event. When the sheepman approached he acted as if he didn't see the two men in devil's clothing and asked why I was having an argument on his place and why I didn't go elsewhere. Our troubles, he said, were none of his business; he was paying his monthly "counter-bution" and he wanted only to live in peace. He asked the other two why they were taking all that gaff from me instead of knocking me down? I said, "You knave! They wanted to steal your sheep!" The farmer answered, "I wish you'd kiss my backside — and those of my sheep, too," and went away.

I insisted on fighting, but the poor Hunter could hardly stand on his feet for fear, and I really felt sorry for him. In fact, he and his friend spoke such moving words that finally I pardoned him and forgave him everything. But Jump-up wasn't satisfied; he made him kiss the rears of three sheep — as many as they had wanted to steal — and scratched his face so that he looked as if he had tried to steal food from a cat's dish. I let it go at that. Soon the Hunter of Werle disappeared, because he was too ashamed. My friends spread the word and asserted with many juicy curses that I owned two real devils who were waiting on me. For this reason I was feared more and loved less.

CHAPTER 3: *The great god Jupiter is caught and discloses the designs of the gods*

I SOON FOUND THIS out, and I changed my former ungodly life and strove for pious virtue. I went on raids as before, but I was so kind and discreet to friend and foe alike that everyone I dealt with thought me different from what they had heard of me. Then, too, I stopped throwing away my money and collected many pretty ducats and jewels, some of which I cached in hollow trees near Soest because that's what the famous fortune-teller of Soest suggested. She said I had more enemies in my own regiment and in town than outside or in the enemy's garrison, and that they were all after my money. And while the news was spreading that the Hunter had skipped the country, I was right on the backs of those who were tickled about it. And before one place really found out that I had struck at another, that same place had reason to feel I was still present, for I got around like a whirlwind, was now here, now there, and more rumors spread about me than had in the days when the other fellow impersonated me.

One time, near Dorsten, I lay in ambush with twenty-five shooting irons and waited for a convoy consisting of several wagons. According to my custom I was on lookout myself because we were close to the enemy. Who came along but a single man, neatly dressed, talking to himself and carrying on a strange argument with his fancy walking-cane. He seemed to say, "Unless the great Numen interposes, I'll punish the world." From this I suspected he might be a great prince, traveling incognito, who wished to learn how his subjects live and who had resolved to punish those that did not live according to his wishes. I thought, 'If this man is of the enemy, he'll fetch a good ransom; if not, I ought to treat him so politely and impress him so favorably that I'll have a friend in a high place for the rest of my born days.' So I jumped out of the bushes, with my gun cocked, and said, "You will please walk ahead of me into the bushes, sir, unless you want to be treated as an enemy." He answered very seriously, "I am not accustomed to such treatment." I urged him on politely and said, "You will not regret doing the inevitable just this once." When I had taken him to my men and replaced the lookout, I asked who he was. He answered very magnani-mously that it would probably matter little to me, if I didn't know already that he was a great god. I thought he might perhaps know me or be a nobleman from Soest pulling my leg, for the Soesters are sometimes kidded about the great god and his golden loin cloth, a huge crucifix they have in their church. But I soon understood: I had caught not a nobleman but an arch-nut who had studied too many things too hard and had gone off the deep end, particularly on the subject of poetry. When he warmed up a little, he claimed to be Jupiter.[1]

By now I wished I hadn't made this catch, but since I had the fool I had to keep him until we moved on. And as time hung heavy on my hands anyway, I thought I'd tune up this instrument and enjoy the sounds it made. So I said to him, "How is it, my dear Zeus, that your Divinity leaves its heavenly throne to descend upon us here? Forgive my question, O Jupiter; you might consider it frivolous, but we too are related to gods, being sylvan folk born of fauns and nymphs, and you can speak frankly to us." "By the river Styx," answered Jupiter, "if you were Pan's own son you wouldn't find out a thing about this, but since you resemble my cupbearer Ganymede[2] to a T, I'll tell you that a big hue and cry about the viciousness of the world has penetrated through

---

[1] This character, claiming to be Jupiter/Zeus, the chief god of Greek my-thology, is used by Grimmelshausen to pronounce some notions of reform al-ready obsolete in Germany around the time of the Thirty Years' War.

[2] Ganymede was the most handsome of mortals. Zeus kidnapped him and made him his cupbearer so that he could always enjoy his company. Observe the extensive use the author makes of irony and satire in this connection.

the clouds to me, and the council of the gods has given me permission to destroy the earth by flood, as in the days of Lycaon.

"But since in my heart I harbor an unaccountable love of the human race and prefer to use kindness rather than severity, I am presently perambulating here in order to explore human behavior. And though I find everything worse than I had expected, I am not about to terminate the human race unconditionally and peremptorily; rather, I'll punish the guilty and try to educate the rest."

I had a hard time keeping a straight face, but I said, "Alas, exalted Jupiter, your care and trouble will presumably be in vain if you don't annihilate people as before, by water or even fire. For if you send a war, all the bad, refractory rascals will get busy killing the peaceable, pious people; if you send hard times, it will mean good business for usurers and wholesalers who have a corner on the market; if you send sickness and death, the misers and survivors will have their heyday since they'll inherit a lot. You will have to eradicate the whole world root and branch if you are out to punish it."

CHAPTER 4: *Concerning the German hero who will overcome the whole world and make peace among all nations*

JUPITER ANSWERED, "YOU SPEAK of this problem like an ordinary human, forgetting that we gods can devise means to punish only the bad and to preserve the good. I shall create a German hero who will accomplish all with the edge of his sword. He will kill all the wicked people and preserve and exalt the good ones." I said, "Such a hero would need soldiers; where soldiers are involved there is war, and where there is war the innocent must suffer with the guilty!" "You terrestrial gods are just like people on earth; you understand practically nothing! I shall send a hero who needs no soldiers and yet can reform the world. In the hour of his birth I shall give him a body stronger and more handsome than that of Hercules; he will be equipped with abundant foresight, wisdom, and understanding. Venus herself will give him a handsome appearance so that he will surpass Narcissus, Adonis, and my own Ganymede; she will endow him (in addition to all his virtues) with a peculiar charm, grace, and personality so that he will become popular with everybody. Mercury will present him with incomparable sense and reason, and the inconstant Moon will encourage rather than hinder him, for he will give him great speed. Pallas

Athene[3] will raise him on Parnassus, and at the astrologically right time Vulcan will forge his weapons, particularly the sword with which to strike down the godless and subdue the whole world — without the help of a single human being having to fight as a soldier. He'll need no help. Every large city will tremble at his presence and every fortress that is otherwise impregnable will fall to his power in the first quarter of an hour. Ultimately he will rule over the greatest sovereigns on earth and set up such a government over land and sea that men as well as gods will love it and praise it."

I said, "How can destruction of the godless and power over the whole world be achieved without strong-armed action? O Jupiter, I frankly confess that I can understand these matters even less than a mortal." Jupiter answered, "I'm not surprised, for you don't understand the wondrous power the hero's sword will have. Vulcan will forge it of the same material he uses to make my thunderbolts, and he'll give it such virtue that my German hero can deprive whole armies of their heads with one stroke through the air, although the men may be behind a mountain and an hour's distance away. The poor fellows will have to lie there headless before they even know what hit them. Whenever he comes to a town or a fortress, he'll use one of Tamerlane's tricks,[4] raising a white flag as a sign that he comes in the interests of peace and the common welfare. If the people come out, well and good; if not, he'll draw his sword, and by virtue of its special power he'll cut off the heads of all warlocks and witches in that town and display a red flag. But if no one presents himself after that, then in the same manner he'll dispatch all murderers, usurers, thieves, rogues, adulterers, whores, and pimps and run up a black flag. Finally, if the ones still left in town don't come to him and act repentant, he'll want to eradicate the whole city and its inhabitants as disobedient and obstinate. But he will execute only the ones who kept the others from yielding sooner. Thus he will go from one town to another, giving to each the countryside around it, to be governed in peace. From each town in all of Germany he will summon the two wisest and most learned men, make a parliament of these, unite the towns forever, abolish serfdom and tariffs, excises, interests, property taxes, and the sales tax throughout Germany, and take such measures that all memory of forced labor, contribution,

---

[3] Pallas Athene-Minerva was the protectress of cities but equally the goddess of wisdom, the entire intellectual side of human life.

[4] Tamerlane, or Timur (*ca.* 1336-1405), a renowned Mongolian conqueror, usually pictured as the incarnation of deceitfulness and atrocity.

confiscation of money, warring, or onetime special taxes will fade among the people, who will be more blessed than the inhabitants of the Elysian fields.

"Then," Jupiter continued, "I shall descend frequently with the whole crowd of the gods to revel among the Germans amidst their vines and fig trees.[5] I shall relocate Helicon[6] inside Germany and transplant the Muses there. I shall bless Germany more abundantly with all sorts of luxuries than Arabia felix, Mesopotamia, and the country around Damascus. I shall foreswear use of the Greek tongue and speak only German, and, in a word, prove such a Germanophile that I shall yield to them (as previously to the Romans) dominance over the whole world."

I said, "Your Highness Jupiter, what will the masters and princes say when the future German hero illegally takes away what is theirs and gives it to the cities? Won't they resist by force or at least protest to men and gods against this seizure?" Jupiter answered, "My hero will bother very little with them. He will divide all the mighty into three groups. Those who live in sin and evil he will punish like commoners, for no earthly power can resist his sword. The others will be given the choice of staying in the country or leaving it. Those who love their land and elect to stay in it will have to live like other common people. But the private life of the Germans will become much happier and more enjoyable than is the life of kings at present. All Germans will be like Fabricius who refused to share the kingdom of Pyrrhus because he loved his fatherland and his virtue and honor too dearly.[7] Those will constitute the second group. The third group, the ones who want to stay rulers, our hero will lead by way of Hungary and Italy into Moldavia, Wallachia, Macedonia, Thrace, Greece, and even across the Hellespont into Asia. Having obtained these countries for them, he will there deposit and make into kings all the military cutthroats of Germany. Then he will capture Constantinople in one single day, will

---

[5] vines and fig trees: Jupiter uses here an Old Testament phrase; cf. Deuteronomy 8, 8; 1 Kings 4, 25; Micah 4, 4; Psalms 105, 33, etc. It signifies good food, peace, and prosperity.

[6] Helicon is a mountain range in central Greece, the home of Apollo and the nine Muses.

[7] Gaius Fabricius Luscinus was a model of ancient Roman integrity; sent to negotiate the release of Roman prisoners of war after the battle at Heraclea (280 B.C.), King Pyrrhus of Epirus tried to bribe him — unsuccessfully.

lay in front of their behinds the heads of those Turks who won't convert to Christianity, and re-establish the Roman Empire.

"Returning to Germany, he (with the two members of parliament summoned from each of the German cities, who will be called the leaders and fathers of the German fatherland) will construct a city right in the middle of Germany. This city will be larger than Manoah[8] in America, contain more gold than Jerusalem in the days of Solomon. Its ramparts will compare to the Tyrolean Alps; its moats, to the straits between Spain and Africa. In the city he will build a temple of diamonds, rubies, emeralds, and sapphires; and in the museums that will be built he will collect the rarest objects from all over the world and the rich gifts that will be sent him by the kings of China and Persia, the Great Mogul of the East Indies, the Great Khan of Tartary, Prester John in Africa, and the Great Czar in Moscow. The Turkish emperor would send him even more — if our hero hadn't taken his realm away from him and given it as a fief to the Roman emperor."

I asked Jove what the Christian kings would do in these rearrangements. He answered, "The ones in England, Sweden, and Denmark (because they are of German blood and family), and the ones in Spain, France, and Portugal (because the ancient Germans once conquered and ruled these countries) will volunteer to receive their crowns, kingdoms, and lands as fiefs from the German nation. Then there will be a constant and everlasting peace among all nations of the world — as in the days of the Emperor Augustus."

CHAPTER 5: *How the hero will unite the religions and mold them into one*

JUMP-UP, WHO HAD BEEN listening, provoked Jupiter and almost ruined the whole game by saying, "And then Germany will be like the land of Cockaigne, where it rains muscatel and six-inch pies grow overnight like mushrooms, where I'll have to chew with both cheeks full like a thrasher's and guzzle malmsey wine until my eyes start watering." "Sure, sure," Jupiter answered, "particularly when I strike you with eternal hunger like Erysichthon, because it seems to me

---

[8] A legendary city in South America famous for its gold; older maps located it on Lake Parima in Guiana until Alexander von Humboldt proved it wasn't there.

you are making fun of my majesty." To me he said, "I thought I was among good fauns, but I see I ran into ridicule personified. One should not reveal the counsels of heaven to such traitors, nor throw precious pearls to the swine. Well, shit on his back and let him use it for a scarf!" I thought, 'What a strange and foul-mouthed idol is this, who, besides the sublime, handles such filthy matters?' Sensing that he disliked laughter, I suppressed it as best I could and said, "Kindest Jove, just because of one rude and immodest faun, please don't conceal from your Ganymede how things will be in Germany." "Oh, no," he said, "but order this godling to hold his faultfinding tongue hereafter, lest I transform him into a rock." Then he said, "Dear Ganymede, the making of gold will be as common in Germany as any other trade — pottery, for instance — and every stable boy will carry the philosophers' stone in his pocket." Then I asked, "How can Germany have an enduring peace with our different religions? Won't the various priests incite their people and provoke another war?" "Oh no," said Jupiter, "my hero will wisely anticipate this matter, and above everything he'll unite the Christian denominations throughout the whole world." I said, "Miracle of miracles, that would be a great and unsurpassable deed! How could it be done?" Jupiter answered, "I'll be glad to reveal that to you. After my hero has created universal peace in the world, in moving words he will address the spiritual and worldly leaders and heads of the Christian peoples and particularly of the churches; and he will eloquently point out to them the harmfulness of the prevailing discord in matters of faith. Through the most reasonable, incontrovertible arguments he will lead them to the point of desiring — on their own — a general reconciliation and of turning the whole matter over to his skilful direction. He will then assemble the wisest, most learned, and most pious theologians of every denomination and assign them a quiet, serene place where they can cogitate without being disturbed; he will furnish them with food, drink, and all other necessities, and order them first to compose the differences among their various religions and then to put down in clear wording the correct, true, sacred Christian religion according to Holy Writ, the ancient traditions, and the approved opinions of the Church Fathers. About that time Pluto[9] will scratch his head long and hard because he'll be worried about the diminution of his realm. In fact, he will initiate all sorts of quibbles, conspiracies, evil, and deceit; he'll advance one amendment after another and try to kill the matter or at least prolong it *ad infinitum* or *indefinitum*.

[9] Pluto, the god of Hades (the lower world) and the dead, is here equated with the devil.

"He will undertake to point out to each theologian, in glowing colors, his vested interests, his status, his peaceful life, his wife and children, his reputation, and whatever is most likely to make him insist on his own opinion. But neither will my brave hero be idle; as long as this council lasts, he will ring all the churchbells to admonish all Christians to pray ceaselessly to the highest Numen to send the spirit of truth to the council. But if he notices that some are perhaps yielding to Pluto's blandishments, he will torture the whole conclave with starvation, and if they won't work to complete the great cause he'll speak to them of hanging or show them his marvelous sword; first with kindness, later with seriousness, terror, and threats, he will bring them to the point at issue, so that they will no longer mislead the world, as they used to, with their obstinacy and false doctrines.

"When unity has been reached, he will arrange a great celebration and publish the refined and improved religion to all the world. He'll make a bloody victim of anyone who is against it, he'll gift-wrap him like a Christmas package and send him to the devil for a New Year's present. Now, dear Ganymede, having heard all you wanted to know, tell me your reason for leaving heaven, where you used to pour many a precious cup of nectar for me."

CHAPTER 6: *What the ambassador of the fleas effected with Jupiter*

I THOUGHT TO MYSELF that the fellow might not be a fool after all, but rather that he might trick us as I had tricked others at Hanau in order to get off more easily. For that reason I tried to provoke him, because you can always tell a fool by the way he acts in anger, and I said, "The reason I left heaven is that you weren't there. I took the wings of Daedalus[10] and flew to earth to look for you. But wherever I inquired I found that your reputation had suffered among people and that you and the other gods had lost credit among men. They called you an adulterous whoremonger full of crab lice and denied you the authority to punish others for such sins. Vulcan, they said, was a pitiful

---

[10] Daedalus had made wings for himself and his son Icarus so that they could escape from the labyrinth which Daedalus had built for King Minos of Crete. Daedalus reached his destination, but Icarus came too close to the sun, which melted his wings; he was plunged into the sea and drowned.

old cuckold who had been forced to accept the adultery of Mars without any particular revenge; they were wondering what kind of armor such a lame-brain might be forging. Venus herself was called a most hateful strumpet because of her lack of chastity, and men wondered what manner of charm and grace she might bestow on others. Mars was called a murderer and a robber; Mercury, an idle gossip, thief, and procurer; Apollo, a presumptuous harlot-chaser; Priapus, a filthy swine; Hercules, a crazy madman. In short, the whole crowd of gods was considered to be so despicable that they ought to be given no other lodging than the stinking Augean[11] stables."

"Ach!" said Jupiter, "would it surprise you if I forgot my customary kindness and smote these hopeless character assassins and sacrilegious detractors of gods with thunder and lightning? What do you think, my dearest Ganymede?" And while he was grumbling and threatening, Jupiter shamelessly pulled down his breeches, in front of me and my whole party, and chased the fleas out. His splotchy skin showed how cruelly these insects had been troubling him. I couldn't imagine what he was driving at until he said, "Shoo! Begone, you little pests! By the river Styx, I swear you shall never be granted what you solicit so eagerly!" I asked him what he meant by these words. He answered that the tribe of fleas, when they heard that he had come down to earth, had sent their ambassadors to transmit their compliments. The fleas had indicated also that, though they had all been assigned to dogs, at times some of their number found their way into the pelts of women, either because they liked it there or because they had gotten lost. But these out-of-bounders, they complained, were treated badly by the women, were captured, and not only murdered but, before death, horribly martyrized and mauled between their fingernails, so that a stone might cry out and take pity on them. "As a matter of fact," Jupiter continued, "they presented their cause in such moving and piteous words that I had to show them my sympathy and to assure them of my assistance, but with the proviso that I first wanted to hear the women too. However, the fleas replied that the women, if allowed to contest the matter, would either prey on my pity and kindness with their poisonous, bitching tongues or would outshout the fleas, bribe me with beauty and lovely words, and seduce me into a false judgment, disadvantageous to the fleas. They prayed, moreover, to be rewarded for the

---

[11] Augias, the very wealthy king of Elis, owned 3000 head of cattle which he had kept in the same stable for 30 years. Hercules was assigned the task of cleaning out the place. He did so by diverting the river Alpheus through the stable and thus flushing out the mess.

humble devotion and loyalty they had always shown and would continue to show, for they had always seen at close range what had been going on with Io, Callisto, Europa and several others, and had never passed the news on to Juno, though they had been very close to her too. But if I would permit the women to hunt and kill them on their own premises, they petitioned to be granted a heroic death, to be killed with a cleaver like oxen or shot like game. I answered, 'You boys must be awfully hard on them, or they wouldn't be so hard on you.' 'That is so,' they said, 'but the ladies won't let us live in our own territory. Some of them take care of their lap dogs with brushes and combs, washing them with soap and lotions, so that we are forced to quit our assigned territories and look for homes elsewhere.' I then allowed them to take refuge on my human body so that I might know of their activities at close range and pronounce my sentence accordingly. Well, this rabble started to exasperate me, so I have to get rid of them, as you have seen. I will defecate my charter right on their noses and let the women trouble and tribulate them all they want to. And if I catch one of these confounded customers myself, I'll give him the identical treatment."

CHAPTER 7: *Once more the Hunter tracks down honor and booty*

WE COULDN'T REALLY LAUGH because, in the first place we did not want to give away our position by making too much noise; secondly, our hallucinator didn't like it. But Jump-up almost exploded. just about that time our lookout in a high tree let us know something was approaching in the distance. Having climbed up, I saw through my telescope that it was the draymen we were waiting for. Their protection consisted of some thirty-odd cavalrymen. I could easily figure that they would not drive through the woods where we were but would go around it, across the open field where we could do nothing to them, though the open road was in very poor shape. I hated to have lain in wait for nothing, with only a fool for our prize; so I quickly made a different plan.

From our camp site a creek bed ran toward the field; one could ride along in it on horseback. Twenty men and I placed ourselves at the point where it left the woods, and I asked Jump-up to keep himself in reserve at the camp site. Then I ordered each of my men to target some specific man in the convoy and whether to fire or hold his shot in reserve. Some experienced hands asked me if I thought the convoy would come here, where they had no business and where there had been no peasants in a hundred years. Others who thought I could work magic expected me to deliver the convoy into our hands by incantation. But I did not need any devilish tricks for it, only my well-trained and clever Jump-up; for when the convoy, which proceeded in strict grouping, was about to pass us, Jump-up, following my orders, started bellowing horribly like an ox and whinnying like a horse so that the woods echoed with the sound, and anyone would have sworn there were droves of horses and cattle in it.

As soon as the convoy heard these sounds, they decided to do a little rustling and to collect a few items that were rare in these parts, for the countryside had been pretty well picked over. All of them rushed helter-skelter into our ambush, as if they were racing for the privilege of being gunned down first. Thirteen saddles were vacated by the welcome we gave them, and we squeezed a few more empty soon afterward.

Then Jump-up ran down the ravine shouting, "Cavalry this way! Cavalry this way!" This so confused and frightened the horsemen that they could ride neither forward nor sideways nor back; they dismounted, hoping to take off on foot, but I managed to capture all seventeen survivors plus the lieutenant who was in charge. Then I rushed to the freight wagons and unhitched twenty-four horses. But I got only some bolts of silk and some Dutch cloth. There wasn't enough time to rob the dead, let alone search the wagons thoroughly, because the drivers had galloped off as soon as the action began. They were sure to sound the alarm at Dorsten, and everything might be taken away from us. When we had packed up, Jupiter came running out of the woods wanting to know whether Ganymede was about to leave him. I said, "Yes" — unless he gave the fleas their charter. "I'd rather see them all in Cocytus[12] first!" he answered. I had to laugh, and because I had several horses free, I asked him to get on one. But since he could stay in the saddle no better than a walnut, I had to have him tied to the horse. He said the skirmish reminded him of the battle between the Lapithae and the Centaurs at Peirithous' wedding.[13]

Now when everything was over and we were hurrying off with our prisoners as if someone were breathing down our necks, the captive

---

[12] Cocytus, Acheron, Styx, and Lethe are the rivers in the lower world.

[13] Peirithous was a Thessalian prince who also ruled over the Lapithae. At his wedding he and his friends had to subdue the Centaurs, who threatened to carry off the bride.

lieutenant got to thinking about the big mistake he had made in delivering the cavalry troop recklessly into the hands of the enemy and sending thirteen good men to the shambles. He became desperate and wanted to force me to have him killed. He thought this dereliction was a blot on his name and would block his future promotion — if he ever got that far and wasn't shot first. I tried to cheer him up by pointing out that fickle Fortune often shows her meanest side to soldiers; yet I had never seen a man downhearted or even desperate on that account. His attitude, I told him, was a sign of faintheartedness. Bold soldiers always tried to make up for losses next time; he would never get me to violate my word of honor and military custom by harming him. When he saw that I was not about to kill him, he started cursing me, in hopes of arousing my anger. He said I had fought with him not honorably but like a highwayman and a cutthroat; I had wrongfully deprived his men of their lives. His own men were greatly startled when they heard him talk this way, but mine got so angry they would have riddled him like a sieve if I had let them, and keeping them from it required considerable effort.

Personally, I didn't even get excited about his talk. I called on friend and foe alike to witness what had taken place, and I had the lieutenant tied up and guarded like a madman. I promised, if my superiors would permit it, to let him have his choice among my own horses and weapons and to prove to him, in a duel, that it is fair in war to practice deception on an enemy. Both friend and foe then said that among a hundred raiders they had never met anyone who would not, after such derogatory remarks, have shot the lieutenant and dispatched the other captives as well.

Early in the morning I brought my booty and prisoners safely to Soest, and I got from this raid more honor and glory than I had ever received. Everyone said, "We'll have a second Johann von Werth[14] in him!" and that tickled me greatly. The commander wasn't in the least inclined to have me fight a duel with the lieutenant. He said I had overpowered him twice before and that was enough. The more my reputation increased, the greater grew the envy of those who were jealous of my good fortune.

---

[14] Johann von Werth (*ca.* 1595-1652) was a famous general of cavalry. He had won his reputation as a swift and terrible leader of forays from about 1633 on. In France he was called Jean de Wert, and his name was used to frighten children into submission.

CHAPTER 8: *How the Hunter finds the devil in a trough, and how Jump-up comes by some fine horses*

BUT I JUST COULDN'T get rid of Jupiter. The commander didn't want him, and said he was giving him to me because he would bring no ransom. Thus I got a personal fool and didn't have to buy one, though only a year ago I had been forced to be one myself. Well, that's the way luck and the times change! Only a little while ago lice were eating me up, and now I had the lord of fleas in my charge. Six months ago I was the stable boy of a lousy dragoon; now I employed two men who called me "master." It wasn't quite a year ago that the gang of boys was running after me to make a harlot of me; now the girls were turning silly because of love for me. Thus I discovered early that nothing in the world is more constant than inconstancy. And I was beginning to worry that Luck, once she vented her spite on me, would really show me a rough time.

Just about then Count von der Wahl,[15] governor general of the Westphalian district, was collecting troops from the various garrisons to lead a campaign through Münster across the Vecht river toward Meppen, Lingen, and such places. He particularly wanted to smoke out two companies of Hessian cavalry at Paderborn that had been giving our men trouble. I was included among the dragoons; and, some troops having been assembled at Hamm, we rode quickly toward the cavalry garrison, a badly fortified hick town, and waited for more of our men to come. The enemy tried a sally, but we chased them back into their nest and offered them retreat without horses and arms but with everything their belts encompassed. They refused and fought us with carbines and muskets.

Thus it came about that I had to try my luck in capturing towns, for the dragoons were advancing for that purpose. I succeeded excellently and Jump-up and I were among the first inside. We soon emptied the streets because whoever among the citizens carried a gun was cut down, and they did not want to fight anyway. Then we went inside the houses. Jump-up said we should pick the house with the biggest pile of manure in front of it, because that meant the richest codgers lived there and officers would be quartered there. Well, we attacked such a house. Jump-up went into the stables and I into the house itself, our

[15] Count von der Wahl came to Westphalia in 1637, one year after the siege and fall of Magdeburg.

understanding being that each would divide with the other what he had liberated. Each lit a candle. I shouted for the master of the house; receiving no answer (because the people were hiding), I stumbled into a room in which I found only an empty bed and a locked chest. I forced it open, hoping to find something precious, but when I lifted the lid a pitch-black something rose up, and I thought it was Old Nick himself. I swear I was never in all my life so scared as when I came on this black devil unawares. After a second of hesitation I shouted, "I'll beat your brains out!" and raised the hatchet with which I had opened the chest. And — I didn't have the heart to strike.

Then he kneeled down, raised his hands, and said, "Dear suh, Ah begs uv you fer God's sake, lemme live!" I knew he was no devil because he had mentioned God and was begging for his life. Accordingly I told him to hurry and get out of the chest. He did, proving to be as naked as God created him. I cut a piece off my candle and let him show me the way. He did so, taking me to a room where I found the owner of the house. He and the domestics were amused at the incident, but they still feared for their lives and begged for mercy. I reassured them; that was easy because we had orders not to harm the civilians. Then the master turned over to me a cavalry captain's belongings (among which was a heavy, locked knapsack) and said the captain and all his men, except the blackamoor and one other, had gone to their posts to fight.

Meanwhile Jump-up had caught the one man and six beautiful horses in the stable. We put them in the house, locked it, asked the Negro to dress, and told the owner what to tell the captain. After the city gates had been opened and the guard had taken their places, our general of ordnance, Count von der Wahl, was admitted; he took lodgings in the very same house we occupied. For that reason, in the middle of the night we had to move and look for other quarters. We found them with our comrades who also had come into town with the attack. We had a good time and spent the rest of the night eating, drinking, and carousing, after Jump-up and I had shared our loot. My share consisted of the blackamoor and the two best horses. One of these was a Spaniard on which a fellow wouldn't be ashamed to be seen by his enemy; later I used it to show off. From the contents of the suitcase I received various precious rings and, in a gold casket studded with rubies, the miniature portrait of the Prince of Orange. These things, valued at no more than half their worth, along with the horses amounted to over two hundred ducats. The darky who had scared the daylights out of me I gave to the general and got a mere two dozen thalers for him.

From there we moved quickly to the Ems river, where we achieved little. As it happened that we were passing by Recklinghausen, Jump-up and I got permission to visit the parson whose bacon I had once stolen. We had a good time reminiscing. I told him that the blackamoor had repaid him and his cook by frightening me the same way I had scared them. I gave him a nice pocket watch that rang the hours — another piece of loot from the captain's portmanteau — and so everywhere I made friends of people who otherwise would have had occasion to hate me.

CHAPTER 9: *An unequal struggle in which the weaker is the stronger, and the victor is vanquished*

MY ARROGANCE INCREASED WITH my good luck, and the upshot of it was bound to be my ultimate downfall. We were camping about half an hour from Rehnen when I and some of my friends sought and obtained permission to go to town in order to have our guns repaired. But we really intended to have a good time together, and we turned in at the best inn and sent for musicians to play snappy tunes to help us down the beer and wine we were drinking. We lived it up and left out nothing that hurt our pocketbooks. I even bought drinks for fellows from another regiment and acted like a young prince who owns land and serfs and has money to burn. Therefore, we were served better than a group of cavalrymen that weren't spending quite so lavishly. This made them mad and they started quarreling with us.

"Why is it that these foot-sloggers throw around their money?" (They thought we were musketeers, and, in fact, there is no animal in the world so much like a dragoon as a musketeer; when a dragoon falls off his horse, a musketeer gets up.) Another shouted, "That milkface is sure to be a clodhopper whose mother sent him some of the milk money. He's spending it on his comrades so they'll help him out of the lurch sometime — or maybe the ditch." These words were meant for me, for they thought I was a young nobleman. The waitress told me this, but since I hadn't heard it myself I couldn't do much about it. Immediately after that I ordered a big beer glass filled with wine and let everyone drink to the health of all good musketeers, and with each toast we made such a racket that no one could hear his own words. This displeased them even more and one of them said, to no one in particular, "What a life these foot-sloggers are leading!" Jump-up answered, "What's it to you, bootblacks!?" That hit home, but he looked so ugly and made such a cruel and defiant face that no one dared cross him. And yet they resented us, and one of them, a clean-cut fellow, said, "If these town-crappers couldn't show off on their own dunghill, where would they show off?" (He thought we were garrisoned here, for our clothes looked fairly clean.) "Out in the field we'd pick 'em off as a falcon picks off doves." I answered him, "We capture cities and fortresses and they are handed over to us to guard. But you horsemen, you don't even stir up the dogs in the tawdriest one-horse town. I don't see why we shouldn't enjoy ourselves in a place that's more ours than yours!" The cavalryman answered, "The master in the field takes the fortresses. And that we are the masters I'll prove by not being afraid of three such gun-toting toddlers as you. Two of 'em I'd stick behind my hatband and the third I'd ask if there are any more where you come from. And if I were sitting a little closer to you, my young squire, I'd slap your face to prove my point."

I answered, "Although I am not one of your cavalrymen, but only a hybrid between them and the musketeers, I think my pistols are as good as yours. But this toddler is brave enough to face a horsy blowhard like you with nothing but a musket and on foot." "Huh, you son of a bitch," said the guy, "I consider you a rascal if you don't live up to your words like a nobleman." I threw a glove at him and said, "Look! If I don't get that back from you, in the open field, on foot, and using only my musket, you can call me what you called me just now." We paid our bill and the horseman readied his pistols and carbine, and I my musket. As he rode off to the place we had agreed on, he advised Jump-up to go ahead and order my funeral. Jump-up told him to have his friends order his own. But he reproached me for my cockiness and said he was afraid my number was up. I only laughed because long ago I had figured out how to deal with a well-equipped cavalryman if one were to attack me.

When we came to the place where this jolly meeting was to take place, I had already loaded my musket with two balls, put on fresh priming, and smeared the cover of the pan with tallow, as careful musketeers do in rainy weather. Before we engaged, our friends on either side agreed that we should attack each other on level ground. One of us was to enter a fenced-in field from the east, the other from the west, and each was to do his best, like a soldier in the face of the enemy. No one was to help his friend, nor was anyone to avenge the death or injury of the other. When all had promised this, my opponent and I shook hands; each forgave the other his death, and each hoped to prove the superiority of his branch of the army in this stupidest of all stupidities in which a reasonable person ever engaged.

With my priming lighted on both ends, I entered the field on the side assigned to me. When I saw my opponent, I acted as if I were throwing off the old priming as I walked. But I was only pretending. My opponent thought the musket had misfired. Eagerly, pistol in hand, he rushed toward me, thinking to pay me for my sins and send me to hell. But before he could say Jack Robinson I had the pan open and the fire going again, was aiming, and welcomed him in such a way that my firing and his fall were one and the same thing.

After this I retreated to my friends who received me almost with kisses. His comrades took him out of the stirrup, behaved honorably toward him and us, and returned my glove with words of praise. But when I thought my honor was at its highest, there came twenty-five musketeers from Rehnen who arrested me and my friends. I was put in chains and sent to headquarters, for all duels had been forbidden on pain of death.

CHAPTER 10: *The general of ordnance restores the Hunter to life and encourages him*

SINCE OUR GENERAL OF ordnance was used to keeping strict discipline, I was afraid I might lose my head. Nevertheless I hoped to get off easy because I had always been a good soldier though still very young, and I had gained a great reputation for bravery. But this was an uncertain hope, for the daily occurrence of such brawls required exemplary punishment.

Meanwhile, our men had attacked a strong redoubt and demanded surrender, but had not obtained it because the enemy knew we had no heavy artillery. For that reason the general, Count von der Wahl, moved up his entire force, let a trumpeter once more demand surrender, and threatened to storm the place. There came a polite letter to the effect that only the eloquence of force would induce the commander to surrender.

While everyone was wondering what to do next, it occurred to me to take this opportunity to get out of jail. So I racked my brain and set my mind to work thinking about how to deceive the enemy, because all we needed was the siege guns. And because something occurred to me immediately, I let my lieutenant colonel know I had an idea how the place could be taken without great trouble or expense, if only I were pardoned and set free. Some old, experienced soldiers laughed and said, "The fellow thinks he can talk his way out of jail. Well, no harm in trying." But my lieutenant colonel himself, and some others who knew me, accepted my words like articles of faith, and went to the general to report concerning my intention and other details they knew about me. Because the count had heard of the Hunter, he ordered me to his house, where for the duration I was released of my chains. The count and my lieutenant colonel were just at table when I came in.

When the general asked what I wanted, I answered, "Your Excellency, although my life is forfeit because of my crime and your Excellency's orders, allegiance to our Imperial Roman Majesty impels me to show how the enemies of our Majesty can be harmed and the armed might of our Majesty strengthened." The count interrupted my speech and asked if I hadn't recently given him the blackamoor. I said I had. Then he continued, "All right, your diligence and faithfulness might possibly suffice to save your life. But what's your plan?" I answered, "Since the place can't hold out against heavy artillery, I think the enemy will be ready to negotiate as soon as they *believe* we have the big guns." "Any fool could have said that," answered the count. "But who will persuade them to believe it?" I answered, "Their own eyes. I saw their lookout with my telescope. We can fool them by loading logs, like wooden pipes, onto wagons and taking then into the field with heavy teams. They'll think these are guns, especially if your Excellency will order some excavations as for gun emplacements." "My dear young fellow," answered the count, "those men are not a bunch of children. They won't believe this humbug — unless they hear the guns. And if the trick doesn't come off," he addressed the officers about him, "we are the laughing stock of the world!" I answered, "Dear sir, let me make those guns sound in their ears. Just let me have a few double-barreled muskets and a sizeable barrel. Nothing will happen except the required sound effect. But if, contrary to expectation, the thing goes wrong and we get laughed at, then I — who must die anyway — as the author of it all, will take the ridicule with me and cancel it with the loss of my life."

Although the count wanted none of my scheme, my lieutenant colonel persuaded him by saying I had a lucky hand in such things and he didn't doubt I'd succeed this time too. Therefore, the count ordered him to arrange everything as could best be done. And he promised jokingly that all the honor gained by this trick would go to the lieutenant colonel.

So three of the hollow logs were prepared and twenty-four horses hitched to each — although two would have been plenty! Toward evening we took these out where the enemy could see them. Meanwhile I also had obtained three double-barreled muskets and a huge cask, which we got from the wine cellar of a castle. I arranged these things to suit myself and at night had them taken out to our mock artillery. I loaded the muskets with twice the normal charge of powder and fired into the cask, the head of which had been removed. This simulated three trial shots. The report was such that anyone would have sworn on stacks of Bibles that we had ten or twenty-five-pound cannon. Our general of ordnance could not help laughing at this elaborate trickery, but once more he offered the enemy terms, adding the information that if they did not surrender tonight they'd have to pay for it tomorrow. Both sides sent hostages, the articles of surrender were signed, and that same night we moved through one of the gates. This benefited me considerably, for not only did the count grant me the life I had forfeited by violating his orders, but he also set me free that same night, and in my presence ordered the lieutenant colonel to make me an ensign at the first opportunity. But this was inconvenient, for he had many cousins and in-laws on the waiting list, and they were all watching to be sure I wasn't promoted ahead of them.

CHAPTER 11: *Containing all sorts of things of slight importance but of great imagination*

IN THAT CAMPAIGN NOTHING more that was remarkable happened to me. But when I got back to Soest, the Hessians from Lippstadt had captured my man, whom I had left behind in my quarters with the baggage; moreover, they had taken one of my horses from the pasture. The enemy learned from this man about my exploits, and they thought more highly of me than before, because until now common report had persuaded them to believe that I could work magic. He also told them he had been one of the devils who had so frightened the Hunter of Werle in the sheepfolds. When the "Hunter" found this out, he was so ashamed that he took French leave once more and went from the Hessians to the Dutch. But my man's being captured turned out to be the greatest stroke of luck for me; this will become clear from a later part of my story.

I started to live a little more respectably than before, because now I had great hopes of soon becoming a junior officer. Gradually I began to associate with the officers and young noblemen who were expecting the exact same thing I imagined I would be getting before long. For this reason they were my worst enemies — except that to my face they acted like my best friends. The lieutenant colonel didn't particularly like me either, because he was under orders to advance me ahead of his relatives. My captain disliked me because I kept better horses, clothes, and weapons than he, and moreover, I no longer came across with gifts for the old miser. He would rather have seen my head chopped off instead of being promised a troop, for he had hoped to inherit my fine horses. And my lieutenant hated me because of *one* word that had slipped out recently.

It happened like this. On our last expedition he and I had been ordered to keep watch together at a difficult post. It had to be done lying down, though it was pitch dark; and when my turn came, he came crawling up to me on his belly like a snake and said, "Sentry, do you notice anything?" I answered, "Yes, sir, lieutenant." "What is it? What is it?" he asked. I answered, "I notice the lieutenant is scared."

From that time on he didn't like me, and I was ordered to go where the situation was most risky. In fact, he was looking high and low for opportunities to "get me" before I became an ensign — that is, while I could not defend myself against him. All the sergeants were my enemies, too, because I was preferred. Even the common soldiers started to waver in their love and friendship for me, because it appeared that I despised them since I kept company with the big wheels — who didn't like me any better. Worst of all, not one solitary person told me how everyone felt about me. I didn't notice anything because to my face each man played up to me, though he would rather have seen me dead. So I kept on living blindly in false security, and as time passed I became more and more conceited. Even though I knew that some people were disgusted when I outdid the nobles and the officers of rank with my showing-off, I did not stop doing it.

After I had become a corporal, I was bold enough to wear a leather tunic worth sixty thalers, scarlet-red trousers, and sleeves of white satin embroidered all over with gold and silver thread — all of which was worn at that time by the highest officers. Of course, everyone took notice. But I was a frightfully stupid fool to manage things this way, for if I had used the money for bribes in the right places instead of squandering it on clothes, I would have become an ensign and not made so many enemies. But that wasn't all: I dressed up my best horse (the one Jump-up had gotten from the Hessian captain) with saddle, bridle, and arms, so that when I sat on him I might well have been mistaken for St. George. Nothing riled me more than the fact that I wasn't a nobleman and couldn't dress my servant and the stable boy in my personal uniform.

I reasoned that everything had to have a beginning; once I had a coat of arms I could have liveried servants, and when I became an officer I would have a signet even though I wasn't a nobleman. I had not entertained this thought very long when I asked an imperial count palatine[16] to give me a coat of arms. It had three red masks in a white field, on the crest the bust of a young jester in calfskin with a pair of rabbit ears, and bells in front. I thought this matched my name perfectly, for after all I was called 'Simplicius.' So I properly became the first of my lineage, family, and coat of arms, and if someone had tried to make fun of this, I would have been quick to unsheathe my sword or to pull a pair of pistols on him.

Although I did not care much for women yet, I went along with the nobles whenever they called on ladies, of whom there were many in town. I wanted to be seen and show off my precious wardrobe, my well-groomed hair, and the plumes on my hat. I must confess that I was preferred to all others because of my good figure, but I also heard that the spoiled females compared me to a handsome, well-carved wooden statue that has little to recommend it besides its beauty. Except for playing the lute I could not produce anything to please the ladies, for as yet I knew nothing of love. But when the men who were popular with ladies twitted me for my clumsiness and wooden manners — I said that, for the time being, it was enough for me to enjoy a naked sword and a good musket. The ladies approved of this speech, and this so enraged the ladies' men that they secretly swore to kill me, though there was no one who had the heart to challenge me or provoke me to challenge him — for which a slap in the face or some insulting words would have sufficed, and I had laid myself wide open for that. From this behavior the ladies inferred that I must be a resolute youth; they said publicly that my appearance and resoluteness spoke louder than all the lisping compliments Cupid had ever invented, and that enraged the gentlemen even more.

CHAPTER 12: *Fortune fortuitously grants the Hunter a noble honorarium*

I H A D T W O F I N E horses, and at that time they were all the joy I had in the world. Every day I was free I rode them on bridle paths and in

---

[16] The designation of count palatine was bestowed on distinguished members of the bourgeois class. Among the privileges of office were those of granting (bourgeois) coats of arms, creating poets laureate, and granting academic degrees.

the riding school. Not that the horses could have learned anything more than they already knew — I did it so people would see that these beautiful creatures belonged to me. When I was prancing through the streets, or rather when the horse was dancing along with me on it, the simple people looked at me and said, "Look, that's the Hunter! What a beautiful horse! What a panache!" or "God Almighty, what a guy he is!" I cocked my ears and enjoyed it as if the Queen of Sheba had compared me to the wise King Solomon in all his glory. But, fool that I was, I did not hear what prudent people thought of me or what my detractors said. In a word, the wisest doubtless considered me a young puppy whose extravagance would necessarily be of short duration, because it was built on a weak foundation and maintained by uncertain loot. And if I am to confess the truth, I must admit that the latter were right, although at that time I did not understand it, for the situation was this: I was able to make an enemy sweat and could pass for a good plain soldier, but I was still only a child. The reason for my greatness was that then, as now: the snottiest stable boy can shoot to death the bravest hero in the world. But if gunpowder had not been invented, I couldn't have whistled that particular tune.

While riding around, it was my habit to memorize all roads, paths, ditches, swamps, bushes, hills, and watercourses in order to use my knowledge of the locality later on, either in offense or defense, if the occasion arose. One time I passed a ruined building not far from town and thought this might be an ideal place for a retreat or a lookout, especially for us dragoons if we were chased or outnumbered by cavalry. I rode into the yard, the enclosing walls of which were pretty much dilapidated, to see if one could retreat there on horseback in case of necessity and if the place could be defended on foot. As I rode past a cellar my horse balked and couldn't be made to move either by force or kindness. I gave him the spurs till I felt sorry for him, but all for nothing. I dismounted and led him down the stairway, but he jumped back, and when I tried to coax him down, I noticed he was sweating from fear and had his eyes glued to one corner of the cellar. As I looked at the trembling horse, I got scared myself and felt as if someone were pulling me up by the hair and pouring a bucket of ice water on me. But I could see nothing. Then I thought that perhaps the horse and I had been hexed and would have to die in this cellar. When I tried to get out, the horse refused to follow and that made me even more frightened and confused, so that I didn't know what I was doing.

Finally I reached for my pistol, tied the horse to a sturdy elderberry bush that had grown up in the cellar, and as I was about to look for help in getting my horse out, it occurred to me that perhaps a treasure was hidden in the ruin and *that* might make the place so eerie. I became convinced of this and looked around more closely, particularly in the area where my horse did not want to go at all. In the corner I noticed a section of the wall about the size of a small window shutter where the masonry was different in color and texture. But when I was just about ready to investigate I again felt as if all my hair was standing on end, and this seemed to confirm my hunch that a treasure-trove must be hidden there. I would have preferred an exchange of bullets in a duel ten — no, a hundred — times more than being in this frightful situation. I was troubled and didn't know by whom, for I could see and hear nothing. Having taken the other pistol as well, I moved to get out, leaving the horse behind, but I couldn't get up the stairs; a strong air current seemed to keep me down. At that point cold shivers started running down my back. Finally I had a bright idea: I would fire the pistols to alarm the peasants who were working in the fields nearby, and they would help me. There was no other way of getting out of the haunted place. But I was so desperate and mad that in firing I aimed at the exact area of the wall where I thought the cause of my strange experience lurked. The bullets made two holes in the masonry as big as a good-sized fist.

After the shots my horse whinnied and perked up his ears, and that made me feel good. I don't know whether the monster or ghost disappeared at that instant or whether the poor horse was glad to hear the shots. My courage returned; I walked up to the place unimpeded and started enlarging the holes in the wall. There I found a treasure in silver, gold, and jewels so rich that I should still be enjoying it — if only I had known how to keep and invest it. There were six dozen old-fashioned silver cups, a large, gold loving cup and several plated ones, four silver salt-cellars and one of gold, an old-fashioned golden chain, several diamonds, rubies, sapphires, and emeralds, some of them mounted in rings and other jewelry, and a whole boxful of large pearls (but all old and no longer of the highest quality); then, in an ancient moldy leather bag, I found eighty of the oldest Joachimsthalers of the purest silver, and 893 gold pieces with the French coat of arms and an eagle. No one could identify these because, as they said, the inscription was illegible. I put the coins, rings, and jewels in my pockets, boots, trousers, and holsters; and since I didn't have a sack with me on this pleasure ride, I cut the blanket off the saddlecloth and put the rest of the silver vessels between the blanket and the lining. I hung the gold chain around my neck and rode happily toward my quarters.

But as I was leaving the yard I noticed two peasants who were about to run away when they saw me. I easily caught up with them because I had three pair of legs and level ground. I asked them why they feared me and wanted to run away. They told me that they thought I was the ghost who lived in the deserted estate and who usually mistreated anyone getting too close to it. When I asked for particulars, they told me that, from fear of the specter (or rather monster), no human being had gone there for years on end, except perchance a stranger who had lost his way. Rumor had it that in the cellar lay an iron trough full of money, guarded by a black dog and an accursed maiden; as their grandparents told it, a strange nobleman who knew neither his father nor his mother would some day arrive to save the maiden, unlock the iron trough with a fiery key, and carry off the hidden money. They told me many more such silly fables, but because they sound too tedious I won't go into them. Then I asked them why they came, since they dared not enter the ruin. They answered that they had heard a shot and a loud scream. When I told them that I was frightened and had fired a shot hoping to summon help, but that I had not screamed, they replied that in this ruin lots of shots might be heard before anybody in the neighborhood would investigate. "For in truth, it is so haunted that we would not believe your Lordship when he said he had been there, had we not seen him with our own eyes when he rode out."

Now they wanted to hear from me whether I had seen the maiden with the black dog and the iron trough. If I had wanted to, I could have told them the worst cock-and-bull story, but I said nothing at all, not even that I had found the treasure. I rode home and looked over my find and was glad all over.

CHAPTER 13: *Simplicius' strange notions and castles in the air, and how he kept his treasure-trove*

THOSE WHO REALIZE THE value of money and consider it their god know what they are talking about. If anyone learned the power, the almost divine virtue of money, it was I. I know the feelings of a person who has a goodly supply of it, and I've found out more than once how it feels not to have a single penny. I venture to prove that money possesses all the virtues, and more, of precious stones:[17] money

[17] Precious stones, metals like gold or silver, and jewels exert their influence on the wearer. Insomnia is assigned here to the garnet but to the amethyst

removes fear and makes people jolly and happy, as the ruby does. It often robs you of sleep, like garnets; on the other hand, it also induces repose and sleep, like the hyacinth. Like the sapphire and amethyst, it strengthens the heart, drives out fright, and makes people joyful, wide-awake, moral, and mild-mannered. It dispels bad dreams, quickens the wit, and if one quarrels makes one win, like the carnelian — especially if one bribes the judge with it. Money allays lecherous and adulterous desires, because one can buy pretty women. In short, one can hardly overstate what money is able to accomplish (as I have already shown in my book, *Black and White*)[18] if only one knows how to use and invest it.

My money — what I had amassed of it by robbery and finding the treasure-trove — was of a strange kind. In the first place, it made me more cocky than I had ever been before, so much that I hated from the bottom of my heart being called just plain 'Simplicius.' Like the amethyst, it kept me from sleeping, for I lay awake many a night worrying about how to invest it and thereby get more. It made a perfect arithmetician out of me, for I calculated how much my unminted gold and silver might be worth and added this to the total of cash hidden here and there or still in my purse. This came to a considerable amount even without the precious stones. It also tempted me with its peculiar trickiness and evil nature, by jolly well interpreting the proverb, "He who has a lot wants more," and making me so stingy that everyone would have been glad to become my enemy. I considered quitting the army, buying a little place somewhere, and twiddling my filthy thumbs all day long. But, in view of the free life I was leading and my hope of becoming a big shot, I soon rejected that plan. Next I thought, 'Simpli, get a patent of nobility; at your own expense, recruit a company of dragoons for the emperor, and you are sure to become a young lord who in time will go places.' But as soon as I considered that a single unlucky skirmish or the end of the war might be *my* end too, I no longer favored this.

Next I wished to be of age, a grown man. If I were, I'd take a beautiful, rich, young wife. I'd buy an estate in the country and lead the quiet life of a gentleman farmer. I would specialize in animal husbandry and have a good income honestly obtained. But since I was much too young for this scheme, I had to give it up too. I had plenty of ideas like

later in this chapter.

[18] Once more Grimmelshausen pretends (as in Book II, 1) that he and Simplicius are identical.

these until I finally resolved to put my most valuable possessions in the hands of a wealthy man in a well-defended city and let him manage them until Fortune decided what to do with me.

At that time my Jupiter was still with me, for I could not get rid of him. At times he was altogether rational and talked very sensibly for weeks on end. He liked me because I had done a lot for him. When he saw me walking around in deep thought, he said, "Son, your dirty money, your gold and silver — give it away." I asked why. He answered, "That way you'll acquire friends and get rid of unnecessary worries." I told him I'd rather have more than give it away. He said, "Then get more, but you will never have peace of mind or friends."

I thought about it and came to the conclusion that what Jupiter said was indeed sensible, but by then greed had such a hold on me that I wouldn't dream of giving anything away. Yet after a while I gave the commander a couple of silver and gold-plated cups, and my captain a pair of silver salt shakers. But these rare antiques only served to whet their appetites for more. I gave twelve silver thalers to my dearest pal, Jump-up. He, in turn, advised me to get rid of my wealth or be prepared for trouble, because officers didn't like common soldiers who have more money than they. He had heard rumors going around about my wealth. If he were in my shoes he'd retire from the wars, go to some quiet place, and let God provide.

I said, "Listen, brother, how can I so easily give up the prospect of having my own troop?" "Ah!" said Jump-up, "don't you see many a good sergeant become old and grey, who should have had a troop before a lot of others — even you?" I had to keep silent because Jump-up was telling the truth, and he meant well by me. But secretly I resented it, for I was awfully conceited at that time.

I considered this advice and that of my Jupiter very carefully, and I remembered I had not a single genuine friend in the world who might assist me in trouble or avenge my death. Yet neither my greed nor my ambition nor my desire for greatness would let me quit the army and seek serenity. But I stuck to my first plan, and when I had a chance to go from Münster to Cologne with a convoy of a hundred dragoons, several merchants, and their freight wagons, I wrapped up my treasure-trove and handed it over for safekeeping to a prominent merchant, in exchange for an itemized legal receipt. There were 74 marks of unminted fine silver, 15 marks of gold, 80 Joachimsthalers, and in a sealed box, various rings and jewelry, which with gold and precious stones weighed altogether eight and a half pounds; there were also 893 antique gold coins, each weighing as much as one and a half gold florins. I took my Jupiter along because he wanted to go and had well-to-do relatives there. He praised me to the skies for all I had done for him, and therefore his kinsmen treated me with much consideration. But he kept advising me to invest my money better, to buy friends who would do me more good than gold in a strongbox.

CHAPTER 14: *How the Hunter is caught by the enemy*

ON THE WAY HOME I thought about arranging my life from now on so that I might regain everyone's favor, for Jump-up had put a restless bug in my ear by persuading me to believe everyone was jealous of me — and in truth, that's how it was. I also remembered what the famous fortune-teller of Soest had told me some time ago and that worried me even more. But these thoughts also sharpened my wits: I noticed that a man who lives without care from one day to the next is really almost like a dumb beast. I tried to find out why this or that person might hate me and concluded that my pride had made more enemies than anything else. For that reason I decided to act humble again (even though I wasn't), to associate once more with the common soldiers, to take off my hat to the higher-ups, and to diminish my wardrobe, until perhaps my status improved.

From the merchant in Cologne I had brought along a hundred thalers, which I was to repay with interest when I returned to claim my treasure. I thought that on the way I'd distribute half the money among the soldiers of the convoy, for I had learned by now that greed makes no friends. I had resolved to change and to make a new start on this trip. But I had reckoned without the host, for when we were passing through the duchy of Berg eighty muskets and fifty horsemen ambushed us at a very favorable spot, just when I had been sent ahead with four other men and a corporal to reconnoiter the road. The enemy kept quiet while we rode into their trap, letting us pass so as not to warn the convoy until it got into their line of fire. But they sent a cavalry officer with eight men who watched us until their group had attacked the convoy and we turned around to join our men at the wagons. Then they pounced on us and asked if we wanted quarter. I for one was well mounted and rode my best horse, but I did not care to run. I swung around to a small plain to see what could be done. Meanwhile the volley our men received told me what we were up against, and flight suddenly appeared attractive. But the ensign had it all figured out; he had cut off retreat, and while I was trying to fight my way out, he — mistaking me for an officer — once more offered me quarter.

I thought that getting off with my life was better than risking it and asked if he would keep his promise of quarter as an honest soldier. He answered, "Yes, honestly." So I handed over my sword and was taken captive. He asked right away who I was, for he thought I was a nobleman and therefore an officer. But when I replied that I was called the Hunter of Soest, he said, "It's your good luck not to have fallen into our hands a month ago. At that time I could not have granted you quarter nor kept my promise, because we thought of you as a known sorcerer."

This ensign was a bold young cavalier and not more than two years older than I. He was overjoyed at the honor of capturing the famous Hunter and for that reason he kept his word — even in the Dutch manner. (It's their custom not to take from their Spanish enemies anything comprised by a man's belt.) In fact, he was even so considerate as not to have me searched; I, in turn, was generous enough to hand him the money in my pockets. When the time came to divide the loot, I told him in secret to make sure he got my horse with saddle and bridle, for the saddlebag contained thirty ducats, and it would be hard to find another horse like mine. For that the ensign liked me as if I were his own brother. He immediately mounted my horse and let me use his. Of the convoy only six were killed and thirteen captured (eight of whom were wounded); the others fled, not having the guts to recapture the enemy's spoils, as they could have, for they were all mounted.

In the evening, after the loot and the captives had been parceled out, the Swedes and Hessians (who had come from different garrisons) parted company. The ensign kept me, the corporal, and three other dragoons, all of whom he had captured. We were taken to Lippstadt, a fortress located somewhat less than ten miles from our garrison. Because I had harassed that place quite a bit, my name was well known there, but my person was feared rather than revered. When we came in sight of the town, the officer sent a cavalryman ahead to announce his arrival to the commander and to let that gentleman know how the ambush had turned out and who the captives were. When the word got around there was quite a commotion, for everyone wanted to see the Hunter. Then some said this and others something else about me, and it was just as if an exalted ruler was about to make his entrance.

We captives were taken straight to the commander, who was greatly amazed at my youth. He asked where I came from and if I had ever served on the Swedish side. When I told him the truth, he asked me if I didn't want to join his side again. I answered that it didn't make much difference to me, but since I had sworn an oath of loyalty to the emperor I thought I ought to keep it. He then ordered us taken to the provost marshal, but the ensign, at his own request, was allowed to invite us for the evening, since I had formerly entertained my prisoners of war, one of whom had been his brother.

That night several officers, soldiers of fortune as well as born noblemen, convened at the officer's and he sent for me and my corporal. To tell the truth, I was extremely well treated by them; I acted as if I had never lost a thing, was the life of the party, and carried on not as one captured by the enemy but as if I were among my best friends. For all that, I behaved as modestly as possible, because I guessed my behavior would be reported to the commander — and it *was*, as I later found out.

Next day we prisoners of war were taken one after the other to the regimental judge advocate, who examined us. The corporal went first; I was next. When I entered the room he was surprised at my youth, and in order to reproach me he said, "My child, what have the Swedes done to you that you fight against them?" That riled me, especially since I had seen soldiers just as young among them, and I answered, "The Swedish soldiers took away my prettiest marbles and I wanted to get 'em back."

Hearing me pay him back, some of the officers having a seat on the examining committee were ashamed, and one said in Latin that he should ask me serious questions, for I was clearly no child. That's how I found out the judge advocate's name was Eusebius, for that's how the officer addressed him. Then he asked me my name, and when I told him he said, "There isn't a devil in hell by the name of Simplicissimus." I answered, "Probably there isn't one named Eusebius, either," and repaid him in kind, as I had previously done with our clerk Cyriacus. But this didn't go over so well with the officers, for they told me to remember that I was a prisoner and hadn't been brought here to make wisecracks. I neither blushed nor apologized, but replied (since they were holding me for a soldier and wouldn't let me get off as a child) that I had answered as I had been asked; I hoped that I was not to blame for that. Then they asked about my home, family, and connections, and whether I had served on the Swedish side; they inquired, furthermore, about conditions in Soest, the strength of the garrison there, and other items like that. My answers to all their questions were brief and to the point; I said no more about Soest and the garrison than I thought I could justify. I kept altogether mum about having been a jester, for I was ashamed of it.

CHAPTER 15: *Under what conditions the Hunter becomes free again*

MEANWHILE, IN SOEST, THEY had found out how the convoy had fared, that the corporal, myself, and several others had been captured, and where we had been taken. The next day a drummer was sent to come and get us. The corporal and the three others were turned over to him, with a letter the commander let me read before dispatching it. It went approximately as follows:

Monsieur, etc.,
    your letter together with the ransom was handed over to me by your drummer, who is returning with the corporal and the other three prisoners. As concerns Simplicius, the Hunter, because he served on our side before, he cannot be released. If I can be of any service in which duty does not interpose, I am and remain,

Your humble servant,
N. de S.A.[19]

I did not half like this document, but still I had to seem grateful for it. I asked to see the commander but was told he would send for me after the drummer had been dispatched the next morning. Until then I would have to be patient.

I had awaited the appointed hour when, around noon, the commander sent for me and for the first time honored me by inviting me to his table. During the meal he drank to my health but did not indicate by even one word what he had in mind for me, and it was not becoming for me to mention it. But after the table had been cleared and I felt a bit tipsy, he said, "Dear Hunter, you saw from my letter what pretext I used to keep you here. Now, I don't intend anything unreasonable, dishonest, or contrary to the rules of war. You yourself told the judge advocate that you used to serve on our side in the main army. For that reason you will have to make up your mind to join my regiment. If you do, and you serve to my satisfaction, in time I shall advance you further than you could hope for on the imperial side. Otherwise I hope you won't mind if I return you to the lieutenant colonel from whom the dragoons took you."

[19] There exists documentary evidence that this N. (= name) de S.A. was Colonel Daniel de St. André (or Andreas).

I answered, "Honored Sir Colonel, since I never swore allegiance to the Crown of Sweden or to its allies, and since I was only the lieutenant colonel's stable boy and never swore allegiance to him, I do not feel bound to go into Swedish service or to break my oath of allegiance to the Holy Roman Emperor. For this reason I humbly beg you to excuse me for refusing this request." "What?" said the colonel. "Do you despise Swedish service? Remember that you are my prisoner, and I'll show you a thing or two before returning you to Soest so you can serve the enemy, or maybe I'll let you rot in jail. Now think that over."

To be sure, these words frightened me, but I did not yield and said I hoped God would protect me from such treatment and keep me from perjury. As for the rest, I'd leave it to the colonel's well-known discretion to treat me like a soldier. "Sure," he said, "I know how to treat you — if I wanted to be severe; but you had better think it over. And don't give me cause to teach you a lesson." After this I was put back in the stockade.

It isn't hard to imagine that I didn't get much sleep that night but instead had all sorts of ruminations. Next morning several officers, including the one who had captured me, appeared, on the pretext of entertaining me, but in truth to bring news that the colonel was about to accuse me of sorcery, since he couldn't get me to comply in any other way. They meant to frighten me and see what I would do, but because I had a clear conscience I reacted rather coldly. Even though we talked little, I noticed that the colonel's main concern was to keep me from going back to Soest. He could easily figure out that I wouldn't leave a place where I was hoping for advancement and where I still had two beautiful horses and other valuables.

Next day he sent for me again and once more questioned me if I had changed my mind. I told him, "I have decided to die rather than commit perjury. But if you will let me off without forcing me into Swedish service, I solemnly promise not to bear arms for six months against either Swedes or Hessians." The colonel was downright pleased with this offer; we shook hands on it, and he forgave me the ransom and ordered the secretary to make out a document in duplicate, which both of us signed. In it the colonel promised me freedom and protection so long as I stayed in the fortress which was entrusted to him. I, in turn, pledged to do nothing harmful to the garrison so long as I stayed in the fortress. The colonel kept me for lunch again and showed me more honor than the imperials ever had done or would do. That's how he gradually won me over, so that I wouldn't have gone back to Soest even if he had set aside my promise and let me go.

CHAPTER 16: *How Simplicius becomes a free lord*

IF SOMETHING IS DESTINED to happen, everything shapes up for it. I thought I was practically married to Lady Luck (or at least was so close to her that even the worst events had to turn out to my advantage), when at the commander's dinner table one day I heard that my servant had come over from Soest with both of my beautiful horses. However, I didn't consider (as it later turned out) that, like the Sirens, fickle Fortune first smiles sweetly on anyone she wants to destroy; then she elevates him all the higher only to hurl him to the ground later.

Because I had done him much good, this servant (whom I had captured from the Swedes) was very devoted to me. Every day he had saddled my horses and ridden out of Soest to meet the drummer who had been sent to bring me and the others back. He had taken my best clothes along, that I might not come back naked or in rags (for he thought I had been stripped bare). When he did not see me and heard I had been asked to accept service with the enemy, he dug his spurs into the horse and shouted, "Farewell, drummer! Farewell, corporal! I want to be where my master is!" Thus he fled from Soest and arrived just as the commander had freed me and was honoring me. The colonel put up my horses at an inn until I should find myself lodgings. He thought me lucky to have such a faithful man and such excellent horses while I was still so young and only a common dragoon. When I took leave of him, he praised one of the horses so highly that I thought he would have liked to buy it from me. And since he was too discreet to ask the price, I said I would be honored to offer it as a gift. But he roundly refused, more because I was in my cups, and he did not want it said that he had talked a drunk out of something he might have regretted afterwards, rather than doing without this horse.

That night I got to thinking about how I would arrange my future life. I decided to stay my six months where I was, that is, to spend the winter, which was approaching, in peace and quiet. I had enough money for this without using any of my treasure at Cologne. I thought it would be a good time to finish growing and to reach full strength. In the spring I could all the more courageously rejoin the imperial army.

Early next morning I did an autopsy on my saddle, which was in much better shape than the one the ensign had received from me. After that I had my best horse taken to the colonel's quarters. I told him that since I had resolved to spend my six warless months here under his protection, my horses would be worthless to me. To let them be ruined by inactivity would be a shame. Therefore, he'd do me a favor by giving this martial nag a place alongside his own, and I'd be happy if he would accept it as a token of my gratitude for all the favors I had received from him. The colonel thanked me very courteously and, through his steward, sent me a fattened live steer, two fat hogs, a barrel of wine, four barrels of beer, and twelve loads of firewood. He had all of these goods delivered to the lodging I had just rented for half a year. He sent word along that these housewarming gifts were to provide a little help in getting my household started.

Seeing that my generosity earned me much credit with the colonel, I wondered how I could enhance my reputation with the common people. So I sent for my man and, in the presence of my landlord, said to him, "Dear Nicholas, you have shown me more loyalty than a master can require of a servant. But now that I have no master of my own and no war in which to obtain the means of paying you as I'd like, and since I won't need a man in the quiet life I intend to lead, I am giving you as your wages my second horse together with the saddle, pistols, and other gear; and I am asking you to be content for the present to find another master. If I can be of service to you in the future, be sure to let me hear from you at any time."

My good Nick kissed my hands. He could hardly speak for tears. He didn't want to accept the horse but thought I should sell it and use the money to support myself. Finally, after I had promised to take him back in my service as soon as I needed someone, he was persuaded to accept it.

This farewell scene so moved my landlord that he, too, could not keep from crying; and as my man praised me among the soldiers, so the landlord praised me to the skies among the citizens. The commander thought I was a very loyal fellow because not only had I kept faithfully the oath I had sworn to the emperor but also I had given up my excellent horse, servant, and weapons — all the better to keep my written promise to him.

CHAPTER 17: *How the Hunter plans to spend six months, and an encounter with the fortune-teller of Soest*

I DON'T BELIEVE THERE is a person in this world who hasn't a screw loose somewhere, for we all come from the same place and when my pears are ripe the other fellow's aren't far from it. But someone might answer, "Ah, you coxcomb, do you think because you are silly others are too?" I don't say that, but I do think that some are better than others at hiding the fool within them. A person with foolish notions isn't necessarily a fool; when we're young we all have such notions. But he who acts them out is thought a fool, for some people show none of their foolishness, and others, only half of it. Those who suppress it altogether are regular sourpusses. But those who give a little indication of it when time and occasion permit — those I consider the best people and the most understanding. Since I was quite independent and had money in my pocket, I probably let my own foolishness show a little too much, for I hired a boy, dressed him like a page in the most outrageous colors — violet-brown, flecked with yellow, no less — and I declared these to be my colors because I liked them. This youngster had to wait on me as if I were a prince of the realm and had never been a dragoon — or, half a year before that, a poor stable boy.

This was my first folly in that town. And though it bulked large, it was not even noticed, much less was I reproached for it. But what's the difference? The world is so full of foolishness that nobody pays attention to it any more, or laughs at it, or is surprised — they're all so used to it. I was reputed to be a smart, professional soldier, not a fool still running around in children's-size shoes. I made arrangements with my landlord for boarding me and the page and I gave him as a down payment all the meat and wood the commander had sent me in exchange for my horse. My boy had to have a key to the wine cellar, for I was pleased to serve wine to my company. And since I was neither a townsman nor a soldier, and thus had no one of my own kind to keep me company, I made friends in both groups and had daily visitors whom I did not want to leave unwined. The organist became a good friend of mine, and since I loved music and had (as I may say, without bragging) an excellent voice, which I wanted to keep from getting rusty, he taught me how to compose, and to play the organ as well as the harp. As I already played the lute masterfully, I bought one of my own and had a lot of fun with it every day.

When I was tired of music, I sent for the furrier who, in Paradise, had taught me the art of self-defense. I practiced it with him in order to become even more perfect, and I persuaded the commander to have one of his master gunners teach me, for a fee, the art of aiming and firing a cannon and the use of gunpowder. As for the rest, I kept very quiet and to myself, so that people were amazed when they saw me poring over books like a student — me, who had been used to robbery and bloodshed.

My landlord was the commander's watchdog and my keeper; he reported everything I did or didn't do. But that suited me well enough, for I hardly gave a thought to soldiering, and if the conversation got around to it I never let on I'd ever been a soldier. I acted as if I were here only for my daily lessons and exercises. I wished my six months were over, but no one could tell where I'd take service after that. As often as I called on the commander he kept me for lunch or supper, and sometimes we got into conversations meant to probe my thoughts and intentions. But I answered so carefully that no one could tell what my plans were.

One day the commander said, "How about it, Hunter? Don't you want to become Swedish yet? Yesterday one of my ensigns was killed." My answer was, "Honored sir, a woman is not expected to remarry immediately after her husband's death. Why shouldn't I have the privilege of waiting out my six months?" With such repartee I always escaped a definite answer and even gained more of the colonel's favor. He permitted me to walk around freely inside and out of the fortress. In time I was allowed to hunt rabbits, quail, and other birds — a privilege not granted his own soldiers. Moreover, I fished in the river Lippe and had such good luck that I seemed to be catching fish and crayfish by magic. Then I had a hunter's suit of middling quality made; dressed in this, I tramped by night all over the countryside around Soest, where I knew every road and pathway. Occasionally I collected the treasures I had hidden in various places, hauled them into the fortress, and let on I wanted to spend the rest of my life with the Swedes.

Once I ran into the fortune-teller of Soest, and she said to me, "Look, son, didn't I advise you well some time ago to hide your money outside the town of Soest? I assure you, it was the greatest stroke of luck for you to have been taken prisoner. If you had come home, certain fellows who swore to kill you because you deprived them of a lady's favor would have strangled you while you were hunting." I answered, "How can anyone be jealous of me when I care nothing for girls and their favors?" She replied, "Surely you will not remain long of this opinion, or the ladies will run you out of the county on a rail. You always laughed at me when I foretold events. Do you again not want to believe me when I tell you more? Don't you find people friendlier where you are now staying than in Soest? I swear, they love you only too well, and such all-powerful love will harm you if you don't accommodate yourself to it." I asked her why, if she knew so much, she didn't tell me more about my parents and if I'd ever find my way back to them. But she should speak in clear language instead of using abracadabra. She said I should ask about my parents after I'd accidentally met my foster father leading the daughter of my wet nurse by a rope. She laughed violently and assured me that she had told me, voluntarily, more than she had revealed to others who had implored her. I gave her a few silver thalers, and when I started kidding her she left hurriedly. Just then the coins were heavy in my pocket, and I also owned many precious rings and other jewelry. These valuables were all the time screaming at me that they wanted to circulate among people. I gladly obliged, for as I was quite a show-off, I paraded my wealth and let my landlord see it without keeping anything secret. He reported even more than he had actually seen! People wondered where I had acquired it, for word had gotten around that I had deposited my treasure-trove in Cologne: the cavalry officer had read the merchant's IOU when he captured me.

CHAPTER 18: *How the Hunter begins courting and makes an occupation of it*

MY PLAN TO MASTER the use of firearms and the art of fencing during these six months was good, and I made excellent progress, but it wasn't enough to keep me occupied, and boredom is the devil's workshop, particularly when there was no one to guide me. Diligently I studied all sorts of books and learned a lot from them. But there were some that helped me like the grass eaten by a sick dog. The incomparable *Arcadia*,[20] from which I hoped to learn polite conversation, was the first that diverted me from wholesome stories to books of love and from genuine history to romances of chivalry. I picked up books of that sort wherever I could, and when I had found one I didn't stop until I'd finished reading it, even though it took me all day and all night. Instead of eloquence, these books taught me how to pitch woo. But at that time my affliction was not so strong or violent that one could have called it a divine frenzy or an oppressive malady, for wherever my love happened to alight, I received what I wanted easily and without special effort, and I had no cause to complain like other wooers and lechers who are full of fantastic thoughts, troubles, desires, secret suffering, anger, jealousy, vengefulness, rage, tears, bragging, threats, and a thousand other manifestations of foolishness, and who in their impatience wish for a thousand deaths. I had plenty of money and did

---

[20] The *Arcadia* (1502) of Iacopo Sannazaro is the outstanding pastoral novel of the Renaissance; however, Grimmelshausen probably means Sir Philip Sidney's *Arcadia* (1590), for since 1629 it was available in German translation.

not mind spending it; I had a good voice and practiced daily on various musical instruments. Instead of dancing, which I never liked, I exhibited a well developed, supple body when fencing with the furrier. Moreover, I had a fine, smooth face and was acquiring a graceful pleasantness of manner so that the ladies of their own accord ran after me even though that made me slightly uncomfortable.

With the approach of Martinmas[21] (when we Germans start the swilling and stuffing that goes on until Lent), officers and civilians invited me to various places to help them eat the Martinmas goose. And that's when things began to happen, for on these occasions I met some ladies. My singing and my lute made them look at me, and when they did, I made such graceful eyes and gestures — in addition to the love songs I had composed myself — that many a pretty girl fell for me and was in love with me before she knew it. Lest I be considered a tightwad I, in turn, gave two parties, one for the officers, the other for high society in town. Thus I gained favor with both sides and entrance to their houses, for my food and drink was of the best. I really cared only for the company of the ladies, and though I might not get what I wanted from one or two (there were still a few who could withhold their gifts), I treated them all alike, so as not to bring suspicion on those who showed me more favor than virtuous maidens should. I made each of them believe that I merely made conversation with the others and that *she* alone enjoyed my favor.

An even half dozen loved me, and I them, but none alone had me or my heart. In one, I liked only her dark eyes; in another, her golden hair; in the third, her lovely charm; and in the others, something that the first three did not have. If I called on still others, I did so because they had something new or strange, and in any case I refused or despised nothing, since I did not intend to stay in the same place for very long. My page, who was an archrascal, was always rushing around with love notes and messages; on the side, he received a lot of favors from the *Fräuleins* and knew when to keep quiet, all of which cost me a pretty penny, since I wasted a fortune by doing this and might well have said, "What's gained by the drum is lost by the fife." In all this I kept my affairs so secret that not one in a hundred knew what a lover-boy I had become, except perhaps the parson, for I didn't borrow half so many religious books as I used to.

[21] St. Martin's feast is celebrated on November 11th.

CHAPTER 19: *How the Hunter wins friends, and the sermon the preacher delivers*

IF FORTUNE WANTS TO cast a man down, she first raises him up high, and the good Lord always sends a warning before the fall. He sent me one, but I refused to accept it. In my own mind I thought my present happy state was so firmly established that no misfortune could touch me, because everyone, especially the commander, wished me well. "What a friendly man the Hunter is," I heard them say. "He talks with the children in the street and has a kind word for everybody."

I often visited the oldest of the town's ministers, from whose library I borrowed many books, and when I returned one, he discussed various subjects with me and we got along well. When the Martinmas goose and the Christmas holidays were past, I gave him, for the New Year, a bottle of Strasbourg brandy, which he sipped with rock candy, as all the Westphalians do. When I stopped off to call on him he was just reading a book called *Joseph*,[22] which I had written and which my landlord had lent him behind my back. I blanched and was ashamed that such a learned gentleman should be reading my attempts at writing, especially as it is well established that a man is best known by what he writes. But he invited me to sit down with him, and although he praised my imagination, he upbraided me for going into so much detail on the amorous adventures of Potiphar's wife. "Out of the abundance of the heart the mouth speaks," he added. "If you did not know from experience how a lover feels, you could not have told so much about this woman's passion." I answered that what I had written was not my own invention; I had copied and excerpted it from other books in order to gain practice in composition. "I am willing to take your word for it," he said, "but you may be sure I know more about your love life than you think!" This sent a chill down my spine, and I wondered if the devil himself had told him about it. When he saw me turn pale, he admonished me to consider what a dangerous road I was taking. He mentioned the proverb, "Young soldiers, old beggars," and warned me against squandering my money on women and in other useless ways. I wasn't used to such talk and became very impatient, but I let on that I was grateful for his paternal concern and promised to think it over. In

---

[22] Grimmelshausen, not Simplicius, wrote the novel *Joseph the Chaste*. Cf. similar references to books by Grimmelshausen in Book II, 1 and Book III, 13. *Joseph* was published in 1666.

my heart I thought, 'What business is it of yours, how I manage my life?!' And as I had become used to the pleasures of love, I did not want to do without them. Such warnings count for nothing when a young man is no longer used to the bridle and spurs of virtue and he rushes headlong to his ruin.

CHAPTER 20: *How Simplicius pulls the wool over the preacher's eyes, so that he forgets to look at Simplicius' life of pleasure*

I WAS NOT YET so stupid nor so immersed in lusts of the flesh that I neglected to keep up my friendships with everyone so long as I was staying in the fortress, that is, until the end of the winter. I also recognized what trouble a man may have if he incurs the hatred of the clergy, for they have great influence among all nations, regardless of creed or denomination. So I racked my brain and returned on the next day to the parson and, using learned words, lied atrociously about how I had resolved to follow his advice. From his reaction I could see how pleased he was. "I feel how much I need an angelic counselor and have needed him for some time — in fact, even in Soest; now I am happy to have found one in your Reverence, learned sir. If only the winter were over or the weather improved so that I could leave." I asked his further advice, particularly about a college where I might enroll. He answered that his alma mater was Leiden, but for me Geneva would be just the place. "Holy Mary!" I answered, "Geneva is farther from home than Leiden."[23] "Alas," he said, considerably shaken, "it seems you are a popish Catholic. My God, how you've pulled the wool over my eyes!" "Why, Reverend?" I said. "Because I don't want to go to Geneva?" "Not at all," he said, "but because you are calling on the Virgin Mary." I replied, "Isn't it becoming for a Christian to call on the mother of his Saviour?" "Certainly," he answered, "but I beg of you to tell me what denomination you belong to." I answered, "You have heard, Reverend, that I am a Christian, for if I were not, I would not have been in church so often. But I confess that I am a follower neither of St. Peter nor of St.

[23] The University of Leiden and the academy at Geneva both were Calvinist institutions.

Paul.[24] I simply believe what is contained in the twelve articles of the common Christian faith, and I will decide when one of the three denominations can persuade me with sufficient reason and proof that *it* has the only true and saving religion. For only one of them can be right; the other two must be wrong. If I were to embrace one without sufficient deliberation I would be eternally sorry. No, I'd rather stay off the road altogether than go astray. If your Reverence will be my guide, I will follow you with deep gratitude and accept that religion which you yourself profess."

He then said, "I see you are caught in pernicious error, but I hope God will enlighten you and help you out of the slough. To this end, I will shortly prove to you from Holy Writ the truth of our faith, so that it will prevail even against the gates of hell." I answered that I was eagerly looking forward to such proof; but secretly I thought, 'I won't mind your faith if only you don't nag me about my love affairs!' From this the reader can see what an ungodly and evil rascal I was at that time, for I caused the good parson a lot of futile trouble just so he would leave me alone in my life of vice; and I thought, 'When you finish with your proofs, I shall long have flown the coop!'

CHAPTER 21: *How the Hunter contracts an unexpected marriage*

ACROSS THE STREET FROM my lodging there lived a lieutenant colonel awaiting reassignment. He had an extremely beautiful daughter who always looked like a noble lady. I had long wanted to meet her, though at first she didn't seem the kind of girl for whom I would give up the others that I might love her alone and cleave to her forever. Yet I often went walking in hopes of meeting her, and many times I made amorous eyes at her. But she was so well chaperoned that I could never talk to her alone. Moreover, I had to be on my best behavior because, for one thing, I was not acquainted with her parents, and for another, the family had a much higher social position than I considered myself to have. I got closest to her when we chanced to meet on the way to or from church. Making good use of my chance, I sighed piteously — something I could do perfectly, though it was all pretense. But she reacted so coldly that I was forced to believe she could not be seduced

---

[24] The followers of St. Peter are Catholics; those of St. Paul, Protestants. Since the Protestants were divided into Lutherans and Calvinists, Simplicius refers to three denominations.

as easily as the daughter of a common burgher. And while I was beginning to doubt that I could ever have her, my desire for her became even more ardent.

The lucky star that helped me to get acquainted with her was the one children carry on a stick ahead of the procession around Christmas to commemorate the fact that the three wise men were guided to Bethlehem by a star. In the beginning I took it as a good omen that a star guided me to her house. When her father summoned me, he said, "Monsieur, I have sent for you because of your position of neutrality between soldiers and citizens. I need an impartial witness for an affair in which I am about to mediate between the groups." I was beginning to think he had something of awesome importance in mind because there were pens and paper lying on the table. But it was nothing more than an invitation to a "royal" party (since the Eve of the Three Kings, or Twelfth-night, was at hand) for which the guests are given various titles, and I was to see that no favoritism was shown and that the offices were distributed by lot without respect to person. His secretary was helping too, and because the lieutenant colonel was something of a merry drinker and it was after supper, he served wine and snacks. The secretary was writing the names down, I was reading them off, and the lady my heart longed for was drawing the slips of paper. Her parents were looking on and complaining about the long winter evenings. That was their way of hinting that I was welcome in their house to help them pass the time after the lamps were lit, since they were not occupied with anything special. This was exactly what I had been hoping for. After this night (when I showed only a moderate interest in the lady) I was trying once more to catch my sweet bird and to make a big fool of myself so that the girl and her parents couldn't help thinking I had swallowed hook and all, though in reality I was only half serious. My aim was, rather, to act like a husband without bothering to get married first. Like a witch, I dressed up only at night when I went to call on her, and throughout the day I kept busy reading romances. From these I copied love notes to my sweetheart, as if I were a hundred miles away or wouldn't see her for years to come. After a while, since her parents encouraged rather than prevented my billing and cooing, I offered to teach her the lute and thus had free access to her, by day as well as by night, and I had to change the ditty —

The bat and I,
By night we fly,

which I had made up, into one in which I congratulated myself on my luck at seeing her by day after many a beautiful evening. I continued the song by complaining that now my nights were made unhappy for lack of daytime pleasures. Though the verses turned out to be somewhat too free, I sang them for my beloved to a sensuous melody and with many deep sighs. In addition, the lute seemed to ask, on my behalf, that the maiden please cooperate in making my nights as happy as my days. But her answer was rather chilly. She was an intelligent girl and had ready answers for all my inventions and conceits. I was careful not to mention marriage, and when the matter came up in conversation I spoke of it vaguely and ambiguously. My lady's married sister noticed this, and, seeing that her sister loved me from the bottom of her heart and that the affair would at length end badly, prevented me from meeting my beloved alone as often as previously.

It isn't necessary for me to go into the details of my courting, because love stories and novels are full of that sort of information. It is enough if the gentle reader knows that I was first permitted to kiss my beloved doll, and after a while to continue from there. I pursued such advances with all the incitements I could think up until I was finally admitted by night into my sweetheart's bedroom. I lay down beside her in bed as if I belonged there. Now, because everybody knows what usually happens next, the reader might surmise that I did something improper. Not me! All my entreaties were in vain and all my promises fell on deaf ears. Such resistance as I encountered I would not have thought possible in a woman, for she was intent solely on honor and marriage, and though I promised her the latter with a thousand sanguinary oaths she wanted to do nothing until after the wedding. But she did let me lie next to her in bed and, worn out by arguing and chagrin, I dozed off. But I was awakened with a vengeance. At four in the morning the lieutenant colonel stood by the bed with a torch in one hand and a pistol in the other. "Croat!" he shouted to his man, who was standing next to him with a drawn sword, "Croat, run and bring a parson." I woke up and saw the danger I was in. 'Golly,' I thought, 'he wants you to make your peace with God before he makes war on you.' There were green and yellow spots before my eyes and I wasn't quite sure whether to open them or keep 'em closed. "You irresponsible rascal, do you want to dishonor my house?!" he said to me. "It would serve you right if I broke your neck — and that of this slut who has become your whore. I'll tear your heart out, you beast, and throw it to the dogs for mincemeat." He rolled his eyes and gnashed his teeth like a rabid dog. I did not know what to do or reply, while my bedmate resorted to copious crying. When I recovered my senses a little, I wanted to defend our innocence, but he ordered me to shut up and I had to let him talk.

Meanwhile his wife came in, and she started a brand new sermon, so that I wished I lay somewhere in a briar patch. I think she would have droned on for the next two hours if the Croat and the minister hadn't arrived. Before they came I tried several times to get up, but the lieutenant colonel threatened my life and made me lie down again. That's how I found out that a man who is caught in an evil deed has no courage at all, and how a thief feels when he's nabbed breaking into a place, even though he has stolen nothing yet. I was thinking of occasions when I would have chased off the lieutenant colonel together with two of his Croats, but now I lay there like a wimp and didn't have the heart to open my mouth, much less use my fists.

"Look at this fine spectacle," he said to the parson, "to which I had to call you to make you a witness of my own shame." He had hardly uttered these words in an ordinary tone of voice when he started raving again and losing his sense of proportion. He ranted about breaking my neck and spilling my blood with his own hand, and so on, and I thought he might shoot me in the head any minute. The parson did his utmost to keep him from a rash deed that he might later regret. "Lieutenant colonel," he said, "use your God-given reason and consider making the best of a bad bargain. This handsome young couple isn't the first or the last to be overcome by the irrepressible force of love. The crime they have committed — if it is to be called a crime — can be easily remedied by them. To be sure, I don't approve of this approach to marriage. Still, our couple deserves neither the gallows nor the wheel, and no disgrace from their action will come to you if you forgive them, keep this peccadillo secret, consent to the marriage, and let them confirm their intention by the customary church ceremony." "What?" he answered, "I am to forgive them, praise them, honor them, instead of punishing them? I'd rather tie them up and drown them before daybreak! You must marry them this moment — that's why I sent for you — or I'll wring their necks like chickens."

Seeing I had no choice in the matter, I considered that I would not have to be ashamed of the girl; as a matter of fact, in view of my family and background, I was hardly worthy of sitting down where she kept her slippers. I swore up and down that we had done nothing sinful together. But I was told we should have behaved so that no one could suspect anything evil; this was no way to remove the suspicion we had raised. Then, sitting up in bed, we were joined in matrimony by the parson; thereafter we were requested to get up and leave the house together. At the threshold the lieutenant colonel told his daughter and me never to darken this door again. Having recovered a little and having my sword by my side, I answered almost in jest, "Dear father-in-law, I don't know why you do everything topsy-turvy. When others get married, their relatives lead them to their bed. You, on the other hand, not only chase me out of bed, but also out of the house after the wedding; instead of wishing me luck in my marriage, you don't even want me to have the pleasure of seeing my father-in-law's face and being of service to him. If that custom were to spread, the institution of marriage would make few friends in this world."

CHAPTER 22: *How the wedding goes, and what the Hunter plans now*

THE PEOPLE AT MY lodgings were surprised to see me bring home this girl who — even greater surprise — went to bed with me without batting an eyelash. And even though the trick played on me put perplexing notions in my head, I wasn't so foolish as to scorn my bride. Now I had my sweetheart in my arms, but my head was full of a thousand thoughts of how to manage and improve my situation. One minute I thought I deserved my fate; the next, that I had suffered the most grievous disgrace on earth and would have to avenge myself for it. But when I considered that revenge would necessarily hurt my father-in-law and therefore also my innocent, kind wife, all my plans came to nothing. I was so ashamed that I decided to keep to myself and show myself to nobody, but then I realized that that would be the greatest foolishness of all. Finally I resolved to regain my father-in-law's confidence and, as for the rest, act as if nothing untoward had happened and everything about my marriage was all right.

Over such thoughts daylight came, and I got up, although I would have liked to stay in bed longer. First I sent for my brother-in-law and informed him of how closely we were now related. I asked him to send over his wife to help us with plans for entertaining at our wedding celebration; and I asked if he would please try to patch things up with my in-laws. Meanwhile I would invite guests who would promote peace between us. He agreed willingly to do what he could, while I went to see the commander and invited him with clever phrases. He promised to come, sent me a deer and a barrel of wine, and said he'd try to bring my father-in-law along. I had a meal prepared that was good enough for princes and had plenty of fine guests, who not only had a good time but even reconciled the parents-in-law with me and my wife in such a way that they wished us as much luck and happiness as they had cursed and sworn at us the night before.

I didn't mind the unusual procedure after all, for if the vows had been said in church, I fear there would have been some members of the fair sex who might have made trouble for me, for among the burghers' daughters there were at least half a dozen who had known me only too well and who were in trouble now.

On the day following, it was my father-in-law's turn to entertain the wedding guests; but since he was on the miserly side, he did not have as much to offer as I. Then he told me how to arrange my life and how to keep house, and I noticed that I had lost my noble freedom and was about to go into bondage. I played the obedient son, as if I really wanted to hear my father-in-law's advice and, if possible, follow it. This attitude pleased the commander, and he said, "Since you are a promising young soldier, it would be foolish for you to take up anything but soldiering in these martial times. Nowadays it is far better to put a horse in someone else's stable than to feed somebody else's horse in your own. As far as I am concerned, you can have a troop any time."

My father-in-law and I thanked him, and I no longer rejected the offer as I used to. Then I showed the commander the merchant's IOU and informed him that I had to go and get the valuables before joining the Swedish service; for if anyone found out that I had gone to the enemy they'd keep my fortune and give me the raspberry in Cologne. This made sense to them, and it was agreed that I should leave for Cologne in a few days, return to the fort with my treasure, and accept my troop. My father-in-law also was to get a lieutenant-colonelcy and a company in the commander's regiment. Since Count von Götz was in Westphalia at that time and had his headquarters at Dortmund, the commander of Lippstadt expected a siege next spring and was looking for good soldiers (though this was all for nothing, because von Götz had to quit Westphalia and face the Duke of Weimar[25] on the upper Rhine the next spring).

[25] Bernhard, Duke of Saxe-Weimar (1604-1639), joined the victorious King Gustavus Adolphus of Sweden in 1631. In 1638 he conquered the important fortress of Breisach. General von Götz was ordered to take it back for the imperial party; he failed.

CHAPTER 23: *Simplicius comes to a city, which he calls Cologne (because it has to have a name), in order to retrieve his treasure-trove*

THINGS HAVE A WAY of happening. One fellow's misfortune comes about piecemeal or by degrees; another's overtakes him by leaps and bounds. Mine had a sweet and pleasant beginning, and I considered it not a misfortune but the best of luck. I had hardly spent a week with my beloved bride when, dressed in my hunter's outfit and armed with a gun, I took leave of her and her friends in order to pick up what I had left in Cologne for safekeeping. I got there without mishap because all the roads were well known to me; in fact, not a soul saw me until I came to the toll gate at Deutz, across the Rhine from Cologne. I, on the other hand, saw many people; I especially remember a peasant in the duchy of Berg who was the spitting image of my knan in the Spessart, and his son was just like me. This boy was herding pigs when I tried to sneak past him; because the hogs heard me and started grunting, the boy cursed them and wished aloud that the devil should fetch them and a hailstorm strike them. The hired girl heard him and she hollered at him to stop cursing or she'd tell his father. The boy answered that she could kiss his backside and spit on her mother. Now his father had heard him too, and he came out of the house with a cat-o'-nine-tails, shouting, "Wait, you so-and-so of a rascal. I'll teach you how to swear!" And grabbing him by the scruff of the neck, he beat him like a dancing bear, and with every stroke he said, "There, you brat, I'll teach you how to cuss; you go plumb to hell; I'll kiss your backside; I'll teach you to spit on your mother," and so on. This sort of education reminded me of myself and my knan; but I was not honest or grateful enough to thank God for removing me from such darkness and ignorance and giving me knowledge and better insight. Why shouldn't the good luck I was enjoying every day last forever?

When I got to Cologne I stayed with my Jupiter, who was quite rational at that time. When I told him why I had come, he said right away that I was probably on a wild goose chase; the merchant to whom I had entrusted my money had declared bankruptcy and skipped the country. True, my valuables were under official lock and key, and the merchant had been ordered to return, but he wasn't likely to come back because he had taken the most valuable part of his assets with him, and a lot of water would flow down the Rhine before the matter was settled. Anybody can imagine how much I liked hearing this news. I swore worse than a trooper, but what was the good of that? It did not produce my property, and there wasn't much hope I'd ever get it back.

Since I had taken along only ten thalers to spend on the journey, I could not even stay as long as the business required. Moreover, there was another danger in staying, for since I was attached to a hostile garrison, someone was sure to turn me in, and I would not only lose my treasure but get into worse trouble. Was I to turn around without doing anything, leave my fortune behind with nothing to show for my trip? That too seemed inadvisable. I decided to stay until a court decision was handed down and to write my bride the reasons for my delay. Then I went to an attorney, explained my situation and asked how much he would charge to help me. I promised him a bonus for hurrying matters along. Because this lawyer expected I would be good for quite a haul, he eagerly accepted my case and let me board at his house. The next day he went with me to the man in charge of bankruptcies, handed in a notarized copy of the merchant's IOU, and produced the original. We were then informed that we would have to wait till the case came up in court, for some of the goods were missing.

Being sure now of considerable leisure, I wanted to see what life in a big city was like. My landlord was, as I said, an attorney and counselor at law, but on the side he kept half a dozen boarders, and in his stable there were always eight horses, which he would hire out to travelers. He also had a German and a French stable boy, either of whom he used for driving or riding and to take care of the horses. With these three, or three and a half, occupations he made not only a living but also a good profit. Since Jews were not allowed in town, he was able to keep a lot of money-making irons in the fire.

During the short time I spent in his house I learned a lot from him, particularly how to diagnose many diseases. And that is the most important part of medicine, for they say that when a disease is correctly diagnosed the patient is already half cured. To my landlord goes the credit for my acquiring this knowledge, for he taught me to observe first his and then other people's physiological make-up. I found that many people are sick unto death without knowing it; others, even doctors, consider them to be in perfect health.

I found some who were sick with anger, and when the disease came over them they made faces like the devil, roared like lions, scratched like cats, clawed about them like bears, bit like dogs, and — worse than savage animals — like utter fools heedlessly threw about everything they could lay their hands on. They say this disease is caused by the gall bladder, but I think it comes about when a fool becomes arrogant. Therefore, if you see an angry man roaring, especially if it is over a trifling matter, you can be sure he has more pride than good sense. From this illness springs much unhappiness, for both the patient and others. One ought not to call those suffering from it *patients*, for patience is exactly what they don't have.

I found that stuffing and swilling is also a disease. It is a trouble caused by habit rather than by opulence. Poverty helps but is not a complete cure, for I saw beggars living in luxury and rich misers suffering the pangs of hunger. It carries its remedy on its own back; it is called 'want,' if not of money then of bodily health, so that in the end these patients grow healthy of their own accord — that is, when because of poverty or other diseases they can no longer stuff themselves. I also found that laughter is a disease. Philemon[26] died of it, Democritus[27] was infected with it till he died, and to this day some of our ladies say they like to laugh themselves to death. Some think it originates in the liver, but I rather think it is caused by an excess of silliness, and excessive laughter is not an indication of a rational human being. No medicine is needed against it, for it is a jolly disease and many times it stops before the patient wants it to.

Of other diseases, like envy, gambling, pride, curiosity, laziness, vindictiveness, jealousy, frailties of love, and other such illnesses and vices I shall not write at this time. For one thing, I don't *intend* to write about them; for another, I want to get back to my landlord, who caused me to think about such imperfections, for he was possessed by greed to the ends of his fingernails.

CHAPTER 24: *The Hunter catches a coney in the middle of the city*

THIS FELLOW, AS I said, had various and sundry ways of accumulating money. He lived off his boarders, not they off him. He could have fed himself and his family well for what the boarders paid him, if he only had used the money for that purpose. But he fed us poorly and held back on everything. In the beginning I ate with his children and the hired help, because I didn't have much money with me. The tiny morsels we received seemed altogether too diminutive for my stomach, which was used to Westphalian helpings. We never got a good piece of meat on the table, only the leftovers of what had been served a week ago to the boarders. It had been gnawed at here and there and was hoary with age like Methuselah. His wife (who did the

[26] Philemon, a writer of Greek comedies (*ca.* 360-265 B.C.), died laughing over one of his jokes.

[27] Democritus, Greek philosopher (460-*ca.* 410 B.C.), laughed at the foolishness of human beings.

cooking, for he wouldn't hire a maid) poured a dark, sour gravy over it and deviled it up with pepper. We licked the bones so clean that you could have made chessmen out of them, but even then they hadn't been utilized well enough. They were put in a special container, and when a certain quantity had accumulated they were broken up and all the fat boiled out of them. I don't know whether it was used to flavor soup or to grease jack boots.

On fast days — there were plenty of them, and they were all meticulously and solemnly observed, for our host was very scrupulous on this point — we had to gnaw on stinky smoked herring, river salmon spoiled by too much salt, rotten kippers and other fish, all superannuated. He bought everything at bargain prices and went to the trouble of visiting the fish market in person to pick out with his own hands what the fishmongers were about to throw away. Our bread was usually black and stale; our drink, a thin, sour beer that like-to cut my insides to ribbons, though the landlord said it was good, aged bock. The German hostler told me that in the summertime things were usually even worse; the bread was moldy, the meat full of maggots, and their best dish was a couple of radishes at noon and a mess of lettuce at night. I asked him why he didn't quit the niggard. He answered that he was away on trips most of the time and was counting more on tips from the travelers than wages from the moldy miser.

One time the skinflint brought home six pounds of beef tripe for soup and put it in the basement pantry. To their delight, his children found a window open, tied a fork to a long stick, and with this contraption helped themselves to the tripe, boiled it in a hurry, and ate it half raw. They told him the cat must have eaten the mess. But this parsimonious skinflint did not believe them. He looked all over for the cat, weighed it, and found out that with hide and hair it was not so heavy as the tripe that vanished! He wasn't at all ashamed of these cheap maneuvers but thought that he was very clever and ought to be admired for the inventions his greed taught him.

Since he acted so shamelessly, I asked to be transferred to the boarders' table and never mind the cost. The food was slightly more magnificent, but that didn't do me much good, for it was only half-cooked. This saved the landlord money in two places — on fuel and on the quantity eaten. Nobody could digest much of it. Then, too, he counted every bite we put in our mouths and looked miserable when we ate well. His wine was considerably diluted and did not aid digestion; the cheese served at the end of the meal was hard as a rock; the Dutch butter was so salty that no one could use more than half an ounce per meal; fruit was carried in and out till it got soft and ripe; and if anyone grumbled, he started a terrific row with his wife so that we could all hear it. But secretly he told her not to change a thing.

One time, one of his clients had brought him a rabbit as a present. I saw it hanging in the pantry and thought we would soon enjoy a piece of game, but the German hostler told me we'd never sink our teeth into it. If I went to the Old Market that afternoon, I would see the rabbit for sale there. I cut a little notch in the rabbit's ear, and at noon, while our landlord was out of the room, I told the boarders that our skinflint had a rabbit he wanted to sell and that I would cheat him out of it. If they would go along, we would not only have some fun but get to eat the rabbit as well. They all agreed to join me, for every one of them would have been glad to play a trick on our landlord.

Therefore, in the afternoon we went to the place where the hired man had said the landlord used to stand whenever he sold something through an agent, and where he would be watching lest he get cheated out of a penny. We saw him there, talking to some people of importance. I had employed a fellow to say to the salesman, "Mister, that rabbit is mine. It disappeared last night from my window, and I am taking it along as stolen goods. If you want to, you can take me wherever you want to go, but at your risk and at your expense." The seller answered that he would find out what to do; the rabbit had been given him by a gentleman who doubtless had not stolen it. And while the two were arguing, a crowd quickly gathered. When our tightwad noticed what was going on, he motioned to the salesman to let the rabbit go, for on account of his many boarders he was afraid he'd be the talk of the town.

The man I had employed made a big show of producing the piece of ear and fitting it in the notch of the rabbit's ear, and the crowd was satisfied that it was his rabbit, and that he was in the right. Now I and my company approached as if we just happened to come along. I sauntered up to the man with the rabbit and started haggling with him over the price. When we had agreed, I sent the rabbit to our landlord, asking him to take it home and have it prepared for our table. The fellow I had employed got a tip worth two mugs of beer and nothing for the rabbit. And so, against his will, our curmudgeon had to serve up the rabbit, and he could not even breathe a word about it, while all of us had a good laugh. If I had stayed longer in his house, I would have played more such tricks on him.

End of the Third Book

Book Four

CHAPTER 1: *How the Hunter was spirited off to France, and the reasons therefor*

*T*rying to put too much edge on a blade spoils it, and drawing a bow too far makes it break. I wasn't satisfied with the rabbit trick I had played on my landlord; rather I continued to punish my host for his monstrous avarice. I taught the boarders to soak the salty butter in water in order to remove excess salt and to grate the hard cheese like Parmesan and moisten it with wine. These practical jokes were like stabs at the heart of the miser. By a special trick I removed the water from the wine on the table, and I made up a song comparing the miser to a hog, from which no good can come until it is dead and hanging in the butcher shop. I sang this song to the sound of my lute and caused him to repay me quickly with the following dirty trick — for, after all, I was ill advised to play tricks on the man in his own home.

Two young noblemen who lived at my landlord's received a check along with orders from home to go to France and learn French there. But the German servant was away, and our landlord did not dare trust his French servant abroad with the horses. He said he did not know him well enough for that, and he was afraid he might forget to come back, thus robbing him of the horses. So he asked me to do him the great favor of taking the noblemen to Paris. My case would not come up for at least a month; and if I would give him power of attorney, he would see to my affairs as diligently as if I were present in person. The noblemen begged me to go; my own desire to see France also urged me on, since I could now do so without any cost to myself; in Cologne I'd be idle for at least another month and would have to spend money for room and board. And so I took to the road as the coachman for these young nobles.

On the way, nothing worth writing about happened. But when we got to Paris and the noblemen cashed their letters of credit at our landlord's agent, not only was I arrested and the horses attached by court order, but also the agent, who said my landlord owed him a large amount of money, had the horses sold — with the approval of the local magistrate and in disregard of my protests. So I sat there like a shorn lamb and didn't know what to think, much less how to retrace the long and (at the time) dangerous road home. The two nobles expressed their sincere sympathy for me in my predicament, gave me a generous tip, and said they did not want to dismiss me until I found a good job or got a chance to get back to Germany. They rented a room and I stayed with them for a few days and looked after one of them who had become indisposed from the long, unaccustomed journey. And since I had done a satisfactory job, he gave me his hand-me-down clothes when he bought a suit tailored in the latest fashion. They advised me to stay in Paris for a few years and learn the language. My money in Cologne would not run away, and our landlord would take care of it in his usual pedantic way.

While I was still making up my mind about what to do, the doctor who came in daily to visit the sick nobleman heard me playing the lute and singing a German song. This pleased him so well that he offered me a good position and free board if I would give music lessons to his two boys. He knew my predicament better than I and was sure I would not refuse a good job. Since both noblemen recommended me highly and advised me to take the job, we soon agreed on the particulars. But I would hire myself out only for three months at a time.

This doctor spoke Italian as if it were his mother tongue and German as fluently as I did. That was another reason why I went to him. When I ate the farewell supper with my noblemen, he was there too, and my head was full of all sorts of thoughts — about my newly wedded wife, the troop promised me, the treasure in Cologne, and the fact that I had been persuaded to leave all this behind me rather irresponsibly. When the conversation got around to our former landlord's avarice, it suddenly occurred to me — and I blurted it out across the table — that he might have gotten me out of the way on purpose so that he could claim my property in Cologne and keep it. The doctor thought this might well be, especially if the landlord considered me a man of low social rank. "No," said one of the noblemen, "if he has been sent out of the country to stay, it is because Simplicissimus always nagged and twitted him about his stinginess." The sick one now thought he knew an even better reason; he had overheard the French hired hand complaining in broken German to our landlord that the Hunter had tattled on him to the landlady for not tending the horses well. But the jealous skinflint must have misunderstood the Frenchman's language; for he had assured the man that he could stay, while the Hunter would be gotten rid of. Since that day, he had looked at his wife askance and had had more arguments with her than before.

The doctor said, "Whatever the reason, I am sure there was a plan to get the Hunter out of Germany and keep him out. But don't let that get you down. I'll see to it that you find a way back. Just write him to take good care of your treasure or he'll have to answer for it in court. What makes me suspicious is that the presumed creditor is a good friend of your landlord and his local agent. I imagine you yourself handed over the paper enabling him to have the horses seized and sold."

CHAPTER 2: *Simplicius gets a landlord who is better than the previous one*

MONSEIGNEUR CANARD (THAT WAS the name of my new employer) offered to help me in every way to hang on to my valuables in Cologne, for he saw how sad I was. As soon as I came to his house, he wanted me to tell him about the state of my business, so he could think up ways of helping me. I imagined my credit wouldn't be worth much if I told him where I came from. So I told him I was a poor German nobleman who had lost his father and mother and who only had a few relatives in a fortress occupied by the Swedes. I said I had been forced to keep this from my landlord and the two noblemen who were of the imperial party, or they would have seized my property for their own use as something belonging to an enemy. I intended to write to the commander of the fortress (the one who had promised me the position of junior officer) and tell him not only how I had been spirited out of the country, but also that he should be good enough to take possession of my money and give it to my friends for safekeeping until I had a chance to get back to the regiment.

Canard was all for it and promised to expedite my letters, even if they were addressed to Mexico or China. Accordingly, I wrote to my dear wife, to my father-in-law, and to Colonel de St. André, the commander at Lippstadt. The letter said that I'd be back as soon as possible if only I had the means to make the long trip. I addressed the envelope to him and enclosed the other two letters. I asked both my father-in-law and the colonel to try and seize my money by military force before the matter was forgotten. Incidentally, I detailed how much there was in gold, silver, and jewelry. These letters I wrote in duplicate, one copy being sent by Monsieur Canard's messenger, the other by mail; in case one did not get there, the other would surely arrive. Thus I regained a joyful outlook and instructed my employer's two sons the more gladly. They were being brought up like young princes, and because Monsieur Canard was very rich and very proud, he wanted to show off. He had caught this malady from great men, for he was daily associating with princes, as it were, and aping them in everything. His house was like the household of a count, and nothing was lacking save the title of "Your Excellency." And his fancy was such that he dealt with a marquis who happened to call on him no better than with his own kind. To be sure, he also treated little people, but he never accepted modest fees. He would rather charge nothing, so he'd be called a generous man. Because I was a bit unusual and since I knew he liked to show off with me when I accompanied him (along with other servants) on his sick calls, I also helped him when he made up medicine in his laboratory. That's where I got to know him better, for he liked to practice his German on me. I asked him once why he did not call himself by the name of a noble estate he had bought near Paris for twenty thousand crowns, and why he insisted that all his sons study so hard to become doctors. Wouldn't it be better, I asked, since he already was a member of the nobility, if he bought them some offices (as was done for other cavaliers), and so let them become full-fledged noblemen? "No," he said, "when I come to a prince, he says 'Doctor, sit down'; but to a nobleman he says 'Wait your turn.'" I continued, "You know well that a doctor has three faces: an angel's when the patient sees him coming; a god's when he helps him; and a devil's when the patient is well again and has to pay the bill. A nobleman has greater honor from standing at the door for his prince than a doctor has from sitting down, because he is always waiting on his prince and has the honor never to be far from him. Besides, the other day I saw you taste something of the prince's — I'd rather stand up waiting for someone for ten years than try the taste of someone else's feces, even if I were asked to sit on roses." He answered, "I didn't *have* to do that. I did it in order to prove to the prince how much trouble I was taking to diagnose his case — and so that I could charge a larger fee. You talk of these matters like a German, and if you were another nationality, I'd say like a damn fool!" I swallowed this because I saw he was about to get angry, and in order to sweet-talk him, I begged him to excuse my ignorance and started discussing something more pleasant.

CHAPTER 3: *Simplicius consents to being used as an actor, and he gets a new name*

DR. CANARD HAD MORE venison to throw out than some folks with game preserves of their own have to eat. Since more meat was given to him than he and his family could eat, he also had many hangers-on, and it almost looked as if he were keeping a free table for everybody. One time the king's Master of Ceremonies and other prominent court personages were eating a princely collation provided by the doctor, who knew where to make his friends — namely, among those who were around the king every day and who were in favor. To show those people his goodwill and to keep them entertained, he asked me to do him the honor of singing a German ditty to the accompaniment of my lute.

I was glad to oblige, for I was in the mood for it and tried hard to give them something special. Consequently, I pleased those present so well that the Master of Ceremonies said it was a shame I didn't know French. Otherwise, he would commend me to the king and queen. But my employer, who feared he might lose me, told him I was a nobleman who did not want to stay long in France and who probably did not care to hire himself out as a musician. Then the Master of Ceremonies told him he had never before seen such perfection of form and voice and such skill on the lute — all in one person. A play was soon to be given in the Louvre,[1] for the king.[2] If I could act in it, he hoped to give me a part in which I could make a great impression. Monsieur Canard translated this and I replied that if I were told the character I was to act and given the songs beforehand, I could learn the words and melodies by heart, as pupils are required to do when they sing and act in Latin. When the Master of Ceremonies saw that I was willing, he asked me to come to the Louvre next day for a tryout. So I presented myself at the appointed hour.

I played the melodies of the different songs directly from the printed music. When I received the French words and the melodies to learn by heart, the texts were translated for me so that I could make the appropriate gestures. None of this was difficult, and I could do it in a

[1] The Louvre, an example of the finest Renaissance architecture in France, was the royal palace until in the '80s the Court moved out of Paris to Versailles.

[2] The king was Louis XIII (1601-1643), who with the aid of Cardinal Richelieu ruled France from 1610 on.

short time — and so well that not one in a thousand would have thought I was anything but a native Frenchman.

And at the first rehearsal of the comedy I acted out my songs, melodies, and gestures so pitifully that everybody believed I was an old hand at playing the part of Orpheus whom I represented and who is making such a lamentable fuss over his Eurydice.

I never had a more satisfying day than the one on which the comedy was performed. Monsieur Canard gave me something to make my voice even clearer, but when he tried to enhance my beauty by means of *oleum talci* and to powder my naturally curly black hair, he found that this only detracted from my appearance. I was crowned with a laurel wreath and had to wear a turquoise-colored toga that left bare my neck, the upper part of my chest, arms up to the elbow, and my legs. Around me I wore a flesh-colored cloak of taffeta that looked more like a military sash. In this outfit I wooed my Eurydice[3] with a pretty song, implored the goddess Venus for support, and finally carried off my beloved in a scene in which I had to sigh and cast loving glances at her. But after I had lost my Eurydice, I dressed in a black costume that was made like the other one, except that my white skin shone like snow because of the contrast. In this garment I lamented the loss of my wife, and I got so absorbed in the act that I started crying in the middle of my sad songs, and for a minute I didn't know if I could go on. But I managed to carry it off until I appeared before Pluto and Proserpine in hell, where I begged them to return Eurydice to me. After I was granted my wish, I turned so happy in song and expression that the audience was quite astonished. But when I lost her a second time, I imagined the greatest dangers a man could get into, and I grew so pale and miserable that I almost fainted. After that, I sat down on a rock and lamented my loss with pitiful words and a sad melody, and I called on every creature for sympathy. All sorts of tame and wild animals, trees, mountains, and so on, came to listen to me. This scene looked as if magic had been used. Nothing went wrong until the end, when I had renounced women, had been strangled by frenzied maenads, and thrown into a lake, where a dragon was supposed to devour me. (I stood behind some

---

[3] The plot of this play — very popular in the days of early opera — runs more or less as stated by Grimmelshausen: Death having robbed Orpheus of his beloved wife Eurydice, the divine musician gets her back from Hades but loses her a second time because he violates a condition of her release by looking back on her before they have reached the upper world. Now Orpheus turns against women and gives up music. He is killed by being torn to pieces by maenads, frenzied women worshippers of Bacchus. For obvious reasons the librettist modified the end.

scenery and only my head was visible to the audience.) Now the fellow who was inside the dragon, working it, couldn't see and so his monstrous mouth nuzzled and nibbled at some greenery next to my head. This struck me as so ridiculous that I couldn't help making a wry face, and some ladies who were watching me noticed it.

Besides generous and general praise, I received not only a considerable cash honorarium but also a new appellation: from now on the French called me by no other name than "Beau Alman."[4] Since it was the carnival season, more such plays and ballets were given, and I was in several of them. But finding that I curried too much favor with the spectators, especially the ladies, and that I made too many enemies, I gave up acting, particularly after I had been battered and beaten more than is customary on stage, while, in the role of Hercules, I was fighting with Achelous for Deianira.[5]

CHAPTER 4: *Beau Alman is led against his will into the mountain of Venus*

THROUGH MY ACTING I became acquainted with persons of quality, and it seemed that Fortune was again smiling on me. I was even offered a job in the king's household, something that doesn't happen every day, even to big shots. One time while I was working in the laboratory, a uniformed servant came, spoke to Monsieur Canard, and handed him a letter for me. (Because I was interested in pharmacy I had learned from my employer how to sublimate, coagulate, calcinate, filter, precipitate, wash, and so on, as was required in the alchemical method by which he prepared his medicines.) "Monsieur Beau Alman," Canard said to me, "this letter concerns you. A gentleman wants to know if you are willing to give his son lessons on the lute. He is asking me to use my influence with you, so you won't refuse this request." I answered that I would do my best to be of service if I could thereby please Dr. Canard. He asked me to dress up a little better and go along with the servant. Meanwhile, he would have something prepared for me to eat, for I'd have a rather long way to go and could hardly get to

---

[4] Grimmelshausen did not observe the rule according to which Simplicius should have been called "Le bel Alman" (*mod.* Le bel Allemand).

[5] After the tragic end of Hercules' first marriage he fell in love with Deianira, the daughter of the king of Calydon. But she was betrothed to the river-god Achelous; Hercules fought with him in single combat and won.

my destination before evening. So I got dressed fairly well and hurriedly bolted some of the snacks that had been prepared, including a couple of delicious little sausages which — it seemed to me — tasted a bit medicinal. Then I proceeded with the servant by curious, roundabout ways, until after about an hour we reached a garden gate that was not quite closed. The lackey pushed it open, and when I had entered after him he banged it shut, bolted the night latch, which was on the inside, and led me to a pleasure pavilion inside the garden. After we had walked to the end of a fairly long passage, he knocked on a door that was immediately opened by a noble old lady. She greeted me very politely in German and asked me to step inside. The lackey, who knew no German, bade me good-by with a deep bow.

The old lady took me by the hand and led me into the room, which was covered with precious tapestry and beautifully appointed. She asked me to sit down and rest while I found out why I had been taken to this place. I was glad to obey and sat down in an easy chair she had placed by the fire, which was burning because of the cold. She then sat down opposite me in another chair and said, "Monsieur, if you know anything about the power of love, which overcomes and dominates the bravest, strongest, and wisest of men, you will not be one whit surprised that it also assumes mastery over members of the weaker sex. It wasn't your lute (as you and M. Canard were persuaded to think) for which you were called, nor did a man call you. It was your unsurpassable handsomeness and the most excellent lady in Paris that brought you here. She is expecting to die should Fortune deny her the happiness of beholding your divine form and of refreshing herself thereby. That is why she ordered me to inform you (as my fellow countryman) and to beg you more ardently than Venus ever begged Adonis to come to her tonight, so that she may take her fill of looking upon your beauty. This, she hopes, you will not deny a noble lady." My answer was, "Madame, I don't know what to think, much less what to say in reply to this. I don't claim to be such that a lady of high quality should desire my humble company. Moreover, as I think of it, if the lady who wants to see me is so excellent and noble as you, my dear fellow countrywoman, mentioned and conveyed to me, why didn't she send for me earlier in the day, instead of having me brought to this forsaken place so late at night? Why didn't she ask me to come straight to her? What do I have to do with her garden? May you forgive me, my dear compatriot, if, as a stranger in a strange land, I become suspicious of being betrayed, especially since I was told to see a gentleman, and everything seems topsy-turvy. The minute I notice foul play I am going to use my blade." "Soft, soft, my dear fellow countryman! Forget these uncalled-for thoughts," she interrupted. "Women are unconventional and cautious in their plans. A man can't understand them at first. If the lady who loves you more than anything in the world had wanted you to know who she is, why, she would not have let you come here first, but straight to her. There's a hood," and she pointed to a table, "which you must put over your head when you are taken to her, because she does not want you to know where or with whom you have been. May I beg and pray of you to behave with this lady in a manner befitting her exalted position and the inexpressible love she bears you. Otherwise, you may expect to find out that she is powerful enough to punish your pride and your disdain of her. But if you treat her as she deserves, you may rest assured that every step you have taken in her behalf will be rewarded."

Meanwhile, it had become dark, and all sorts of worries and fearful thoughts plagued me so that I sat there like a graven image. I imagined vividly that I would not leave this place except by consenting to everything I was asked. So I said to the old lady, "All right then, my dear compatriot, if it is as you told me, I'll entrust myself to your inborn German honesty, in hopes that you will not permit any treachery to befall a guileless German. Go ahead and do what you have been told to do with me. The lady you mentioned probably won't kill me by looking at me" "Heavens, no," she said, "it would be a shame if such a well proportioned body — one that might be called the pride of our nation — were to perish so soon. You will find more pleasures than you have ever dreamed of."

The minute she had my consent she called for Jean and Pierre, who stepped out from behind some tapestry, each wearing a large shiny cuirass and armed from head to foot with halberd and pistol. I was so taken aback that I turned pale.   The old lady noticed and said with a smile, "A man ought not to be so frightened when he's on his way to a lady." She then told the men to take off their cuirasses and to light the way for me, with only pistols in hand. She slipped the black velvet hood over my head, took my hat, and guided me out by the hand. I noticed that our way led through many doors and along a street paved with cobblestones. After perhaps ten minutes, I had to climb a short stairway, and a narrow door opened; I walked along a paved passage, up a winding staircase, then down a few steps; and finally, about six steps farther on, another door opened. When I had stepped through it the old lady pulled off the hood and I saw that I was in a room decorated in exceedingly good taste. The walls were hung with beautiful paintings, the buffet sparkled with silverware, and the bed, which stood off to one side, was trimmed with hangings of brocade. In the middle of the room stood a table, luxuriously set, and by the fireplace was a bathtub that looked nice enough — but a little out of place, I thought.

The crone said to me, "Welcome, countryman; do you still think you are being trapped? Put side your indignation and act as you did on stage the other day when Pluto returned your Eurydice to you. Let me assure you, you'll find a prettier one here than you lost there."

CHAPTER 5: *How Beau Alman fared there, and how he came back out*

FROM THESE WORDS I gathered that I was supposed to do more in this place than allow myself to be looked at. So I told my old compatriot that a thirsty man gets little comfort from sitting by a forbidden well. She said that in France people weren't so grudging as to forbid anybody the enjoyment of the water, especially when there was plenty of it. "Well, madame," I answered, "such talk is easy, but I am a married man!" "Fiddlesticks!" replied this sinful woman. "Nobody will believe you tonight. In the first place, married noblemen seldom go off traveling in France, and even if it were so I don't think you are such a simpleton to die of thirst rather than drink from a stranger's well, particularly if the stranger's is perhaps even jollier and holds better water than your own."

This was our conversation while a lady in waiting, who was tending the fire, took off my shoes and stockings, which had gotten dirty on the way over, for Paris is a very dirty town.[6] A minute later an order came that I was to be given a bath before supper. (The little lady in waiting was running in and out, preparing the bath and carrying in perfumed soap and towels of the finest cambric cloth trimmed with expensive Dutch lace.) I was ashamed and did not want the old girl to see me naked, but there was no way out of it; I had to undress and she washed me all over. The maid had to step outside for a while.

After the bath I was given a soft undershirt; I had to put on a purple taffeta housecoat and a pair of silk hose of the same color. My slippers and night cap were embroidered with gold thread and pearls, and after my bath I sat there resplendent as the king of hearts. While the old lady was drying and combing my hair — she treated me like a prince or a baby — the above-mentioned maid brought in the food, and when the food had been placed on the table, there entered three statuesque young

[6] Those in the know recognized the last six words, not as a statement of fact but as a hackneyed pun: the Latin name of Paris is *Lutetia*; this calls up the adjective *lutea* (filthy).

ladies whose alabaster-white breasts were considerably visible, but whose faces were completely masked. All three seemed to be perfect beauties; but still one was much more beautiful than the others. I silently bowed very deeply to them; they curtsied to me in turn. These ceremonies looked, of course, as if a number of mutes were trying to act like speaking characters. The three of them sat down at the same time so that I could not guess which one took precedence, much less which one I was to oblige. The conversation opened with the question of whether I could speak French. My compatriot said no. Then one lady asked her to tell me please to sit down. When this had been done, the third asked the interpreter to sit down too. Again I could not figure out who was the foremost. The crone and I sat exactly opposite the three ladies, and there's no doubt that I looked twice as handsome beside that old bag of bones. All three looked at me with grace, love, and goodwill, and I could have sworn they sighed a hundred times. Because of the masks, I could not see the sparkle of their eyes.

My old dame — she was the only one who could talk to me — asked me which one of the three I considered most beautiful. I answered that I couldn't really see them, but as much as I *could* see of them, none of the three was ugly. The ladies at once wanted to know what the crone had asked and I had replied. She interpreted it and added the lie that I had said the lips of each were worth kissing a hundred thousand times (for from my seat I could very well see their mouths under their masks, especially that of the one who sat right across from me). With this fib the crone got me to consider my vis-à-vis as the noblest, and I looked at her more eagerly from then on. This was all of our table conversation, and I carefully pretended that I knew not one word of French. Since it was so quiet and a quiet meal is not much fun, we quit all the sooner. The ladies then bade me good night and were on their way. I could not accompany them farther than the door, which the crone immediately bolted after them.

When I saw that, I asked where I was to sleep. She answered that I would have to make shift with her in the bed in this room. I let her know I did not mind the bed if only one of those three angels were in it. "Well," she said, "you won't have any of them tonight." While we were bantering like this, a beautiful lady who was lying in the bed drew back the curtain a little and told the crone to quit chattering and go to bed. I picked up the candle and tried to see who was in the bed. But the old hag blew it out and said, "If you want to keep your head on your shoulders, don't you dare look at the lady! Just lie down, and let me assure you if you make a serious effort to look at this lady against her will, you will never leave this place alive." With these words she left and locked the door from the outside. The maid, who had been keeping up the fire, extinguished it completely and left the room through a door hidden by an arras.

Now the lady in the bed said, "Allez, Monsieur Beau Alman, go to bed, my sweet 'art gome to mee!" The crone had taught her to say that much in my language. I advanced to the bed, to see how the situation might be handled, and as soon as I got there she was on my neck, welcomed me with many kisses, and for ardent desire almost bit off my lower lip. In fact, she started unbuttoning my housecoat and almost tore off my shirt. She pulled me down to herself and from unrestrained love acted in such a way that words fail me. She only knew one other phrase, "Gome to mee, sweet 'art!" The rest she let me know by gestures.

Certainly, I thought of my dear wife at home, but what good did that do me? Unfortunately, I was a human being, and with such a well-proportioned creature, so full of loveliness, I would have had to be a clod to try and get off chaste. In this fashion I spent eight days and eight nights in this place, and I think the other three also slept with me, because they didn't all talk like number one and didn't act so crazy either. Though I spent a week with these four ladies, I was never permitted to see the face of any of them save through veils, which they wore except at night when it was dark. When the time was up, I was set down in a coach with the windows closed and the curtains drawn. On the way the old lady untied my eyes, and after letting me out at the house of my employer, the coach drove off quickly. My honorarium was the sum of two hundred pistoles, and when I asked the crone whether to give any tips from this money, she said, "Absolutely not. If you did that, it would insult *les dames*. In fact, they would think you imagined you had been in a whorehouse, where one has to pay for everything." Later I had a few more customers like these, and some of them asked so much of me that I finally had to give up this sort of foolishness because I couldn't do it any longer.

CHAPTER 6: *Simplicius takes French leave. He thinks he has the French disease but learns better*

THROUGH THESE ACTIVITIES I amassed so much money, from payments in cash and in kind, that it frightened me. I was no longer surprised that women take to brothels where they make a trade of their bestial lust — it's good business. But I got to thinking — not from piety or pangs of conscience, but from worry that one of these days I'd be caught in one of these escapades and get my comeuppance. For that reason I tried to get back to Germany, and especially when the commander of Lippstadt wrote me, first that he had captured a number of merchants from Cologne whom he would not set free unless my property were given back to me, and secondly, that he was still holding the troop whose command he had promised me. He was expecting me before spring; if I were not back then he would let someone else fill the vacancy. My wife also sent along a little letter in which she gave loving assurance of her great longing for me. If she had known about my fine style of living, she would have whistled a different tune.

I could easily imagine that Dr. Canard would hardly consent to letting me go. Therefore, I planned to take French leave as soon as an opportunity arose. It soon did, much to my sorrow. One day I ran into some officers of the Weimar army. I told them I was an ensign in Colonel de St. André's regiment, had been in Paris on private business, and wanted to get back to my troop. I requested permission to join them on the way home. They told me the day of their departure and were glad to have me go with them. I bought a nag and outfitted myself for the trip as secretly as possible, packed up my money — about five hundred doubloons, all of which I had earned from shameless hussies, by sinful work — and without Canard's leave departed with the officers. On the way I wrote him, but I dated the letter from Maastricht, so that he would think I had headed for Cologne. I said farewell to him and told him that it had been impossible for me to stay longer; I just couldn't take any more of his aromatic sausages.

On the second night out of Paris I felt like someone who had caught the plague. My head hurt so frightfully that I couldn't possibly get up. We were in a godforsaken village where no doctor was available, nor was there anyone — and this was worse — who might nurse and help me. Early in the morning the officers started on their way to Alsace and left me behind like a sick dog, not caring what happened to me since I was not of their party. But before leaving, they commended me and my horse to the innkeeper and left word with the mayor to look after me because I was an officer in the king's service.

So I lay there for a few days and lost consciousness of myself and the world; I was raving like a madman. They brought the priest, but he couldn't get anything sensible out of me. And when he saw he couldn't cure my soul, he considered helping my body. He had me bled, prepared a sudorific, and had me put in a warm bed for sweating. This did me so much good that I regained consciousness that night and recalled where I was, how I had gotten there, and how I had become ill. Next morning the priest came back and found me in black despair, not only because all my money had been stolen, but also because I thought

I had the French disease. I had this coming to me, I thought, rather than so many pistoles, and now I was spotted all over like a tiger. I couldn't walk, stand, sit, or lie. I had no patience, for as I couldn't believe God had wanted me to keep the lost money, now I was so mad that I said the devil had stolen it. I cursed a blue streak; in fact, I acted like a man out of his mind with despair, and the good minister had his work cut out cheering me up, for my shoe was pinching badly in two places at the same time. "My friend," he said, "even if you can't be a pious Christian, act like a reasonable human being in your misfortune. What are you doing? In addition to losing your money, do you also want to lose your life, and, what's more, your eternal soul?" I answered, "I don't give a hoot for the money, if only I didn't have this damned horrible disease. I wish I were in some decent place where I could get a doctor and be cured!" "You must have patience," answered the divine. "Consider the poor little children in this village, of whom more than fifty are sick." When I heard that children had the same disease, I immediately took heart, for I could easily figure out that children wouldn't get the awful disease I thought I had. So I went through my knapsack to see what I might find. Except for some shirts and underwear there was nothing valuable but a little box with a lady's portrait, the frame studded with rubies. Some beauty in Paris had given it to me. I took the picture out, sent the frame to the clergyman, and asked him to sell it in the nearest town so that I might have something with which to buy food. I realized less than a third of the frame's value, and since the money was soon spent, I had to sell my horse next. The money from it barely lasted me till the scabs started forming and I began to feel better.

CHAPTER 7: *Simplicius thinks over his life so far, and learns to swim when the water comes up to his nostrils*

WHAT A MAN SINS with, he is usually punished with. My case of smallpox mauled me so badly that from now on women left me severely alone. My face was so pitted that it looked like a barn floor where they'd been threshing peas. In fact, I got so ugly that my nice, curly hair, in which many a damsel had become entangled, became ashamed of me and dropped out of sight. In its place grew something like pigs' bristles, and I was forced to wear a wig. And just as there was no beauty left in or on my skin, my lovely voice also left me, for the pox had been in my throat too. My eyes, until lately never without the fire that could inflame a lovely woman, now looked inflamed themselves and watered like those of an octogenarian hag with cataracts. And to top it all, I was abroad in a foreign land, unknown to man or beast, did not know the language, and hadn't a penny in my pocket.

Only then did I start thinking back and regretting the many wonderful opportunities for advancement that I had let slip by me through carelessness or indolence. Looking back, I realized that my extraordinary good luck in the wars and the treasure-trove had been no more than the cause and preliminaries of my misfortune. I could never have fallen so low if good luck had not previously smiled on me so falsely and elevated me so high. I even felt that the good I had encountered, and had considered truly good at the time, was evil and had led me to extreme disaster. I had no hermit, anymore, who wished me well, no Colonel Ramsay to give me a home in my misery, no parson to advise me — in short, there wasn't a single soul who would lift a finger for me. Now that my money was gone everybody said that I had better go too, and look for a chance elsewhere, even if I must herd the swine like the prodigal son. Only now I remembered the parson's advice to use my time and money for a college education. But it was much too late to clip the bird's wings with those shears, because the bird had flown the coop. Oh, quick and unexpected change for the worse! A month ago I had been a man who had moved princes to admiration and women to ecstasy; common people had looked upon me as a masterpiece of nature, like an angel, even; now I was so unworthy that the dogs peed on me.

I developed a thousand and more different ideas about what to do next, for the innkeeper wanted to get rid of me the minute I ran out of money. I would have been glad to join an army, but the recruiters wouldn't have me, for I looked like a scurvy cuckoo. I couldn't take a job because I was still too weak and — what's worse — had never become used to regular work. My best consolation was that summer was coming, and in a pinch I could sleep behind a hedge when no one wanted to put me up in his house. I still wore the good suit of clothes I had ordered for the trip, and my knapsack was full of good linen shirts and underwear, but nobody wanted to buy any of this from me for fear of catching my disease. So I buckled on my backpack, took sword in hand, and started making tracks. The first place I came to was a small town, barely big enough to have an apothecary shop. That's where I went to have an ointment made to help me get rid of the red splotches on my face. And since I had no cash I gave the apothecary's clerk a nice shirt for it, but unlike the other fools who wouldn't have my clothing, he wasn't squeamish and took it. My thought was to get rid of the marks first, in hopes of getting rid of my bad luck later. And when the apothecary consoled me that in a week's time I'd look almost all right except for the deep marks the pocks had eaten into my skin, I felt much encouraged. It was market day just then, and a medicine man was making lots of money while palming off useless trash. "You fool," I said to myself, "why don't *you* start that kind of business? You've been with Dr. Canard long enough, and if you haven't learned by now how to cheat a simple peasant and make a living by it, you are a hopeless beetle-brain."

CHAPTER 8: *How Simplicius becomes a huckster and a quack who cheats people*

AT THAT TIME I was as hungry as a horse, and my stomach demanded more of me than I could give it. I had left only a single gold ring with a diamond, worth about twenty crowns. Having disposed of it for twelve, I could easily figure out that that wouldn't last very long, since nothing more was coming in. So I decided to become a doctor. I bought the ingredients for a common theriac[7] and made it up for sale in the villages and market towns. For the country people, I took some juniper jelly and mixed it with leaves of oak and willow and other bitter drugs. Then I made a green ointment of all sorts of herbs, roots, butter, and some aromatic oil; it was good for various sores in human beings and galled horses. From calamine, pebbles, crayfish eyes, emery, and pumice I mixed a toothpowder. From lye, copper, sal ammoniac, and camphor I made a blue liquid for the scurvy, bad breath, toothache, and sore eyes. I acquired plenty of small containers of tin and wood, paper sacks, and glass jars in which to package my merchandise. In order to give me the proper airs, I had a French handbill printed, which told what all and sundry were good for. When, in about three days, this work was finished, I had invested not quite three crowns for drugs and containers. I packed up my goods and left town, intending to make my way by peddling my wares from one village to the next, as far as Alsace. In Strasbourg, a neutral city, I hoped to board a merchant ship for Cologne and from there to grope my way back to my wife. My intention was good, but I failed miserably.

At first I offered my quack remedies in front of a church, but the take was small, because at that time I was much too shy. I didn't speak

---

[7] theriac(a): In old medicine an antidote for snakebite and poison. It was prepared from powdery substances and mixed with honey to make an electuary, i.e. a pasty mass. The best kind was produced in Venice, hence the designation *Venice treacle*.

the barker's blatant language yet, and I saw at once that I'd have to do better if I wanted to dispose of my rubbish and make money. I took my merchandise to an inn, and while I was eating I heard the innkeeper say that in the afternoon a group of people would be meeting under the linden tree in front of his house. If my stuff were any good I might sell a lot of it. But the country was full of cheats, and the customers were not spending anything unless they could see that the theriac was unusually good.

When I had found out what the trouble was, I bought half a glass of good strong gin, caught myself a toad of the kind called "moamy," the sort that sits and croaks in shallow puddles in the spring and early summer; they are gold or almost orange colored, speckled black underneath, and no beauties to look at. I put one of these in a wine glass full of water and placed it among my merchandise on a table beneath the linden tree.

When the people had gathered in droves about me, some thought I would pull teeth with a pair of tongs I had borrowed from the innkeeper's kitchen. But I started orating: "Messieurs et mes amis," (my French wasn't very good yet), "I do not weesh to pull ze teeth. But I have much good liquor for ze eyes, for curing discharge from red eyes." "Ho-ho!" said one heckler. "Look at your own. They glow like two will-o'-the-wisps!" I answered, "Zat is true, but if I had not used my liquid on zem, zey would have become blind. Usually I don't sell the liquor. I sell ze theriac, ze powder for white teeth and ze ointment for sores. The liquor I give you free. I am no *trompeur*, and I no desire to chit ze people. I offer ze theriac. I prove eet is good, but if you don't like, eet is not necessary you buy." Then I had one of the bystanders select one of my theriac jars; I put a small quantity of the medicine — about the size of a pea — into the gin glass, which the people thought was full of water, and stirred it well. With the tongs I lifted the moamy out of the water glass and said, "Look here, good peoples, if this poisonous toad drink my theriac and not die, then eet is no good and you better no buy it." With these words I stuck the poor toad — born and bred in water and incapable of tolerating alcohol — into the gin, covering the glass with cardboard so the beast couldn't jump out. Then the creature started kicking wildly and acting up worse than if I had thrown it on red hot coals, for the gin was much too potent for it. And after it had carried on like this for a while, it croaked and gave up the ghost.

The farmers were dumbstruck when they saw this certain proof and started buying wildly. As far as they were concerned, there wasn't a better theriac in the whole world, and I could hardly wrap the stuff in handbills and collect the money for it fast enough. Some bought three, four, five, even six jars, so that they might not be without such precious medicine in an emergency; they even bought for friends and relatives who lived elsewhere! Though it wasn't even market day, that evening my reckless method of selling brought in ten crowns — and less than half of my stock was sold. That same night I moved on to the next village, for I was afraid some peasants might get curious and try out the theriac by putting a toad in water, and when the experiment failed I'd get a sound thrashing.

In order to prove the excellence of my electuary in still another way, I prepared two poisons: a yellow arsenic from flour, saffron, and gallic acid; and sublimate of mercury from flower and vitriol. In order to present my proof, I put two identical glasses full of fresh water on a table before me. The water in one of these was mixed with a lot of *aqua fortis*, or sulfuric acid; into this glass I put a little of my theriac. Into both glasses I sprinkled enough of my two poisons to make the water that contained no theriac (and no *aqua fortis*) as black as ink. The other glass stayed perfectly clear because of the *aqua fortis*. "Aha!" said the people. "This is a strong theriac indeed, and for so little money." When I poured the two glasses together, the water became clear again. After such proof my good farmers untied the strings of their purses and bought. This not only helped my hungry stomach, but also it put me on a horse again and yielded a neat little penny for my trip; and so without a mishap I got back to the German border. Therefore, my dear peasants, do not trust these foreign mountebanks. They'll cheat you, for they don't care a rap for your health — only for your money.

CHAPTER 9: *The "Doctor" gets a musket and practices starvation*

WHILE PASSING THROUGH LORRAINE I ran out of merchandise, and since I was afraid of garrisoned towns I had no chance to replenish my stock. So I had to do something else until I could make up more theriac. I bought two quarts of brandy, colored it with saffron, filled some half-ounce vials with it, and sold it as a precious goldwater, good for fever. This brandy netted me thirty guilders. When I was almost out of vials, I heard of a glass factory near Fleckenstein, and there I hoped to replenish my supply. But while I was going there on a byway, I happened to be picked up by a raiding party from Philippsburg that was quartered in Castle Wagelnburg. So I lost everything I had obtained on my trip by cheating the people; and because the peasant who was showing me the way said I was a doctor, to give the devil his due, I was taken for a *real* doctor in Philippsburg.

There I was questioned. I wasn't a bit shy about telling them who I was, but they didn't believe me and wanted to make more of me than I possibly could have been. They wanted to make a doctor of me! I had to swear that I had belonged to the imperial dragoons at Soest, and under oath I told everything that had happened to me from then until now and what I intended to do. They said the emperor needed soldiers in Philippsburg as well as in Soest, and they'd keep me until there was a chance to send me on to my own regiment. If I did not like the smell of this suggestion I would have to be satisfied with living in the stockade. Until they let me go again they'd treat me there like a medical doctor, since that is how they had caught me.

Thus, I came down off my high horse onto a jackass and had to become a musketeer, though it all happened without my cooperation. This was a hard nut for me to crack; for one thing, they were keeping a lean larder there, and the bread rations were frightfully small. I say "frightfully" on purpose, for it frightened me every morning when I received my loaf, because I knew I would have to make it last all day, though I could have eaten it at one meal. Truth to tell, a musketeer is a miserable creature who has to live this way in a garrison and who has to get by on dry bread — and not half enough of that. He's no better than a prisoner who is prolonging his poor life with the bread and water of tribulation. In fact, a prisoner is better off, for he does not have to stand watch, go the rounds, or do sentry duty; he stays quietly in bed and has just as much hope as a sad garrison trooper of getting out of his prison in time. There were a few who, by various means, had it a little better; but none of these ways of getting a bite more to eat were to my liking. In their misery, a few troopers took on wives (some of these former two-bit sluts) who could increase their income by such work as sewing, washing, spinning, or by selling second-hand clothing or other junk, or even by stealing. Among the women was a female ensign who drew her pay like a corporal! Another was a midwife, and she was given many a good meal for herself and her husband. Another took in laundry and ironing; she washed shirts, socks, nightshirts, and other apparel for the bachelors among the officers and men, and she had quite a reputation. Others sold tobacco and furnished pipes for those who needed them. Still others sold brandy; it was generally thought that they were adulterating it with water distilled by their own bodies — but that didn't change the color of the liquor in the least! Another was a seamstress who was able to earn money through hem-stitching and embroidery. Still another could pick a living off the field; in the winter she dug up snails, in spring she picked salad herbs, in summer she took the young out of birds' nests, and in fall she could gather hundreds of other tidbits. Some sold kindling wood, which they carried to market like donkeys; others peddled other merchandise. To earn my keep that way was not for me, since I already had a wife. Some of the men made a living by gambling (which they could do better than professional sharps), and with loaded dice and a stacked deck they got what they wanted from their simple-minded fellow soldiers. I despised such machinations. Others, like dumb beasts, labored at building fortifications or did other odd jobs; for this I was too lazy. Some carried on a trade, but I had learned none. If a musician had been needed I could have served, but this starvation district got along on pipes and drums. Some took over others' guard duty and stood watch day and night. I would rather have starved than wear out my body that way. Some made both ends meet by going on raids, but I wasn't even permitted to step outside the gates. To make it brief, no matter where I turned, I could pick up nothing with which to fill my stomach. And what made me furious was having to take it when the gang said, "You're a doctor and don't know how to cure starvation?"

Finally, necessity made me juggle a couple of good-sized carp out of the moat into my hands as I stood on the rampart; but as soon as the colonel heard of it I was in dutch and he forbade further prestidigitation on pain of hanging. At last, others' misfortune turned out to be my luck. Having cured a few cases of jaundice and fever — these patients must have had special faith in me — I was allowed to wander out of the fortress to gather (so I said) medicinal roots and herbs. But instead I set snares for rabbits and was lucky to catch two the first night. These I took to the colonel and he gave me not only a thaler as a present but also permission to go out after rabbits when I was off duty. Since the country was rather deserted and nobody was catching these animals that had multiplied over the years, the rabbits brought grist to my mill, especially as it seemed that they turned up everywhere or that I could charm them into my snares. When the officers saw that they could trust me, I was allowed to go raiding with the others, and I resumed the life of Soest, except that I could not be in charge. For that, one had to know all the roads and byways and the course of the Rhine.

CHAPTER 10: *Simplicius survives a miserable bath in the Rhine*

I WANT TO TELL a few more adventures before I let you know how I was rescued from carrying a musket. One story deals with danger to life and limb, from which I escaped by the grace of God; the other, with danger to my soul's salvation, in which I did not fare so well. I want to conceal my vices no more than my virtues, not only because I want the reader to know the whole story, but also so that he knows what strange characters populate this world — characters that give little thought to God.

As I said toward the end of the previous chapter, I was allowed to go on raiding parties along with the others, and this is something granted not to every stumblebum but only to good, reliable soldiers. One time nineteen of us were moving through the country northeast of Strasbourg to wait for a ship from Basel reportedly carrying contraband and some Weimar officers. Above Ottenheim we got hold of a fishing boat to put us on an island where oncoming vessels could be forced to land. Ten of us had already been taken across, but when one of the remaining nine, who was a good oarsman, was rowing the rest across, the boat suddenly capsized and we were in the river before you could say Jack Robinson. I didn't worry much about the others but looked to my own safety. And though I made every effort and used all the tricks of good swimmers, the stream played with me as with a bundle of rags, throwing me helter-skelter now to the bottom, now to the surface. Struggling heroically, I managed to come up for breath frequently, but if it had been a little colder I could not have survived. Time and time again I tried to swim ashore, but the eddies that carried me from one side to another would not let me land. When I had passed the country beyond Goldscheur and had already resigned myself to taking the Rhine bridge at Strasbourg either dead or alive, I noticed a big tree whose branches were sticking out of the water not far from me. The current went right in that direction and I did my best to reach it. Luckily I succeeded, and through the force of the water and my own exertion I managed to cling to the largest branch (which I thought at first was the whole tree). But the current and the waves were constantly twisting and turning the tree and moving it up and down. My stomach became so upset from this motion that I wanted to spit out liver and lights. Barely able to hold on, I was beginning to faint and would have been glad to slip into the water again, except I felt I wouldn't have the courage to endure a hundredth part of the misery I had just been through. So I hung on, hoping for an uncertain rescue that God might chance to send me if I were to get off alive. But in regard to this hope, my conscience furnished me scant comfort; it reproached me for having foolishly rejected God's gracious help over the last few years. Yet, now I hoped for the best and started to pray as fervently as if I had been raised in a monastery; I resolved to live more piously and made several vows: I renounced the life of a soldier and promised never to go raiding again; I threw away my pack and ammunition and let on that I wanted to become a hermit once more, to repent of my sins, and to thank God's mercy for my hoped-for salvation until my dying day.

After two or three hours spent between hope and fear on the branch, I saw the ship I was supposed to help capture coming down the Rhine. With a piteous cry in the name of God and doomsday, I called for help, and since they had to sail right by me and saw my plight, everyone in the ship was so moved to mercy that they made for shore and deliberated on how to rescue me. Because of the eddies around me and the many roots and branches, no one could safely swim to me or come close with a boat, and so it took a long time to decide how to rescue me. You can easily imagine how I felt all this time. Finally they sent two stout men in a boat, who floated a rope toward me from upstream. They held on to one end while I managed to tie the other around my midriff. Like a big fish on a line, I was then pulled into the boat and taken to the ship.

Having thus escaped death, it would have been reasonable for me to fall on my knees and thank divine mercy for my rescue, and also to start leading a better life, as I had sworn and promised in my utmost misery. But far from it! When they asked me who I was and how I had gotten into this trouble, I lied like a dog to these fellows, for I thought if I told them that I had wanted to rob them, they'd throw me right back into the Rhine. So I said I was an organist, driven out of my village because of the war and now on my way to Strasbourg in order to look for a job in connection with schoolteaching or anything else. A raiding party had picked me up, robbed me of everything, and thrown me in the Rhine, which had deposited me in the tree. And since I spieled off these lines without the least embarrassment and swore I was telling the truth, they believed me, gave me food and drink, and showed me every kindness — all of which I needed badly.

Most people went ashore at the customs office in Strasbourg, and so did I, once again thanking all. In the crowd I noticed a young merchant whose walk and gestures made me think that I had seen him before, but I couldn't remember where. His way of talking made me think that he was the ensign who had previously captured me, but I couldn't figure out how such a brave young soldier had turned into a merchant, particularly since he was a born cavalier.[8] My desire to find out whether my eyes and ears were deceiving me made me go to him and I said, "Monsieur Schönstein, is it you or isn't it?" He answered, "I am no von Schönstein, but a merchant." Then I said, "In that case I am not the Hunter of Soest, either, but an organist, or rather a roving bindlestiff." "Brother," he said, "what in the devil's name are you doing here? Where are you keeping yourself?" I said, "Brother, if heaven has destined you to preserve my life (as now has happened a second time),

---

[8] See Bk. III, 14; the ensign's name was not previously mentioned.

my fate requires me to be fairly close to you." We embraced each other like two good friends who had previously promised to love each other till their dying day. I had to come to his lodgings and tell him everything that had happened to me since I had left Lippstadt for Cologne to collect my treasure. I did not conceal from him how I and my fellows had planned to ambush the ship and how things turned out. But I did not breathe a word about how I had carried on in Paris, for I was afraid he might gossip about it in Lippstadt and my wife would make my life miserable.

He in turn confided to me that the Hessian general staff had sent him to Bernhard, Duke of Weimar, to report on matters of great importance relating to the war and to confer about future plans and the coming campaign. He had accomplished this, and now he was returning disguised as a merchant. Incidentally, he told me that my beloved wife had been with child when he left and that she and her relatives had been in good health. He also said that the colonel was still holding the troop for me, and he teased me that the pocks had so spoiled my looks that neither my wife nor the other ladies in Lippstadt would recognize me for the Hunter. Finally we agreed that I should stay with him and take this opportunity of returning to Lippstadt, which was just what I wanted. And since I had only rags to wear, he advanced me money so I could buy some clothes to make me look like a salesman.

But they say that if a thing is not to be, it won't happen. I found this out when we were traveling down the Rhine and the ship was searched at Rheinhausen. The Philippsburgers recognized me, picked me up, and returned me to Philippsburg, where I had to tote the musket again. Though this hurt my good ensign as much as me, he could do little for me; he had a hard enough time getting away himself.

CHAPTER 11: *Why preachers should not eat rabbits that were caught in a snare*

THE GENTLE READER HAS heard in what physical danger I had been; concerning the danger to my soul he must know that as a musketeer I was an awfully crude being who didn't give a damn for God or Holy Writ. No meanness was beyond me; all grace and kindness I had ever received from God was forgotten; I prayed for matters neither temporal nor eternal but lived unreformed, like a beast. No one would have believed that a pious hermit had brought me up.

I seldom saw the inside of a church, and I never went to confession. And as the salvation of my soul was nothing to me, so I troubled my fellow men all the more; wherever I could trick someone, I did — and boasted of it! Almost no one was exempt; and I often got my comeuppance and was threatened with whippings and the strappado, but this did no good. I persisted in my godless way as if I were rushing straight to hell. And though I committed no crime worthy of hanging, I was so dastardly that (aside from witches and sodomites) no worse man could be found.

Our regimental chaplain took note of this, and because he was quite a zealot, around Easter time he sent for me to find out why I hadn't come to confession and communion. After he had finished his well-meaning admonitions, I treated him like the minister in Lippstadt, and the good man could do nothing with me. Concluding that Christ and baptism had been wasted on me, he summarized: "Alas, you miserable man, I thought you were going astray through ignorance, but now I know you are continuing to sin from evil intention. Do you think anyone will have pity on your poor, damned soul? As for me, I protest before God and the world that I have no part in your damnation; I have done — and shall gladly continue to do — all that's needed for the salvation of your soul. But, presumably, when your poor soul leaves its damned abode, I won't have to do much more than have your body taken to the place where the dead animals are buried or where the godforsaken and desperate are put away."

This serious admonition did no more good than previous ones, simply because I was afraid to go to confession. What a great fool I was! I would often tell my knavish exploits to the assembled company, and lie to boot, but now that I was to repent and humbly confess my sins to a single person, in lieu of God, in order to receive absolution — now I was stubborn and silent as a stick. I use the word "stubborn" deliberately; I stayed stubborn, for I said to the chaplain, "I am serving the emperor as a soldier, and should I die like a soldier it won't surprise me if — like other soldiers, who are not always buried in holy ground but must make shift in the fields, in a ditch, or in the stomachs of wolves and ravens — I'll have to get along outside the churchyard." So I left the parson, who with all his anxiety for my soul deserved only this of me: I refused to give him a rabbit that he wanted very much; I said that the hare had hanged himself by a cord and since one who died by an act of desperation could not find rest in holy ground, he couldn't have it.

CHAPTER 12: *To his surprise, Simplicius is delivered from the musket*

THUS, NO CHANGE FOR the better was seen in me; rather I became worse as time passed. The colonel once told me he'd like to kick me out like a rogue, for I was no good. But as I knew he didn't mean it, I said I wouldn't mind being dismissed, but he should send the executioner along to keep me company. So he let me get by, for he could easily see that if he sent me away I'd take it as a favor rather than as punishment. Accordingly, I stayed a musketeer against my will and suffered the pangs of hunger far into the summer. But Count von Götz was approaching with his army, and so did my deliverance; for when Götz had his headquarters at Bruchsal, the general staff sent my good friend Heartbrother (whom I had faithfully helped out with money in the camp at Magdeburg) with some orders to our fortress, where he was treated with great honor and respect. I happened to be on sentry duty before the colonel's quarters, and even though Heartbrother wore a black velvet coat, I recognized him at first sight, but I didn't have the heart to address him then. I was afraid he'd be ashamed of me (as things go in this world) or even refuse to recognize me, because by his wardrobe he appeared to be a man of high rank and I was only a lousy musketeer. After I had been relieved, I asked his servants about his name and rank, so that I wouldn't perhaps address the wrong man; and yet I didn't have the courage to speak to him. Instead, I wrote him this letter, which I had his valet deliver in the morning:

Monsieur, etc.
    if it should please my gracious master through his overwhelming influence to rescue one whom he previously delivered out of fetters and bonds through bravery in the battle of Wittstock — if it should please him to rescue him now from the most wretched state in the world, a state to which he came as a plaything of fickle Fortune — this act would cost him little and would make a lifelong servant of his faithful, now most forsaken and deserted,
                    S. Simplicissimus.

As soon as he had read this, he asked me to come to his room, and he asked, "Fellow countryman, where is the man who gave you this letter?" I answered, "Sir, he is a prisoner in this fortress." "All right," he said, "go to him and tell him I will help him even if the noose is already around his neck." I replied, "Sir, there's no need to bother going: I am Simplicius, and I have come to thank you for my rescue at Wittstock, as well as to ask you to rid me of the musket that I am forced to carry against my will." He didn't let me finish my sentence, but showed me by an embrace how much he wanted to help me. He did everything a true friend can do for another; and even before he asked me how I had been placed in this fortress and in such bondage, he sent a servant to a Jewish trader to buy me a horse and clothing. Meanwhile, I told him how I had been since his father had died at Magdeburg. When he heard that I was the Hunter of Soest (of whose exploits he had heard so much), he regretted not having known this before, for he might well have been able to help me to a company.

When the dealer arrived with a whole pack of soldiers' clothing, he picked out the best pieces, let me put them on, and together we went to the colonel. "Sir," he said, "in your garrison I've found this man, to whom I am so greatly obliged that I cannot leave him in his present state (even though he doesn't deserve better). I beg you, therefore, to do me the favor either of promoting him or permitting me to take him along, so that I can get him such advancement in the army as there may not be a chance for here."

Upon hearing me praised the colonel was so dumbfounded that he made the sign of the cross and answered, "Worthy sir, forgive me if I believe that you are only testing my willingness to serve you as you deserve. If this is so, please demand anything that is in my power and you will see me ready. But as to this fellow, he belongs not to me but — as he says — to a regiment of dragoons; and besides, he's such a devil that he has given my provost more trouble than a whole company. I think water would refuse to drown him!"

But this wasn't enough for Heartbrother; he asked the colonel to condescend to invite me to his table, and his wish was granted. He did this so he could tell the colonel about me in my presence what so far he had heard only as mere conversation in Westphalia, from Count von der Wahl and the commander at Soest. He told it in such a way that all listeners had to think of me as a good soldier. All this time I behaved so modestly that the colonel and his officers (who knew me well) could not help thinking that I had put on a new man with my new clothes. And when the colonel asked how I had come by the title of Doctor, I described my whole trip from Paris to Philippsburg and my method for cheating the peasants in order to have something to chew. This made them laugh hard. Finally, I openly confessed that I had wanted by all sorts of deviltry to irritate and wear down the colonel to the point of dismissing me from his garrison so that he might live in peace and hear no more complaints about me.

After that, the colonel related all sorts of dirty tricks I had played since the day I had come into the garrison: how I had poured lard on top of boiled peas and sold the potful for pure lard; how I had sold, as salt, sacks partly filled with sand; how I had made a monkey of practically everyone; and how I had composed satirical verses about people. Throughout the meal they were talking only about me. But if I hadn't had such an influential friend, my exploits would have been worthy of only one thing — punishment. This showed me what happens at court when a rogue gains the prince's favor.

When the meal was ended, the dealer did not have a horse that Heartbrother thought good enough for me. And since Heartbrother enjoyed so much esteem and the colonel wanted his favor, the colonel gave him one of his own horses, with saddle and bridle. And while milord Simplicius, together with his friend Heartbrother, joyfully rode out of the fortress, some of his comrades shouted after him, "Good luck to you! Good luck!" But the others, moved by envy, hollered, "The worse the s.o.b., the better his luck!"

CHAPTER 13: *Dealing with the Order of the Marauding Brothers*

ON THE WAY HEARTBROTHER and I agreed that I should pretend to be his cousin. So that I might have more status, he would get me a second horse and a servant and put me in Colonel Neuneck's regiment where I could stay as a volunteer until an officer's position became vacant; then he'd help me get it. Thus, in no time at all, I turned into a man who resembled a good soldier. But during that summer I engaged in few exploits except helping to steal a couple of cows in the Black Forest; besides, I got to know the Breisgau and Alsace pretty well. But again, I wasn't very lucky, for when men of the Weimar army captured my servant and horse at Kenzingen, I had to use my other horse all the harder and when he gave up the ghost, I joined the Order of the Marauding Brothers — that is, I robbed on foot. My friend Heartbrother would have gotten me another mount, but since I had done away with the first two horses so quickly, he did not exactly rush in but left me up in the air in order to teach me a lesson. I didn't press him, either, for my companions were such a pleasant gang that I did not even want to change until it was time to move into winter quarters.

Now I'll tell what sort of people the Marauders are. There are doubtless some people, especially those who are ignorant of war, who don't know about them. Neither have I yet run into an author who treats of their habits, wonts, rights, and privileges, though it is a matter well worth knowing, not only for our generals but also for the peasants. Concerning the name of the group, when a certain gentleman brought in a newly recruited regiment, the men were so weak and debilitated that they could hardly march or stand up under the hardships of soldiering. When they were found hiding behind fences and hedges and were asked what regiment they belonged to, they would answer, "*Merode*" (which is French for sick, out of order).[9] From this sprang the custom of calling "Merode Brothers" all those who trot along behind and out of step, even if they are not sick or wounded. One can see them in droves behind hedges, in the shadow or in the sun or about a fire, being lazy and smoking, while an honest soldier under his flag has to endure heat, thirst, hunger, cold, and other miseries. Ahead of the army, alongside, and behind it, the marauders pick up everything they can lay their hands on, and what they can't use they spoil, so that the regiments moving into camp or quarters often can't find a good drink of clean water. When they are forced to stay with the baggage train, it becomes more numerous than the army proper. When they are together or marching in gangs, they have no sergeant major, no color sergeant or corporal who keeps order; they live like masters and are scot-free. They do not keep watch, they do not labor at digging trenches, they do not attack, they are found in no battle line — and yet they make a living! Well, I was one of these brothers, and I stayed one till the day before the battle of Wittenweier. At that time I went with some pals of mine to steal oxen and cows, and we were caught by Weimar troops. They knew what to do with us; they put us under a musket and distributed us among the various regiments. I was assigned to Colonel Hattstein's regiment.

CHAPTER 14: *A perilous fight for life in which both contestants escape death*

AT THAT POINT I came to see that I was born only for misfortune. About a month before the battle, I heard some of General Götz's officers discussing the war; one of them said, "This summer there's sure to be a battle. If we beat the enemy, we'll have to spend next winter taking Freiburg and the forest cities; but if we get beaten we'll enjoy winter quarters just the same." I drew the correct conclusion from this prophecy, and I said to myself, 'You will drink the good wines of the Neckar or of Lake Constance, and you will enjoy whatever is coming to the Weimar troops.' But I was badly mistaken. Because I was a Weimar man myself now, I was predestined to help lay siege to Breisach, and such a siege was undertaken full tilt right after the battle

---

[9] Grimmelshausen is here pulling his readers' leg. The word comes from the French *marauder*, "to plunder." Other explanations have been suggested, none very satisfactory.

of Wittenweier.[10] Like the other musketeers I had to stand guard duty and dig trenches day and night. This only taught me how to get at a fortress by way of trenches — something to which I had paid no attention at Magdeburg. As for the rest, I was in lousy shape: two or three of us lived in cramped quarters; my purse was empty; wine, beer, and meat were rarities; apples and half rations of bread had to do for venison.

This situation was hard to bear and gave me reason enough to think back to the fleshpots of Egypt, that is, the Westphalian hams and knockwurst in Lippstadt. I no longer thought of my wife except when I lay in my tent and was stiff from frost and cold. Then I often said to myself, 'Alas, Simplici, don't you think it would serve you right if someone did to you just what you did in Paris?' And such thoughts worried me, as they would any cuckold, though I knew my wife was faithful and virtuous. At last I became so impatient that I told my captain how my personal affairs stood. I also wrote to Lippstadt. The reply was that letters from Colonel de St. André and my father-in-law to the Prince of Weimar had resulted in orders to my captain to issue me a pass for a visit to Lippstadt.

A week or so before Christmas I was walking down the Breisgau, carrying my trusty gun; I was hoping to receive twenty thalers that my brother-in-law had deposited to my credit in Strasbourg. There I would join some merchants and travel down the Rhine, where there were a number of imperial garrisons. When I had just passed Endingen and was approaching an isolated house, someone shot at me and the bullet tore a hole in the brim of my hat. That instant a big burly fellow came running toward me, shouting that I should drop my gun. I answered, "Not to please you, I won't, country cousin!" and I cocked the gun. He whipped out an object that looked more like an executioner's sword than a dagger and rushed toward me. When I saw that he meant business, I let him have it, hitting him in the forehead so that he spun around and finally fell down. Taking advantage of his position, I twisted the sword out of his hand and tried to run him through. But the sword wouldn't pierce, and he jumped unexpectedly to his feet again and grabbed me by the hair. I did the same to him. I had already thrown his sword out of reach, and now we began to wrestle so hard that the embittered strength of both of us showed plainly. Yet neither could get the better of the other. Now I was on top, now he; now both of us got on our feet again, but not for long because each tried his best to kill the other. Since he was so grimly after my blood, I gathered up

[10] Breisach fell on December 19, 1638; the battle of Wittenweier took place on July 30, 1638.

what was oozing from my nose and mouth and spit it in his face. This was a help because it kept him from seeing clearly. That way we worked on each other in the snow for about an hour and a half. This exercise was so tiring that it seemed that one's exhaustion could not completely overcome the other's weariness, at least not by the use of fists; nor could one kill the other without a weapon.

Wrestling, which I had learned at Lippstadt, came in very handy; otherwise, I should have come out on the short end, for my enemy was much stronger than I, and sword and bulletproof besides. Finally, when we had almost worn each other out, he said, "Brother, stop; I yield to you." I said, "You should have let me pass by in the first place." "If I die, what good will it do you?" he asked. "And if you shot me dead, what good would it have done you, since I haven't a penny in my pocket?" Then he begged my pardon, and I gave in and let him get up. But first he had to swear solemnly that he would not only keep the peace but also be my faithful friend and servant. I would never have believed or trusted him, however, if I had known about the wanton deeds he had previously committed.

When both of us had gotten up, we shook hands and agreed that all these events should be forgotten. Each was surprised to have found his match, and the other fellow thought me just as big a rascal as he. I did not disillusion him, lest he try again once he recovered his gun. He had a big bump on the head from my shot; I had lost a lot of blood; and we both complained about our necks, which had been so ill-treated that we couldn't carry our heads upright.

Since evening was approaching and my opponent told me I would not meet a cat or a dog, much less a human being, on my way as far as the river Kinzig,[11] I was persuaded to go with him. He said he had good drink and some food in his house, not far from the road. On the way he sighed many times and assured me he was sorry to have hurt me.

CHAPTER 15: *How Oliver thinks he can justify his criminal sylvan doings*

WHAT A STUPID OX is a resolute soldier who risks his life or sets a low value upon it! Among a thousand men, not one would have had

---

[11] This river arises in the Black Forest and empties in the Rhine at Kehl (near Strasbourg). Another river by the same name flows through Gelnhausen and into the Main at Hanau.

the courage to go to an unknown place with a ruffian who had murderously attacked him only a short time before. On the way, I asked him what army he belonged to. He answered that for the time being he belonged to none, but was warring on his own account. Then he asked me the same question. I told him I had been one of the Duke of Weimar's men, had been dismissed, and was on my way home. He asked for my name and when I answered "Simplicius," he turned around (for I had him walk ahead, because I didn't trust him) and gave me a hard look. "Aren't you also called Simplicissimus?" "Yes," I answered. "Whoever denies his own name is a rogue. But what's your name?" "Alas, brother," he answered, "I am Oliver, whom you remember from the days of Magdeburg." With these words he threw down his gun, fell on his knees to ask my forgiveness for having wanted to hurt me, and told me that now he imagined he'd never have a better friend in the world than me, since according to old Heart-brother's prophecy I would courageously avenge his death. For my part, I continued to express surprise at our strange meeting. But he said, "That's nothing new; mountain and valley don't run into each other. What's strange is how we two have changed: I've turned from a secretary into a fisherman of the woods, a footpad; and you, from a fool into a brave soldier! Let me tell you, if there were ten thousand of us, we'd relieve Breisach tomorrow, and in the end we'd be masters of the whole world."

With such talk we came at dusk to a small, out-of-the-way hut that might have belonged to a day laborer, and though I did not approve of Oliver's braggadocio I said he was right, particularly because I knew his false and roguish mind. Though I did not trust him in the least, I followed him into the shack, where a peasant was just heating up the room. Oliver asked him whether supper was ready. "No," said the peasant, "but I still have the cold leg of veal that I brought from Waldkirch today." "Well, then," said Oliver, "go and get what you have and bring along the small keg of wine."

When the peasant was gone, I said to Oliver, "Brother," (I called him this in order to be on the safe side) "you have a willing host." "May the devil thank the rogue!" he said. "I take care of him and his wife and children. On top of that, he does all right with his own booty. I give him all the clothes that come my way, to use as he sees fit." I asked where the fellow's family was. Oliver explained that he had taken them to Freiburg, where he visited them twice a week. From there he brought back food and powder and shot. Moreover, Oliver told me that he had been in this freebooter's trade for a long time; it paid much better than serving a master, and he was not about to stop until he had lined his purse well. I said, "Brother, you ply a dangerous trade; if you got picked up for robbery, what do you think would happen to you?" "Ha," he said, "you are still the same old Simplicius. You don't have to tell me that I am running a risk; on the other hand, they've got to catch me before they hang me. My dear Simplicius, you haven't read your Machiavelli[12] yet. I am an upright man, and I carry on my trade openly and without subterfuge. I fight, I risk my life like the heroes of old; and since I am risking my life, it follows undeniably that to carry on this handicraft is meet and proper."

I answered, "Assuming that robbery and theft are permitted (or are not), I nevertheless know they are against the law of nature, which wants us to do to others as we would have them do to us. Such iniquity is also against worldly law, which says that thieves should be hanged, robbers beheaded, and murderers broken on the wheel. And finally it is against God, and that's most important, for He leaves no sin unpunished." "It is as I told you," replied Oliver. "You are still the Simplicius who hasn't studied his Machiavelli. If I could set up a monarchy in my own way, I wonder who would preach against me then?" We would have argued longer, but the peasant had returned with food and drink. So we sat down together and fed our stomachs, for I was hungry as a bear.

CHAPTER 16: *Oliver interprets Heartbrother's prophecy to his own advantage and thus loves his worst enemy*

OUR FOOD CONSISTED OF the finest bread and a cold leg of veal; we drank good wine and sat in a warm room. "You have to admit, Simpli," said Oliver, "that this is better than the slit trenches at Breisach." I said that was true — if only one could enjoy such life with a certain amount of safety and honor. This made him explode with laughter. "Are those poor devils in the trenches safer than we? They have to worry every moment about a sudden attack. My dear Simpli, I see you have put aside your fool's cap, but you have kept your foolish head, and you can't tell good from bad. If you were anybody but the man who, according to old Heartbrother's prophecy, is to avenge my death, I'd make you admit that I lead a nobler life than a baron." I

---

[12] Niccolò Machiavelli (1469-1527), Florentine statesman and author. In his *Il Princepe* (*The Prince*) he tries to show that Italy can regain its ancient preeminence only through autocratic princes. Popular misunderstanding attributed to Machiavelli the notion that in the acquisition of power, especially for political reasons, ethics has to take a backseat.

thought, 'What will come of this? I'll have to think up something different; otherwise, with the help of the peasant this brute will exterminate me.' So I said, "Who ever heard that the chicken is smarter than the hen? Brother, if your life is as happy as you say, let me share in your happiness — I need it." Oliver answered, "Brother, I love you as I love myself; why should I refuse you anything? Stay with me if you like; I'll take care of you. If you want to leave, I'll give you a nice sum of money and accompany you wherever you go. And to prove that these words come from my heart, I'll tell you why I think so much of you. You remember how true old Heartbrother's prophecies were. At Magdeburg he said to me, 'Oliver, look at our fool any way you like; he will frighten you by his bravery and play the worst trick on you. And you will cause him to do it at a time when you don't recognize each other. But not only will he spare your life; after a while, he will come to the place where you will be slain, and there he will avenge your death.' On account of this prophecy I am willing to share the heart in my body with you, dear Simplici; for as one part of the prophecy has been fulfilled, I don't doubt the rest will also come true. From your revenge I must conclude, dear brother, that you are a good friend. If you were not, you wouldn't undertake it; and that's how I feel about it. Now tell me what you intend to do." I thought, 'May the devil trust you, not I! If I accept money you'll kill me on the way; if I stay with you I'll be drawn and quartered too.' I resolved to trick him and said that if he liked me I'd stay with him for a few days in order to see how I'd get used to that kind of life. If I liked it, he'd have a faithful friend and a good soldier in me; if not, we could part in kindness any time. After that he plied me with drink, but since I didn't trust him I pretended to be drunk before I really was, in order to find out whether he would hurt me when I couldn't defend myself.

Meanwhile, those big, sturdy lice I had brought with me from Breisach started acting up; in the warmth of the room they crawled from my rags to look for a good time outside. Oliver noticed and asked if I had lice. I said, "Sure, more than I'll ever have ducats in all my life." "That's no way to talk," said Oliver. "If you stay with me, you'll probably get more ducats than you now have lice." My reply was, "That's as impossible as getting rid of the lice right now." "No, it isn't," he said, and he ordered the peasant to bring me some clothes that were hidden in a hollow tree not far from the house. He brought a gray hat, a jerkin of elk skin, a pair of red breeches, and a gray coat. He would give me shoes and stockings tomorrow, he said. When I saw this generous gift, I trusted him a little more and fell asleep happy.

CHAPTER 17: *When Simplicius goes out robbing, his thoughts are more pious than Oliver's in church*

IN THE MORNING, TOWARD daybreak, Oliver said, "Get up, Simpli; let's see what in God's name we can pick up." 'O my God,' I thought, 'am I to rob in thy holy name? Heavenly Father, how I have changed! What will become of me if I don't turn to thee? Check my course, for I'll go to hell if I don't repent.' With these thoughts I followed Oliver to a village in which there was not one living creature. To get a better view, we climbed up the church tower. There Oliver had hidden the shoes and stockings that he had promised me the night before, and also two loaves of bread, several pieces of smoked meat, and half a keg of wine. With these rations one man might survive for a week. While I was putting on my gift shoes and stockings, he told me that he used to watch from this hiding place whenever he thought something good was coming along. He mentioned that he had several other places stocked like this one, so that if one produced no loot he might try at another. I praised his wisdom, but I let him know that I disapproved of defiling a consecrated building. "What?" he said. "Defile? If churches could talk they'd say that what I do in them is nothing compared to the vices committed there by others. How many people who step into a church under the pretext of serving God come only to show off their new clothes, their beautiful figures, their worldly positions, or something similar? Here is one strutting like a peacock in front of the altar, and yet he acts as if he would pray the leg off a saint; there is one in the corner sighing like a publican in the temple, but the sighs are meant for his sweetheart, whose face he is staring at and for whom he came to church in the first place. More than one man could not carry on an illicit affair if the church didn't help him. Many a loan shark who hasn't taken time all week to figure out new angles does so during the sermon. Some only sit there and sleep as if they had hired the place for it. I won't mention the stories I have read, but I must bring up one more thing: people not only make a mockery of churches while they are alive, but they fill them with vanity and foolishness even after death. As soon as you enter a church you see gravestones and epitaphs of people whom the worms have eaten long ago. When you look up you catch sight of shields, helmets, weapons, swords, flags, spurs, and such. Small wonder that, in this war, in some places the peasants made fortresses out of churches to defend their possessions. Why shouldn't I make a living by the church that so many people live on? Had I known of your scruples about lying in wait in a church, I would have thought up a better answer than this, but until I give you a better one, put this one in your pipe and smoke it."

I would gladly have told Oliver that those other folks who be-smirched the church were as dishonorable as he and would get their reward. But because I did not trust him and did not want to get into another argument, I agreed with him. After a while he asked me to tell him how I had been doing since we parted at Wittstock, and why I was wearing jester's clothes when I arrived in the camp before Magdeburg. But since a sore throat made me miserable, I asked to be excused and requested that he tell me his life (which presumably was full of strange wrinkles). He agreed and started to recount his heinous life, as follows.

CHAPTER 18: *Oliver tells about his family and his youth, and particularly about his deportment in school*

"MY FATHER WAS BORN of simple people, not far from Aachen. Because his folks were poor, as a young man he had to work for a rich dealer in copper goods, who taught him to read and write and figure, and put him in charge of his whole business, as Potiphar did Joseph. This was to the advantage of both parties, for as time went on the merchant became richer by way of my father's industry and foresight; because of his success my father became more and more proud so that he grew ashamed of his parents and despised them. They often deplored it, but in vain. When my father had passed his twenty-fifth birthday, the merchant died, leaving behind his elderly widow and an only daughter. The latter had run into bad luck, having become pregnant by a shop clerk, but the child soon followed its grandfather. When my father saw that the daughter had lost her father and her child, but not her money, he did not hold it against her that she could never again wear virgin's white. He considered her wealth and got next to her, an arrangement that her mother gladly permitted, not only because her daughter's honor would be restored, but also because my father knew the trade inside out and was a sharp businessman who never lost sight of Number One. Through this marriage my father became a rich merchant overnight, and I his heir. Because of his wealth I was well brought up; I was dressed like a gentleman, fed like a baron, and as for all the rest, treated like a count. All this I owe to copper and brass rather than to silver and gold.

"Before I was eight, my mettle already showed (for even small nettles can sting and the sting gets worse). No deviltry was too big for me, and whenever I could pull a nasty trick on someone, I did. Neither my father nor my mother would discipline me. With my fellow hoodlums I wandered up and down the streets picking fights, sometimes even with boys who were bigger than I. When I took a licking my parents would say, 'It's a shame for a big bruiser to beat up our child!' But if I got the better of my enemy — I used to scratch and bite and throw rocks — they said, 'What a scrappy boy our little Oliver is turning out to be!' This encouraged me. I was still too small for prayers; but when I cursed like a fishwife, they said I didn't know what it was all about. So I grew worse, until they sent me to school, where I readily performed what the other bad boys had thought up but did not dare to do themselves. When I had ruined or torn my books, my mother bought me new ones, lest my stingy father get excited. I was a pain in the neck to my teacher; he didn't dare handle me as I deserved because he received many valuable gifts from my parents, and he knew they were spoiling me.

"In summer I caught crickets and released them in school, where they chirped and sang. In winter I stole sneezing powder and scattered it in the room where the boys were being whipped. Whenever a stubborn soul kicked up some dust, my powder made everybody happier by causing everybody to sneeze. After a while I considered myself to be above such ordinary jokes and specialized in the following trick: I stole something from somebody and put it among the belongings of somebody else, whom I wanted to get in trouble. I did this frequently and was almost never caught. I don't want to go into detail about the gang wars we had; I usually was a leader, and my face was often bleeding from scratches, and my head full of bumps and bruises. People know what boys are up to, and from what I have told you, you can easily imagine what else I did during my schooldays."

CHAPTER 19: *Oliver as a student at Liège and his experiences there*

"AS MY FATHER'S WEALTH increased daily, there were more and more freeloaders and parasites around, who praised my intellectual abilities. They kept mum about my vices (or at least found excuses for them), for they rightly suspected that neither my father nor my mother wasted much friendship on anybody who did otherwise. So my parents took great joy in me and hired a private tutor to accompany me to Liège. I was sent there more to learn French than to engage in formal studies, for they wanted to make a merchant out of me and not a theologian. The tutor had orders not to be too strict with me, lest I develop a servile attitude. He was to introduce me to other students and see to it that I did not become shy or monklike, for they wanted me to develop into a man of the world who knows what's what.

"My tutor, being bent on all sorts of devilment himself, didn't need these directives. Why should he forbid me anything *he* was doing or reproach me for a small fault when he was to blame for greater ones? He was particularly fond of drinking and lewdness; I preferred fighting and scuffling. So we went roaming the streets together at night, he and his gang and I; and in a short time I learned more lechery than Latin from him. In my studies I relied on my good memory and native wit and let the work slide, but I was saturated with vices, roguery, and knavishness. Even then my conscience was so wide that a wagonload of hay could have passed through it. It caused me no qualms if, during the sermon in church, I read Berni's lewd love stories or Burchiello's comic poems or Aretino's licentious sonnets.[13] The words I liked best in all of the service were, 'Ite missa est.'[14]

"At this time I made a point of dressing in the latest fashion. Since every night was Mardi Gras for me, and since I carried on like a nobleman and spent not only my father's generous allowance but also the extra money my mother secretly sent me, the ladies were paying attention to us, particularly to my tutor. These females taught me to play around, to neck and pet. I had known how to fight before and my tutor did not keep me from gorging and guzzling, because he enjoyed it too. This jolly life lasted a year and a half before my father found out about it from his agent. The latter received orders to watch us more closely, to dismiss the tutor, to pull my reins tighter from now on, and to keep down my expenses. This discouraged us considerably, but though the tutor had been fired, the two of us still were together day and night. Since we couldn't spend so lavishly as before, we fell in with a gang that robbed people of their overcoats at night or even drowned them in the Meuse. What we picked up in this desperate way we squandered on our whores. Our studies were practically forgotten.

"One evening when, as usual, we were loitering about in order to snatch overcoats off students, we were pounced upon, my tutor was stabbed to death, and I was arrested along with five others who were regular thieves. The next day when we were questioned I mentioned my father's agent, who was a man of importance. He was summoned, and I was released on his bond, but until further notice I had to stay at his house under arrest. The tutor was buried; the other five were

[13] Francesco Berni (d. 1536), Burchiello (d. 1448), and Pietro Aretino (d. 1556) were Italian writers of humorous or licentious works.

[14] "Go now: Mass is over."

punished as thieves, robbers, and murderers. My father, who had been
sent a report on my troubles, hurried to Liège and smoothed over
everything with money. He lectured me on the distress I was causing
him and reproached me for driving my mother to the brink of despair
by my actions. Then he threatened to cut me off with a shilling and to
send me straight to hell if I didn't mend my ways. I promised to do
better and rode home with him. That was the end of my university
days."

CHAPTER 20: *The good student's return and farewell, and how he
sought advancement in the war*

"AFTER I HAD BEEN home a while, my father realized that I was
a rotten apple. I had not become a respectable gentleman, as he had
hoped, but a wise guy and a windbag who thought he knew it all. I had
hardly gotten warm at home when he said to me, 'Listen, Oliver, the
more I look at you the more I see you are a jackass. You are too old to
learn a trade, too impertinent to serve a master, and not good enough
to take over my business. All the money I have spent on you, and
what's become of you?! I hoped to make a man of you and be happy,
but I had to ransom you out of the hangman's hands. Oh, the shame of
it! Maybe I should put you in a treadmill until you sweat vinegar and
blood, or until your luck changes after you have done penance for your
sins.'

"I had to listen to such lectures every day, until I got tired of them
and told my father that I was not the only one to blame; it was his fault
and that of the tutor who had misled me. It was only fair for him to be
unhappy with me because his parents hadn't been happy with him
either, for he had practically let them go begging and starve to death.
He was about to reach for a stick to pay me for telling him the truth,
but instead he swore long and loud and said he'd send me to the
penitentiary in Amsterdam. This was more than I could take; that night
I went to a farm he had recently bought, watched for my chance, and
rode off to Cologne on the best stallion in his stable.

"I sold the horse and again joined a group of con men and thieves,
similar to the ones I had left behind in Liège. They recognized me at
once by the way I gambled, and I recognized them: both of us had the
professional touch. I joined their gang at once and helped them make
their nocturnal hauls wherever and whenever I could. But when, after
a while, one of us was caught in the Old Market relieving a noble old
lady of her heavy purse, and when I saw him standing for six hours in

the pillory with an iron collar around his neck, and his ear was cut off and he was whipped, I decided to change occupations and become a soldier. Our colonel, the one under whom we served at Magdeburg, was recruiting for his regiment, and I became one of his boys. Meanwhile, my father had found out where I had gone. He wrote his agent to get in touch with me, but when he did I had already taken the king's shilling. The agent reported this to my father, who ordered him to bail me out, no matter the price. When I heard that, I was afraid of the penitentiary again, and for once I did not care to be free. The moment my colonel found out I was a rich merchant's son, he raised the price so high that my father left me where I was. He thought he'd let me kick around in the wars and maybe I'd change for the better.

"It didn't take long for the colonel's clerk to kick the bucket, and I was asked to take his place, as you remember. At that time I raised my sights and hoped to advance step by step, perhaps to become a general. From the regimental secretary I learned how to behave, and my ambition to become important made me act like a man of honor and reputation — in contrast to my previous behavior. But I did not succeed very well until the secretary died. Then I tried to get his position: I spent money where I could, for when my mother found out that I was doing better, she secretly sent me money again. But because young Heartbrother was the colonel's favorite and was preferred, I tried to get him out of the way, particularly when I noticed that the colonel was about to give him the appointment. When I was not promoted, I became so impatient that I had myself made bulletproof by our provost so that I might provoke a duel with Heartbrother and dispatch him. But I could never find an acceptable way of getting at him. The provost was not in favor of my plan, either. 'If you get rid of him,' he said, 'it will hurt you more than it will help you, because you will have murdered the colonel's favorite man.' Instead, he suggested that I should steal something while Heartbrother was present and conceal it on him; then the provost would see to it that Heartbrother lost the colonel's goodwill. I followed this suggestion. At the christening I stole the colonel's gold-plated cup, gave it to the provost, and with it he got Heartbrother out of the way. You remember how, in the colonel's big tent, he made puppies crawl out of your clothes too."

CHAPTER 21: *How Simplicius fulfilled Heartbrother's prophecy about Oliver while neither recognized the other*

WHEN I HEARD OUT of Oliver's own dirty mouth how he had done in my best friend, I saw red. Yet, I could not take revenge and had to suppress my desire for it. I asked him to tell me how he had fared after the battle of Wittstock.

"In that engagement," said Oliver, "I acted not like an inkslinger who is only paid to write, but like a regular soldier. I was well mounted, absolutely bulletproof; and since I was not assigned to a squadron, I showed off my bravery as an individual who is determined to advance by his sword or die. I scurried about our brigade like a hurricane, partly in order to warm up, partly to show that I was better suited for fighting than for writing. But it didn't do any good. Luck ran in favor of the Swedes, and I had to share in the misfortune of our side, for I had to ask for quarter, which a little while ago I had not been willing to grant to anybody.

"So, like other prisoners of war, in order to recuperate I was shoved into an infantry regiment garrisoned in Pomerania. Since there were many new recruits and I gave indications of great courage, I was made a corporal. But I had no intention of sticking around. I wanted to get back to the imperials, whom I liked better, though I would have advanced faster with the Swedes. I arranged my escape this way: I was sent with seven musketeers in order to extract contributions in some of our out-of-the-way places. When I had received more than eight hundred florins, I showed the money to my men and aroused their desire for it. We agreed to divide it among ourselves and to go AWOL with it. When we had done so, I persuaded three of them to help me shoot the other four. Having killed them, we divided the loot — two hundred florins each. With this we started out for Westphalia. On the way I persuaded one of the three to help me kill the other two, and when we were supposed to divide the money once more, I garotted the last one. With this money I arrived safely at Werle, where I joined the army and lived the life of Riley.

"Although I wanted to continue to live high off the hog, my money was running low; then I heard a lot about a young soldier at Soest who was making wonderful booty and acquiring quite a reputation. I was encouraged to follow his example. On account of his green clothing they called him the Hunter. So I, too, had a green suit made for myself, and under his name I robbed and committed atrocities on our side as well as on his, so much so that both of us were about to be forbidden to go on raids. The other fellow stayed home, but I carried on in his name as much as I could. For this reason he challenged me, but — it would have required the devil to fight with him. (They told me the devil really was in him and showed in his hair.) In that case, how could I be sure of being bulletproof any more?

"But I was not able to escape the Hunter's wiles, for with the aid of a servant he got me and my fellows into a sheepfold where he tried to force me into a fist fight in the moonlight, with two real devils looking on. But because I wouldn't fight, they made me do the most disgraceful thing in the world. And when one of my friends spread the news of this occurrence, I was so ashamed that I took French leave and went to Lippstadt, where I let the Hessians recruit me. But since they didn't trust me I trundled on and joined the Dutch army. The pay was good, but their war was not my cup of tea; we were kept like monks and were supposed to live lives as chaste as nuns'.

"Since I dared not show my face among either the imperials or the Swedes or the Hessians — unless I wanted to get into trouble, having deserted from all of them — and since I could no longer stay with the Dutch because I had gotten a girl in trouble (having criminally assaulted her, an offense that would soon see the light of day), I thought I'd take refuge with the Spaniards. From them I hoped to go home and see what my parents were doing. But when I was about to do that, I got my directions mixed up and landed among the Bavarians. With them I marched among the Marauding Brothers from Westphalia to the Breisgau and lived on gambling and stealing. When I had something in my pocket I spent my days gambling, my nights in the taverns. When my pockets were empty I stole what I could lay hands on. Some days I rustled two or three horses, either from the pasture or out of the stables. I sold them and gambled away what I got for them. Then at night I'd slip into people's tents and relieve them of their most valuable possessions even if they had concealed them under their pillows. When we were marching I kept a sharp eye on the knapsacks that the soldiers' wives carried. In some narrow pass I'd cut these off their backs; and so I got along until the battle of Wittenweier. There I was taken prisoner, once more shoved into an infantry regiment, and thus made a Weimarer. But because I didn't like the camp at Breisach, I quit after a short time and went off to fight my own war, as you see me doing now. Let me assure you, brother, that I have laid to rest many a proud man. I have prospered with loads of money, and I don't intend to stop until I see there's nothing in it for me any more. And now it's your turn to tell me about your life."

CHAPTER 22: *What happens when a person has doggone and cat-gone bad luck*

WHEN OLIVER HAD FINISHED his story, I could not help marveling at Divine Providence. I saw how the good Lord not only had protected me like a father from this monster, while I was in Westphalia, but even had made him shun me in terror. Only now did I see what a trick I had played on Oliver. To be sure, old Heartbrother had foretold it; but Oliver had interpreted the prophecy differently, much to my advantage, as may be seen from chapter 16. For if this brute had known that I was the Hunter of Soest, he would have retaliated for what I had done to him in the sheepfold. I also considered how wisely and ambiguously Heartbrother had worded his prophecies, and I weighed in my mind the fact that it would be difficult for me to avenge the death of a man who deserved to die by hanging and the wheel, though Heartbrother's prophecies usually had come true. I also considered how healthy it had been for me not to tell him the story of my life first, for that way I myself would have told him how I had insulted him. While I was letting these thoughts run through my mind, I noticed on Oliver's face a number of scratches that he hadn't had at Magdeburg. I imagined that these scars were the marks made by Jump-up, when he, in the shape of a devil, had scratched Oliver's face. So I asked him where these scars came from, adding that I might infer by this omission he had withheld the best part of his life's story. He answered, "Alas, brother, if I were to tell you *all* my tricks and dirty dealings we'd both get bored. But in order to show you that I don't want to conceal anything from you, I'll tell you the truth, even though it seems the joke is on me in this case.

"I firmly believe that from my mother's womb on I was predestined to have a scarred face, for as a child other boys always scratched me when I fought with them. One of the devils attending the Hunter also scratched the hell out of my face; I felt his claws for more than six weeks! But all that healed up nicely. The stripes you see now have a different origin. When I was still with the Swedes in Pomerania, I had a pretty mistress. I made my landlord and his wife give up their bed so we could lie in it. But the cat, which also used to sleep there, came every night and bothered us no end. She didn't want to give up her regular place so easily as the bed's owners had donne. This made my mistress so mad — she couldn't stand cats anyway — that she swore she wouldn't do a thing for me until I got rid of that cat. I wanted to enjoy her favors a while longer, and by pleasing her I wanted to get even with the cat, but in such a way that I'd have a little fun along with it. So I put the cat in a sack, called my landlord's two sturdy dogs (they did not like the cat, either), and went to an open pasture for a bit of amusement. I thought the dogs would chase the cat around in the pasture like a rabbit; there was no tree to which she could retreat, and this would be fun to watch. But dammit! My luck was not only doggone bad (as they say) but even cat-gone lousy (as they would say if more people had had my experience). When I opened the sack, the cat saw only the open field with two strong enemies and no high place to which to retreat for safety. That was no reason for the cat to give up and have her skin shredded. She took to my head, that being the highest place far or near. When I tried to remove her I lost my hat, and the harder I tried to drag her off, the more firmly she fastened her claws in me to hold on. The dogs couldn't look on idly for long. They too got into the act, and with open jaws they jumped at me to get at the cat — in front, behind, and on the sides. The feline did not care to budge; she hung on as best she could by clawing into my face or any other part of my head. And if by chance she took a swipe at a dog with her thorny-gloved arm, I got *that* for sure, too. Since occasionally she also hit the noses of the dogs, they tried their best to paw her down with their front legs, and that way I got many unfriendly pawings in the face. When I tried to reach for her with my hands to get her down, she bit and scratched for all she was worth. So the cat and the dogs together waged war on me, scratching and abusing me so frightfully that I hardly resembled a human being any more. But worst of all was the danger of splitting my nose or an ear, or losing it, when the dogs were snapping at the cat. My collar and coat looked as bloody as a blacksmith's stall when he is bleeding horses on St. Stephen's Day. I had to think up something altogether new to get out of this fix. Finally I dropped to the ground so that the dogs could get at the cat and my fine head would no longer be a battleground. To be sure, the dogs strangled the cat, but I did not have half the fun I had hoped for, only mockery and a face like the one you are looking at. I was so mad I shot both dogs and beat up my mistress, who had caused all this foolishness. She left me, probably because she could no longer love my mask of a face."

CHAPTER 23: *An example of the trade that Oliver plied, of which he was the past master, and to which Simplicius was to be apprenticed*

I WOULD HAVE BEEN glad to laugh at this story of Oliver's; yet I had to express my sympathy. Just as I was beginning to tell him the story of my life, we saw a coach accompanied by two horsemen coming up the road. So we descended from the steeple and sat down in a house that was close to the road and very convenient for attacking passers-by. I kept my loaded gun in reserve, but before they even noticed us Oliver had killed a horseman and his horse with one shot. The other horseman immediately fled, and while I, with my gun cocked, made the coach-man stop and get down, Oliver jumped on him with his broad sword and split his head down to the teeth. Right after that he wanted to cut down the women and children who were traveling in the coach and who already looked more like corpses than living human beings; but I absolutely wouldn't let him and told him if he wanted to do it, he would have to strangle me first. "Ah, you foolish Simpli!" he said. "I would never have believed that you are as hopeless as you let on." I answered him, "Brother, why do you want to butcher innocent children? If they were men who could defend themselves, that would be something else." "Hoity-toity!" he said. "Scramble the eggs and they won't hatch. I know these young blood suckers well enough. Their father, a major, is a regular slave driver and the worst tyrant in the world." After these words he was about to murder some more, but I kept him from it until he finally gave in. There were a major's wife, her maids, and three pretty children whom I pities with all my heart. To prevent them from giving us away, we locked them in a cellar where there was nothing to eat except some dried fruit and turnips. We were hoping somebody else would let them out. Then we looted the coach and with seven beautiful horses rode off into the thickest part of the woods.

When we had tied them up and I was looking around a little, I saw someone standing rigid as a pikestaff by a tree not far off. I pointed him out to Oliver and wondered if we hadn't better look out. "Stupid!" he said. "That's a Jew; I tied him to the tree, but the bum croaked recently and now he's frozen stiff." He went over to him, patted his chin, and said, "Ha! You old dog, you brought me many nice ducats!" And when he moved the jaw of the corpse, several doubloons dropped out of his mouth. The poor fellow had tried to hold on to them even after death. Then Oliver reached into his mouth and fished out twelve more doubloons and a precious ruby. "Simpli," he said, "I owe this booty to you." And he gave me the ruby, while he pocketed the money and went to get the peasant. He told me to watch the horses and not to let the dead Jew bite me. That was his way of telling me that he had more courage than I.

While he was away, I worried about the dangerous situation in which I was living. I decided to take one of the horses and be gone, but I was afraid Oliver would catch me in the act and shoot me, for I figured that this time he was only testing my good faith and was standing by to watch me. Then I thought I'd run off on foot, but I had to consider that I could not escape the peasants in the Black Forest (who had, at that time, the reputation of being hard on soldiers), even if I got away from Oliver. 'If you take all the horses,' I thought, 'so that Oliver has no means of pursuing you, and if you are caught by the Weimar troops, then you will be broken on the wheel as a convicted murderer.' In short, I had no assurance of getting away, particularly as I was in a wild forest where I knew neither the highway nor the trails. Then my conscience began to bother me because I had held up the coach and been a cause of the coachman's pitiful death, and also a cause that the women and innocent children had been locked in the cellar, where they might starve and perish, like the Jew. In turn I tried to console myself with my innocence, saying that I was being held by Oliver against my will. But my conscience reproached me: for the evil deeds previously committed, this inveterate murderer and I deserved being delivered into the hands of justice. Now I'd get my due reward, and perhaps it was God's just will to have me punished in this way. Finally, having regained some measure of confidence and hope, I prayed to God in his kindness to deliver me from this troublesome situation; and when this pious mood came over me, I said to myself, 'You fool, you are not tied down or locked up. The whole wide world is open to you. Don't you have horses enough for flight? Or if you don't care to ride, your legs will carry you away quickly enough.'

While I was still in doubt and torment and could reach no decision, Oliver and our peasant came along. He took us to a farm where we fed the horses and took turns sleeping for a few hours. After midnight we rode on and by noon we reached the Swiss border, where Oliver was well known, and where we had a big meal served. While we were enjoying it, the innkeeper sent for two Jews, who bought the horses for something like half their value. Everything was arranged so neatly and precisely that few words were exchanged. The horse-traders' biggest question was whether the horses had been imperial or Swedish. When they heard they came from the army of Weimar, they said, "We have to take them to Swabia for the Bavarians, not to Basel." I was amazed at their easy familiarity with these things.

We had a royal banquet and I greatly enjoyed the fresh trout and excellent crayfish. When dusk came we started back. Our peasant was loaded like a donkey with roast meat and other food. So we arrived next day at a single farmstead where we were welcomed and put up in a friendly way. Because of a storm we stayed a few days. After that, having used lonely roads through the woods, we reached the same little house where Oliver had taken me when I first met him.

CHAPTER 24: *Oliver bites the dust, and so do six more*

WHILE WE WERE SITTING there feeding our faces and resting, Oliver sent out the peasant to buy food, shot, and powder. When he had left, Oliver took off his coat and said to me, "Brother, I don't care to haul all this damned money around with me any longer." So he untied a couple of rolls or sausages of it, which he was carrying on his bare body, threw them on the table, and continued, "You will have to trouble yourself with this until I quit the business, and then both of us will have enough. The cockeyed money has chafed and galled me." I replied, "Brother, if you had as little as I, it would not irritate you." "What?" he interrupted. "What's mine is yours; and whatever we take in from now on, we'll divide fifty-fifty." I picked up both rolls and found them good and heavy, for the coin was solid gold. I told him it was not so well packed as it might be, and if he liked, I would sew it up in such a way that wearing it would be little or no trouble. When he agreed, I went with him to a hollow oak tree where he kept scissors, needle, and thread; and from a pair of trousers I made a scapular or shoulder garment for each of us and sewed up many a gold penny in it. And since we wore the scapulars under our shirts, it was just as if we were armed with gold in front and back. When I wondered why he had no silver coin, he answered that he had more than a thousand thalers deposited in a tree. From this he let the peasant pay the household expenses and never asked for an accounting, because he placed no value on such sheep droppings.

The money having all been sewn up, we went to our lodgings and cooked all night and stretched out in the warmth of the stove. About an hour after daybreak, when we were least prepared, six musketeers with their corporal came into the hut, their guns cocked and ready to fire. They burst through the door and shouted for us to surrender. But Oliver (who, like me, had his musket always ready for action and his sharp sword by his side — he was sitting behind the table, while I stood behind the door by the stove) answered them with a couple of bullets that knocked down two of the men. I got the third one and wounded the fourth with another shot. Then Oliver whipped out his trusty sword which was as sharp as a razor and could be compared to Caliburn,[15] King Arthur's sword in England) and split the fifth man from shoulder to belly so that his entrails spilled and he dropped down

---

[15] *Caliburnus* is the medieval Latin form of the name of King Arthur's sword; in English it is known as *Excalibur*.

next to them. Meanwhile I hit the sixth over the head with the butt of my gun, so *he* didn't move much any more. But Oliver received the same kind of blow from the seventh. The blow was so severe that Oliver's brain was splattered all over, but I returned the favor in kind, and so number seven joined his comrades in the dance of death. When the man whom I had in the beginning injured with a shot noticed these blows and saw that I was coming at him with the butt of my gun, he threw his musket away and started running as if all hell were after him. The whole skirmish took no longer than it takes to say the Lord's Prayer; in this short space of time seven brave soldiers bit the dust.

Seeing that I was the master of the field and the sole survivor I checked Oliver to see if there might still be life in him. When I found him completely without breath, it seemed downright foolish to leave all that gold on a body that couldn't make use of it. So I skinned off the gold jacket that I had finished only last night and put it on over my own. Because I had broken my musket, I picked up Oliver's; I also appropriated his sword in case an emergency might arise. Then I decamped by the road along which our peasant would have to return. I sat down in a quiet place to wait for him and to consider what to do next.

CHAPTER 25: *Simplicius comes out rich, but Heartbrother shows up as a pitiful specimen of mankind*

I HAD NOT BEEN waiting half an hour when the peasant came toward me, running and wheezing like a bear. He did not notice me until he was close upon me. "What's the hurry? What's up?" I said. He answered, "Get out of here quick! A corporal and six musketeers are coming to raid the place. They have orders to bring you and Oliver dead or alive to Lichteneck. They caught me in order to use me as a guide, but I managed to break away. I am warning you." I thought at once that the rogue had squealed on us, in order to get the money Oliver kept in the hollow tree. But I did not let on that I suspected anything, for I wanted him to show me the way. I told him that Oliver and the party of soldiers that were supposed to capture him were dead. But when the peasant did not want to believe it, I took the trouble to go back with him and let him see the awful sight of seven corpses. "The seventh soldier," I told him, "I let escape, and I wish to God I could bring these back to life." The peasant turned white with fear and asked me what to do. I said, "My mind is made up. You have a choice of three alternatives: either you take me by safe trails out of the forest to

Villingen; or you show me Oliver's money that's hidden in the tree; or you die here and keep these present corpses company. If you take me to Villingen, you can keep Oliver's money for yourself; if you show me the money, I'll divide it with you; if you do neither, I'll shoot you and go where I please." The peasant would have liked to run off, but he was afraid of my musket. So he fell on his knees and asked to guide me out of the woods. We started at once and hurried on that day and all the following night, which, as luck would have it, was bright; nor did we stop for food and drink or for rest, until toward daybreak we saw the town of Villingen before us; and there I dismissed the peasant. His reason to hurry was fear of death; mine, the desire to get out of there with my money. I can almost believe that gold gives a man great strength, as they say, for though it was heavy enough to carry, I did not feel especially tired.

I took it for a good omen that when I reached Villingen the gates were just being opened. The officer of the watch looked me over, and when he heard that I was a volunteer trooper of the same regiment to which Heartbrother had appointed me while he was at Philippsburg, and that I was coming from Weimar's camp at Breisach (by whose men I had been captured at Wittenweier and made to serve), and that now I wanted to get back to my regiment among the Bavarians, he assigned me a musketeer and had me taken to the commander. He was still asleep, for military concerns had kept him awake more than half the night, and I had to wait about an hour and a half in front of his quarters. The people just returning from early Mass crowded around me, and civilians and soldiers wanted to know how things were going at Breisach. The noise awakened the commander, and he ordered me to come in.

He started to question me and I answered just as I had done at the city gate. Later he asked me about some special points concerning the siege, and I confessed everything; how I had stayed about two weeks with a fellow who had also deserted; how he had held up and robbed a coach, hoping we'd get enough booty from the Weimarers to buy mounts, in order to return well equipped to our regiments; but we had been surprised and attacked by a corporal and six men sent to arrest us; how my comrade and six enemies had been killed; how the seventh had escaped as well as I; and how each had gone to his own party. But I said nothing about having intended to go home to my wife in Westphalia or about my wearing the two well-padded scapulars; nor did it bother my conscience to conceal this information, for it was none of his business. He didn't even ask about it, but he was amazed and almost wouldn't believe that Oliver and I had slain six men and chased off the seventh, though my partner had not survived. In this conversation I had occasion to mention Oliver's sword, which I praised and carried with me. He liked it so well that I had to give it to him in exchange for another, because I wanted to get out of there with a passport.

When he dismissed me (having ordered a passport made out for me), I went to the nearest inn, but I did not know whether to sleep or eat first. I needed to do both. I decided to appease my stomach first and ordered something to eat and a drink. Then I worried about how to arrange matters in order to get safely back to my wife in Lippstadt with all my money, for I intended as little to find my regiment as to break my neck.

While I was thinking about this, a fellow came limping into the room; he walked with a stick, his head was bandaged, one arm was in a sling, and the clothes he wore were so ragged that I would not have given him a penny for the lot. Immediately on seeing him, the waiter wanted to kick him out because he smelled bad and there were enough lice crawling on him to populate the Swabian moors. The fellow begged to be allowed, for God's sake, to warm himself a little, but he got nowhere with the waiter. When I took pity and put in a good word for him, he was grudgingly allowed to sit by the stove. It seemed to me he was watching me with great appetite and devotion while I was tackling my meal. He let out a sigh or two, and when the waiter went out to get me a piece of roast, he sidled up to my table and extended a little earthenware penny-pot, so that I could easily imagine why he had come. I took his pot and filled it from my jug of wine before he had a chance to ask. "Oh, my friend," he said, "for Heartbrother's sake, give me something to eat, too." When he said that, I felt a stab in my heart and I knew it was Heartbrother himself. I almost fainted when I saw him in such misery; but I managed to embrace him, asked him to sit with me, and then we both started crying, I for pity, and he for joy.

CHAPTER 26: *The last chapter in this book, for none follows after*

OUR UNEXPECTED REUNION ALMOST took away our appetites; each only asked how the other had been doing since our last meeting. But since the innkeeper and the waiter were constantly coming and going, we could tell each other nothing of a confidential, private nature. The innkeeper was surprised that I put up with this lousy individual, but I told him that in wartime this was the custom among honest soldiers and comrades in arms. When I found out that Heartbrother had been staying in the poorhouse, was now living on hand-outs, and that his wounds were badly cared for, I rented a separate room in the inn, put Heartbrother to bed, and sent for the best local surgeon. I also let a seamstress and a tailor dress him properly and thus snatch him from the jaws of the lice. In my purse I happened to have the doubloons that Oliver had knocked out of the dead Jew's mouth. I threw them on the table, and within hearing of the innkeeper I said to Heartbrother, "Look, brother, this is my money. I'll spend it on you; we'll use it up together." That made the innkeeper more attentive. I showed the barber-surgeon the ruby, which also came from the Jew and which was worth about twenty thalers, and told him he could have it if he would cure my friend completely. He was satisfied and went to work diligently.

So I cared for Heartbrother like for my other self and had a plain suit of grey cloth made for him. But first I went to the commanding officer on account of the passport. I told him I had met a badly injured comrade from the same regiment and wanted to wait until he had completely recovered; with due regard for my regiment, I did not want the responsibility of leaving him behind. The commander praised my loyalty and gave me permission to stay as long as I wished, and he offered to give each of us a valid passport as soon as my friend could travel.

When I returned to Heartbrother and sat with him at his bedside, I asked him to tell me frankly how he happened to have met with such a sorry fate. I imagined that he might have lost his former position of dignity on account of some important cause or omission. But he said, "Brother, you know I was Count von Götz's factotum and his dearest, most intimate friend. On the other hand, you also know well what rotten luck he had in his last campaign. Not only did we lose the battle of Wittenweier, but we couldn't raise the siege of Breisach either. Since on this account there is all manner of nasty talk going around (especially now that Count von Götz has been summoned to Vienna to answer charges), I voluntarily live in this humble state, partly from shame and partly from fear. Often I wish I could die in this misery, or at least keep myself concealed until the count's innocence has been proven. As far as I know, he has always been loyal to the Holy Roman Emperor. And I imagine the absence of good luck last summer is to be attributed to Divine Providence (that parcels out victories where it pleases) rather than to the count's incompetence.

"When we tried to relieve Breisach and I saw that on our side everything was done listlessly, I armed myself and proceeded to the pontoon bridge as if I expected to finish the job all by myself; and yet, at that time, it was neither my responsibility nor my duty. I did it as an example for the others and because we had achieved nothing all summer. My luck (or rather misfortune) had it that I was one of the first men on the bridge to see the whites of the enemy's eyes. There was heavy fighting, and as I had been among the first to attack, I became one of the last when we could not resist the violent attacks of the French.[16] I fell into the hands of the enemy, and I was shot once in the right arm, and again in the thigh, so that I could neither run away nor use my sword any more. And since the narrowness of the place and the heat of the skirmish did not permit much talk about giving or receiving quarter, I took a blow on the head that sent me sprawling to the ground. Being well dressed, I was robbed of my clothes and thrown into the Rhine for dead. In this trouble I cried to God and left all to His holy will, and after making several vows, I received His help. The Rhine washed me ashore, where I stanched my bleeding wounds with moss. And though I nearly froze to death, still I felt in myself a strange strength that made me crawl away. With God's help — though I was badly wounded — I reached some Marauding Brothers and soldiers' wives who took pity on me although I was a complete stranger to them. They all despaired of the relief of Breisach, and that hurt me worse than my wounds. They dressed and refreshed me near their fire, and before I could bandage my wounds, I saw that our people were preparing for a shameful retreat and giving up their cause for lost. This hurt me so much that I resolved to tell no one who I was, lest I incur mockery. For this reason I joined some wounded men of our army, who had a surgeon with them. I gave him a gold cross, which was still around my neck, and for that he has bandaged my wounds until now.

"Dear Simpli, this is the miserable life I've had to live. Nor do I intend to reveal my identity until after Count von Götz's difficulties have been resolved. Your kindheartedness and faithfulness have been a great consolation to me; they are a sign that God has not yet forsaken me. When I came from early Mass this morning and saw you standing in front of the commander's quarters, I imagined that God had sent you instead of an angel to help me in my poverty." I consoled Heartbrother all I could and confided to him that I had even more money than the doubloons he had seen and that all of it was at his service. Then I told him of Oliver's death and how I had been forced to avenge it. This so revived his spirit that his body also benefited, for every day his wounds got better.

End of the Fourth Book

---

[16] Shortly after the death in 1632 of Gustavus Adolphus of Sweden, the French, under policies devised by Richelieu, entered the Thirty Years' War on the side of the Protestants.

Stultorum
imaginatio
et
Probatio.

Schau deß Simplex
Albertäten.
Zu getraifst mit Hasen-
Schröten
In Gebärden, Thun, ü.
Reden.

Book Five

CHAPTER 1: *How Simplicius becomes a pilgrim, and how he goes on a pilgrimage with Heartbrother*

After Heartbrother had regained his strength and his wounds were healed, he confided to me that in his deadly peril he had vowed to make a pilgrimage to Our Lady of Einsiedeln. Because he was so close to Switzerland, he wanted to make it now, even if he had to do it by begging along the way. This was music to my ears, and I offered him my money and company; in fact, I wanted to buy two nags and make the trip on horseback. Of course, it wasn't devotion that impelled me; I wanted to see the Swiss Confederation,[1] because it was the only country still inhabited by beloved peace. Then, too, I was glad of the chance to wait on Heartbrother during this trip, for I loved him almost more than myself. But he turned down my help and my company, saying that his pilgrimage had to be made on foot and with peas in his shoes. If I were his companion, I would not only prevent his devotion but also expose myself to a lot of discomfort on account of his slow and laborious gait. He said this only to rebuff me, because to live during such a pious trip on money gained by robbery and murder was against his conscience. Furthermore, he did not want to involve me in too much expense, and he told me frankly that I had already done more for him than I owed him, or than he could hope to repay. At this point we got into a friendly disagreement, which was so pleasant that I have never heard such a sweet argument. Each merely reminded the other that he had not yet given all that friendship demanded — had not, in fact, half repaid the other's favors. But this

---

[1] Switzerland, though in 1639 still part of the Holy Roman Empire and thus technically under Habsburg rule, had enjoyed increasing independence from the late 13th century on. Amazingly the Swiss Confederation had been spared armed conflicts associated with the Reformation and even now was prosperous and at peace. Complete independence came with the Peace of Westphalia in 1648.

Einsiedeln is a renowned place of pilgrimage in the canton of Schwyz.

exchange did not move him to put up with me on the pilgrimage. Finally I realized that Oliver's money and my godless life were equally disgusting to him. So I lied a little, telling him that a desire to lead a better life prompted me to go to Einsiedeln. If he were to keep me from this good work, and I were to die, he would hardly be able to answer for it. My arguments persuaded him to let me visit the holy place in his company, particularly when I displayed great remorse (also a lie) about my past life and told him that I, too, had imposed on myself the penance of walking to Einsiedeln with peas in both shoes.

This dispute had hardly ended when a new one arose, for Heartbrother was too scrupulous; he objected to my asking the commander for a passport made out to my regiment. "What?" he said. "Don't we intend to become better Christians by journeying to Einsiedeln? And you want to start out with a falsehood; you want to pull the wool over people's eyes? If all the martyrs and witnesses of Christ had done that, there would be few saints in heaven. Let us, in God's name and under His protection, go where our pious intention and desire call us. God will lead us where our souls will find peace." I rebuked him, saying that it was prudent not to tempt God but to go with the times and make use of the inevitable, especially since making pilgrimages was an unusual activity among soldiers; that if we told of our journey, we would be treated as deserters rather than as pilgrims; and that this would plunge us into trouble and danger; and that the Apostle Paul (to whom we could not well compare ourselves) had made wondrous use of the customs of his time. Heartbrother finally allowed me to get a passport for traveling to my regiment. With this document and a reliable guide we left town, just as the gate was being locked, and started out for Rottweil. After a short distance we turned into byways and crossed the Swiss border that night. Next morning in a village we equipped ourselves with long, black coats, pilgrim's staves, and rosaries; and having paid the guide well, we sent him back.

In comparison with other German lands, the country appeared very strange to me — as if I were in Brazil or China. I saw country people trading and going about their business in peace. The barns were full of cattle; in the farmyards chickens, geese, and ducks were plentiful; the roads were safe and used by many travelers; in the taverns sat customers who enjoyed life. Nowhere was there fear of the enemy, no terror of looting, and no anxiety of losing one's goods, life, or limb. Everyone lived securely under his vines and fig trees and — unlike other German districts — in pure joy and delight, so that I considered this country an earthly paradise, though by nature it was harsh enough. All along the way I did nothing but gape, while Heartbrother counted his beads. For this he reproached me; he wanted me to pray continuously, but I couldn't get used to it.

In Zurich he found me out and very smartly told me off. At Schaffhausen, where we stayed overnight, my feet hurt badly from the peas. Next morning I was reluctant to walk on peas again, and I had them boiled and put back into my shoes; and that's how I got to Zurich without sore feet. But my friend acted very nasty and said to me, "Brother, by the great grace of God you have walked well in your shoes despite the peas." "Yes," I replied, "my dear and honored Heartbrother, I had them boiled. Otherwise I couldn't have done so well." "Alas," he answered, "may God have pity on you. What have you done? It would have been better to forget your vow entirely than to make a mockery of it. Forgive me, brother, for using plain language with you and telling you in brotherly love that the salvation of your soul is in utter jeopardy unless you change your ways before God. I gladly confess and speak the truth when I say that I love no one in the world more than you. But I also do not deny that unless you change, continuing that love would burden my conscience." I was struck dumb and could not recover my breath for a while. Finally I openly confessed that I had not placed the peas in my shoes from devotion but only to please him, so that he would take me along on this trip. "Alas, brother," he said, "I see you are a long way from holiness, peas or no peas. May God help you to improve, for otherwise our friendship cannot endure."

From this point on, I followed sadly after him, like one being led to the gallows. My conscience started bothering me, and I thought of all the mean tricks I had ever played on anyone in my life. It was then that I first lamented the loss of that innocence which I had brought with me out of the woods and which I had frittered away on so many occasions. My sorrow was increased by the fact that Heartbrother would no longer talk much with me. He only looked at me and sighed, and that struck me as if he knew I was damned, and pitied me.

CHAPTER 2: *After being frightened by the devil, Simplicius gets religion*

WE ARRIVED IN EINSIEDELN and entered the church just as a priest was exorcising a man possessed by an evil spirit. That was new and strange to me. So I let Heartbrother kneel and pray all he wanted, and I went over to watch this sight. I had hardly approached when the spirit cried out of the poor man, "Oh-ho, my friend, does bad luck bring you here? I thought I'd find you with Oliver, at home in hell, when I got back; but I see you are here, you adulterous, murderous whoremonger. You think you can escape us? Oh, you priests, do not accept him; he is a hypocrite and a worse liar than I. He is only fooling himself and making a mockery of God and religion." The priest ordered the spirit to be silent because he was an archliar and would not be believed.

"Yes, indeed," he answered, "just ask this runaway monk's traveling companion. He will tell you that this atheist did not shrink from boiling the peas on which he promised to walk here." When I heard this and everybody looked at me, I didn't know which way my head was screwed on. But the exorcist punished the spirit and made him cower in silence; yet he could not drive him out that day. Meanwhile Heartbrother came over, just when I looked more like a corpse than a live person and was so terrified that, between hope and despair, I did not know what to do with myself. Heartbrother comforted me as best he could and assured the bystanders (and especially the fathers) that I had never been a monk but rather was a soldier who had probably done more good than evil. He added that the devil was a liar who had exaggerated the incident of the peas far beyond what it was. I myself was so bewildered that I already seemed to feel the pain of hell upon me, and the priests had quite a time calming me. They advised me to go to confession and communion, but once more the evil spirit cried from the man possessed, "Take heed, he will make a fine confession. He does not even know what confession is. And what will you do with him? He is a heretic and belongs to us. His parents were Anabaptists, not Calvinists," and so on. The exorcist again ordered the spirit to be still and said to him, "It will annoy you all the more then if this poor lost lamb is snatched out of your jaws and numbered among the flock of Christ." Hearing this, the spirit started to roar so savagely that it was terrifying to hear him. Yet I derived my greatest comfort from this repulsive outcry, for I thought the devil would not rant so if I had already lost God's grace.

Though I was not at that time prepared for confession (it had never entered my mind until then, and I had always been as afraid of it as the devil is of the holy cross), still I felt such remorse about my sins, such a desire to do penance and to improve my vicious and godless life, that I asked for a father confessor. Heartbrother was altogether glad at this sudden conversion and improvement, for he knew that so far I had not joined any church. There and then I publicly embraced the Catholic faith, went to confession, and after absolution partook of the Eucharist. After this I felt so relieved and easy about my heart that I cannot express it. The most remarkable thing, however, was that henceforth the spirit in the possessed man left me in peace, though before confession and absolution he had reproached me specifically with various misdeeds, so that I suspected he had been ordered to do nothing but observe and record my sins. But, he being a liar, the bystanders did not believe him, particularly because my honorable pilgrim's garb presented me in quite a different light.

We spent all of two weeks in this town, which abounded in grace; I thanked God for my conversion and looked at the miracles that had taken place there. All of this induced in me a mood of considerable reverence and piety. But it lasted only a short while, for since my conversion had not sprung from a love of God but rather from fear and dread of damnation, by and by I turned lax and lukewarm, because I gradually forgot the terror with which the fiend had struck me. After we had sufficiently looked at the relics of the saints, the vestments and other sights of the church, we went on to Baden to spend the rest of the winter there.

CHAPTER 3: *How the two friends spent the winter*

THERE I RENTED A cheerful parlor and bedroom, which in the summer were usually occupied by visitors to the baths, mostly rich Swiss who go there more to show off and have a good time than to improve their health. I also arranged for our board, and when Heartbrother saw that I was living it up, he advised me to be economical and reminded me of the long winter ahead of us. He was afraid my money would not last: I might need my resources in the spring when we had to leave; even a large sum of money would soon be gone if a person only spent it and added nothing to it. Money disappeared like smoke, he said, and so on. After such well-meaning counsel I could no longer conceal from Heartbrother how well-lined my pockets were. I also told him that I wanted to spend the money for our benefit, especially since I had acquired it in a way so unworthy of God's blessing that I did not intend to buy a farm with it. And even though I did not want to invest it just to entertain my dearest friend on earth, it was only fair that he, Heartbrother, enjoyed Oliver's money, in order to make up for the disgrace he had suffered from Oliver at Magdeburg. And because I knew we were in a safe place, I peeled off both my scapulars, took out the ducats and pistoles, and told Heartbrother that all this money was at his disposal; he should invest it or spend it as he thought might profit us best.

When he realized that, along with my trust in him, I had so much money that I could have been quite an important person regardless of him, he said, "Brother, as long as I've known you, you have done nothing but to show me your love and trust. How can I ever repay you? It is not only money with which you put me under obligation — that might in time be repaid, perhaps; it is your love and trust and especially your absolute confidence in me, all of which are beyond material values. I blush for shame that I would never trust a person as much as you have trusted me. I assure you, brother, that this proof of your true friendship binds me to you more than to a rich man who might give me thousands. However, I beg you, brother, yourself to stay the master, keeper, and disburser of your money. For me, it is enough to have you as my friend." My answer was, "What strange words are these, dear Heartbrother? You assure me with words that you are obliged to me; yet you warn me not to spend our money for nothing." And so we talked back and forth — foolishly, almost, for each was intoxicated with love for the other. And Heartbrother became simultaneously my steward, treasurer, servant, and master. During this leisurely time he told me of his life: how he had become know to Count von Götz and how he had been advanced. Then I told him how I had fared since his late father died. Until now we had never taken the time to do this. And when he heard that I had a young wife in Lippstadt he reproached me for running off to Switzerland with him instead of going to her first, as was my duty. My excuse was that I could not have left him, my very dearest friend, alone in such utter misery. He persuaded me to write my wife and let her know that I would come to her at the earliest opportunity. I wrote and begged her pardon for not returning earlier: all sorts of untoward events prevented me, though I had wanted to come back before this.

Now when Heartbrother found out from the newsletters[2] that Count von Götz was doing well — particularly, that he would succeed in vindicating himself before his imperial majesty, would be released, and would even get back the command of an army — he wrote to Vienna concerning himself, sent for his equipment, which was still with the Bavarian army, and began to hope that his own luck would improve. On account of these developments we decided to part next spring, he to go to his count, and I to my wife in Lippstadt. In order not to spend the winter idly, we learned from an engineer to build — on paper — more fortresses than the kings of Spain and France combined could

---

[2] Newsletters, the forerunners of newspapers, were printed publications for the dissemination of newsworthy events.

have erected. Furthermore, I got acquainted with some alchemists who suspected that I had money and wanted to teach me how to make gold, if only I'd pay for the start-up expenses. I think they would have talked me into it if Heartbrother had not shown them the door. He said that whoever knew *that* art wasn't likely to go around like a beggar asking others for money.

Though Heartbrother received a favorable reply and excellent promises from his count in Vienna, I never got a single line from Lippstadt, though on some mail days I sent off letters in duplicate. That infuriated me so much that I did not start out on my journey to Westphalia in the spring. I got Heartbrother's permission to go with him to Vienna, where I would join in his expected good fortune. So with my money we equipped ourselves like cavaliers, with clothes, horses, servants, and weapons, and proceeded by way of Constance to Ulm, where we took a boat on the Danube and after a week safely reached Vienna. On the way I did not observe much except that the women who lived along the banks did not answer the oral greeting of passers-by in kind, but rather gave them visual proof of their femininity by hoisting their skirts. That way a fellow gained much deep and valuable insight.

CHAPTER 4: *How Heartbrother and Simplicius enter the war once more, and how they get out of it again*

STRANGE THINGS HAPPEN IN this changeable world. They say that a man who knew everything would soon be rich. I say that the man who could always adjust to the times would soon be great and powerful. Many a skinflint or curmudgeon — these titles are bestowed on misers — soon gets rich because he knows how to use one or two advantages. But for that reason he is not great; rather, he receives (and will always receive) less respect than he had when he was poor. On the other hand, riches closely follow the man who knows how to make himself great and powerful. Fortune, which is accustomed to granting might and riches, looked at me with a winsome smile, and after we had been in Vienna for a week, she gave me several chances to climb up the ladder of importance. But I didn't do it. Why? I suppose because my fate had decided on something else, namely, that to which my fatuousness led me.

Count von der Wahl, under whose command I had previously distinguished myself in Westphalia, happened to be in Vienna when

Heartbrother and I arrived. He was having a banquet with Count von Götz, several important councilors, and others, when the conversation turned to all sorts of unusual characters, soldiers, and famous raiders. They mentioned the Hunter of Soest, and several of his daring exploits were so well told that some were amazed that so young a fellow could have achieved them. Others deplored the fact that the sly Hessian colonel, de St. André, had framed him with a wife so that he would have either to lay aside his sword or to join the Swedish army. Count von der Wahl said he had found out how the colonel had tricked me. My beloved Heartbrother, who happened to be present and who wanted very much to see me advance, requested permission to speak. He said he knew the Hunter of Soest better than any other person on earth. The Hunter was, he continued, not only a good soldier, used to the smell of powder, but also a good horseman, a perfect swordsman, an expert in artillery and musketry, and, in addition, one who rivaled any engineer in building fortifications. He had left behind in Lippstadt not only his wife (with whom he had been so shamefully saddled), but also everything he owned, and had sought imperial service again; for in the last campaign he had been under the command of Count von Götz, and when captured by Weimarers, he had wanted to return to the imperials. He and his friend had killed a corporal and six musketeers who had pursued them in order to bring them back; he had made excellent booty and was now in Vienna and willing to take up arms once more against the enemies of His Imperial Majesty, but only under conditions commensurate with his reputation, for he no longer wanted to serve as a common soldier.

By that time, those present were so inspired with drink that they wanted to satisfy their curiosity by taking a look at the Hunter, and Heartbrother was sent out by coach to go and get me. On the way he instructed me how to behave in the presence of these illustrious men, for my advancement and future depended on it. When I arrived, I answered their questions briefly and to the point, so that they began to take notice of me as one who only spoke what was necessary and who used emphasis in a clever way when he did speak. To put it in a nutshell, I made a pleasant impression on everybody, and besides, Count von der Wahl had already praised me as a good soldier. After a while I got tipsy too, and perhaps in that condition I showed how little I really knew of life at court. The upshot of it all was that an infantry colonel promised me a company in his regiment, and I didn't refuse. I thought, 'To be a captain, that's something.' But the next day Heartbrother rebuked me for being too easily pleased; if I had held out I could have bettered my rank.

And so I was presented as their captain to a company which, though complete in its officers (including me), counted no more than seven soldiers for sentry duty. My NCOs were for the most part such decrepit old codgers that I could only wonder and scratch myself behind the ears. So, in the next engagement (in which Count von Götz lost his life[3] and Heartbrother's testicles were shot away), we were miserably beaten, though I was only slightly wounded in the thigh. For a cure and recovery we went to Vienna, where, incidentally, I had deposited my money. Besides our wounds, which healed soon enough, Heartbrother found himself in a dangerous condition, which the doctors could not diagnose at first: he became paralyzed in his extremities, like a choleric person who is bothered by his gall. And yet he was not in the least inclined to that complexion, nor to being angry. Still, he was advised to take the waters, particularly those at Griesbach in the Black Forest.

This is how our luck changed overnight. Only recently Heartbrother had wanted to marry a young lady of quality and have himself made a baron, and me a nobleman. But now he had to think of something else, for he had lost the wherewithal to propagate a new generation; and since, in connection with his paralysis, he was threatened with a lengthy illness (during which time he needed good friends), he had his will drawn up. In this he designated me as the sole heir of his property, chiefly because he saw that for his sake I was throwing my own fortune to the winds and giving up my captaincy in order to go with him to a health resort, where I would stay until he was completely cured.

CHAPTER 5: *Simplicius pretends to be a messenger and, being addressed as Mercury by Jove, learns what the great Numen has in mind concerning war and peace*

WHEN HEARTBROTHER WAS ABLE to ride again, we exchanged our cash (for now we kept but one purse between us) for a letter of credit on a bank in Basel. We bought horses, hired servants, and rode up the Danube as far as Ulm and, since travel was pleasant in May, proceeded from there to the spa. We rented rooms, and I continued to Strasbourg, in order not only to cash the check we had had transferred from Basel, but also to look for experienced doctors who could prescribe medicines and work out a schedule for taking the waters.

[3] This was the battle of Jankau, March 6, 1645.

Several of these doctors came with me and found that Heartbrother had been poisoned. But since the poison had not been strong enough to kill him outright, it had gone into his arms and legs, from where it had to be removed by drugs, antidotes, and steam baths. Such a cure would take from one to eight weeks. Then Heartbrother recalled immediately when and by whom he had been poisoned, namely, by those who would have been glad to take over his position in the army. And when he heard from the various doctors that this cure would not have required visiting a spa, he firmly believed that his field surgeon had been bribed by his rivals to send him this far out of the way. However, Heartbrother decided to complete his cure at the resort, especially since the air was salubrious, and the company of the other guests pleasant and agreeable.

I did not want to waste this kind of time, and since I was anxious to see my wife again, and Heartbrother did not particularly need me, I disclosed my plan to him. He approved and advised me to go, the sooner the better. He gave me some precious jewelry that I should present to my wife in his name; also I was to beg her pardon, on his behalf, for delaying my return. So I rode to Strasbourg, and there I not only provided myself with money, but also inquired about the safest way of making my trip. I found out that it could not be done on horseback and alone, for raiding parties sent out by the garrisons of the two enemies made the roads unsafe. I hired a courier, obtained a passport for him, and wrote up several letters to my wife, her sister, and her parents, which I asked to have delivered in Lippstadt. Then I pretended to change my mind, got the courier to give me his passport, returned my horses and the servant, disguised myself in a red and white livery, and took a boat to Cologne, which was then neutral.

There I first went to see my old Jupiter, in order to find out about my sequestered property. But at that time he was totally unhinged in his mind and disgusted with the human race. "Oh, Mercury," he said, when he saw me, "what news do you have from Münster?[4] Do these humans think they can make peace without my compliance? Never! They had it; why didn't they keep it? Weren't all the vices flourishing when they induced me to send them a war? And why do they deserve peace now? Have they improved since then? Haven't they rather become worse and rushed into war as if they were going to a fair? Or did they repent because of the famine I sent, in which many thousands died of hunger? Or did the savage epidemics that cut down so many millions terrify them, so that they became better? No, no, Mercury, the

---

[4] Preliminary peace negotiations at Münster started as early as 1644.

survivors who see the misery and distress with their own eyes are not only unrepentant; they have grown much worse than they ever were. If they have not changed after so many severe penalties, but continue their godless life amid wretchedness and vexation, what will they do if I were to send them delectable, golden peace? I should have to worry that they would take it upon themselves to deprive me of heaven, as the titans did before. But I will prevent such insolence betimes and let them linger woebegone in war for a long time to come."

Because I knew how to treat this god if one wanted to put him in the right frame of mind, I said, "Alas, great god, all the world is moaning for peace and promising to mend its ways. Why should you withhold it from them any longer?" "Indeed, they are moaning," answered Jupiter, "but not for my sake, only for theirs. They don't want to praise God, each under his vines and fig tree, but merely to enjoy the fruits of them in peace and lechery. The other day I asked a louse-ridden tailor whether I should give them peace. But he answered, what did he care?! He would keep as busy in war as in peacetime. I got a similar answer from a foundryman. He told me that if he did not cast church bells in peacetime, he'd cast cannon and mortars in wartime. A blacksmith said, 'If I don't have plows and farm wagons to work on in peacetime, I have plenty of artillery horses to shoe and army wagons to take care of in wartime. I can do without peace.' Look, dear Mercury, why should I grant them peace? Surely there are a few who want it, but only for the sake of their bellies and their convenience. There are, however, also some who want to keep the war going, not because it is my will, but because it is to their profit. And just as the masons and the carpenters want peace so that they can get rich by rebuilding and repairing the burnt-out towns, so others, who do not believe in earning an honest living by manual *labor*, wish a continuation of the war in order to have a better opportunity for manual *theft*."

Since my Jupiter was concerned only with these affairs, I took it that he could give me no news about my family. Therefore, I told him nothing, but proceeded resolutely on familiar byways to Lippstadt and asked for my father-in-law as if I were only a messenger. But I found out at once that he and my mother-in-law had departed this world half a year ago, and that my beloved wife, after she had been delivered of a boy (who was with my sister-in-law) had also passed away right after his birth. I handed my brother-in-law the letters that I had written myself to my father-in-law, my dear wife, and to him, my brother-in-law. He offered me lodging so that he might find out from me — the messenger — how Simplicius was. For the same reason my sister-in-law talked a long time with me about myself, and I spoke of myself and told her as many pleasant things about me as I knew, for the pock-marks had so changed and marred me that no one recognized me any more, except Herr von Schönstein;[5] but being an old, trusted friend, he kept mum.

When I told my sister-in-law in great detail that my master Simplicius owned many fine horses, had numerous servants, and was a man of importance, wearing a black velvet coat adorned all over with gold, she said, "Really? I always thought he was of better descent than he admitted. By making substantial promises, the commander here persuaded my deceased parents that they should deceitfully palm off my late sister, who indeed was a virtuous woman, on Mr. Simplicius. I could never see any good come of this. Nevertheless, he made a good impression and promised to go into Swedish — or rather Hessian — service, in this garrison. For this purpose he went to Cologne in order to bring his valuable possessions here. But the proceedings bogged down, and he, having been spirited off to France, left my sister (who had been married only a month) pregnant — also about a dozen burghers' daughters. They all gave birth to boys; my sister was the last.

"Since my father and mother are dead, and my husband and I expect no children, we have adopted my sister's child, and we expect to make him the heir of all we own. With the help of our commander here, we have collected his father's assets in Cologne — amounting to perhaps three thousand florins — so that this youngster, once he is old enough, will have no cause to complain of poverty. My husband and I love the child so much that we wouldn't give him to his own father, if he should come by to pick him up. Moreover, he is the handsomest among all his stepbrothers and resembles his father as if he were cut from the same pattern. I know that if my brother-in-law knew what a handsome son he has here, he couldn't deny himself the pleasure of looking at the little darling, even though he might not relish running into his other children, the bastards."

These and many other matters were brought up by my sister-in-law, and I could easily see that she loved my child, who was skipping about in his first pair of breeches and making my heart glad. For that reason I rummaged through my pockets for the jewelry Heartbrother had given me to present to my wife. "My master Simplicius," I said, "asked

---

[5] Von Schönstein was the cavalry officer who had captured Simplicius and taken him to Lippstadt (Bk. III, chap. 14). Later he had been on the boat that rescued Simplicius from the tree in the Rhine. Though von Schönstein had tried to get Simplicius out of the imperial army, he failed because he was on a secret mission (Bk. IV, chap. 10).

me to give these jewels to his beloved wife as a greeting; it is only fair to leave them for his child." My brother-in-law and his wife received the gift joyfully and concluded that I was not living in want, but rather that I must be a man different from the kind they had imagined before. So I asked permission to return, and when I received it, I requested the favor of kissing young Simplicius in the name of the old one, so that I might tell his father about it as a token. When this was done (with my sister-in-law's permission), both my nose and the child's started bleeding.[6] My heart was about to break, but I concealed my emotions; and in order not to have much time to think about the cause of this sympathetic event, I left at once, and after two weeks of much trouble and danger arrived at the spa in beggars clothes, for I had been stripped bare on the way.

CHAPTER 6: *A practical joke that Simplicius played in the spa*

UPON ARRIVING, I NOTICED that Heartbrother had gotten worse rather than better, though the doctors and druggist had plucked him cleaner than a fat goose. He seemed to be childish and could hardly walk upright. I cheered him up as best I could, but he was in poor condition, and the way his strength was failing he probably suspected that he would not last long. His greatest comfort was that I would be with him when he closed his eyes.

I, on the other hand, enjoyed life and sought my old accustomed pleasures where I could find them, but in such a way that Heartbrother missed none of his care. And since I knew I was a widower, leisure and youth again induced me to run after women. The shock of my life which I had received at Einsiedeln was forgotten. At the resort there was a very beautiful lady[7] who let it be known she was of nobility, but as I figured it she was even more *mobilis* than *nobilis*. I busily paid court to this man-trap, for she seemed to be a good dish. After a short time

[6] Folk belief has it that a nosebleed after kissing is a sign of close relationship.

[7] This is the adventuress Libushka, who tells her life story in Grimmelshausen's *Trutz Simplex: Oder ausführliche ... Lebensbeschreibung der Ertzbetrügerin ... Courasche*, (Trutzsimplex or the Life of the Archcheat and Runagate Courage), a book that inspired Bertolt Brecht's *Mother Courage, a Chronicle Play of the Thirty Years' War* (1939).

I received free access not only to her house, but also to any other enjoyment I might have wished and hoped for. But from the beginning I was disgusted with her easy ways and wondered how to get rid of her without giving offence, for she seemed to be more interested in fleecing my purse than in marrying. Whenever I was with her she showered me with loving, ardent glances and other manifestations of her fiery affection, so that I was ashamed for both myself and her.

There was also a rich Swiss nobleman at the spa. Not only had his money been stolen, but also his wife's jewelry, consisting of gold, silver, pearls, and precious stones. Now since it is as unpleasant to lose such things as it is hard to come by them, the Swiss sought all the counsel and help he could in order to recover them. He sent for the famous devil-conjurer of the goatskin, who by his conjuring harassed the thief to the extent that he personally had to return the stolen goods to their proper place. For this service the wizard received ten thalers.

I would have been happy to confer with this sorcerer; but I was afraid it could not be done without loss of dignity (for at that time I thought I was a big wheel). So, having heard that he was a great toper, I asked my servant to drink with him that evening in order to become acquainted with him, and perhaps I could find out a thing or two that would come in handy; for the stories told about him were so strange that I could not believe them unless I heard them from him in person. Having disguised myself as a traveling quack who sells ointments, I sat down at his table, intending to find out whether he could guess (or whether the devil would tell him) who I was. But I did not notice anything peculiar about him, for he just kept pouring wine down his throat, and he thought I was what my clothes indicated. He even drank to my health a few times, and he showed more respect to my servant than to me. He told him in all confidence that if the man who robbed the Swiss had thrown the least little part of the loot into running water, thus giving the accursed devil his share of it, it would have been impossible to name the thief or to recover the loss.

Hearing these silly things, I was amazed at how the sly, deceptive fiend can get his clutches into poor humans by means of such insignificant trifles. I could easily imagine that this was part of the pact made between the conjurer and the devil, and that such a trick would not help the thief if another conjurer were called in, one whose pact did not contain this clause.

So I ordered my servant (who could steal more skillfully than a gypsy) to get the fellow good and drunk, steal his ten Reichsthalers, and throw a few pennies of it into the river Rench. The man did as he was ordered. When the conjurer missed his money next morning, he went to a wild part of the Rench, there, no doubt, to confer in this matter with his familiar. But he was so mishandled that he came back with a black eye and scratches all over his face. I felt so sorry for the poor rascal that I had his money returned to him with this message: Seeing what kind of evil and deceptive guy the devil was, he might henceforth quit his company and service, and return to God. But for me this admonition turned out like the grass that the dog eats; from this time on I had nothing but bad luck. Soon afterward my two fine horses dropped dead from sorcery. And what could have protected me? I lived as godless a life as an epicurean and never commended my possessions unto God's protection. Why should this sorcerer not have taken revenge on me?

CHAPTER 7: *Heartbrother dies, and Simplicius starts pitching woo again*

THE LONGER I STAYED in the resort the better I liked it; for one thing, the number of guests increased daily, it seemed; for another, the place itself and the style of living there struck me as pleasant. I became acquainted with the jolliest people and started using courteous phrases and compliments, the existence of which I had never noticed before. I was thought to be a nobleman, for my servants called me captain, and soldiers of fortune do not commonly attain that rank at my age. For that reason the rich fops sought not only my acquaintance but also my sworn friendship, and I theirs. All manner of entertainment, gambling, gluttony, and drinking were my greatest worry and concern. They took away many a pretty ducat without my noticing it especially or worrying about it, for my purse was still heavy enough from Oliver's legacy.

Meanwhile, Heartbrother's condition went from bad to worse, so that he finally had to pay the debt of nature: the doctors had left him after extracting their share from him. He confirmed his last will and testament and made me the heir of what he expected to receive of his late father's inheritance. I had him buried in great style and dismissed his servants, after buying them mourning clothes and giving them a sum of money.

His death was a painful blow to me, particularly since he had been poisoned; and though I could not change that, it changed me. I stayed away from all social gatherings and only sought solitude, there to meditate upon my sad thoughts. For this purpose I would sometimes hide in a thicket, there to contemplate not only what a friend I had lost,

but also the fact that I would never again find one like him. In this
connection I also made all sorts of plans for my future life, but without
deciding anything definite. Now I wanted to get back in the army; but
then I considered that the lowliest peasants in this part of the country
were better off than a colonel, for no raiders ever came into these hills.
I could hardly imagine what an army would have to do in order to ruin
this part of the world, where all the farms were still standing, well
built, as in peacetime, and all the stables were full of cattle — though
in the plains there wasn't even a cat or a dog left in the villages.

One time when I had been enjoying myself listening to the prettiest
song of the birds and thinking that the nightingale was fascinating the
other birds into silence by the loveliness of its song, when on the other
bank, there approached a beauty who moved me more than a well-
accoutered demoiselle could have done, though she wore only the
traditional dress of a farm girl. From her head she took a basket in
which she was carrying a roll of fresh butter that she hoped to sell in
the spa. She put it in the water so it wouldn't melt in the hot sun. Then
she sat down in the grass, took off her peasant hat and kerchief, and
wiped the perspiration from her face. So I had plenty of time to look at
her and to satisfy my inquisitive eyes. It seemed to me that in all my
born days I had not seen a prettier girl: the proportions of her body
appeared to be faultless and beyond reproach, her arms and hands
white as snow, her countenance lovely and pert, her dark eyes full of
fire and exciting glances. She was wrapping up the butter again when
I shouted across to her, "Ah, maiden! To be sure, with your pretty
hands you have cooled the butter in the water; but with your bright
eyes you have set my heart on fire." As soon as she saw and heard me,
she, without having spoken a word, ran away as if pursued, leaving me
behind filled with all those foolish notions with which an enamored
simpleton is usually tormented.

My desire to have this sun shine upon me did not let me stay in the
solitude I had sought, but made me regard the song of the nightingale
as no better than the howling of wolves. For that reason, I too trotted
toward the spa, sending my page ahead to talk to the country girl and
haggle with her until I arrived. He did what he could; and after
arriving, I did what I could. But I found a heart of stone and such
reserve as I would never have thought possible in a farm girl. But this
only increased my ardor, though as one who has been around I could
have told myself that she would not be one who was easily fooled.

At that time I should have had either a bad enemy or a good friend:
an enemy who would have forced me to concentrate my thoughts on
him and to give up my foolish love; or a good friend who would have

advised me differently and kept me from the folly I was about to commit. But, alas, I only had my money to dazzle me, my blind desires to mislead me because I did not restrain them, and my own rashness to ruin me and drive me into misfortune. Fool that I was, I should have judged from the black color of our clothing (an evil omen) that her love would be my misery. Since Heartbrother and the girl's parents had died, both of us were dressed in mourning when we first saw each other. What joyfulness could there have been in our courtship? In a word, I was caught in a fool's snare, and therefore I was blind and without reason, like the boy Cupid himself. And as I did not dare to satisfy my animal urge in any other way, I decided to marry her. "Heck!" I said to myself, "you are only a peasant boy and will never own a castle. This is a noble part of the country which, in comparison to other places, is enjoying wealth and prosperity. Anyway, you still have enough money to buy the best farmstead hereabouts. You ought to marry this honest Fanny from the country and get yourself a peaceful gentleman's place among the farmers. Where would you find a jollier home than near the spa, where you can see a different world every six weeks — on account of the guests, who come and go. On the basis of this you can imagine how the world changes from one century to the next." This and a thousand other thoughts went through my head, until I finally asked for the hand of my beloved in marriage and received her consent, but not without a struggle.

CHAPTER 8: *Simplicius contracts a second marriage, meets his knan, and learns who his parents were*

I ORDERED A BIG wedding, for I was in seventh heaven. And I not only bought the farm where my bride was born, but I improved it with a beautiful new building, as if I wanted rather to hold court there than keep a courtyard. Before the wedding I bought thirty head of cattle and put them on the place, for that was the number the farm could support throughout the year. In brief, I arranged everything in the best possible manner, including the most expensive household furnishings that my folly could select. But the bubble burst quickly, for when I thought I had set my sail for Angel-land I only got to Hell-land and then — much too late — I found out why my bride had been so reluctant to marry me. And what hurt me the worst was that I could not weep on anybody's shoulder about this shame of mine. It was no more than fair for me to pay for past sins, but this knowledge did not make me a bit more patient or pious. Rather, because I found myself so cheated, I planned to cheat my cheater and started grazing where I could find greener pasture. Thus, I was more often in pleasant company in the spa than at home. In short, I let my household go to rack and ruin.

On the other hand, my wife was just as slovenly: a beef that I had slaughtered she salted down like pork; she wanted to roast trout on a spit and grill crayfish! By these few examples one can easily see how she kept house. She also liked to drink a glass of wine and to share it with others, and that was a sign of my approaching disaster.

Once I was promenading down the valley with some dandies to visit friends in the lower baths. There we met an old peasant leading a goat that he wanted to sell. And because I had a feeling that I had seen this person before, I asked him where he was coming from with the goat he was leading on the rope. He took off his hat and said, "Sir, I dasn't tell ya." I said, "Well, surely you didn't steal it?" "No," he said, "I come from the town down in the valley, the one I dasn't mention to the gentleman because we are talking in the presence of a goat."[8] This made everyone laugh, and because I got white as a sheet they thought I was annoyed or ashamed that the peasant answered me so neatly. But my thoughts were elsewhere, for by the big wart which the peasant had in the middle of his forehead, like a unicorn, I was assured that he was none other than my knan from the Spessart. So I decided to act the prophet before I told him who I was and presented him with a son who was fully grown and as well dressed as I was at that time. I said to him, "My good old man, don't you come from the Spessart?" "Yes, sir," answered the peasant. I continued, "About eighteen years ago troopers looted and burned your place." "Yes, God ha' mercy," answered the peasant, "but it isn't quite that long ago." I continued asking, "At that time did you not have two children, a grown-up daughter and a young boy who herded your sheep?" "Sir," replied the peasant, "the daughter was my child, but the boy was not. I wanted to raise him as my own." From this I gathered that I was not the son of this coarse yokel. That made me partly glad, but it also saddened me, because it occurred to me that I might be a bastard or a foundling. So I asked my knan where he had gotten the boy, and why he had wanted to raise him as his own child. "Alas," he said, "that was strange: the war gave him to me and the war took him away." Now I was getting worried that some unpleasant fact about my birth might come out, and I turned the

---

[8] The town is called Gaisbach, and Geiss (a variant spelling of *Gais*) means "goat." The peasant is pretending that the goat should not hear this word lest her feelings be hurt.

conversation back to the goat and asked him if he had sold it for meat to the lady who kept the hotel. That would be strange, for the guests in the spa didn't usually eat old goat meat. "Ah, no, sir," answered the peasant, "the lady has plenty of goats and won't pay me much for anything. I am bringing it for the countess who is taking the waters. Dr. Busybody has prescribed some herbs that the goat must eat. The doctor then takes her milk and adds some medicine to it. The countess, she has to drink the milk and get well from it. They say there's something wrong with her insides, and if the goat can cure her, she can do more than the doctor and his gravediggers combined." During this conversation I wondered how I could continue talking with the peasant, and I offered him one thaler more than the doctor or the countess would pay for the goat. He agreed at once (for a slight profit quickly persuades most people), but with this proviso that he would first tell the countess of my higher offer. If she should raise her bid to equal mine, she was to have preference; if not, he would bring the goat that evening and tell me about the deal.

So my knan went on his way, and, I, with my company, went mine. But I could not, and did not want to, stay with the group any longer. I turned aside and found my knan still with his goat, for the others would not give as much for it as I (which surprised me in such rich people, but their niggardliness didn't make me more stingy). I took him to my newly-bought farm, paid for the goat, and after I had got him half drunk, asked him where he had got hold of the boy we had been discussing today. "Well, sir," he said, "the Mansfeld war gave him to me and the battle of Nördlingen took him away again." I remarked that that must be a good story and asked him to tell it, since we had nothing else to talk about. He began, saying, "When the Mansfelders lost the battle at Höchst, the defeated troops scattered far and wide, for many did not know where to retreat. Many came to the Spessart, where they wanted to hide in the woods. But after escaping death on the plains, they found it with us in the hills, and since both warring parties considered robbing and killing each other, on our grounds, as fair play, we reached out for them, too; at that time hardly a peasant went abroad without his shooting iron (for we couldn't always stay at home with our plows and hoes). In this hubbub in the tremendous, wild forest not far from my farm, I had heard several shots. Shortly afterward I noticed a beautiful, young noblewoman on a stately horse. First I thought she was a man, for she rode like one; but when she raised her eyes and hands to the sky and I heard her call on God in a pitiful voice, in French, I lowered and uncocked my gun, for her gestures and her prayer assured me that she was a woman in distress. We approached each other, and when she saw me, she said, 'Alas, if you are an honest Christian, I beg you, in the name of God and his mercy, to take me to some married women who, with God's help, can aid me in delivering me of my body's burden.' These words, together with her way of speaking and her sad but exceedingly beautiful and graceful figure, moved me to pity; I took her horse by the reins and led her through hedges and bushes to the very densest thicket, where I had concealed my wife and child, the hired hands, and my cattle. There, in less than half an hour, she was delivered of the boy we were talking about today."

My knan took a drink, indicating that the story was ended. I offered him more wine, and when he had emptied the glass, I asked him what had happened to the woman. He answered, "When she had given birth, she asked me to be the boy's godfather and to have him baptized as soon as possible. She also told me her name and that of her husband, so they could be recorded in the baptismal register. She opened her satchel, which contained some precious things, and gave my wife and child, the maid, and another woman so much that they might well be satisfied. While she was thus busy, having told us of her husband and commended the child to our care, she died on our hands. There being so much confusion in the country that no one could stay at home, we could hardly find a parson for the funeral and the christening. But when both were done, our mayor and our parson ordered me to raise the child to manhood; for my trouble and expense I was to keep the woman's legacy, except several prayer books, precious stones, and some odds and ends, which I was to hold in trust for the child. So my wife raised the boy on goat's milk, and we were glad to keep him, thinking that when he grew up we'd give him to our daughter in marriage. But after the battle of Nördlingen we lost the girl and the boy and everything we owned."

I said to my knan, "You have told me a nice story, and yet you forgot to tell me the most important part: you didn't tell the names of the woman or the husband or the child." "Sir," he answered, "I didn't think you wanted to know. The lady's name was Susanna Ramsay, her husband was Captain Sternfels von Fuchshaim, and since my name is Melchior, I had the boy baptized Melchior Sternfels von Fuchshaim, and that is how he's recorded in the register."

From this story I found out that I was the son of the hermit and Governor Ramsay's sister, but much too late, for my parents were both dead; and about my Uncle Ramsay I could learn only that the people of Hanau had sent him and his Swedish garrison packing, and that this had made him madder than a hornet.

I completely drowned my godfather in wine, and the next day I sent for his wife. When I made myself known to them, they did not want to believe me until I showed them the hairy birthmark on my chest.

CHAPTER 9: *How Simplicius suffers labor pains and becomes a widower once more*

NOT MUCH LATER I rode down into the Spessart with my godfather, in order to get definite information and to obtain documents concerning my birth; these were given to me without trouble, on the basis of my godfather's statements and the entry in the baptismal register. I also stopped to see the parson who had been in Hanau and taken care of me there. He gave me a written testimonial concerning the place where my father had died, the fact that I had been with him until his death, and finally, that for a while I had been with Mr. Ramsay, the governor of Hanau. In fact, I collected various statements from witnesses and had my life history written up and certified by a notary public, for I thought that one never knows where it will come in handy. This trip cost me more than four hundred thalers, for on the way back we were caught, mugged, and robbed by a foraging party, and my godfather (or knan) and I, having lost our shirts, barely came away with our lives.

Meanwhile, matters at home were getting worse, for when my wife found out that her husband was a nobleman, she not only played the great lady but also let the household go completely to pot. Since she was pregnant, I put up with it in silence. Moreover, some cattle disease had killed off most of my best animals.

I could have taken all this in my stride; but, Jupiter Pluvius, it never rains but it pours! When my wife had been delivered, the hired girl was also brought to bed with child. Her baby looked like me, to be sure; but the one my wife bore was the exact image of the hired man. On top of that, the same night the lady mentioned above[9] deposited a baby at my doorstep with a written message saying I was the father, so that all at once I had three children on my hands and expected more to come crawling out of the corners. This gave me a lot of gray hair; but that's how it is when one leads a godless and wicked life, as I had done by yielding to beastly lust.

[9] As Courage tells it, the pseudo-elegant Simplicius was a deceiver whom she deceived; the child she deposited at his door was not hers at all, for she was barren. The child was the result of a union of her maid and a total stranger.

What could be done? I had to have the children baptized and, in addition, pay the fine for fornication. And because the Swedes were in command at that time and I had served under imperial colors, I was fined much more heavily. Yet, all this was only a prelude to utter ruin, which was approaching. Though these many unfortunate accidents troubled me profoundly, my darling wife made light of them; in fact, she joked day and night about the handsome gift that had been laid at my door, and about my having been fined a pretty penny. If she had known about me and the hired girl, she would have treated me worse. But that good creature was nice enough to let me (and an amount equal to the fine I would have had to pay) persuade her to designate as the father of her child some dandy who, about a year ago, had been at our house for my wedding, but whom she had otherwise hardly known. Still, she was dismissed, for my wife suspected what was on my mind concerning her and the hired man. But for all that, she could not say anything; for otherwise I could have reproached her, telling her that I could not have been with her and the hired girl at the same time. However, what worried me was the fact that I should bring up the hired man's child, while my own would not be my heir, and, moreover, that I had to keep still and be glad that no one else knew about it.

Every day such thoughts tormented me, while my wife was swilling wine at all hours, for since our wedding she had become so used to drink that she seldom was without it and never went to bed sober. This soon caused her child's death and inflamed her intestines so much that they failed her and she died, making me a widower once more. I took this so much to heart that I almost laughed myself sick.

CHAPTER 10: *What the peasants tell about the weird Mummelsee*

WHEN I SAW MYSELF thus restored to pristine freedom — but with a purse almost empty of money and a household burdened with many head of cattle and servants — I adopted my godfather Melchior as my father; my godmother, his wife, as my mother; and the bastard Simplicius who had been placed at my door, for my heir. To these two old folks I handed over my house, lands and all property, except a very few gold coins and jewelry, which I had saved up for emergencies. Since my bad experiences with them, I so loathed the company and cohabitation of women that I made up my mind never to get married again. But the old couple, who were hard to equal in farm experience, immediately rearranged my household: they got rid of those hired hands and animals that were no good and brought in whatever produced a profit. My old knan and mither spoke of better things to come and promised (if I let them manage) always to have a good horse in the stable for me and to earn enough to allow me to sit down over a bottle of wine with any honest man. I noticed right away what kind of people were running my farm: my godfather and the hired hands did the field work — he was sharper than a Jew when he sold livestock, timber, or resin; and my godmother supervised the raising of animals and knew how to get dairy money and hold onto it better than ten wives of the sort I had had. Therefore, after a short time, my farm was stocked with everything necessary, including animals large and small, and it was soon considered the best in the country. Meanwhile, I went walking for pleasure and indulged in all sorts of meditations, for when I saw that my godmother realized more from the bees, through wax and honey, than my wife used to get from beef, pork, and such, I was satisfied that she would not be caught napping in other matters.

One day I was walking to the spa, intending more to take a drink of fresh water than to get acquainted with the dandies (as I used to do), for I had begun to imitate the economizing of my old folks, who advised me against associating much with people who wantonly waste their parents' substance and their own. Just the same, I fell in with a group of middle-class people, while they were talking about an odd subject, to wit, the Mummelsee, a bottomless lake located on one of the highest mountains in the neighborhood. They had sent for some old-timers who were telling fascinating things they had heard about this unusual body of water. Listening to their reports gave me great enjoyment, though I considered them no more than old wives' tales, and some sounded as mendacious as some of Pliny's stories.[10]

One peasant said that if an odd number of items — peas or pebbles or something else, it didn't matter what — were tied in a handkerchief and dipped in the water, the count was changed to even; likewise if one dipped in an even number, an odd number would come out. Someone else (and almost everybody with him) asserted and confirmed by examples, that if one rock or several were thrown in, no matter how serene the sky had been before, immediately a severe thunderstorm would arise, with frightful rains, hailstones, and gusts of wind. From this topic they proceeded to all sorts of stories of strange happenings at

[10] The Roman author Pliny the Elder (*ca.* A.D. 23–70) was an author of encyclopedic interests. In his *Naturalis historia* he reports some facts that can not be verified, but in the 17th century his reputation as a teller of tall tales was greatly exaggerated.

this lake: fantastic appearances of earth and water sprites, and what they had said to people. One man told how once, while some herders were grazing their cattle by the lake, a brown bull had come out of the water. He had mixed with the other cattle, but a little man had come after him to drive him back into the lake; and when the bull did not want to return, the little man had wished all the troubles of mankind on him. Then the bull and the little man had gone back into the water. Another said that once when the lake was frozen over, a peasant had driven his ox team with a load of timber safely across; but when his dog came after him, the ice broke and the poor dog went down and was never seen again. Still another asserted as true the story of a hunter who, following the tracks of his quarry and passing by the lake, had seen a water sprite sitting on the surface with a whole lapful of gold coins, which he was playing with. When the hunter had been about to fire at the sprite, the latter had ducked and shouted, "If you had asked me to help you in your poverty, I would have made you and your family rich."

I listened and laughed at these and similar stories, which sounded like fairy tales for entertaining children, but I did not believe even that such an abyss could exist on a high mountain. But there were others, old and trustworthy peasants, who said that in their own and their fathers' memories, august, princely persons had gone up to see the lake; one ruling duke of Württemberg had had a raft built, on which to go out on the lake to measure its depth. After the measurers had dropped a plumb with nine thread-nets (that's a length of yarn, about which the peasant women in the Black Forest know more than I or any surveyor) and still had not hit bottom, the raft had started going down — contrary to the nature of wood — so that those on board had had to give up their undertaking in order to save themselves by swimming to shore. In commemoration of this event, one could still see pieces of the raft on the lake shore, and the Württemberg arms and other designs carved in stone there. Still others, quoting many witnesses, proved that an archduke of Austria had wanted to drain the lake, but many people had dissuaded him, and the petitions of the county people had thwarted his plan; they were afraid the whole countryside might perish and drown. Furthermore, the nobles already mentioned had put several barrels of trout into the lake, but all of them had died within an hour, right before their eyes, and had floated out the mouth of the lake, regardless of the fact that such fish are in the river in these hills and the outlet of the lake flows into that same river.

CHAPTER 11: *Unheard-of gratitude from a patient almost causes Simplicius to have holy thoughts*

THE LAST STORY ALMOST made me believe the earlier ones, and my curiosity was so aroused that I decided to have a look at this miraculous lake. Concerning its name, those who had been talking gave different and contradictory opinions. I said the German name "Mummelsee" meant that the lake wore a mummery or disguise, as at a masquerade, so that not everyone could fathom its true nature or depth (which had never been fathomed, even though important personages had tried).

Then I went to the place where, a year ago, I had seen my late wife and for the first time swallowed the sweet poison of love. I lay down once again in the shade and the green grass, but I no longer paid any attention to what the nightingales were piping; rather, I contemplated the changes I had suffered lately. I considered that at this very place I had begun to turn from a free man into a slave of love; that since then I had changed from an officer into a peasant, from a rich farmer into a poor nobleman, from Simplicius into Melchior, from a widower into a husband, from a husband into a cuckold, and from a cuckold back into a widower; and that likewise I had turned from a peasant's son into the son of an honest soldier, and again into the son of my knan. I pondered how, since then, fate had robbed me of Heartbrother and replaced him with an aged couple. I thought of my father's blessed life and death, of the pitiful death of my mother, and of the various changes to which I had been subjected all my days, and I could not keep from crying. And while I was thinking of all the money I had owned and squandered during my life (and regretting it), along came two topers or winebibbers (they were taking the waters for their palsy) and sat down near me, finding this a good place to rest. They were telling each other their troubles, for they thought they were alone. They were disgusted with their doctors, but I won't go into that, because the doctors won't like me if I did, and next time they might give me a purge that would expurgate my soul. I mention this only because one of these oldsters was thanking God for not having more money. That expression of gratitude removed from my mind all the sadness I felt at the time. I resolved to strive neither for honor, nor for money, nor for anything else the world loves. I decided to take up philosophy, to endeavor to live a godfearing life, and especially to repent my recalcitrance and try, like my late father, to climb the highest rungs on the ladder of virtue.

CHAPTER 12: *How Simplicius travels with the sylphs to the center of the earth*

MY DESIRE TO SEE the Mummelsee increased when my godfather told me that he had been there and knew the way. But when he heard that I had set my mind on seeing it, he said, "What good will it do you to go there? You and I will see nothing but the image of a pond that's located in the middle of a vast forest. And when you have paid for your present enthusiasm with laborious disenchantment, you will have regrets and tired feet (for no one can *ride* there), and the trip down for the trip up. Nobody could have dragged me there if I had not been forced to hide there when Dr. Daniel (he meant the Duc d'Enghien)[11] was marching down to Philippsburg." But I and my curiosity paid no attention to his advice, and I found another guide to take me there. Now, when he saw I was serious, he said that since the oats were in the ground and there wasn't much to do on the farm, he would go with me to show the way, for he loved me and did not want to let me out of his sight. And because the people in the neighborhood believed I was his own son, he liked to show me off and behaved toward me and others as might a common poor man whose son has become great solely through good fortune and without the father's help and furtherance.

So we hiked together over hills and valleys, and before we had walked six hours we came to the Mummelsee, for my godfather kept walking like a beetle and was as fit as a youngster. There we ate the food we had taken with us, because the long way and the climb had made us hungry and tired. Having finished, I looked at the lake and saw lying in it several pieces of hewn timber that my knan and I recognized as parts of the Württemberg raft. I surveyed the length and width of the lake by means of geometry, since it was very difficult to walk around it and measure it in paces or feet. I entered its dimensions in my notebook and made a sketch of it on a reduced scale. And when I had finished with that, I wanted to find out if it were true or an old wives' tale that a thunderstorm came up whenever a rock was thrown in: the sky was clear, and the air calm and warm. I had already found by the mineral taste of the water that no trout could live in it.

[11] Philippsburg was captured in succession by the Swedish, the French, the imperials (under von Götz), and again by the French in 1644. The Duc d'Enghien is Louis II, the Great Condé, who commanded French armies with Turenne.

In order to start work on my experiment, I walked along the left-hand side of the shore to a place where the water, which is crystal clear otherwise, appears to be pitch black, because of the depth of the lake. For this reason it looks so frightening that the very sight terrifies a person. Here I started throwing in rocks so big I could hardly carry them. My godfather or knan not only refused to help me, but even warned and begged me to quit, but I eagerly continued. Rocks that were too large and heavy to carry I rolled toward the lake until I had thrown in about thirty of them. Then black clouds began to cover the sky and violent thunder was heard. My godfather, who stood on the opposite shore by the outlet and deplored my work, shouted to me to find a safe place lest the rain and the storm or even worse misfortune overtake us. But I answered him, "Dad, I want to stay and see the end of this, even if it rains pitchforks." "You," answered my knan, "behave like all these reckless brats who don't give a damn if the whole world goes to pieces."

While listening to his grumbling, I did not turn my eyes away from the deep part of the lake, so that I might notice if bubbles or air rose from the bottom, as usually happens if one throws rocks into deep water. But I saw nothing of the kind. Rather, far away in the direction of the abyss I saw several creatures fluttering about in the water. Their shape reminded me of frogs, and they flitted about as sparks fly from a rocket that's rising into the air. And as they approached me more and more closely, they seemed larger and taller and shaped more like human beings. I first felt great amazement and then, because they were so close to me, terror and repugnance. Moved by horror and wonder, I said to myself, yet so loud that my knan, standing on the opposite shore, could hear me above the thunder, 'Alas, how great are the creations of our Maker, even in the bowels of the earth and the depths of the water!' I had hardly finished speaking when one of these sylphs appeared on the surface of the water and answered, "Behold! This you acknowledge before you have seen anything of it. What would you say if you were in the center of the earth and saw our dwellings, which your curiosity has disturbed?" Meanwhile, similar small watermen emerged like ducks bobbing up. They all looked at me and returned the rocks I had thrown in. This amazed me. The first and foremost among the sprites, whose clothing glittered with gold and silver, threw me a sparkling stone the size of a pigeon's egg, green and transparent like an emerald, and said, "Take this jewel so that you have something to tell about us and this lake." I had hardly picked it up and put it away when I felt as if the air was suffocating or drowning me. I could no longer stand up but reeled about like a yarn windle and finally fell into the lake. No sooner was I in the water than I recovered, and by virtue of the stone I used water instead of air for breathing. Like the little waterman, I could easily locomote in the lake and moved with the sprite into the deep part. The whole thing reminded me of a flock of birds descending in curves from the uppermost parts of the air to the ground.

My knan, having seen this marvel in part (namely, the part that took place above the surface), together with my sudden fit, took off from the lake and headed for home as if his head were on fire. There he told the whole sequence of events, but particularly how, during the thunderstorm, the sprites had brought up the rocks I had thrown into the lake and put them in their old places; and how, in turn, they had taken me down with them. Some people believed him, but most thought it was a cock-and-bull story. Still others suspected that, like a second Empedocles (who jumped into the crater of Mt. Etna), I had drowned myself in the lake and asked my father to spread these tales so that I should gain notoriety, because they had noticed that for some time I had been in melancholy humor, almost desperate, and so on. Others wanted to believe that my adopted father had murdered me (except I was stronger than he), so that the old miser would be sole owner of my farm. So, at this time the conversation in the spa and the surrounding countryside was about nothing but the Mummelsee, about me, my departure, and my godfather.

CHAPTER 13: *The prince of the Mummelsee tells of the sylphs' life and origin*

[Summary: The prince of the Mummelsee takes Simplicius down to the center of the earth, a distance of 4,500 miles. On the way they talk, and the prince tells him that lakes have a threefold purpose: first, to fasten the oceans to the earth, as with nails; secondly, to allow the water sprites to distribute the oceans' waters to the earth through wells, creeks, lakes, rivers, and so on; and thirdly, to permit the sprites to live in them like reasonable creatures of God, attend to their business, and praise the Creator. If the sprites were to cease working, the world would perish and regenerate itself through a fire started by the heat of the sun. They are mortal creatures who rank below human beings (the scale being: angels, humans, sprites, and animals), for Christ has not redeemed them. They know the will of God, are always healthy and therefore long-lived, free, knowledgeable in sciences and arts, not sinful and hence not subject to punishment or God's anger. Simplicius is bursting with questions. How can the sprites be free if they have a king? How are they born, and how do they die? Female sprites, he is told, conceive without pleasure and bear without pain; death to a sprite is painless — as if a light has gone out. Their freedom is unimpaired, for they can traverse fire, water, air, and earth without effort and without fatigue. Simplicius concludes that the sprites must be happier than men, but he is corrected: men have souls; they are able to aspire to eternal bliss and to look upon the face of God. In this sight men enjoy in one moment more happiness than the whole tribe of the sprites has had or will have from the beginning of creation till doomsday.]

CHAPTER 14: *What Simplicius discussed with the prince en route, and the strange and marvelous things he heard*

[Summary: Simplicius is informed by his companion, the "little prince," that the rocks which people throw into lakes have to be removed so that the communication between one body of water and another is not impeded; and in order to discourage human beings from needlessly throwing in rocks, the sprites create thunderstorms.]

[In answer to Simplicius' question about the difference in waters, the prince explains that the waters assume diverse qualities as they pass through metals or semi-elements like sulphur, salts of various kinds, vitriol, alum, antimony, and so on. Fire in the earth warms the water. Much of this information is provided in great detail.

[Simplicius asks if he could leave by a different outlet than the Mummelsee. "Of course," is the reply. Ancestors of the sprites guided some Canaanites to America: they had escaped the sword of Joshua and in despair had thrown themselves into a lake.[12] When Simplicius is amazed by this, the little prince is astounded at his amazement, and Simplicius asks whether the sprites don't find humans astonishing. "No," he says, "the only thing amazing about humans is the way they throw away their chances of eternal bliss. If only the sprites had this human privilege of proving themselves worthy in the sight of God." Toward the end of this discussion Simplicius and the little prince are approaching the king's court.]

CHAPTER 15: *What the king discussed with Simplicius, and Simplicius with the king*

[Summary: In contrast to royal courts on earth, the king of the sprites keeps a simple household. Yet all the princes of the various lakes and seas are present, and all are dressed in their national costumes; it's like a picture book. The king asks why Simplicius created a disturbance in his realm and is astonished to learn that the culprit has already resigned himself to dying for the offense. The king then asks Simplicius why humans persist in vice, though the millennium is reported to be near. If the earth must perish by fire, the sprites will also suffer death. As a Christian, Simplicius may have more precise information than that which is available to the sprites and sylphs. Simplicius pleads ignorance of such high matters; nevertheless, the king urges him to tell what he knows about conditions on earth.

[In obvious satire, Simplicius describes the priests, rulers, merchants, doctors and pharmacists, craftsmen and others, as they should be, not as they are. On earth, he says, pride, envy, anger, lechery, debauchery,

---

[12] According to Olfert Dapper, *America*, (trans. J. C. Beer, 1673), p. 15, the story goes that the first human beings in the Americas arose from Lake Titicaka in Bolivia.

laziness, and so on, are unknown. Wars are caused only by excessive zeal on God's behalf.]

CHAPTER 16: *News from the depths of the bottomless sea called Mare del Sur*

[Summary: Simplicius goes on a sight-seeing tour through the subterranean realm. A delegation is just leaving for the Mare del Sur,[13] and Simplicius joins them. While traveling he is to think of a keepsake he would like to take back to earth.

[On the bottom of the South Sea he marvels at coral growths as big as oak trees. From these the sylphs gather food. He also sees giant snails, and pearls big as hens' eggs — and just as edible. The ground is strewn with emeralds, turquoise, rubies, diamonds, sapphires, and other precious stones, many as big as the rocks one finds in mountain streams on earth. Projecting cliffs are inhabited by strange crawling, stationary, or walking creatures, and the fish that swim about remind him of birds. Since it is night, he can see the full moon, the stars, and the antarctic pole. The various water inhabitants are dressed in different national costumes, but all speak German and understand Simplicius perfectly. This easy communication is possible because the sprites had nothing to do with that terrestrial aberration, the Tower of Babel. Thus they have been spared the consequences thereof.]

When my convoy had picked up enough food, we returned through another shaft from the ocean to the center of the earth. On the way I said to someone that I thought the center of the earth was hollow and that the Pygmies[14] were running around in it, as on a treadmill, and thereby turning the earth so that all of it received the rays of the sun (which, according to the opinion of Aristarchus and Copernicus, stood still in the middle of the heavens).[15] I got the horselaugh for this idea and was told to consider the opinions of the two scholars quoted, plus

[13] The Pacific Ocean.

[14] Dwarfs of Greek mythology.

[15] Aristarchus of Samos (*ca.* 250 B.C.) was the first to maintain that the earth moves around the sun, a theory that Copernicus confirmed in 1530. The water people have not yet heard of it.

my own notion on the subject, as no more than a silly dream. Instead
I should think of the gift I wanted from their king, lest I return empty-
handed to the shores of earth. I replied that the marvels I had seen up
to that point had so confused me that I could think of nothing at all,
and I asked to be advised about what I might request from the king.
My own idea was to ask for a spring with medical properties, to be
located in my own back yard, for wasn't their king the ruler of all the
fountains in the world? The regent of the Pacific Ocean and its abysses
replied that to grant this would be beyond the king's power, and even
if he could do it, and wanted to please me, such fountains never lasted
long. I asked him the reason for this. He answered that throughout the
earth there are empty pockets which gradually fill up with all sorts of
metals generated there by various exhalations. Sometimes water from
the center seeps into these pockets, where it stays many centuries and
assumes the noble virtues and medicinal properties of the metals. As
the water presses on from the center and seeks and finds an outlet on
the surface, that part of the water which was enclosed by the metals for
so many hundreds, even thousands, of years gushes out first and acts
on human bodies with the miraculous effects observed in newly
discovered spas. But as soon as the metallically charged water has
flowed off, common water follows. To be sure, it too has come through
the same passages, but in its rapid flow it cannot take on the virtues
and powers of the metals, and thus it cannot be as effective as the first
liquid. I thanked him for this information and told him I'd like nothing
better than to own such a well. This would help my fellow humans,
would bestow honor on their king, and would enhance my name and
keep me in eternal remembrance. The prince then answered that if this
was what I wanted, he would support my request, though their king
paid no attention whatever to the reputation he might enjoy on earth,
be it good or bad. Now we had come again to the center of the earth
and within the king's court, where he and his courtiers were about to
eat. It was a light meal, at which neither wine nor strong drink was
served. As we ate raw or soft-boiled eggs, the guests consumed pearls
that had not yet hardened; these provided good nourishment and
strength.

I observed that the sun shone on one sea after another, sending its
rays all the way down into these abysmal depths, so that the sprites
were never without light. The sun shone at this distance as brightly as
we see it on earth, and the shadows were sharply outlined. For the
sylphs, the seas are like windows through which they receive both light
and heat. And if the sun does not come through directly (some seas
being rather bent and crooked), reflection takes over, for nature has

placed whole rocks of crystal, diamonds, and garnets in such a way that they convey the light downward.

CHAPTER 17: *Return from the earth's center; strange notions, castles in Spain, the making of schedules, and a reckoning without the host*

MEANWHILE THE TIME FOR my departure was approaching, and the king ordered me to let him know how he could do me a favor. I spoke up and said he could do me no greater favor than sending a regular mineral spring to my farm. "Is that all?" answered the king, "I would have thought that you might have brought along several large emeralds from the American sea and asked permission to take them with you to earth. Now I see that there is no greed among you Christians." And with these words he handed me a stone of strangely varying color and said, "Put this in your pocket. Wherever you deposit it on earth, it will begin seeking the center. It will proceed through the most convenient minerals until it returns to us. We shall then send you a medicinal fountain of the first water, which will enhance and advance you to the extent that you have merited by revealing the truth to us." Then the prince of the Mummelsee asked me to follow him, and together we returned through the same passages by which we had come.

This return trip seemed much farther than the journey down, because the prince and I did not talk much, except for his telling me that the sprites got to be three, four, or five hundred years old and lived all that time without illness. Moreover, in my mind I had already become rich through my mineral spring, and I was occupying all my sagacity and thought in wondering where to locate it and how to make the most of it. I was already drawing up plans for the substantial buildings which would be needed to accommodate the guests and which would enable me to charge dearly for lodgings. I was thinking of the palm grease which would persuade the doctors to favor my new miracle spa to all others (even the one at Schwalbach),[16] so that I'd have mobs of rich guests. I was already moving whole mountains in order that people arriving or departing could not complain about wretched roads. I was hiring clever factotums, frugal cooks, circumspect housemaids, watchful hostlers, neat attendants of baths and fountains.

[16] Schwalbach (now called Langenschwalbach) was and is a popular spa.

I was thinking of a place right in the middle of wild mountains, not far from my farm, where I would create a beautiful, parklike garden with all sorts of rare plants, a place in which foreign guests and their ladies could promenade, where the sick could recover, and the healthy find delight in games and outdoor exercises. Then I'd pay the doctors to compose an eloquent booklet detailing the precious medicinal qualities of my spring. This, together with an attractive frontispiece showing my farm, both as a sketch and in ground plan, I'd get printed up and by merely reading it, a prospective patient would find half his health restored and hope for the rest by checking in. I sent for all my children in Lippstadt and let them learn all sorts of trades and professions that would be of use in the new resort. But I wanted none of them to learn how to be a bloodletting barber-surgeon; I'd do all the bloodletting myself — if not of bodies, then of purses.

Being absorbed in such multifarious thoughts and overly happy with planning, I returned to the air, for the prince put me ashore, at the edge of his Mummelsee, in completely dry clothes. I had to put away the jewel he had given me when he first called for me, or I would have either drowned in air or have had to put my head under water to breathe. When I had given the jewel back, we took leave of one another as people do who will never see each other again. He ducked under the water and returned with his retinue to the deep; but I, happy about the stone that the king had given me, walked away with it as if I had carried off the Golden Fleece of Colchis.

But, alas, my joy, which was mistakenly based on an everlasting regularity on earth, did not endure very long. For I had hardly left the miraculous lake when I got lost in the vast forest, because when my knan had taken me here I had not paid enough attention. I had walked quite a distance before I noticed my predicament, for I was still hard at work planning the spa and becoming rich without getting my hands dirty. So I got farther and farther away from the place where I wanted to go, and — even worse — I didn't notice it until the sun was down, and I didn't know what to do next. There I stood, Henry Helpless in the middle of the wilds, with nothing to eat and no gun, either of which would have been good to have as night fell. But the rock I had brought from the bowels of the earth consoled me. I said to myself, 'Patience, patience, Simpli; this pebble will make up for all your suffering. Rome was not built in a day, and great projects are not completed without toil and sweat. Otherwise, without puffing and without mopping his brow, any numbskull could develop such an elegant spa as you are carrying in your pocket.'

When I had thus encouraged myself, I felt better and used my feet faster, though night had already come. There was a bright, full moon, but the fir trees kept out the light better than had the deep sea earlier that day. Still, I made headway, and around midnight I noticed a fire in the distance and I went straight for it. I knew it was peasants who had something to do with resin, and though such fellows can't be trusted at all times, necessity and my own inclination made me address them. I sneaked up on them and suddenly said to them, "Good night or good day, good morning or good evening, gentlemen! First tell me the time, so I'll know how to greet you properly." All six of them stood or sat there shaking and didn't know how to answer. Because I am rather tall and was in mourning on account of my wife's recent death, and because I carried a frightening cudgel on which I was leaning like a wild mountain-man, I appeared like a terror to them. "What?" I said. "Does no one want to answer?" They still kept quiet for some time. Finally one had sufficiently recovered to ask, "End who ish the chentleman?" I gathered that he was a Swabian (they are often considered doltish, though for no good reason), and I said I was a traveling scholar who had just now returned from the Mountain of Venus, where I had learned a heap of strange tricks. "Ho-ho!" said the oldest peasant. "Now I think I'll live to see the time of peace return, for the students are beginning to travel once more."

CHAPTER 18: *Simplicius plants his spring in the wrong woods*

THAT'S HOW WE ENTERED into conversation. They asked me politely to sit down by the fire with them. They offered me a piece of black bread and some cheese made of skim milk, both of which I accepted. In the end they became so friendly that they asked me, as a student, to tell their fortunes. And since I have some knowledge of palmistry and physiognomy, I started pulling their leg, telling each what I thought he would like to hear, lest I lose face among these wild men of the woods, with whom I did not feel altogether comfortable. They also wanted to learn smart tricks from me, but I put them off till next day, saying that I wanted to sleep a while first. After I had thus played the role of a gypsy, I stepped aside a little and lay down, more to listen to them and to find out what they thought of me than to sleep, though my appetite for that was great enough too. The louder I snored, the more agitated they became. They put their heads together and took turns guessing who I might be. They didn't think I was a soldier because of my black clothes, and they didn't think I was a burgher because I dropped in on them here at such an unusual time and so far from civilization. They finally agreed that I must be a journeyman who had at one time been a college student, because I could soothsay so well. "But," said one, "he didn't know everything. I think he's a soldier in disguise who wants to spy on us and drive off our cattle. I wish we knew; we'd rock him to sleep so he'd forget to wake up!" Another quickly said that he thought I was something else. Meanwhile I lay there, keeping my ears pricked up and thought, 'If these hayseeds attack me, two or three of them will have to bite the dust before they lay me out.'

While the peasants were deliberating and I was worried with fear, I suddenly felt as if someone had peed in bed, for the spot where I lay got all wet. Oh, horrors! Then I realized that Troy and all my exquisite plans were lost, for by the smell I knew it was my mineral spring. Anger and chagrin put me into such a rage that I almost went after the six peasants in order to beat them up. "You goddamn louts!" I shouted, jumping up and shaking my cudgel at them. "This mineral spring, coming up here in the place where I was sleeping, will tell you who I am. For two cents I'd skin you alive and let the devil take you to hell with him. You and your evil thoughts!" The ghastly expression on my face terrified them all. But soon I came to and realized the folly I was committing. 'No,' I thought, 'it is better to lose the mineral spring than to lose my life; and that would be easy to do if I attacked these rednecks.' So I spoke kindly to them once more, and before they could think of something, I said, "Get up and try the wonderful mineral spring that, from now on, you and all the other forest workers will be able to enjoy because I was here." They couldn't make head or tail of what I was saying and were looking at each other like animated dried cod, until they saw that I — sober as a judge — took the first drink of water from my hat. Then one after the other got up from the fire around which they had been sitting, looked at the miracle, and tried the water. But instead of being grateful for it, they started cursing and saying they wished that I and my mineral spring had gotten lost somewhere else, for if their master of the manor found it out, the whole county of Dornstedt would have to do forced labor and build roads, and that would be a great hardship upon them. "On the other hand," I replied, "you will all benefit. You can sell your chickens, eggs, butter, beef, and so on, at better prices." "Naw," they said, "the master will install a manager here, and he'll get rich while we must take the short end and keep up the roads and trails; and we won't even get a 'thank you' for it."

After a while they disagreed; two of them wanted to keep the spring, and four wanted me to get rid of it. If it had been in my power I would have done the latter, even without their suggestion, whether they liked it or not.

Since daylight had come and I had nothing else to do there, and since, moreover, there was the risk of a fight if the argument went on, I said, "If you don't want all the cows in the valley of Baiersbrunn to give red milk as long as the mineral spring is running, you had better show me the way to Seebach." They agreed and sent two fellows along with me, for one man alone with me would have been too frightened.

So I left, and although the whole region is infertile and bears nothing but pine cones, I felt even more like cursing it, for I had lost all my hope there. But I went quietly off with my two guides until I came to the highest place in those hills, from which I could tell approximately where I was. There I said to them, "Gentlemen, you can make a good thing out of your new mineral spring. Go to your lord and announce the discovery, and he'll give you a good reward. The prince will develop it as a showplace and an asset of his land, and he'll make it known to the whole world, in order to enlarge his income." "Well," they said, "what kind of fools do you think we are? Shall we offer him the rod with which to wallop our buttocks? We'd rather have you go to hell with your damn mineral spring. You heard why we don't like it."

I answered, "Oh, you hopeless drips, I ought to call you lazy beggars because you have left the ways of your rugged ancestors far behind. They were so loyal to their prince that he boasted he could lay his head in the lap of any of his subjects and safely go to sleep.[17] But you lazybones are far different, just because you are afraid of a little work, for which in time you will be repaid, and which all your descendants would amply enjoy. To disclose the presence of this spring would be in the interest of your prince, and to the benefit and health of many suffering sick people. What's the difference if each of you spends a few days at forced labor?" "What?!" they shouted. "We'd rather kill *you* with forced labor, to keep your mineral spring hidden." "You crazy loons," I said, "that would require more than the two of you!" And, brandishing my cudgel, I chased them off in the name of St. Velten.[18] Then I went downhill, and after much trouble I got back to my farm

[17] Eberhard the Bearded (1445-1496), Duke of Württemberg, was held in such high esteem by his people that he could make this claim.

[18] St. Velten is a euphemism for the devil.

about nightfall. Thus I found out by experience what my knan had told me earlier, namely, that I'd have tired legs from this pilgrimage, and the trip down for the trip up.

CHAPTER 19: *A short chapter on the Hungarian Anabaptists and their manner of life*

AFTER MY RETURN HOME I kept pretty much to myself. My greatest joy was to pore over books, of which I acquired many. I studied all sorts of subjects, especially those demanding thought and reflection, but I soon tired of what the schoolmasters and pedants know. Arithmetic also bored me, and music became as hateful as the plague: soon I dashed my lute to smithereens; I put up with mathematics and geometry, but as soon as they led me into astronomy, I gave them up and pursued astronomy and astrology. For some time I enjoyed these, but then they appeared so false and uncertain that I no longer wanted to bother with them. Now I reached for the *Ars magna* of Raymundus Lullus,[19] but I found it to be a lot of hot air and little substance; and because I considered it a *topica* I soon gave it up and got busy with the Hebrew cabala and Egyptian hieroglyphics. In the end I found that among all the arts and sciences none is better than theology so long as it teaches a person to love God and serve him. According to its precepts I devised for people a kind of life that could be more angelic than human. A group of married as well as unmarried men and women would have to join together and, under a wise leader, earn their living by manual labor like the Anabaptists; the rest of the time they would exert themselves in the praise of God and the salvation of their souls.

In Hungary I had seen this kind of life on the Hutterite farms.[20] I

[19] Ramon Lull (*ca.* 1235-1315) was a Catalan philosopher who invented the *Ars magna*, an arrangement in which the letters of the alphabet designate basic concepts, while their interrelation is indicated by geometrical figures. *Topica* is the title of one of Aristotle's works. It deals with the various general forms of argument employed in probable, as distinguished from demonstrative, reasoning, and the sources from which arguments may be derived or to which they may be referred.

[20] The Hutterites have practiced their form of Christian communal life since the time of the Reformation. Their enemies called them Anabaptists, and after some excesses on their part under Thomas Münzer at Münster, they were

would have joined them if these good people had not become mixed up in, and dedicated to, a false and heretical doctrine contrary to the general Christian church. At least I considered their life the most blessed on earth, for they appeared to me in their activities very much like the Essenes described by Josephus and others.[21] First of all, they had treasures laid up and more than enough to eat; yet they wasted nothing. One heard no grumbling or cursing among them, not even unnecessary words. I saw craftsmen working in their shops as if they were paid for piecework. Their schoolmaster taught the children as if they were all his own. Nowhere did one see men and women together: each sex was doing its assigned work in its assigned place. I saw lying-in rooms where there were only young mothers, who were well taken care of — as were the babies — by other young mothers, without recourse to their husbands. Other special rooms contained nothing but babies in cradles; women spoonfed the babies and kept them clean and cared for them. The mothers came in only three times a day in order to breast-feed the infants. Only widows were used as caretakers of young mothers and babies. In another hall women were working at more than a hundred spinning and carding wheels. Some women were exclusively laundresses, some bed-makers, cattle-feeders, dishwashers, waitresses, in charge of china or linen, and so on; each had her job and knew how to do it. Similarly, younger and older men had their assigned activities. If a person got sick, he or she had a special nurse; and there was a doctor and pharmacist for the group, though because of good food and healthy living hardly anyone became ill. I saw many an old person living quietly to an extreme age among them, and that is seldom found elsewhere. They had their appointed hours for eating, for sleeping, for working, but not a single minute for play or for promenading, except for the youngsters. After each meal, for the sake of health, the youngsters went walking for an hour with their teacher. During this time they also had to pray and sing hymns. There was no anger, no zealotry, no vengefulness, no envy, no enmity, no worry about worldly goods, no pride, no regret. In short, there prevailed such lovely harmony as

violently persecuted in Germany. Their Hungarian community flourished until, under Maria Theresa's direction, all Hutterites were forcibly converted to Catholicism. Many of them escaped to Russia; and when pressure there drove them out, they came to Canada, the United States, and Paraguay. At present, communities exist in Manitoba, Alberta, Ontario, South Dakota, Montana, and near Primavera.

[21] The Essenes, a Jewish sect described by Josephus in his *Jewish War* (II. 119-161 and elsewhere), in many ways resembled the early Christians.

seemed to purport nothing but the honorable increase of the human race and of God's kingdom. No man saw his wife except when he met with her at the appointed hour in their bedroom, which contained nothing but their well-made bed plus a chamber pot, a washbasin, a pitcher filled with water, and a white towel, so that he could fall asleep and go to work next morning with clean hands. They all called each other "brother" and "sister," and yet such familiarity never caused any lewdness.

I thought that if I could initiate such a commendable Christian way of life, under the protection of my sovereign, I'd be a second St. Dominic or St. Francis. Oh, if only I could convert the Anabaptists so that they might in turn teach our fellow Christians their way of living, how blessed I would be! Or if only I could persuade my fellow Christians to lead such a (seemingly) Christian and commendable life as do the Anabaptists, what an achievement I would have to my credit! To myself I said, 'You fool, why do you bother about other people? Become a Capuchin monk; you are through with women anyway.' But then I considered that tomorrow I might feel differently, and who knows what means I might require to walk rightly in the way of Christ. Today I might be inclined to celibacy; tomorrow I might burn.

For a long time I went around with such thoughts; I would have been glad to dedicate my farm and my entire fortune to such a Christian association, and I would gladly have been a member of it. But my knan frankly predicted that I'd never assemble such a group.

CHAPTER 20: *An entertaining promenade from the Black Forest to Moscow in Russia*

THAT AUTUMN, FRENCH, SWEDISH, and Hessian armies were approaching our part of the country in order to recuperate there and at the same time to keep blockaded the neighboring imperial free city of Offenburg. Therefore, everybody fled with his cattle and his most precious belongings into the deepest forests. I followed my neighbors' example and left my house quite empty. A Swedish colonel awaiting reassignment was quartered there, and he found a few books in my room, for in the general hurry I had not been able to get everything out of the way. Among these were handbooks on mathematics and geometry, some on the theory of fortification (such as engineers use), and he concluded that the house couldn't belong to an ordinary peasant. So he made inquiries and tried to meet me. By a mixture of courteous invitations and threats he got me to come to my own farm, where he treated me quite politely and ordered his people not to destroy or to ruin anything of mine wantonly. Through such friendliness he got me to tell him of my background, particularly about my family and descent. He was greatly astonished that I was living among peasants right in the midst of the war, that I was willing to look on while someone else tied his horse to my fence rail since it behooved me to tie mine to someone else's. He said I should take up the sword once more and not let the gifts that God had bestowed on me languish behind the stove and the plow. If I were to take Swedish service, he vouched that my qualifications and my knowledge of the science of war would soon advance me. I played it cool and said that advancement was rather an uncertain thing — unless a person had friends who helped him by their influence. He repeated that my qualifications would make friends and assure my advancement. Moreover, I would doubtless meet relatives in the Swedish army, for there were many Scottish noblemen in the Swedish forces. Torstensson[22] had promised him a regiment and when the promise was made good (as it doubtless would be), he would make me his lieutenant colonel. This and similar speeches made my mouth water. And since there was no hope of peace, and additional soldiers would surely be quartered on my farm, so that I would be ruined, I decided to join up once more. I promised the colonel I'd serve under him if he would keep his promise and give me the lieutenant-colonelcy in his expected regiment.

Everything was settled. I sent for my knan (or godfather), who was with my cattle in Baiersbrunn, and deeded the farm to him and his wife. After their death my natural son Simplicius, the one who had been placed at my doorstep, was to inherit the farm with all appurtenances, since no legitimate offspring were on hand. Then I got my horse and what I still owned in money and jewels, and after I had settled all my affairs and arranged for the education of my natural son, the blockade was unexpectedly lifted and we had to start for the main army sooner than anticipated. I acted as a steward for this colonel: I maintained him, his servants, his horses, and the entire household by stealing and robbing. In military parlance this is called "foraging."

General Torstensson's promises, of which the colonel had boasted on my farm, were not half so great as he had pretended. In my opinion, the colonel was rather looked down upon. "Ha!" he said to me, "I wonder who the dirty dog was that slandered me at headquarters. I

[22] Lennart Torstensson (1603-1651) was general of the Swedish forces from 1631 to 1645.

won't stay here much longer." And since he suspected I would not stay long with him either, he concocted some letters, according to which he was ordered to recruit a new regiment in Livonia, where his home was. He thus persuaded me to embark at Wismar and go to Livonia with him. Once we were there, everything turned out to be a flash in the pan, for not only was there no regiment to recruit, but he also proved to be a desperately poor nobleman, and what he owned came from his wife's dowry.

Though I had been twice deceived and had allowed him to drag me this far off, I fell for him a third time: he showed me letters he had received from Moscow in which (as he said) high military positions were offered him (that's how he translated the letters for me), and he boasted of excellent and regular pay. Since he immediately started out with his wife and children, I thought he could hardly be going on a wild goose chase. So, full of high hopes, I joined him, since for the present I had neither ways nor means of returning to Germany. But as soon as we crossed the Russian border and met some discharged German soldiers, particularly officers, I became alarmed and said to my colonel, "What in devil's name are we doing? Are we moving away from the seat of the war and going to a peaceful country where soldiers are discharged and considered a nuisance?!" But he reassured me, saying that I should let him worry; he knew what to do better than these fellows of no account.

When we arrived safely in the big city of Moscow, I saw immediately that everything had gone wrong. My colonel was conferring daily with the magnates, but more with high church dignitaries than with important noblemen. This seemed Greek to me and caused me a lot of worry, for I could not figure out what he was up to. Finally he notified me that the war business had fallen through and that his conscience was urging him to embrace the Greek Orthodox religion. He advised me most sincerely to follow his example, since he could no longer help me as he had promised. His majesty the czar had already received good accounts of my personal qualifications and would graciously condescend — if I embraced the Orthodox faith — to invest me as a cavalier with a sizeable estate and many serfs. This most gracious offer could not be refused, for it was better to have, in this grand monarch, a most gracious lord than an offended prince.

I was quite perplexed and did not know what to answer. In another place I would have given the colonel an answer he could have felt rather than heard; but being practically a prisoner, I had to whistle a different tune, so I was silent a long time while I thought of an answer. Finally, I said that at his suggestion I had come to serve his majesty the czar as a soldier. If my military service was not needed, I could not help that; nor did I blame my long journey on the czar, for he had not summoned me. But that the czar so graciously designed to show me his favor, that was something to boast to all the world rather than to accept, for at this time I could not decide to change my religion. I wished, rather, to be back on my farm in the Black Forest, where I'd be no trouble to anyone. The colonel answered that I should do as I liked; however, he did think that if God and good fortune smiled on me I should be properly appreciative. But if I did not want to be helped nor yet to live like a prince, he hoped I realized that he had spared no effort on my behalf. After this speech he made a low bow, turned on his heel, and left me holding the bag. He wouldn't even let me accompany him to the door.

While I was sitting there dazed and wondering about my condition, I heard two Russian carriages in front of my lodgings. When I looked out the window I saw my good colonel and his sons get into one, his wife and her daughters boarding the other. The carriages and servants were the czar's; some priests were also present, and they showed their good will by practically waiting on this family.

CHAPTER 21: *Further news of Simplicius in Moscow*

FROM NOW ON I was shadowed by several gentlemen of the czar, but I was not even aware of it. I no longer saw my colonel or his family, and I did not know where they were. At that time I developed strange notions and sprouted a lot of grey hair. I became acquainted with the German merchants and craftsmen who ordinarily live in Moscow, and I complained to them of how I had ben spitefully deceived. They gave me advice and instructions on getting a ride back to Germany, but as soon as they heard that the czar was determined to keep me in Russia, they all clammed up; they completely ignored me and I had a hard time finding room and board, for I had already eaten up my horse, plus saddle and bridle, and I was taking the ducats one by one out of the lining of my suit, where I had cleverly sewed them up. In the end I also turned my ring and jewels into money, in hopes of surviving until I had an opportunity to return to Germany. Meanwhile a quarter of a year went by, at the end of which time my colonel and his family were baptized for the second time in their lives. Then he was given a fine country estate with many serfs.

At that time a law was passed, equally applicable to natives and foreigners, that no idlers were to be tolerated under pain of severe penalty. Foreigners who did not want to work had to leave the country within a month, the city within twenty-four hours. So about fifty of us banded together for the purpose of traveling with God's help by way of Podolia to Germany. But not quite two hours' distance from the city we were overtaken by several Russian cavalrymen who informed us that his majesty the czar was displeased because so many of us had banded together and were traveling through the country at our own pleasure and without passports. Moreover, the czar could send us to Siberia for our crude behavior. On the way back to town I found out how matters stood with me, for the leader of the troop told me that the czar did not want me to leave the country. His well-meant advice would be to conform to his majesty's most gracious will, to change my religion as the colonel had done, and not to spurn a nobleman's country estate. He assured me that if I refused, declining to live like a lord among them, I'd be forced to work like a serf. His majesty the czar would be a fool for allowing a man so experienced as the colonel had pictured me to leave the country. I belittled myself and said the colonel had probably ascribed more arts, virtues, and sciences to me than I was actually capable of. Certainly I had come into the country to serve his majesty the czar and the great nation of all the Russians against their enemies, even at the cost of my lifeblood; but I could not yet make up my mind to change my religion. Nevertheless, if I was able to serve the czar in any way without burdening my conscience, I would not hesitate to do my best.

I was separated from the others and lodged at the house of a merchant, where I was now openly watched but also provided daily with excellent food and drink from the court kitchens. A number of people called on me and occasionally invited me to their houses. There was one especially who, no doubt, was ordered to look after me. He was a smart man who every day conversed with me in a friendly way (for I had already learned quite a bit of Russian). He mostly discussed mechanical arts with me; war machines and others, the theory and practice of fortification, artillery, and so forth. Finally, after he had hinted several times I should take up the czar's suggestions (but I had given no hope that I would change my mind), he wanted me — in honor of the great czar — to communicate and impart something of my knowledge to his nation, even if I did not want to become naturalized. The czar would acknowledge my willingness with imperial grace. I assured him that it had ever been my intention to serve the czar; that's why I had come. My intention had never changed, though I noticed that

I was virtually kept prisoner. "Oh, not at all," he answered. "Rather, the czar loves you so much that he would not like to do without you." "But why," I said, "am I being watched?" "Because," was the answer, "the czar is afraid something bad might happen to you."

When he had clearly understood what I was willing to do, he explained that the czar wanted to have saltpeter produced and gunpowder manufactured in his own country. But since there was nobody among them who could handle the matter I would do the czar a great service if I set up the factory. I would be given enough money and workers, and he for one wanted to make sure I did not turn down this proposition, for their information indicated that I was the man who could do it.

I answered, "Sir, I say now as I said before: If I can serve the czar in anything (provided he leaves me alone in matters of religion), I shall do my best." Now this Russian, who was one of the most exalted nobles, became so merry that he drank more toasts with me than any German ever did.

Next day two noblemen and an interpreter came from the czar to draw up a contract. They brought along an expensive Russian wardrobe for me. A few days later I started looking for a saltpeter mine and taught the Russians assigned to me how to separate the saltpeter from ordinary dirt and how to refine it. Then I drew up a plan for a powder mill and taught others how to prepare the charcoal. And after a short time we made considerable quantities of the best powder for muskets and ordnance. I had plenty of workers and my personal servants besides, who were to wait on me (or rather, to keep watching me).

When things were going so well, the colonel, dressed in Russian clothes and magnificently attended by many servants, came to me; it seemed that all his flashiness was to persuade me to be rebaptized too. But I knew well enough that the clothes came from the czar's wardrobe and had only been lent to him to make my mouth water, for that's the usual thing at the czar's court.

And in order to make the gentle reader understand how that was handled, I want to give an example. Once I was busy working in the powder mill I had built outside of town by the river. Suddenly an alarm was sounded because the Tartars on a hundred thousand horses were devastating the country only twenty miles away and were advancing steadily. I and my people had to go to court immediately, and there we were given arms and horses from the czar's armory and stables. Instead of a cuirass I wore a quilted breastplate of silk, which might have stopped an arrow but not a bullet. I was given boots, spurs, a princely headgear with a heron's plume, and a sword all decorated with gold and jewels and sharp enough for splitting hairs. I had never seen, let alone ridden, a horse like the one given me from the czar's stables. I and the horse's gear glittered with gold, silver, precious stones, and pearls. By my side hung a steel mace which shone like a mirror and was so well made and so heavy that I could easily kill anybody merely by tapping him with it. The czar himself was not better mounted or equipped. I was followed by a white flag with a double eagle, and from all the nooks and crannies people flocked to it, so that we numbered forty thousand horse before two hours had passed and sixty thousand after about four hours. With these we advanced against the Tartars. Every quarter hour I received oral orders from the czar, but they were always the same: Having passed myself off as a soldier, I was to prove one today, for then his majesty could consider me so and recognize me as one. Our army was increasing every minute: people of major and minor importance, individuals as well as groups, were joining us. But amid all this hurry and confusion, I could not see a single man who would take charge of the mob and direct the battle.

Well, I don't want to go into too much detail because the encounter is not very important for my story. I only want to say that we suddenly came upon the Tartars in a valley or low-lying area. They were burdened with loot, their horses were tired, and they did not expect us. We attacked them from a number of places and scattered them in a few moments. At the time of the first attack I shouted to my followers in Russian, "Come on! Everybody do like me!" They all shouted this to each other while I rode toward the enemy at full speed. First I ran into a prince's son (called a *mirza*), and I bashed his head in, so that the brain stuck to my steel mace. The Russians followed my heroic example; the Tartars could not withstand their attack and turned in general flight.

I acted like a madman, or rather like one who is desperately seeking death and cannot find it. I clubbed down everyone I met, Tartar or Russian, and those whom the czar had ordered to watch me were so close behind me that my back was protected at all times. The air was buzzing with arrows, as if bees or hornets were swarming, and I caught one in the arm, for I had rolled up my sleeves — all the better to kill and maim with sword and mace. Before the arrow stuck in me, my heart had laughed at the bloodshed; but when I saw my own blood flowing, laughter turned to blind rage. When the savage enemy was routed, some noblemen ordered me to report to their emperor how the Tartars had been vanquished. Therefore, on their authority I turned back with about a hundred horsemen. I rode through town to the royal palace, and everyone received me with rejoicing and congratulations.

As soon as I had finished my report (the czar already knew everything), I had to take off my imperial clothes. They were immediately returned to the czar's wardrobe, though like the horse's trappings, they were spattered and soiled with blood, and as good as ruined. I thought the clothes and the horse should have been given to me as a reward for fighting so bravely in this battle. But from this indication I could well imagine how the Russians, like my colonel, managed their elegance of dress. All these goods were borrowed from the czar; they, like everything else in all of Russia, belonged to the czar.

CHAPTER 22: *The short and jolly journey back to his knan*

WHILE MY WOUND WAS healing I was treated like a prince: I walked around in a gown made of gold brocade and lined with sable, though my injury was neither mortal nor dangerous. In all my days I never enjoyed food so rich as what I ate there. But this was the only reward for my labors, except the praise of the czar, and that was spoiled by the envy of some nobles.

When I had completely recovered, I was sent down the Volga by boat to Astrakhan in order to set up a powder mill there, just as I had done in Moscow, because it was not always possible for the czar to supply these border fortresses outside of Moscow with fresh, usable powder, which had to be shipped by water at great risk. I was glad to be of use, for the czar had promised to return me to Holland after the completion of my business, and to give me a sum of money commensurate with his majesty's gratitude and my just deserts. But alas! when we think we are most assured and safe in our hopes and in the ideas we have conceived, unexpectedly there comes a wind that blows down all the unsubstantial trumpery we have been building up over a long time.

The governor of Astrakhan treated me as if I were the czar himself, and in a short time I had everything going nicely: I remade, as it were, his stale, ruined ammunition, which was spoiled and no good, in much the same way that a tinner makes a new spoon from the metal of an old one. At that time among the Russians, this process was unheard-of; and because of this and other tricks I knew, I was considered by some as a sorcerer, by others as a new saint or prophet, and by still others as a second Empedocles or Gorgias Leontinus.[23]

[23] Greek philosophers, living in Sicily in the fifth century B.C., who were given credit for unusual skills.

One night, when I was in the middle of my work in a powder mill outside the fortress, I was kidnapped by a gang of roving Tartars. They took me (and others) a long way into their country, and there I not only saw the sheep-plant borametz,[24] but I was even permitted to eat of it. The Tartars traded me for Chinese merchandise to some Tartars of Nuichi, who gave me as a special present to the king of Korea, with whom they had just concluded an armistice. In Korea I was valued highly because there was no one like me in fencing, and because I taught the king how he could hit the bull's eye with the gun over his shoulder and his back to the target. For this he liked me a lot, and on my most humble petition he gave me my freedom and sent me by way of Japan to the Portuguese in Macao; they, however, paid little attention to me. For this reason I moved among them like a sheep that has strayed from its own flock. At last I was captured in a strange manner by Turkish or Mohammedan pirates, who, after carrying me around for about a year among strange foreign peoples that populate the East Indian islands, sold me to some traders from Alexandria in Egypt. They took me, along with their merchandise, to Constantinople, where the Turkish emperor was readying several galleys against the Venetians. And as oarsmen were needed, many Turkish merchants had to give up their Christian slaves (for indemnity, though). Being a strapping young fellow, I was drafted and so had to learn how to row; but this slavery did not last more than two months. Our galley was taken in the Levant by the brave Venetians, and I and all my fellow slaves were released from the power of the Turks. The galley was brought to Venice with rich booty and several Turkish captives of high rank, and I was freed. Since I wished to make a pilgrimage to Rome and Loreto, in order to see these places and to thank God for my liberation, I easily obtained a passport and a considerable sum of money from honest folk, particularly Germans; and so I was able to start on my journey equipped with the long staff of the pilgrim.

I went to Rome by the shortest route, and there I was lucky, for I received good alms from important as well as plain people. After staying there for about six weeks, I joined other pilgrims (among them Germans, and particularly several Swiss who were going home) for the trip to Loreto. From there, by way of the Gotthard Pass and Switzerland, I returned to the Black Forest and my knan, who had kept the farm for me. I did not bring anything special home with me except a beard, which I had grown abroad.

---

[24] Legendary plant mentioned by contemporary travelers. It is essentially cotton to which mutton has been gratuitously added.

I had been away for three years and several months, during which time I had crossed several oceans, seen many nations, but generally had experienced more evil than good. I could write a whole book about it. Meanwhile the German peace[25] had been proclaimed, and I was able to live in ease and quiet with my knan. I let him worry and manage, while I sat down to my books again, which were both my work and my delight.

CHAPTER 23: *This chapter is nice and short: it only concerns Simplicius*

I ONCE READ THAT when a Roman delegation had asked how to govern their nation in peace, the oracle of Apollo had answered, "Nosce te ipsum," that is, "Let everyone know himself." This made me reflect, and now, having nothing else to do, I demanded from myself a reckoning of my past life. I said to myself: Your life has been no life but a death; your days have been a heavy shadow, your years a bad dream, your desires grievous sins, your youth a phantom, your well-being an alchemist's treasure that flies up the chimney and is gone before you are aware of it. Through grave danger you ran after the wars, where you experienced much good luck and much bad; you have been now up, now down; now great, now small; now rich, now poor; now joyful, now sad; now well-liked, now hated; now honored, now despised. But, my poor soul, what did you gain from all this journey? This much: I am poor in possessions; my heart is heavy with care; I am loath to do good, lazy and corrupt; and, what's most miserable, my conscience is burdened and fearful. But you, my soul, are weighed down with sin and horribly befouled. My body is weary, my reason confused; my innocence is gone, the better part of my youth is frittered away, precious time is lost, there is nothing that gladdens me, and I am an enemy to myself. When I entered the world after my blessed father's death, I was simple-minded and clean, upright and honest, truthful, humble, diffident, modest, chaste, shamefaced, pious, and devout. But soon I became mean, false, lying, proud, restless, and godless in every respect. And all these vices I learned without a teacher. I guarded my honor, not for its own sake, but for my advancement. I became conscious of time, not so that I might use it well for my salvation, but in order to profit my body. I exposed my life to danger many times,

---

[25] The Peace of Westphalia, 1648.

and yet I never exerted myself to improve it so that I might die comforted and blessed. I only looked to the present, to my worldly profit, and never once thought of the future, let alone that I would someday have to render an account of myself in the sight of God.

Such thoughts tormented me every day, and just then several books by Guevara[26] came to my attention. From these I must quote here, because their sentiment was powerful enough to make me disgusted with the world.

CHAPTER 24: *This is the very last one. It tells how and why Simplicius leaves the world once again*

"FAREWELL, O WORLD, FOR you cannot be trusted, nor is there anything to be expected of you. Within your house the past has disappeared, the present is vanishing under our very hands, and the future has never begun; the most constant is falling down, the most powerful is breaking to pieces, the most eternal is coming to an end, so that you are a corpse among corpses, and within the course of a century you hardly let us live an hour.

"Farewell, World, for you take us captive and do not release us; you tie us down and never loosen our bonds; you sadden us without consoling us; you rob us without restoring; you accuse us without cause; you condemn us without a hearing, so that you may kill us without sentence and bury us without waiting for our death! With you there is no joy without sadness, no peace without discord, no love without suspicion, no rest without fear, no abundance without poverty, no honor without stain, no possession without a bad conscience, no occupation without complaint, and no friendship without falsehood.

"Farewell, World, for inside your palace promises of gifts are made without the intention of giving; people serve without pay; they caress in order to kill, elevate to cast down, help in order to cut down, honor in order to dishonor, borrow never to return, punish without pardon!

"May God bless you, World, for in your house great lords and favorites of princes are hurled down; unworthy creatures are preferred; traitors, looked upon with favor; faithful men, pushed into a corner;

---

[26] Antonio de Guevara (*ca.* 1490-1544), Spanish moralist and court preacher to Charles V, died as bishop of Cadix. The extensive quotation, which is of central importance to *Simplicius*, comes from the *Menosprecio de corte*, in the German translation of Aegidius Albertinus (Munich, 1598, and later).

evildoers, left unimpeded; the innocent, condemned; the wise and qualified, dismissed; bunglers, given great rewards; crafty men, believed. Plain and honest men gain no credence; each does what he pleases, not one as he ought.

"Farewell, World, for in your domain no one is called by his right name: the headstrong are called bold; the faint-hearted, careful; the willful, diligent; and the negligent, peaceful. A wastrel is called magnificent; and a miser, self-sufficient; a crafty tattler and prater, eloquent; the quiet man, a fool or visionary. An adulterer or despoiler of virgins is called an amorous blade; a person with a dirty mind, a courtier; a vengeful one, a zealous partisan; a gentle mind, a dreamer. You are selling us the pleasant for the unpleasant, and the unpleasant for the pleasant.

"Farewell, World, for you mislead everyone: you promise honor to the ambitious, change to the restless; to the climber, the favor of princes; to the easygoing, offices; to the miser, great treasure; to gluttons and lechers, goring and venery; to enemies, revenge; to thieves, secrecy; to youths, long life; to court favorites, unwavering princely favor.

"Farewell, World, for within your palace neither trust nor truth can find lodging; whoever speaks with you is made shameless; whoever trusts you is cheated; whoever follows you is misled; whoever fears you is most badly mistreated; whoever loves you is rewarded with evil; and whoever relies on you absolutely is ruined absolutely. You repay no gift that is given to you, no service shown to you, no kind word spoken to you, nor faith nor friendship kept with you; rather, you deceive, cut down, put to shame, besmirch, threaten, devour, and forget everyone; for that reason everyone cries, sighs, laments, complains, and is undone; and everyone comes to an end. In your house one sees and learns only to hate to the point of strangulation, talk to the point of lying, love to the point of despair, carry on commerce to the point of stealing, beg to the point of cheating, and sin to the point of death.

"God be with you, World, for while one follows you, one idles away one's time in forgetfulness, one's youth with running, racing, jumping over fences and across footpaths, roads and lanes, over hill and dale, through woods and wilderness, across lakes and oceans, in snow and rain, heat and cold, wind and weather. A man's strength is worn down with mining the ore of metals and smelting it, with cutting and shaping rocks, clearing land and building, planting and cultivating, with thinking, scheming, and longing; with advice, arrangements, cares, and troubles; with buying and selling, quarreling, feuding, warring, lying, and cheating. Old age is spent in misery and care: the spirit grows weak, the breath begins to stink, the face becomes wrinkled, a straight body bent; eyes grow dim, limbs tremble, the nose begins to drip, the head grows bald, hearing deteriorates, the sense of smell grows weak and disappears, and taste goes away. A man sighs and complains, is lazy and weak; in sum, he has nothing but misery and labor until his death.

"Farewell, World, for within your bounds no one wants to be pious. Every day murderers are executed; traitors drawn and quartered; robbers, thieves, and holdup men hanged; homicides beheaded; sorcerers burned; perjurers punished; and rebels exiled.

"God be with you, World, for your servants have no other job or pastime than that of being lazy, of irritating and scolding one another, courting virgins, waiting on beautiful women, making eyes at them, playing cards and dice, dealing with pimps, making war on neighbors, gossiping, thinking up evil schemes, going after profit, inventing new fashions, originating new tricks, and introducing new vices.

"Farewell, World, for within your bounds no one is satisfied or contented. If a man is poor, he wants to own something; if rich, to be considered a great personage; if lowly, to rise high; if insulted, to avenge himself; if in favor, to lord it over others; if full of vice, to be in a happy mood.

"Farewell, World, for with you nothing is constant. High towers are struck by lightning; mills are carried away by water; wood is eaten by worms, grain by mice, fruit by caterpillars, and clothes by cockroaches; cattle grow worthless with age, and mankind with disease: one man has scabies, another cancer; a third has lupus; a fourth, syphilis; a fifth, arthritis; the sixth has gout; the seventh, dropsy; the eighth, kidney stones; the ninth, gravel; the tenth, consumption; the eleventh, a fever; the twelfth, leprosy; the thirteenth, epilepsy; the fourteenth is insane. Within you, O World, one person never does what the next does, for when one is crying the other is laughing; one is sighing, the other is joyous; one is fasting, the other is stuffing himself; one is having a feast, the next is starving; one is riding, the other is walking; one is talking, the other is silent; one is playing, the next is working; and when one is born, another is dying. Nor does one live like another: one is the master, the other is the servant; one is a pastor of men, another is pasturing his hogs; one follows the court, another the plow; one is sailing across the seas, another is journeying over land to the weekly markets or annual fairs; one is working in fire, another inside the cool earth; one is fishing in water, another is catching birds in the air; one is hard at work, another lives off the land as a robber or thief.

"May God bless you, O World, for within your house one cannot live a holy life, or suffer death uniformly. One person dies in the cradle; another, in his youth in bed; the third, by the rope; the fourth, by the sword; the fifth is broken on the wheel; the sixth is burned at the stake; the seventh dies in a wine glass; the eighth, in a watery river; the ninth suffocates in a pork barrel; the tenth is killed by poison; the eleventh dies suddenly; the twelfth, in battle; the thirteenth, through witchcraft; and the fourteenth drowns his poor soul in an inkwell.

"May God keep you, O World, for your conversation disgusts me; the life you give us is a miserable pilgrimage, an inconstant, uncertain, hard, harsh, fleeting, and unclean life full of poverty and error; it is to be called death rather than life; for we all die in it every moment, through the many imperfections of inconstancy and through death's various approaches. You are not satisfied with the bitterness with which you are permeated and surrounded; but in addition you cheat most people by your flattery, your incitements and false promises; from the golden chalice that you hold in your hand, you dispense bitterness and falsehood and make people blind, deaf, drunk, and insensitive. Oh, how happy are those who reject your community, despise your sudden momentary joys, spurn your society, and refuse to be lost in the company of such a malicious impostress; for you make of us a gloomy abyss, a miserable clod of dirt, a child of anger, a stinking carrion, an unclean vessel in a dung pit, a vessel of putrefaction full of stench and abomination; for after you have long harried and troubled us with flattery, caresses, threats, beatings, tribulation, martyrdom, and pain, you surrender the worn-out body to the grave and deliver the soul to an uncertain chance. For although nothing is more certain than death, a man is never sure how, when, and where he will die, and — what is most pitiable — where his soul will go and how it will fare. But woe unto the poor soul that has served you, O World, has obeyed you and followed your luxuries and lusts; for after such a poor, sinful, and unconverted soul has departed its miserable body in a sudden and unexpected fright, it is not surrounded by servants and acquaintances (as was the body, while alive), but it is led to the judgment seat of Christ by a drove of its most ghastly enemies. Therefore, O World, may God be with you, for I am sure that in time you will forsake me, not only when my poor soul must appear before the face of the severe judge, but also when the most frightful sentence of all is delivered and pronounced, 'You who are condemned, go to the eternal fire,' and so on.

"Farewell, World, you vile and wicked world, O you stinking, miserable flesh; for because of you, and because the ungodly unrepentant followed you, he is condemned to eternal damnation where, in all eternity, nothing is to be expected but suffering without solace, in exchange for all the pleasures enjoyed; thirst without quenching, for all the drinking; hunger without fulfillment, for all the gluttony; darkness without light, for all the magnificence and splendor; pain without alleviation, for all the voluptuous pleasures; howling, gnashing of teeth, and complaints without surcease, for all the domination and triumph; heat without coolness, fire without extinction, cold without measure, and misery without end.

"God be with you, World, for instead of your promised joys and lusts, evil spirits will lay hands on the unrepentant and condemned soul, and they will rush it to the pit of hell where it will see and hear nothing but the frightful shapes of the devils and the condemned, unrelieved darkness and smoke, fire without brightness, cries, howls, gnashing of teeth, and blasphemy. Then all hope of grace and forgiveness is past; there is no respect of persons: the higher a man climbed or the harder he sinned, the deeper he is cast down, the greater is the pain he must suffer. Much is asked of him to whom much was given; and the more one made himself to shine within your bounds, O vile and wicked World, the more torment and suffering is meted out to him, for divine justice requires it thus.

"God be with you, World, for although the body stays awhile with you in the ground and decays there, yet it will rise on doomsday, and according to the final judgment, there will be eternal hellfire. Then the poor soul will say, 'World, be accursed! For through your blandishments I forgot God and myself, and I followed you all the days of my life in voluptuousness, evil, sin, and shame. Accursed be the hour when God created me! Accursed be the day when I was born into your domain, you evil and wicked World! O you mountains, hills, and rocks, fall on me and hide me from the grim anger of the Lamb, from the countenance of Him who sitteth in the seat of judgment. Ah, woe is me, and woe again in all eternity!'

"O World, you unclean world! For these reasons I pray, I beg, I ask, I admonish you, and I protest against you. May you have no part of me any more. I, for my part, do not desire to place any hope in you, for you know I have determined to put an end to care. Hope and fortune, farewell!"

All these words I pondered diligently and constantly. They caused me to leave this world and to become a hermit once more. I would have liked to live near my mineral spring, but the peasants of the neighborhood did not want me, though the lonely woods suited me well. They feared that I might give away the secret of the spring and get their lord to build trails and a road to it, now that peace had come. Therefore, I went to another wild place and resumed the life I had led in the Spessart. It is not certain that I, like my late father, shall keep it up until the end. May God grant us all the favor of obtaining from Him what is of greatest value to us, namely, a blessed

End.

Book Six:

Continuation and Conclusion

O motion wondrous strange, O most inconstant rest!
A man who thinks he stands is straightway onward pressed.
   O most elusive rest, so restless in repose.
   Our downfall rushes in, descent we never chose,
Even as death itself. Inconstancy that took
Great toll of me is found described here in this book.
   Inconstancy doth lurk within each moment's gladness;
   Inconstancy alone outlives our very sadness.

CHAPTER 1: *A little preface and a brief report on how the new hermit's life agreed with him*

IF ANYBODY IMAGINES I am relating the story of my life merely to while away the time or to make people laugh (as jesters and mountebanks do), he is greatly mistaken. Too much laughter is disgusting to me, and whoever kills that noble, irreplaceable asset, time, badly wastes the divine gift which is granted to us, so we may work out the salvation of our souls. Why should I help anybody to such vain foolishness and, without being asked, become other folks' Secretary of Entertainment? As if I didn't know that by doing so I would participate in other people's sins? Dear reader, I consider myself above such business; and whoever wants a fool, let him buy two and he'll have one to spare. The reason I am presenting my story with a dash of humor is that some delicate tenderlings can't swallow pills that are good for them unless they have been coated with sugar and gilt, not to mention the fact that even the most sober-sided of men will put down a serious book, whereas they keep reading one that makes them smile ever so little every once in a while.

If I am charged with making satirical attacks, I plead "Not guilty." Many folks would rather see general vices berated and scored in a general way than have their own deficiency of virtue corrected in a friendly way. Unfortunately, Mr. Everybody (to whom I am addressing my story) does not enjoy the theological style either. One can see how mountebanks and medicine men nowadays draw more of an audience when their clown begins to shout and caper than can the most enthusiastic minister of the gospel who is calling his flock together, by having all the church bells rung three times in a row, so that he may deliver a wholesome sermon.

Be that as it may. Let me protest to the world that I am innocent if someone takes offense at my having dressed up Simplicissimus in the fashion demanded by the people themselves, when they want to be taught something useful. If here and there a reader is satisfied with the husks and disregards the kernel which is hidden underneath, he will have a jolly story to content him, but he will miss by far that which I had really wanted him to get. So I'll start where I left off at the end of the fifth book.

There the gentle reader learned that I became a hermit once more, and why. Now I must tell how I carried on in this state. The first few months, while my ardor was still strong, everything went well. From the start I easily put a damper on my carnal desire (i.e. lust, an even better designation might be "lack-lust"), to which I had been dedicated, for since I no longer worshipped Bacchus and Ceres, neither did Venus care to visit me anymore. But still I was far from perfect; I had my temptations, a thousand every hour. For instance, when, in order to make myself feel remorseful, I thought of the practical jokes and tricks I had played on folks, in days gone by, the lust of the flesh which I had enjoyed then, came back to haunt me. That wasn't always good for me, nor did it help my spiritual progress. I have since concluded that idleness was my greatest enemy, and freedom (for I was not subject to a clergyman who would minister to me and watch over me) was the chief cause of my failure to persist in the life I had determined to lead.

I lived on a high mountain range called the Moss, a part of the Black Forest that is covered by somber firs. I had a beautiful view eastward into the Oppenau valley and its branches, and south into the valley of the Kinzig and the county of Geroltseck, where the lofty castle rises among the neighboring heights, like the king in a game of ninepins. To the west I could survey upper and lower Alsatia; to the north in the direction of lower Baden, down the Rhine, the city of Strasbourg, with its high cathedral tower, stands out like the heart enclosed in a body. I spent more time looking at the beauty of the view than praying; my telescope, which I had decided not to give up, was a powerful encouragement in this. After dark, when I could no longer use the glass, I picked up the instrument I had invented for the reinforcement of hearing and listened, e.g., to dogs barking several hours away or to some game stirring closer by. This is the kind of foolishness in which I engaged, and in time I neglected work and prayer, two activities by which the old Egyptian hermits had maintained themselves physically and spiritually.

In the beginning, while I was still new, I went about the neighboring valleys, from house to house, looking for alms in order to stay alive. I took no more than what I barely needed, and I especially shunned money, an attitude that my near neighbors viewed as a great miracle, even as a kind of apostolic holiness. But as soon as my abode became known, everybody who came into the woods brought me something to eat. These people bragged about my holy and unusual life, so that folks from farther away, impelled by curiosity or veneration, also came to see me. Thus I suffered no scarcity of bread, butter, salt, cheese, bacon, eggs, and other vittles; I even had too much! But that did not make me any more blessed. Rather, the longer I lived, the worse I became, growing lazier and less charitable. I could well have been called a hypocrite, a holy faker. For all that, I did not give up thinking about virtues and vices and considering what I would have to do if I wanted to go to heaven. But all this went on without system, without good counsel, and without the firm resolve to be as serious as my status and its improvement required.

CHAPTERS 2-18: *Summary*

[Simplicius, asleep, reports a vision or dream: The Prince of Darkness receives word that the Thirty Years' War has ended and that peace on earth is greeted with the joyous singing of "Gloria in excelsis" and "Te deum laudamus." This news drives Lucifer almost insane with rage. He lashes out at various devils for having wasted their chances through laziness. But Belial points out that peace also produces a respectable crop of vices and that all is not lost. Lucifer's fury has attracted many other spirits of hell, who are now lectured by their prince and promised rewards if they redouble their efforts.

[The pep talk over, a dispute arises between Extravagance, a gorgeous female, and Avarice, a ragged old man, concerning who can serve hell better. Instead of receiving a verdict, they are sent out into the world to substantiate their respective claims. Extravagance is assigned to a rich, young English lord; Avarice, to his steward. The lord wastes a fortune, while the steward fraudulently amasses one. In the end they join the army of Charles II and after his defeat become robbers. After their capture, the master is beheaded, the servant hanged. Thus the quarrel remains undecided and Simplicius wakes up.

[On a walk through the woods Simplicius finds a life-sized statue. It looks like an old German hero; and when he tries to turn it over, it begins to speak, saying its name is "Soondifferent," who has always been with him and who will not leave him until he dies. It gives Simplicius a recipe for conversing with lifeless objects and, as if for fun, changes into about a dozen different shapes, but always remains its own true Soondifferent self. Having changed into a bird, it flies away.

[Simplicius feels that he is not really serving God or man; and after reading some saints' lives he decides to make another pilgrimage. His costume and hairy appearance help him in making an easy living, but he is hardly better than a hobo: in Schaffhausen a rich burgher gives him a night's lodging, and in turn he tells fanciful tales about his travels and gives the burgher a foolproof coded recipe against being hit by bullets: "Stand where no one is shooting and you will be safe." His conscience bothers him, however, and in order to keep the man from a false sense of security, he informs him by letter that he has played a hoax on him.

[Along his way, Simplicius tells the most egregious and fantastic lies. He has culled them mostly from ancient writers like Pliny, but he leads his listeners to believe that he has personally seen and experienced everything.

[In a castle owned by a former acquaintance, Simplicius exorcises a ghost. For this service he is offered valuable gifts, which he refuses. He only accepts a lining for his threadbare old cloak. However, the owner secretly sews pieces of gold into it.

[In another burst of humility and devotion Simplicius visits the holy places of Loreto and Rome, and when he discovers the gold coins in his cloak, he decides to journey to Jerusalem. In Genoa he takes a boat for Alexandria, where war prevents further progress. While sight-seeing in Egypt — in Cairo he sees pyramids, and mummies, and machines that raise chickens without hens — he is captured by Arabian robbers and taken to the Red Sea. But whereas the other Christians are sold as slaves, Simplicius is exhibited as a wild and wooly cave man from Arabia Deserta. Under threat of death he is to keep silent while on exhibit. Simplicius doesn't mind his life too much, but in a large commercial city, before an audience consisting partly of Europeans, he blurts out in Latin that he is being held against his will and would appreciate being rescued. A riot ensues, and the local ruler decides Simplicius must be freed; his former masters are sentenced to toil as galley slaves, and part of their confiscated property is to go to Simplicius as payment for damages. Simplicius renders thanks to his European rescuers and wonders what to do next.]

CHAPTER 19: *Simplicius and the carpenter come away with their lives and, having suffered shipwreck, are provided with a land of their own*

MY FELLOW COUNTRYMEN ADVISED me to buy a new set of clothes, and because I had nothing else to do I sought the acquaintance of all the Europeans; they liked to have me about, both for reasons of Christian charity and because of my unusual experiences. Since there was little hope that the Damascene war in Syria and Judea would soon end, enabling me to resume and complete my journey to Jerusalem, I changed my mind and decided to go home via Portugal in a large Portuguese galleon that was ready to leave. Instead of the pilgrimage to Jerusalem, I would make one to St. James at Compostela, and then I would retire somewhere and use up what God had granted me.

In order to sail without special expense (for as soon as I had plenty of money I started pinching pennies), I made an agreement with the head merchant on the galleon: he was to take over all my money and use it to his advantage; he was to return it to me in Portugal, but instead of interest I was to receive free passage and to eat at his table; furthermore, I was to do all sorts of jobs aboard ship and ashore, as occasion and necessity required. But I reckoned without my host, for little did I know what the good Lord had in mind for me. I undertook this long and dangerous journey all the more eagerly because the previous trip across the Mediterranean had gone so well.

When we had boarded the ship and moved with a favorable wind out of the Arabian Gulf (or the Red Sea) into the ocean, we set our course for the Cape of Good Hope and sailed for several weeks, enjoying weather that could not have been any better. When we thought we were close to the island of Madagascar, there suddenly arose a storm so violent that we hardly had time to take in sail. The storm grew worse, and as time passed it got so bad that we had to cut off the mast and abandon our ship to the capricious force of the waves. They took us up almost to the clouds and the next moment dropped us down into an abyss, and those up-and-down movements took as long as half an hour. This very collectively taught us how to pray. Finally the waves threw us with such violence on a hidden cliff that the ship broke to pieces with a horrible crash, and a pitiful cry arose all around. The area was instantly strewn with boxes, bales, and parts of the ship. On the crests and in the depths of the waves woeful human beings were clinging to objects which they had happened to grasp in their predicament. With ghastly screams they deplored their end or commended their souls to God.

A carpenter and I were lying on a large piece of the ship, a sort of raft held together by beams. We clung to them and encouraged each other. Gradually the cruel storm subsided, and little by little the raging waves grew calm and smooth. But pitch-dark night came, bringing with it a sudden shower. It now appeared that in the middle of the ocean we were to be drowned from above. The rain lasted till midnight, and we suffered greatly. Then the sky became clear again, so that we could see the stars; and by them we could tell that the wind, coming from Africa, was drifting us out to sea in the direction of unexplored Australia; and that gave us quite a shock.

Toward daybreak it got dark again so that we couldn't see each other, though we were not far apart. We continued drifting in this dark and miserable state until we suddenly noticed that we had run aground and stopped. The carpenter, who had a hatchet in his belt, probed the depth of the water and when he found it was less than a foot deep on one side we were greatly relieved; we had hopes that God had helped us to reach land. When we recovered, we noticed a fragrance of flowers, indicating the same thing. But because it was so dark and the two of us were so tired, we did not have the heart to look for shore, though we thought we could hear birds singing (as, in fact, we could). As soon as day broke in the east we saw close by in the dim light some land and bushes. So we dropped off into the water, which became shallower as we waded, until, overjoyed, we finally stepped onto dry land. There we fell on our knees, kissed the earth, and thanked God in heaven for preserving us like a father and guiding us to this shore. And that's how I came to the island.

At first we did not know whether we were on an inhabited or an uninhabited part of the mainland, or only on an island.[1] But we noticed right away that the soil must be very fertile, for every square foot of it was so covered with bushes and trees that we could hardly get through. When it was completely light and we had made our way through the undergrowth for about a quarter of an hour without seeing even the slightest trace of human habitation, we concluded that we must be on an unknown but very rich island. Many strange birds approached us without fear; we could even catch them with our hands. We found lemons, oranges, and coconuts — fruits we enjoyed very much. When the sun rose we came to a plateau that was full of palm trees (from which palm wine can be made). This delighted my comrade no end, for

---

[1] About here begins the part of the novel which reminds the modern reader of Defoe's bestseller *Robinson Crusoe* (1719 ff.) Actually Grimmelshausen's account is based on Henry Neville's *The Isle of Pines*, a German translation of which appeared in Frankfurt in 1668.

he loved to drink. There we rested in the sun and dried our clothes, which we had taken off and draped over some bushes; meanwhile, we walked around in our underwear. My carpenter struck his hatchet into a palmetto and found that it was full of cider. Unfortunately we had no vessel in which to catch it, for both of us had lost our hats in the shipwreck.

When the sunshine had dried our clothes, we put them back on and climbed to a high, rocky peak, located on the right side, toward the north, between the plains and the sea. Looking around, we discovered that we were not on a large mass of land but on an island no bigger around than an hour and a half's walk. And when we could see no other land far or near, but only water and sky, we both became sad and lost all hope of ever seeing human beings again. On the other hand, we were consoled that God's kindness had sent us to this safe and fertile place, and not to a barren spot inhabited by cannibals. Then we started to consider what we would have to do (or avoid doing) in order to survive. And since we had to live together on this island almost like prisoners, we swore each other eternal loyalty.

On the mountain we had climbed were many and various kinds of birds, and their nests were so full of eggs that we could hardly stop marveling. We ate some raw and took a supply with us to a spring of sweet water, which flowed toward the sea with enough volume to drive a small mill wheel. Again we felt joyful and decided to build our house near this spring. For our new household the two of us had no other equipment than one hatchet, one spoon, three knives, one fork, and a pair of scissors. There was nothing else. To be sure, my comrade had some thirty ducats that we would gladly have spent for a lighter if we had only known where to buy one. But the money was of absolutely no use to us; in fact, it was worth less than my powder horn, which was filled with tinder that had become soft and gooey. I dried this tinder in the sun and put part of it on a flat stone; over it I spread some easily combustible material, of which there was plenty — moss and fibers from the coconut trees. Then I ran my knife through the powder and struck a fire. This made us as happy as our rescue from the sea. If we had only had salt, bread, and a drinking cup, we would have considered ourselves the luckiest fellows in the world, though twenty-four hours before we could have been counted among the most unfortunate. Such is God's faithfulness and mercy toward men. His be the honor in all eternity. Amen.

We caught some of the birds that were all around us, killed, plucked, and washed them, and stuck them on a wooden spit. I turned the roast while my comrade brought in timber and started building a hut to protect us from rain (which is rather bad for health in this part of the world). To make up for the lack of salt, we seasoned our food with lemon juice.

CHAPTER 20: *They hire a pretty cook, and with God's help they get rid of her*

THIS WAS OUR FIRST meal on the island; having finished it, we collected dry wood to keep up our fire. We would have liked to explore the whole island; but because of exhaustion, sleep pressed in upon us and we slept without interruption until early next morning. Then we followed the brook to the place where it pours into the sea, and we saw with great amazement that a vast number of fish, all the size of medium salmon or large carp, was moving up the sweet water of the little river. It looked like a large herd of hogs crowding ahead. When we also found some bananas and sweet potatoes — both good eating — we thought we had struck it lucky, though we missed four-legged animals and wished we had company to help us enjoy the fruits, fish, and fowl of this island. But we could not discover a single vestige that men had ever been there.

We were walking along the shore, wondering how to arrange our household and especially how to get pots and pans for cooking, and for fermenting and keeping palm wine so that we could really enjoy it, when out at sea we saw something drifting that we could not make out because of the distance, though it looked bigger than it turned out to be. When it came closer and drifted ashore, it proved to be a half-dead woman. She lay on a box and her hands were stuck through its handles. Christian compassion caused us to pull her ashore; and when we figured out from her clothing and other indications that she must be an Abyssinian Christian, we were all the more anxious to bring her around. Observing the proprieties, as is becoming with honest women, we held her, head down, until a considerable quantity of water had run out of her. And though we had nothing save lemons with which to revive her, we squirted under her nose the oil contained in the peel, and shook her until finally she began to move and speak in Portuguese. As soon as my comrade heard this, and after a little color had returned to the woman's face, he said to me, "This Abyssinian woman sailed in our ship as the maid of a great Portuguese lady. I knew both of them well. They embarked at Macao[2] and were headed for Annabon."[3] When the woman heard this, she showed great joy, addressed the carpenter by name, and not only told about her trip but also spoke with amazement at their both being still alive and meeting here, ashore and out of danger. The carpenter asked what might be in the box. She answered that it contained some Chinese cloth, some small arms and weapons, and several large and small pieces of china (which were to have been sent by her mistress' husband to a great prince in Portugal). We were very glad, because we needed all of these things badly.

After that she asked us to be kind enough to keep her with us: she would cook for us, do the laundry, and generally act as our maid — even be like a slave to us — if only we would protect her and provide her with the necessities of life, as much as good fortune and the nature of this country permitted. With much effort and exertion the two of us carried the sturdy trunk to the place we had chosen for our house. There we opened it and found in it implements so practical that, in the present condition of our household, we could not have wished for anything better. We unpacked and dried everything in the sun, and our new cook proved very helpful and diligent. After that we butchered poultry, which we boiled and fried. Meanwhile, the carpenter went to get palm cider, while I walked to the nearby mountain to gather eggs, which we used hard-boiled in place of our daily bread. On the way I thankfully contemplated God's great gifts and benefices, which His providence had lovingly furnished us and would continue to provide. I prostrated myself and thanked the good Lord with outstretched arms and a heart gratefully uplifted. Then I gathered as many eggs as we needed and returned to our hut, where the evening meal was already set out on the very chest that we had fished out of the sea and were now using as a table.

While I had been away getting eggs my comrade (who was twenty-odd years old, while I was over forty) had made an agreement with the cook which was to turn out badly for both him and me. Being alone together, they had talked of old times and the fertility and abundance of this island, which could be called truly blessed; and they had become

[2] Macao, the Chinese seaport held by the Portuguese since 1557; Simplicius had embarked there on his way home from Russia (V, 22). The original text read Anacao, probably a misprint that went uncorrected until 1921 when H. H. Borcherdt made the emendation.

[3] Annobón, a small island in the Gulf of Guinea. It was discovered on January 1, 1473, (hence the name) by the Portuguese and held by them until ceded to Spain in 1778.

so close that they were considering marriage. But the Abyssinian girl would not hear of it unless my comrade, the carpenter, got me out of the way and made himself the sole ruler of the island. She said it was impossible to have a happy, peaceful marriage if a single man were around; and she made him consider how suspicion and jealousy would plague him if an old fellow were talking with her every day, though he might never even intend to cuckold him. "But I have a better plan," she said. "If I should ever marry and increase the human race on this island, which can easily support a thousand or more people, let the old fellow marry me. Then it's only a matter of some twelve or fourteen years until we'll have a daughter whom you can marry." The carpenter would still not be as old as I was now, and the firm expectation that one would become the other's father-in-law (or son-in-law) would prevent any ill feeling or danger. Of course, she would rather have a young man than an old one, but under the circumstances they would have to act as necessity required and play it safe for the sake of herself and the children to be borne by her. This conversation was more drawn out and used more words than I have in reporting it here. But it and the quick movements and beauty of the alleged Abyssinian (who looked much more impressive by firelight) so captivated and bedeviled my good carpenter to the extent that he offered to throw the old fellow — meaning me — into the ocean, for he would sooner wreck the island than give up a lady like her. That's when they made the agreement I mentioned before. But he was to kill me with his ax, treacherously, while I was asleep, for he was afraid of my strength and my club, which he himself had made for me, in the shape of a Bohemian earpick.

The two having made their arrangement, the woman showed my comrade a deposit of good potter's clay not far from our hut, and promised to make beautiful pottery from it — just like that of the Indian women who live on the shores of Guinea. She also proposed various ways of advancing herself and her descendants, to nurture them on this island, and provide a peaceful, enjoyable life for a hundred generations to come. She could hardly stop enumerating all the good she would derive from the coconut trees. From their fibers she wanted to make clothing for herself and her children and grandchildren, and so on.

And now I, poor man, returned, being completely in the dark about their evil agreement and foul business. I sat down to enjoy what had been prepared, and according to Christian custom and praiseworthy tradition I said grace. But as soon as I made the sign of the cross over the food and my table companions and asked for divine blessing, our cook and the trunk disappeared with all that had been in it. Left behind was a stench so strong that my comrade fainted.

CHAPTER 21: *How they dwelt on the island, and how they became accustomed to such a life*

AS SOON AS HE had recovered a little and come to his seven senses, he knelt down in front of me, folded his hands, and for perhaps ten minutes repeated nothing but the words, "Ah, father! Ah brother! Ah, father! Ah brother!" While he kept repeating these words, he cried and sobbed and could not utter anything sensible. I was beginning to think that fright and the stench had deprived him of reason. When he did not stop but kept on asking my forgiveness, I demanded, "Dearest friend, what shall I forgive you? You never hurt me. Tell me how I can help you." "I ask your forgiveness," he replied, "for I have sinned against God, against you, and against myself." And then he repeated again and again his previous lament, until I told him that I knew of nothing sinful in him, but if he had indeed done something that weighed on his conscience, not only would I forgive and forget from the bottom of my heart (as far as it concerned me), but I would also join him in calling on God's mercy and forgiveness. At these words he embraced my legs, kissed my knees, and looked at me so sorrowfully that I fell silent, for I neither knew nor could guess what was the matter. But when I had cheerfully taken him into my arms, embracing him and begging him to tell me what was on his mind and how I might help, he reported in great detail his conversation with the pseudowoman from Abyssinia and the resolve he had made against me, in defiance of God and nature, of Christian love and the oath of true friendship solemnly sworn. And he uttered this with words and gestures that definitely indicated true repentance and a contrite heart.

I consoled him as best I could by saying that God had probably inflicted this as a warning to us so that in the future we might better resist the devil's snares and temptations, and live in constant fear of God. After I had talked with him in this way, he felt consoled a little, but he was not satisfied and begged me most humbly to impose a penance for his crime. In order to restore his downcast soul as much as possible, and because he was a carpenter and his ax was still good, I asked him to erect a cross near the place on the shore where we — and the diabolical cook — had landed. This deed would not only be a penance pleasing to God, but in future would also prevent the fiend (who shuns the sign of the holy cross) from invading our island so easily. "Alas!" he answered, "I shall build and erect not only one cross on the plain but also two on the heights, if only I may regain your grace and favor, O father, and may hope for God's forgiveness." He went to work eagerly and did not stop until he had finished the three crosses.

We erected one on the seashore, the other two separately on the highest peaks of the mountains. The inscription read: *To honor Almighty God and in defiance of the enemy of mankind, Simon Meron from Lisbon in Portugal, with the advice and aid of his faithful friend Simplicius Simplicissimus, a German, has made and here in Christian intent erected this token of the passion of our Saviour.*

From then on we lived a little more religiously than we had before, and for a calendar I carved a notch in a stick for each day and a cross for Sunday. To keep the Sabbath and celebrate it, we sat together talking of holy and divine matters. I had to use this method of keeping track of time because I had not yet thought of how to record anything verbal without the use of paper and ink.

In concluding this chapter I want to reminisce about something that happened on the evening after our good cook's departure. The first night we had not noticed it, for because of exhaustion and fatigue we had fallen asleep at once. The new event that frightened and distressed us was this: We still had vividly in mind how the accursed fiend, in the guise of the Abyssinian, wanted to destroy us by a thousand sly tricks, and we could not sleep. We lay awake a long time; mostly, we prayed. As it grew dark we saw innumerable lights hovering about us in the air. They shone so brightly that we could tell the difference between leaves and fruit in the trees. Thinking that this might well be another temptation of the devil, we fell silent and kept very quiet. But in time we found that it was a kind of firefly or lightning bug (as we called them back home), which comes from a special sort of rotting wood that is found on the island. These bugs are so bright that they can be used in place of brightly burning candles. Later I wrote long passages of this book by their light. If they were as common in Europe, Asia, and Africa as they are here, the candlemakers would lose a lot of business.

CHAPTER 22: *Further consequences of such events; how Simon Meron quit life and the island, and how Simplicissimus remained its only master*

SINCE WE SAW THAT we had to stay where we were, we also arranged our housekeeping differently. My companion made hoes and shovels out of a black wood that becomes almost as hard as iron when it dries out. We used them, first of all, to dig holes for the crosses. Then we made ponds for sea water, in which salt could form (as I had seen in Alexandria, Egypt). Third, we started a pleasant garden, for we considered idleness the beginning of the end. Fourth, we channeled the brook, so that we could direct it as we liked, enabling us to dry up the old bed and thus pick out, with dry hands and feet, so to speak, as many fish and crayfish as we wanted. Fifth, we found extremely good potter's clay next to the brook, and though we had no potter's wheel, or a drill and other tools with which to build one, and though we had never learned this skill, we figured out a way of making what we needed. After we had kneaded and prepared the clay we made it into sausages about as long and thick as British tobacco pipes. We stuck these coils on top of each other like snails and so made earthenware vessels — large and small crocks and dishes for cooking and drinking. After the first firing turned out well, we had no more cause to complain about any lack of supplies. And though we had no bread, we had plenty of dried fish, which we now used in its place. In time the scheme of producing salt also succeeded, and then we really had nothing to complain of — we lived like people of the golden age.

Little by little we learned how to make a delicious cake from eggs, dried fish, and lemon peel, by grinding the last two ingredients between two stones to make a tender meal and baking it with grease from the so-called dodo. My partner learned how to make palm wine by gathering the juice in large jars and letting it stand for a few days until it had fermented. Then he drank so much of the stuff that he staggered, and toward the end he did this almost every day, regardless of how much I spoke against it. He argued that the cider turned to vinegar when you let it stand too long; and there's truth in that. When I asked him not to make so much at once, only a sufficient quantity, he answered that to despise God's gifts was sinful; the palm trees had to be tapped, or they would choke on their own juice. I had to let him run the gamut of his desire, or he would have reproached me for begrudging him what we had in abundance.

And thus, as I said above, we lived like the first men in earth's golden age, when without the least labor a bountiful heaven produced everything that is good for man. However, as no life in this world is so sweet and happy that at times it is not made bitter by the gall of suffering, so it happened to us, too. Insofar as our household improved daily, to that extent our clothing deteriorated from day to day until it rotted on our bodies. Fortunately, until now we had never noticed any winter, not even the slightest cold spell, though at the time when we began to go naked, we had been on the island more than a year and a half, according to my tally. At all times the weather was like that of Europe during May and June, except that about August or a little earlier we had hard rains and thunderstorms. From one solstice to the other the length of days never varied more than an hour and a quarter. Although we were by ourselves on the island, still we did not want to go naked like brute animals but wished to be clothed like European Christians. If we had had quadrupeds, we could have used their skins for covering; lacking them, we skinned large birds, like penguins and dodoes, and made ourselves trousers. But because we had neither the tools nor the necessary chemicals to prepare the skins, they turned hard, became uncomfortable, and deteriorated before we knew it. The coconut palms furnished us with enough fibers, but we could not spin or weave them. My pal, who had been in India for several years, showed me a spine like a sharp thorn on the tips of leaves. If it is broken off and pulled along the stalk of the leaf (more or less as is done with string beans), then there remains connected to the thorn a thread as long as the leaf which can be used in place of a needle and thread. This gave me an opportunity to make trousers from leaves, which I sewed together with thread from their own growth.

While we were living together in this manner and had progressed to the point where we had no reason to complain about overwork, waste, want, or trouble, my comrade daily kept on drinking his palm toddy, as he had become used to it, until finally his liver and lights became inflamed; and before I knew it he quit me, the island, and the palm wine by reason of an early death. I buried him as best I could, and while contemplating the inconstancy of human beings and similar topics, I made him the following epitaph:

> The reason I am here and not at sea,
> Nor yet in hell, is that there fought for me
>   Three things: the first was raging ocean;
>   The second, mankind's fiend, hell's cruel Satan.
> These two I did escape with help of God;
> But palm wine put me underneath the sod.

Then I became the sole master of the island, and once more I began the life of a hermit. For this I had not only ample opportunity but also a stubborn will and determination. To be sure, I made use of the gifts and goods of the place (for I was grateful for God's mercy and omnipotence that had granted me such abundance); but I also tried my best not to misuse these riches. I often wished that some of those honest Christians who had to suffer want elsewhere might be present to enjoy the bountiful gifts of God; but since I knew well that it would be easily possible for God (if that were his will) to transport any number of human beings to this place, by means more miraculous than the one by which I had come here, I humbly thanked Him and His divine providence for caring for me like a father and placing me in this serene situation ahead of thousands of others.

CHAPTER 23: *The hermit concludes his story and makes an end of these six books*

MY COMRADE HAD NOT been dead a week when I noticed a spook near my abode. 'All right, Simplicius,' I thought, 'you are alone. Why shouldn't the Evil One dare to trouble you? Don't you imagine this malicious mischief-worker enjoys spoiling life for you? Why do you let him disturb you, when God is your friend?'

For a few days I walked around with such thoughts; they helped me considerably and made me more pious. I was expecting an encounter with the evil spirit, but this time I was mistaken; for one evening when I heard something suspicious I stepped out of my hut, and there by a rock wall, near the largest spring of the brook that runs from the mountain into the sea, I saw my comrade standing and scrabbling with his fingernails in the cracks of the cliff. I was considerably frightened, but I took courage, made the sign of the cross, commended myself to God's protection, and went to the ghost. I thought that since I would have to do it eventually, today was as good a time as any. I used words that are customary on such occasions, and I soon found out that my late

companion, while still alive, had hidden his ducats there, thinking he'd get them out and take them with him when, sooner or later, a ship came to the island. He also gave me to understand that he had relied on this amount of money more than on God for getting home. This was why he had been punished with restlessness after death and been forced to cause me trouble, for which he was sorry. At his request I took out the money, which I valued at less than nothing. (Since I could use it for nothing, one may easily believe me.)

This was my first fright while alone. Later, ghosts other than this one troubled me, but I want to say nothing of that. With God's help and mercy I got to the point where I no longer noticed any enemy except my own thoughts, which were most variable, for thoughts are hard to control, being scot-free; yet in time a reckoning even of these will have to be made.

In order to have my account less heavily charged with sin, I tried to avoid what did not improve me, but I also assigned myself a daily physical task, which I had to do along with my usual prayers. For just as man is born for work (as a bird for flight), so idleness causes illness of body and soul and, in the end, when one least expects it, death. Therefore, I made a garden, though I needed it less than a wagon needs a fifth wheel, since the whole island could justly have been called a lovely pleasure-garden. Nor was my work good for anything but introducing a more complete order here and there, though many a person would have considered the natural disorder of the plants far more charming. But as I said, it did away with idleness.

Oh, how often I wished for books of spiritual instruction: after I had tired my body and needed rest, I wished to console, edify, and delight myself. But books were not to be had. Now, since I had read in some holy author that the whole wide world is a great book, in which he recognized the wondrous works of God and through which he was encouraged to praise Him, I remembered the crown of Christ when I saw a thorny bush; when I saw an apple or a pomegranate, I thought of the fall of our first parents and mourned it; when I drew palm cider from a tree, I imagined how my Savior had mercifully spilled his blood for me; when I saw a mountain or the sea, I recalled the miracles our Lord had worked in these places, or his experiences there; when I picked up a rock to throw, I visualized how the Jews wanted to stone him; when I was in my garden, I thought of the anxious prayer on the Mount of Olives or of Christ's grave and how he had appeared to Mary Magdalene in the garden, after the Resurrection, and so on. Such thoughts were my daily occupation: I never ate without thinking of the Last Supper, and I never cooked my food without reminding myself of the eternal pains of hell.

At last I found that I could write very well on large palm fronds with the juice of lemons mixed with that of Brazil wood (of which tree there are several kinds on the island). This greatly delighted me, for now I could take notes and write down regular prayers. While regretfully considering my entire life, all the nasty tricks I had played since the days of my childhood, and how a merciful God, disregarding all my coarse sins, had until now not only preserved me from eternal damnation but even granted me the time and the chance to better myself, to convert, to ask forgiveness, and to thank Him for His kindness, I wrote down everything that came to my mind in the book that I made from palm fronds. This, together with my comrade's ducats, I put in a place where people who might sometime come here would find it and be able to tell who had previously inhabited this island. If someone should find the book and read it (sooner or later, before or after my death), I beg him not to take offense if he should find words in it unbecoming to the mouth, not to mention the pen, of a person bent on improvement. Let him remember that the telling of easygoing stories requires easygoing words. An honest Christian reader will marvel all the more, and praise God's mercy, when he finds out that, for all this, such a rogue as I received enough of God's grace to withdraw from the world and live in such condition that he may hope to find eternal glory and by the sufferings of our Redeemer to attain everlasting bliss and a blessed

End.

CHAPTERS 24-27: *Summary*

[The last four chapters constitute a report written by John Cornelissen, a Dutch sea captain from Haarlem, the capital of North Holland, for a friend in Germany:

[On the way from the Moluccas to the Cape of Good Hope, bad weather separates Cornelissen's ship from the others in the fleet. While looking for St. Helena, Cornelissen sights an island marked by two crosses on its highest point, though the maps show no land at all in that part of the ocean. A boat, sent to investigate, returns with water, fresh poultry, and quantities of fresh fruit. The only inhabitant of the island has retreated into an inaccessible cave. He is thought to be an outcast and probably insane. Further exploration reveals that pious messages, mottos in various languages, and crosses are attached to trees or carved into their bark. When a grave and a third cross are found, the sailors call the place the Island of the Crosses.

[A number of sailors now start behaving like madmen, and the captain determines to speak with the hermit in the cave. The second attempt to penetrate into the cavern is no more successful than the first: flares and torches go out, and only when the men are at the point of complete frustration does the hermit shout at them. The invaders, he tells them, are welcome to everything the island offers, but after what happened yesterday he is afraid for his safety. It turns out that the first group of sailors had looted and destroyed Simplicius' hut and threatened his life. The ship's chaplain apologizes and asks advice on curing the madness of the sailors. The hermit assures the captain and his men that he is ready to repay evil with good, and after he has been promised that he will not be taken off to Europe and that the location of the island will not be revealed, he appears, shakes hands all around, and guides them out of the cave. The light he uses comes from dried specimens of big lightning bugs, which he has fastened all over himself.

[The madness among the sailors had increased so much that now hardly a sane man is left. They are given the kernels of the plumlike fruit that induced the madness in the first place, and within the hour all are normal again. The chaplain calls the men together and gives them a stern lecture on looting. Thereupon the sailor who has stolen Simplicius' most precious possession, the palm-leaf book, returns it together with the thirty ducats in cash which he had also taken. Simplicius gives the book to Captain Cornelissen as a personal gift and asks him to distribute the money among the poor of Haarlem.

[Simplicius is very skillful in treating and nursing the ship's sick. His help is as much appreciated as he enjoys giving it, but to show their gratitude, the officers invite him to a sumptuous meal. Unlike any German Cornelissen had known, Simplicius eats only the plainest food and drinks water instead of wine. He states his reasons for refusing to return to Europe: when he left, the place was filled with war, arson, murder, pillage, rape, and fornication. But when God took away these evils, removed plagues and famine, and once more sent noble peace to profit the poor people, there arose all sorts of vices such as voluptuousness, gluttony, drinking, gambling, whoring, sodomy, and adultery which drew the whole swarm of the other vices after them. The worst of it is that there is no hope of improvement because everyone thinks he is a good Christian when he goes to church once a week at best and to communion once a year. Simplicius is afraid that God who had shown him the grace of putting him on this island would treat him like Jonah if he tried to leave it after living there for fifteen years. On the island he has freedom from want and vain desires. When the captain asks him whether he is not afraid to die there alone, he answers that the absence of men does not disturb him so long as God is with him.

[After all the sick have recovered and supplies have been taken aboard the merchantman, Cornelissen sets sail on the sixth day and rejoins his fleet at St. Helena. Before leaving, the ship's carpenters rebuild Simplicius' hut and the captain gives him a magnifying glass which he has requested for making fire from the rays of the sun. They also leave behind an ax, a shovel and a hoe, two bolts of cotton cloth, a dozen knives, a pair of scissors, two copper pots, and a pair of rabbits, to see if they will multiply on the island.]

The End